OUT OF BATTLE

Jon Silkin

OUT OF BATTLE

The Poetry of the Great War

It seemed that out of battle I escaped
Down some profound dull tunnel, long since scooped
Through granites which titanic wars had groined.

Wilfred Owen

London
OXFORD UNIVERSITY PRESS
1972

Oxford University Press, Ely House, London W.1

GLASGOW   NEW YORK   TORONTO   MELBOURNE   WELLINGTON
CAPE TOWN   SALISBURY   IBADAN   NAIROBI   LUSAKA   ADDIS ABABA
BOMBAY   CALCUTTA   MADRAS   KARACHI   LAHORE   DACCA
KUALA LUMPUR   SINGAPORE   HONG KONG   TOKYO

ISBN 0 19 211804 8

© Oxford University Press 1972

Printed and bound in Great Britain at The Pitman Press, Bath

CONTENTS

PREFACE

I should like to thank the many people who have helped with this book since it was begun in 1959, the year of the Rosenberg Exhibition held at the University of Leeds, then under the Vice-Chancellorship of Charles Morris. The exhibition was opened by the late Herbert Read, and prepared jointly by the late Maurice de Sausmarez and myself. I should like to thank the University libraries of Leeds and Newcastle, and also the library of the Newcastle Literary and Philosophical Society, for all their help and kindness during the writing of this book. I am especially grateful to Geoffrey Matthews, who worked with me on the initial stages of the book; and Catherine Lamb, who read and re-read the early draft and co-operated on some of the research. At a later stage, John Press gave the text a close reading and made valuable suggestions for its reduction and improvement. Jon Stallworthy further assisted with the work of condensation; his constant questioning and sympathy helped it over the last lap on its way to the printer. I am grateful to Mrs. Phyllis McDougall, who prepared the index. I have also to thank John Smith for his patience with the book, and Ken Smith, who at all times encouraged me to persist with those insights which have shaped it. I am equally grateful to Geoffrey Hill for discussing Rosenberg and Owen with me over a long period, and to those other critics and friends who have helped me towards an understanding of the poets and the poetry here discussed.

The section on Rosenberg's God first appeared in *European Judaism* (1970); brief versions of work on Owen, Rosenberg, and Sassoon first appeared in *Stand* (1960, 1965).

J.S.

vii

ACKNOWLEDGEMENTS

Thanks are due to the publishers and copyright holders listed below for permission to quote from the following works:

RICHARD ALDINGTON, *Complete Poems* (1949): Mme Katherine Guillaume and Rosica Colin Ltd.

EDMUND BLUNDEN, *Poems 1914–1930* (1930) and *Undertones of War* (1928): the author and A. D. Peters & Co.

RUPERT BROOKE, *Poetical Works*, edited by Geoffrey Keynes (1946): Sidgwick & Jackson Ltd. and Faber & Faber Ltd.; *Letters*, edited by Geoffrey Keynes (1968): Faber & Faber Ltd. and Harcourt Brace Jovanovich Inc., New York.

FORD MADOX FORD, *Buckshee* (Cambridge, Mass., 1966) and *Selected Poems*, edited by Basil Bunting (Cambridge, Mass., 1971): Miss Janice Biala, David Higham Associates Ltd., and the Pym-Randall Press, Cambridge, Mass.

IVOR GURNEY, *Severn and Somme* (1917), *War's Embers* (1919), and *Poems*, edited by Edmund Blunden (1954): the author's literary Estate, Mr. Leonard Clark, Chatto & Windus Ltd., and Sidgwick & Jackson Ltd.

THOMAS HARDY, *Collected Poems* (1930, reprinted 1952) and *The Dynasts* (1924, reprinted 1930): the Trustees of the Hardy Estate, Macmillan London and Basingstoke, and The Macmillan Company, New York.

DAVID JONES, *In Parenthesis* (1937, reprinted 1963) and *Epoch and Artist*, edited by Harman Grisewood (1959): the author, Faber & Faber Ltd., and Chilmark Press Inc., New York.

RUDYARD KIPLING, *Rudyard Kipling's Verse*, Definitive Edition (1940): Mrs. George Bambridge, A. P. Watt & Son, and Doubleday & Company Inc., New York.

WILFRED OWEN, *Collected Poems*, edited by C. Day Lewis (1963), Copyright Chatto & Windus Ltd. 1946, © 1962: the Estate of the late Harold Owen, Chatto & Windus Ltd., and New Directions Publishing Corporation, New York.

HERBERT READ, *Collected Poems* (1966) and *The Contrary Experience* (1963): Faber & Faber Ltd. and Horizon Press, New York.

Isaac Rosenberg, *The Collected Works*, edited by Gordon Bottomley and
D. W. Harding (1937), and *Isaac Rosenberg 1890-1918: Catalogue with
Letters*, edited by Maurice de Sausmarez and Jon Silkin (Leeds, 1959):
Chatto & Windus Ltd.; *Collected Poems* (1949; New York, 1950): Chatto
& Windus Ltd. and Schocken Books Inc., New York.

Siegfried Sassoon, *Collected Poems* (1947): Mr. G. T. Sassoon and Faber
& Faber Ltd.; *The Complete Memoirs of George Sherston* (including
*Memoirs of a Fox-hunting Man; Memoirs of an Infantry Officer; Sherston's
Progress*) (1937): Faber & Faber Ltd., Stackpole Books, Harrisburg, Pa.,
and The K. S. Giniger Co. Inc., Chicago.

Charles Hamilton Sorley, *Marlborough and other Poems* (Cambridge,
1922, reprinted 1932): the author's Executor and the Cambridge University Press.

Edward Thomas, *Collected Poems* (1936): Mrs. Myfanwy Thomas and
Faber & Faber Ltd.

and to the copyright holders for brief extracts quoted from the following:
Bernard Bergonzi, *Heroes' Twilight* (1965): the author and A. D. Peters &
Co.; Robert Graves, *Goodbye to All That* (1929, reprinted 1960): the
author and A. P. Watt & Son; *John Clare/Selected Poems*, edited by Geoffrey Grigson (1950): Geoffrey Grigson for a passage from his Introduction; F. R. Leavis, *New Bearings in English Poetry* (1932, reprinted 1963):
the author and Chatto & Windus Ltd.; Bertrand Russell, *Freedom versus
Organization, 1776-1914* (1965): George Allen & Unwin Ltd. and W. W.
Norton & Co. Inc., New York; C. K. Stead, *The New Poetic* (1964): the
author and the Hutchinson Publishing Group Ltd.

CHAPTER ONE

INTRODUCTION

A book about the poets of the First World War raises certain preliminary critical questions. One is that their preoccupations are also ours, so that in searching for a satisfactory critical approach one is tempted to examine their work as history, reducing poems to documents that might yield solutions to our own problems. Such a case-book approach, extracting the poet's representative attitude from the poem, inevitably limits the reader's response. Another and no less limiting approach is to examine the poem as an item in the 'community of literature', viewing one literary era as progenitor of another. Contingent on this is the danger of bringing one taste to every poem, so that one reads the poem not only without context but, more damagingly, without its inherent moral values. On the other hand, the context that produced the poem should not make us more sympathetic in our responses than we would normally be: that would make it difficult to distinguish between, say, Nichols and Rosenberg. Clearly, however, in war poetry the context is an inescapable impingement, so much so that for the poets it is the subject of the poems and elicits very direct and powerful responses. If this is the case—as Owen claimed it was—then the 'subject' will also need some understanding, just as the poem will itself offer some insight into the context. Ideally, poem and context will generate a reciprocal relationship.

I shall suggest that some of the forces which developed in the nineteenth century emerged in the First World War and influenced the poets. These external social pressures will be considered in the context of the poetry—an approach that I have already objected to; but I hope to show that my reading of the poets' work is not merely as case-book study. I shall read their poems partly by evaluating those forces of which the war itself was a product. In so far as I can evaluate the poems, I will sometimes prefer those which seem to emerge from the generalized consciousness of their period and change or modify the prevailing attitudes. Modifying those attitudes, such poems modify ours, and in such a way as to dislodge the idea that there is one literature of the past and another of the present.

Even where a poem's subject may not now be ours, the poet's response to his subject and his situation may well be relevant to our own.

This is as true of certain poets writing near the end of the eighteenth century as of the poets of the First World War, and I begin by briefly considering Wordsworth and Coleridge because both were intermittently, but intensively, concerned with the problems of the revolutionary and Napoleonic periods. An interpretation of their poems and of the events that prompted them is necessarily complex because both the poets and the events were in a state of flux. If, for instance, one regards early revolutionary France as fighting the combined reactionary monarchical powers, which is how Wordsworth and Coleridge originally understood the situation, one would say that their sympathies at first seem to be with France and against the forces of reaction, one of which is England. This is, of course, to simplify their view of the situation both at the time and afterwards, but the value of politics is that they force clear-cut decisions upon us, just as the value of poetry may be that it permits us to qualify our allegiances. If both poets rejected their earlier allegiances, one might say that their problem was partly one in which patriotism and inter-national radicalism[1] presented mutually exclusive demands. The choices were excruciating, and neither poet solved the problem. Revolutionary France did, of course, change from fighting defensive wars against conservative powers to fighting expansionist wars inspired by Napoleon. At what stage the character of the struggle changed I feel unequipped to say, but Shelley's 'Feelings of a Republican on the fall of Bonaparte' sensitively indicates the change and the dilemma. One might suppose that Wordsworth and Coleridge recognized the changes France was undergoing in the immediately pre-Napoleonic period, and that their change in allegiance altered correspondingly; yet the realigning of their sympathies was not a simple case of the (British) patriot conveniently finding that an apparently acceptable nation (in ideological terms) had changed in such a way as to permit a realignment with his own nation. Both poets abandoned their early beliefs on the grounds that what subsequently happened to France showed that those beliefs and their consequent loyalties had been from the start misplaced; that earlier revolutionary France was all the time latter-day Napoleonic Gaul; that they had been previously

---

[1] Radicalism *between* nations.

deceived but now saw rightly. Such a description is of course too
sweeping, and the change in attitude can be traced, especially in
Wordsworth's case, through more gradual and subtle revisions.

Hazlitt described the 'lake school of poetry' as having 'its origin
in the French Revolution, or rather in those sentiments and
opinions which produced that revolution', and he connects the
literary with the political upheaval. Of their poetry he says that 'all
was to be natural and new'. The political ideas of the Revolution
are 'the cause and principle' for those ideas, guiding or inspiring
the choice of the agricultural worker or poverty-stricken victim as
central figures in the poems. At the same time, these figures
authorize an 'outrageous simplicity' in the language they are bodied
in. Hazlitt's remarks are generalized but shrewd. In *The Spirit of
the Age* he individualizes Coleridge's radicalism: 'he hailed the
rising orb of liberty, since quenched in darkness and in blood, and
had kindled his affections at the blaze of the French Revolution,
and sang for joy when the towers of the Bastille and the proud
places of the insolent and the oppressor fell.' Hazlitt, like Shelley,
acknowledges the rise of liberty in the Revolution and its extinction
in Napoleon and he notes that Coleridge heard 'the voice of God at
the top of [liberty's] ladder'. This brief estimation of Coleridge's
early radicalism, which he was subsequently to deny in *Biographia
Literaria*, seems just, if related to Coleridge's poetry:

> When slumbering Freedom roused by high Disdain
> With giant Fury burst her triple chain!

Yet even here, in 'To a Young Lady with a Poem on the French
Revolution', one notices that Coleridge does not distinguish
between the Revolution's egalitarian ideals and those French
patriotic ones excited in part by the coalition attacks. Similar
sympathies are shown in 'To a Young Ass: its Mother tethered
near it', also written in October 1794. There is, in the earlier poem,
a crucial ambiguity which, consciously or not, reveals certain of
Coleridge's political responses:

> Fallen is the Oppressor, friendless, ghastly, low,
> And my heart aches, though Mercy struck the blow.

The ambiguity resides in 'though'. Does the heart ache *in spite of*,
but, or *even if* 'Mercy struck the blow'? If the first, then the heart

continues to ache for the killed although they were not of the side
to which the revolutionaries/Mercy belonged; that is, the heart
aches even though Mercy killed them. If *but* is meant then the heart
has at length been pacified, because of the poet's sympathies with
the revolutionaries, who struck the blow. *Even if* is the most remote
of the three possibilities, but the most prophetic perhaps of
Coleridge's subsequent attitudes; it suggests that he had expected
better of the Revolution and wonders whether, if such bloodshed
is involved, it may claim its moral rightness. The revolutionaries'
Mercy (on behalf of those it fights for) sheds the tyrants' blood.
Even if is hard to distinguish from the first reading; but suppose
that first says: my heart aches because someone has been executed
(even though a tyrant, and even though Mercy struck him down).
The third suggestion takes the second line of the quotation apart from
the previous one and insists that the heart aches and cannot find
comfort: the fact that Mercy killed them does not soften the blow.
Principles involving the sanctity of human life have been violated,
quite apart from the lives themselves. This last reading invites the
question what kind of Mercy is it that kills. Coleridge's intention
is made no clearer by the preceding lines:

> Red from the Tyrant's wound I shook the lance,
> And strode in joy the reeking plains of France!

Clearly the pacifism expressed by the previous quotation does not
accord with the 'joy' in this, unless it is that Coleridge is revealing
an unfolding self-awareness.

I have examined one word at such length to suggest conflicting
attitudes in at least two of the poems in *Sibylline Leaves*: 'France'
(1798) and 'Fears in Solitude' (1798). Both seem clear assertions,
and revelations, of Coleridge's moral and political dilemmas. When
France

> Stamped her strong foot and said she would be free,
> Bear witness for me, how I hoped and feared!

Coleridge exults and fears and, when Britain joins the coalition
against revolutionary France, he recalls how he 'hung [his] head and
wept at Britain's name'. The 'slavish band' are such because they
support a tyranny endorsed both by England and the French
monarchy, and because they are unable to think in those revolutionary terms which have been shown by France to the labouring

classes of Europe. Yet even here 'France' has different meanings.
Not all France, clearly, said she would be free. Differing classes
demanded different and often conflicting freedoms. At one moment
France is said to be monarchical and enslaved; at another, republican. In a third context she is depicted as tyrannical, causing the 'loud
lament, / From bleak Helvetia's icy caverns'. When France, having
struggled for her own freedom, violated that of the Swiss, Coleridge
had to reconsider his Gallic sympathies. But he was still thinking,
or choosing to think, in terms of a country as a whole, rather than
of a national organism divided into competing power groups.
Freedom, however, is the operative word in 'France'. He deplores
'Blasphemy's loud scream' but had thought, he confesses, that

> ... Wisdom [shall] teach [France] lore
> In the low huts of them that toil and groan!

The 'cruel foes' of both freedom and Helvetia are rendered in

> The Sensual and the Dark rebel in vain,
> Slaves by their own compulsion! In mad game
> They burst their manacles and wear the name
> Of Freedom, graven on a heavier chain!
> O Liberty! with profitless endeavour
> Have I pursued thee, many a weary hour. ...

The sentence beginning 'In mad game ...', its strong conclusion
reinforced by rhyme, uses the technique of an eighteenth-century
verse whose movement is deployed in argument and reason. The
last two lines of the quotation, exclamatory and confessional,
belong to a later mode, and the two components indicate the
various tools at Coleridge's disposal, as well as the ways in which
he chose to deal with the problems. The exclamatory mode is self-
accounting and follows a rational condemnation; it can therefore
be discounted as part of an attempt to interpret or solve the problems. The earlier lines contain the gravamen of the accusation and,
though the argument is ultimately circular, it has to be dealt with.
The 'Sensual' and the 'Dark' were so, it is implied, the whole time
('graven on a heavier chain') and he had been deceived in thinking
they might ever have become otherwise. They cannot cast off their
own oppressive and debased nature. The revolution from within is
a sharp but of course relevant shifting of tactics; if only Coleridge
could have considered such a possibility earlier he would not have

been so abruptly disillusioned. But the shift is also crucial, and Freedom is finally seen not as inhabiting 'forms of human power' but in Nature. It required a tougher and more patient belief in humanity and a more flexible political rationality than Coleridge possessed to deal with the frustration of his social ideals and accept the change that France underwent, a change in part forced on her by the combination of nations ranged against her.

The situation was complex in that, although the coalition was fighting not France so much as the Revolution, the Revolution by its very success, could be said to have become France. This at least is what each nation expediently asserted when putting an army against her. Each had to find a patriotic pretext for fighting an ideological war. France, on the other hand, could find no other way to answer the allies' aggression than via the nationalistic mode with which she had been attacked; she therefore opposed these national-istic modes partly by calling up corresponding ones in herself. Napoleon was perhaps the product of these forces, which he in turn opportunistically manipulated.

In 'Fears in Solitude' ('written in April 1798, during the alarm of invasion'), which represents the crux of Wordsworth's and Coleridge's dilemma as radicals and patriots, Coleridge returns to the conflicts outlined in the previous paragraphs. A description of the landscape in which he is resting yields awareness of 'Religious meanings in the forms of Nature', and he thus completes the circle of thought comprising God and Nature, God and Liberty, Liberty and Nature. Such cohesion is also of course an image of the unity of the imagination. Much of the poem is taken up with the fear of invasion, but however much Coleridge refutes his earlier political attitudes, as expressed in the *Biographia Literaria* (July 1817), in this poem he exposes his conflicts. He sees England as responsible for what may soon be happening:

> We have offended, Oh! my countrymen! . . .
> The wretched plead against us; multitudes
> Countless and vehement,

which probably refers to his own country's proletariat, as well as those in other countries against which England directly and indirectly fought. He then moves through some of the concerns of enlightenment, colonialism and slavery, and speaks of the vices of our own civilization which we have transmitted through conquest.

The passage indicting war is exact,[1] and anticipates the attacks made by Sassoon and Owen on those at home who are unable through lack of imagination, or who refuse, to consider what those who are fighting endure. Coleridge was perhaps the most perceptive, in that he was not a combatant and the realities of war would then have been felt less, at home, than during the First War.

> Secure from actual warfare, we have loved
> To swell the war-whoop, passionate for war! . . .
> The which we pay for as a thing to talk of,
> Spectators and not combatants! . . .
> We send our mandates for the certain death
> Of thousands and ten thousands! Boys and girls,
> And women, that would groan to see a child
> Pull off an insect's leg, all read of war,
> The best amusement for our morning meal! . . .
> As if the soldier died without a wound;
> As if the fibres of this godlike frame
> Were gored without a pang; . . .
> As though he had no wife to pine for him,
> No God to judge him! Therefore, evil days
> Are coming on us, O my countrymen!
> And what if all-avenging Providence,
> Strong and retributive, should make us know
> The meaning of our words. . . .

Civilian apathy and lack of imagination are here delicately indicated by the insistent commentary surrounding the image of the child and the dismembered insect. The suffering of the soldier (and his wife) is qualified by a God who judges him as both agent of suffering and sufferer,[2] but who, it is implied, will judge the English nation at home the most severely. What follows judgement is the retribution of invasion, brought on by ourselves. Coleridge then faces up to such a possibility, and declares:

> Stand forth! be men! repel an impious foe,
> Impious and false, a light yet cruel race,
> Who laugh away all virtue. . . .

It is hard to see in what sense, after the passage indicting England, France may be said to be 'impious'. It is not so much the encouragement to resist invasion that one wonders at (although one wishes

---

[1] See below.
[2] Compare with Wilfred Owen's 'Exposure', p. 202.

that Coleridge had here unfolded the complexity of his position)
as the shrillness that apparently contradicts what has preceded it;
as though England were suddenly the righteous party. In this abrupt
transition one feels the contradictory pressures of his position. A
quiet or implicit assertion of resistance would have emphasized,
not annulled, the sensitive insights of the earlier passage; it is
permissible perhaps to see oneself as culpable but also be determined to resist with 'moderate force', as Simone Weil puts it. This,
in contradictory fashion, is what Coleridge also advises:

> . . . may we return
> Not with a drunken triumph, but with fear,
> Repenting of the wrongs with which we stung
> So fierce a foe to frenzy!

He counsels moderation, and humility, only after expected victory.

I suggest that these are the conflicting attitudes of a man dis-
tracted by the rival claims of patriotism (and its concomitant social
pressures) and inter-national radicalism. What destroys the tragic
sense of irreconcilable concerns is the shrill, self-righteous patriotism,
so much in contrast with the long passage quoted above. It destroys
the shaded, bewildering character of the struggle which these lines
uncover; and what causes his shrillness perhaps is not only the fear
of invasion but the impotent and intermittent awareness that neither
country is innocent, and that the conflict is not susceptible to clear-
cut judgements. Perhaps the shrillness provides one measure of
Coleridge's involvement. He was surely aware that conflict, which
inspires retaliation, solves neither the moral part of the problem nor
the excruciating impossibility of dividing oneself between radical
and patriot. The struggle forced him to choose between morally
unsatisfactory alternatives, a situation in which one's allegiance
tends to become the more assertive once it has been decided. The
disappointed idealist then turns on those whom he feels have
betrayed their ideals, especially since those ideals were his also.

At last bereft of any truly moral society in which he could believe,
Coleridge invests Nature with those sacred ideals humanity has
betrayed: 'All adoration to the God in nature'—Nature seen in
England. Not that he would have disputed that French Nature was
equally God's handiwork, but such inter-national deism did not
solve for Coleridge the social problems; it merely rerouted a
troubled mind. Hazlitt said of him that 'He is a general lover of art

and science, and wedded to no one in particular', an opinion that supports the sense of impotence to be felt in his later work, resulting in part perhaps from the conflicting political attitudes. Not that Coleridge did not finally, again and again, publish his revisions: 'I often recall with what affectionate pleasure the many respectable men who interested themselves for me. . . . They will bear witness for me how opposite even then my principles were to those of Jacobinism or even democracy. . . .'[1] Such advertisement is costly. As a man and a poet he had committed himself to radicalism; not deeply enough, some may feel, but deeply enough for him to be unable to defect without self-damage. The earlier commitments leave traces of their original idealism which no mature conservatism can quite destroy. Two decisions of mutually exclusive character annul the energies of the man and injure him as a whole: 'The Sensual and the Dark rebel in vain.'

The discussion is complicated in that it works in two directions. Jacobin opinion in England supported revolution in France, not because it was French but for what it represented ideologically. Dr. Price, speaking in November 1789 at the annual dinner of the Society for Commemorating the Revolution in Great Britain, 'disdain[ed] national partialities and rejoiced in every triumph over arbitrary power'. He moved the French National Assembly be congratulated on 'the Revolution in that country and on the prospect it gives the first two kingdoms in the world of a common participation in the blessings of civil and religious liberty'. The first quotation relegates nationalism in favour of democratic liberty, and the second recognizes countries as entities in which such liberty is built. Liberty is transmuted, through its ideas, from country to country. The British Jacobins would initially locate their ideals in France, and those opposed to such ideals would naturally see France as hostile. Immediately therefore, as I have suggested, the struggle came to be fought in nationalistic terms, corroboration of which may perhaps be seen in the coalition wars. Those who supported the Revolution were accused of being Gallican, so that a reformer came to be regarded as treasonable. This is perhaps why the government agent was sent to Nether Stowey in 1797 to spy on Wordsworth, his sister, and Coleridge. As a corollary to this, if one were anti-Bonaparte, a pressure which even Jacobins found it hard to resist, one opposed reform because of its French associations.

[1] *Biographia Literaria*, ed. J. Shawcross (1907), vol. I, p. 119.

Thus, what was constantly happening was that inter-national radicalism became subsumed in French nationalism, as an issue involving patriotism.

Wordsworth encountered these difficulties, and retractions and modifications are to be detected in his political attitudes; as, for example, in his changing view of France. At first she is seen as a nation of revolution and a victim of tyrannical coalition comprised of reactionary forces; then, with qualification, as a nation involved with terror; hope returns with the fall of Robespierre, only to die at last. The poet turns to principles of justice abstracted by reason, but here seems to suffer a breakdown, and in the course of recovery denies reason as an instrument and returns to Nature. She becomes increasingly his touchstone and preceptress, until the promptings of duty again impel him into taking an active—vocal—part in the struggle against France.

An important change in Wordsworth's political concerns may be seen in his revised attitude to reform, which is of course linked with his concern with France. He identifies liberty and political justice for the labouring classes with revolution. As the Revolution disappoints, Wordsworth changes his view of reform. He never abandons his sympathies for the poor, but their effectiveness becomes gradually modified by his caution towards reform. What began in indignation (with Wordsworth wishing for a large readership among the working classes) subtly changes to a sympathy, strong but different in that it advocates not revolt of any kind but gradual reform, and, in the meanwhile, fortitude on the part of the labouring class.

Despite his qualifying wish for the sparing of the convent of Chartreuse, Wordsworth records his sympathy for the opening phases of the Revolution; although even in Book VI of *The Prelude*, he has a tendency to promote Nature as the antagonist of his sympathies for the Revolution:

> We crossed the Brabant armies on the fret
> For battle in the cause of Liberty. . . .
> I wanted not that joy, I did not need
> Such help; the ever-living universe,
> Turn where I might, was opening out its glories. . . .
>
> (VI. 764–75)[1]

---

[1] All quotations from *The Prelude* are from the text of 1850.

With his confrontation with the royalist officers at Blois, his sympathies for the Revolution are strengthened. He is subsequently moved by the 'domestic severings', by the willingness of those who fight for the Revolution to suffer separation from their families, which he sees as evidence of their revolutionary sincerity. His meeting with Beaupuy enlarges his sympathies, and these are intellectually strengthened by the discussion between them. Nothing in *The Prelude* stands out as strongly as the humanitarian commitment, which Wordsworth carefully preserves, perhaps not only to balance any intellectual commitment he may be censured for making, but also to indicate the positive acceptable basis of his earlier sympathies. Beaupuy and he chance

> ... to meet a hunger-bitten girl,
> Who crept along fitting her languid gait
> Unto a heifer's motion, by a cord
> Tied to her arm, and picking thus from the lane
> Its sustenance, while the girl with pallid hands
> Was busy knitting in a heartless mood
> Of solitude, and at the sight my friend
> In agitation said, ''Tis against *that*
> That we are fighting,' I with him believed
> That a benignant spirit was abroad
> Which might not be withstood, that poverty
> Abject as this would in a little time
> Be found no more. . . .
> All institutes for ever blotted out
> That legalized exclusion. . . .   (IX. 510–26)

Wordsworth was writing about this incident after he had revised his view of the Revolution, so that there is an interesting comparison with Coleridge's revisions as they occur in Chapter X of *Biographia Literaria*. What moves one in this passage is Wordsworth's compassion, Beaupuy's generous commitment, and Wordsworth's involvement with both, as with the girl's poverty. 'I with him believed' is ambiguous, however, because it reminds us that the event is being recollected. Is Wordsworth recording what he then felt and still feels; or can he no longer own these feelings; or does he own the feelings but not the political commitment that then went with them? My feeling is that he regards his impulses, however mistaken they may subsequently have been shown to be, as the product of a generous humanitarian spirit, but that the

spirit needed control and direction. Of course, such spirit was
directed subsequently, for ill, by Napoleon; the need for control
and direction is vulnerable to dictatorship. Wordsworth was convinced that the Revolution might have had a good issue after the
death of Robespierre, but scattered through Books X and XI of *The
Prelude* are the forebodings and the realizations of fresh massacres.

> . . . would I at this time with willing heart
> Have undertaken for a cause so great
> Service however dangerous.   (X. 152–4)

However, through lack of money (so he says) he left France in
December 1792, although he still retained his revolutionary
opinions in London. War broke out between England and France
in February 1793 and, in July that year, he saw the English fleet in
the Solent. His response is comparable with the passage quoted,
on page 7 above, from Coleridge's 'Fears in Solitude'. Wordsworth
confesses:

> I rejoiced,
> Yea, afterwards—truth most painful to record!—
> Exulted, in the triumph of my soul,
> When Englishmen by thousands were o'erthrown. . . .
> A conflict of sensations without name, . . .
> When, in the congregation bending all
> To their great Father, prayers were offered up,
> Or praises for our country's victories; . . .
> I only, like an uninvited guest
> Whom no one owned, sate silent, shall I add,
> Fed on the day of vengeance yet to come.
>   (X. 283–99)

In the phrase 'conflict of sensations' we have an explicit confession
of Wordsworth's contradictory position, such as never becomes
explicit or conscious, I believe, in Coleridge's work. The kind of
verse that Wordsworth was writing in *The Prelude* permitted a
more flexible, complex analysis of the effect of war—on France, on
England, and himself; and in Book X (351–5) he indicates with
subtlety that tyrants *in* France, rather than France as a whole, may
use the war as an excuse for greater extremes: 'The goaded land
waxed mad. . . .' (X. 336).

> Domestic carnage now filled the whole year
> With feast days. . . .
>   (X. 356–7)

Yet with the fall of Robespierre in 1794:

> From that time forth, Authority in France
> Put on a milder face; . . .
> . . . in me, confidence was unimpaired; . . .
> . . . in the People was my trust. . . .
> I knew that wound external could not take
> Life from the young Republic. . . .   (XI. 1–14)

Inserting into the context later attitudes, Wordsworth goes on to explain how he originally made his errors: that through his opposition to Britain's war with France he felt 'out of the pale of love', his natural affections (for his country, and for Nature, presumably) 'soured and corrupted'. Faced at last with the problems that Coleridge also had to face, and seeing his ideals betrayed, he does not abandon the ideals but turns instead to reason:

> Frenchmen had changed a war of self-defence
> For one of conquest, losing sight of all
> Which they had struggled for. . . .   (XI. 207–9)

There follows a passage in which he explains how he abstracted his adherence to liberty, from an explicit situation into a code of reasoned ideals (presumably aided by Godwin's *Political Justice*, 1793). This apparently satisfied in him the need for the rational exposition of his ideals where the turmoil of events offered none. He adds that at the same time it acted as a cloak impeding his (and many others') recognition of their emotions for what they really were:

> Tempting region *that*
> For Zeal to enter and refresh herself,
> Where passions had the privilege to work,
> And never hear the sound of their own names.
>
> (XI. 228–31)

He sought 'To anatomize the frame of social life' and finally, demanding that everything yield 'formal proof' contained in a system organized by reason, he 'Yielded up moral questions in despair'.

> This was the crisis of that strong disease,
> This was the soul's last and lowest ebb; I drooped,
> Deeming our blessèd reason of least use
> Where wanted most. . . .   (XI. 306–9)

Wordsworth healed himself by immersion in Nature, and Books
XII and XIII as well as 'Tintern Abbey' are explicit on this point.
In addition, both the latter poem and a passage in Book XI testify
to the healing influence of his sister:

> She whispered still that brightness would return,
> She, in the midst of all, preserved me still
> A Poet, made me seek beneath that name,
> And that alone, my office upon earth. . . .   (XI. 345–8)

Yet in reading these last two lines we touch on some sense of
contradiction. The closing years of the Napoleonic Wars show
Wordsworth as a patriot, anything but the poet (in his sense of the
word here) 'and that alone'; yet in the passage above he secures for
himself, I am almost certain, a specialized image of the poet, one
that in some ways refutes the arguments advanced in the Preface to
the *Lyrical Ballads* (1800), which assert that 'The [social] theme is
indeed important!' This exclamation surely embodies a political, or
at least social, meaning comparable with Owen's statement: 'My
subject is War, and the pity of War.' On the other hand, in the
passage from *The Prelude* quoted above, Wordsworth seems to be
stripping the poet of social attitudes and preserving him in the peaceable moral aura of Nature. Similarly, his revisions to 'The Female
Vagrant' constitute a political act at variance with his earlier
radicalism. To disenfranchise oneself politically is an act that
affects politics and may in itself constitute a political act. In Wordsworth's case, it led to the latter. He seems to have recognized that
the political impasse he had reached had brought him his despair,
'a strong disease', and that if he was to survive as a poet and a man
then it had (for the moment) to be as a poet of restricted range. I
am not sure that a political change of direction is consciously
accounted for in the withdrawal at this stage, although, with hindsight, this is precisely what it led to. For Wordsworth did not
keep with himself this compact of withdrawal, as his contribution
to the struggle against Napoleon instances. What is interesting,
however, is his modified attitude to reform, since it is here that we
see the pressures of patriotism and radicalism making their exclusive
demands.

Clausewitz formulated the idea—which Lenin borrowed—that
'War is a continuation of state policy by other means' and, where

the competitive interests of states cannot be resolved in compromise, war will emerge as the only 'solution'. The formula has
internal application also, in that the monarchs and ministers who
formed a coalition against republican France did so because the
example of French 'treason' offered to their own subjects had to
be shown to be unprofitable. Pitt's own domestic repression surely
corroborates this. Wordsworth, because he thought reform could
excite a desire to overthrow governments, came to believe, in his
reading of the French Revolution and its excesses, that reform must
be very gradual indeed if it was not to agitate those very grievances
it was intended to dispel. And if the whigs could preach pacifism
towards the French, Wordsworth could reinterpret their peaceable
message as an example for the poor. He would have endorsed
Coleridge's condemnation of those who 'plead to the poor and
ignorant, instead of pleading *for* them' (my italics). At the same
time he had to convince the ruling class that poverty and suffering
must be mitigated. A single text had to work for two increasingly
opposed factions. He had to pacify those suffering every kind of
deprivation and at the same time move towards gradual reform
those who could effect it, without creating an inflammatory situation.
Thus, increasingly, what he spelt out to the poor was fortitude (as in
'Resolution and Independence'), since this could hardly offend the
ruling class and it offered the poor the notion of sympathy and the
glimmerings of eventual alleviation:

Circumstances have forced [*sic*] this nation to do, by its manufacturers,
an undue proportion of the dirty and unwholesome work of the globe.
The revolutions among which we have lived have unsettled the value of
all kinds of property, and of labour, the most precious to all, to that
degree that misery and privation are frightfully prevalent. *We must bear
the sight of this, and endure its pressure*, till we have by reflection discovered
the cause, and not till then can we hope to palliate the evil [my italics].

The italicized part of the last sentence indicates, if the reader has
not already realized it, that Wordsworth is not principally addressing
the working classes, but the Government and the industrial holders.
Yet his first terse explanation of why 'misery and privation are . . .
prevalent' is strangely wounding; far from the sentiments of 'The
Female Vagrant' or the 'girl and heifer' passage in *The Prelude*.
The assertion of 'we' is at least disingenuous, because although the
appeal is made to those who in principle accept reform (as well as

those who do not yet do so), those who endure the privation suffer more than those witnessing it. To ask the witnesses to endure the sight reveals a qualified compassion for the sufferers. Wordsworth has the right to be as distant as he pleases, but in a public statement supposedly pleading for the poor, as well as for gradualism, it is dismaying. He appears to imply that the struggles of the poor have been taken over by the educated, more privileged, more fortunate and articulate witnesses, and that the battle is now between those who wish for immediate reform and those who want gradual alleviation. Against this must be set the compassion for the *rural* poor that is a constant factor in Wordsworth's work. Nevertheless patience is easier for those who witness than for those who suffer.

In 1799 Wordsworth finally withdrew to Grasmere with his sister, and this withdrawal corresponds to his turning to Nature:

> Knowing that Nature never did betray
> The heart that loved her; . . .
> . . . for she can so inform
> The mind that is within us, so impress
> With quietness and beauty, and so feed
> With lofty thoughts, that neither evil tongues,
> Rash judgements, nor the sneers of selfish men,
> Nor greetings where no kindness is, nor all
> The dreary intercourse of daily life,
> Shall e'er prevail against us. . . .

The conclusion of a benevolent Nature to which these lines from 'Tintern Abbey' point is also the context in which the poor are seen to labour and suffer. One contrast, therefore, with Nature pointing the difference, is between Nature and the malign relations current between men:

> To her fair works did Nature link
> The human soul that through me ran;
> And much it griev'd my heart to think
> What man has made of man.

One of the most wounding depreciations of Shelley is that which seems to praise him—Arnold's notion that he was 'a beautiful *and ineffectual* angel beating in the void his luminous wings in vain' (Arnold's italics). If Shelley's ideas are 'ineffectual', and he is a poet of ideas whatever else he is, we should not therefore feel contempt for him. Much nineteenth- and twentieth-century culture mobilized in various ways against contemporary barbarism —war, capitalism, state power—*seems* almost entirely ineffectual in its results. If, as I hope, it is still too early to see whether culture has modified the savageness in society today, the same may perhaps be said for Shelley, who faced problems that are still ours and which may have been the worse but for his intervention. Arnold's own attitude, as expressed in *Culture and Anarchy*, was that 'the lovers of culture may prize and employ fire and strength [to defend it]'; an attitude alien to Shelley. But it remains to be shown that Arnold's method has in any sense been effective in defending civilization; that indeed it has not weakened and eroded the things it wished to defend; and, moreover, that such a separation of culture from people is not a violation of both and a dilution of the former. Arnold is of course struggling with the common-sense notion that if you have barbarians you must, forcibly if necessary, prevent them from destroying what is precious to humanity, but common sense in social problems often involves philistinism and sometimes violence. It was not Shelley's want of a social context that made his ideas unacceptable to Wordsworth.[1]

Shelley's language has been attacked for its lack of concreteness, which is not the same as to charge him with working in a void without social contexts, and Arnold's 'luminous' cleverly fixes this. To express his idea of change, movement, energy, Shelley often uses images of water, air, fire. These are, of course, less substantial but no more abstract than wood and steel, but before we condemn the language we should see it as a part of his themes. The word abstract seems just to the extent that, although there is detail in his work, Shelley's vision is on the whole synoptic, and the reader, offered the whole vision, obtains the idea rather than the detail of which it is made. Thus W. K. Wimsatt writes of the Romantics as 'discerning the design which is latent in the multiform sensuous picture' and, although speaking of 'Tintern Abbey', his comment that there is 'always something just out of sight or beyond definition' is relevant to Shelley also. For Shelley, the ideal society was, as it is for us, 'out of sight', although not for him 'beyond definition'. Here as much as anywhere, Shelley might be labelled abstract, I suppose, but one might add that in *The Revolt of Islam* and *Prometheus Unbound* the utopias were not vaguely wished for. In the former

[1] See E. J. Trelawny, *Records of Shelley, Byron and the Author* (1858), pp. 4–5.

poem, it is only after counter-revolution has successfully and savagely recovered the country from the revolutionaries, and barbaric punishment been delivered, that Laon and Cythna accept that 'this is the winter of the world', and that an ideal state ordered by love and liberty has to exist, temporarily, in the minds of its lovers alone. Prometheus suffers for his refusal to betray mankind to the tyrant Jupiter, and has moreover no belief that submission would improve anything, except perhaps his own present torment:

> Evil minds
> Change good to their own nature.
>
> (*Prometheus Unbound*, I. 380–1)

Resistance is not an abstract problem, and was in any case ubiquitously relevant in the nineteenth century wherever the problems of nationalism or democracy rose and were opposed. Shelley's Platonism might be labelled abstract, and certainly, with or without Godwin's help, in *Prometheus Unbound* he envisages an ideal society and cosmos, in a manichaean universe where both good and evil were created and struggle against each other. These 'elements' in man are only, as in this sense the men themselves are, extensions or expressions of eternal elements and forms:

> For know there are two worlds of life and death:
> One that which thou beholdest; but the other
> Is underneath the grave, where do inhabit
> The shadows of all forms that think and live
> Till death unite them and they part no more;
> Dreams and the light imaginings of men,
> And all that faith creates or love desires. . . .
>
> (I. 195–201)

Yet 'the light imaginings of men' also reminds us that what man is struggling with is larger and more continuous than his particular problems at that moment. The phrase may, however, be taken syntactically to contrast with 'dreams' (not for Shelley a pejorative word), where to dream means to desire the better side of society to emerge and develop. Whatever the interpretation of such Platonism, it here initiates a distant view of society, although perspective is substantiated by the drawing up of the large permanent forms of which society is the shadow. Again, of course, good and bad are terms we avoid, accounting for our actions in relation to appetites, for instance; and yet we think of them as good or bad as it is expedient for us to do so. I treat this question of abstraction at some length, because I wish to suggest that we have still not found fundamentally acceptable alternatives for these judgemental terms, even though the tone of our judgements has considerably altered. Finally, Shelley's Platonism did not operate in a political void. Whether in his work he believed the permanent forms were fed by man's actions, or the reverse, is not easily answerable, but he clearly had political commitments.

According to H. N. Brailsford, Godwin disliked revolution and approved of gradual reform concurrent with change through education. Wordsworth only temporarily entertained abstraction, 'Tempting regions these', and turned to Nature for his permanent forms. Shelley belonged to a later generation, perhaps unscathed—as Wordsworth was not—by revolution; but this is only to confirm that Shelley's forms are social and political, or to put it otherwise, that they are given political substance.

In *The Cenci* these forms are given dramatic being. Beatrice is tragic not only because she suffers, but because circumstances work on her to produce immoral action alien to her nature. Her tragedy is that a person more 'good' than 'evil' is nevertheless worked on by evil, in the form of the Cenci and the Church, to commit evil; it is this that both must finally be accountable for. This is presumably what Shelley means when he says that she 'appears to have been one of those rare persons in whom energy and gentleness dwell together. . . . The crimes and miseries in which she was an actor and a sufferer are as the mask and the mantle in which circumstances clothed her'. It is nothing to the Church that Beatrice's father has raped her, and murdered other members of his family. These are crimes among several that may be hushed up in tax:

> That matter of the murder is hushed up
> If you consent to yield his Holiness
> Your fief that lies beyond the Pincian gate.—
>
> (I. i, 1–3)

In condemning Beatrice and her accomplices to torture and death, what motivates the Pope is not their moral offence, but the idea

that the murder of her father instances one more attempt by the
rebel on authority:

> Parricide grows so rife
> That soon, for some just cause no doubt, the young
> Will strangle us all, dozing in our chairs.
> Authority, and power, and hoary hair
> Are grown crimes capital.　　　　　　　　(V. iv, 20–4)

The irony is complex. For the Pope the defence of authority is not
a moral question but, as Shelley has indicated throughout the play,
one of self-interest. On the other hand, Beatrice sees her crime as
justified; while Shelley indicates that, although she has committed
one retaliatory and immoral action, he condemns her father's
sadism, and, even more, the scheming retaliatory self-protectiveness
of the Pope. Retaliation does not undo offence, although the Pope
in any case is not concerned with the morality in question but his
own power. The irony grows more complex when we realize that
for Shelley authority and power had indeed become criminal, and
that the old perhaps resorted to the substance of authority rather
than openly consider the problems raised by the younger and more
active members of society. It is in the context of these ironies that
Beatrice's fear rushes up:

> If there should be
> No God, no Heaven, no Earth in the void world;
> The wide, gray, lampless, deep, unpeopled world!
> If all things then should be . . . my father's spirit. . . .
> 　　　　　　　　　　　　　　　　　(V. iv, 57–60)

She is courageously and fearfully encountering the possibility that
the world is not only without any moral guardian, but without any
of the permanent forms of which 'good' is at least one. The idea of
the world as 'lampless' is a terrifying one to a nominally Christian
society, but Shelley does not flinch from considering it.

> No, Mother, we must die:
> Since such is the reward of innocent lives. . . .
> 　　　　　　　　　　　　　　　　(V. iv, 109–10)

Although she cannot see her offence or its retaliatory nature, we
must feel with Shelley that she is a 'tragic character', a victim of
evil drawn into its area. Moreover, we may surmise that if we

should condemn her offence, we are to sympathize with her as a rebel against evil authority, and understand her motives. In a world otherwise void of morality the 'lamp' would have been represented by people such as Beatrice, if she had not committed murder, which would have been 'better'; or if she had recognized and evaluated what she had done, which would have been 'wiser'. Society is the poorer for her incapacities. Yet she is as it were the lamp she cannot see with, tempted into avenging evil (in both senses), and where this happens Shelley means us to understand that evil has entirely triumphed.

As tragic drama, *The Cenci* contained the less familiar ingredient of indignation. The pity we feel for Beatrice relates to the unjustness of her fate. We feel not only punishment in general but her punishment in particular is unjust; the play excites both pity and indignation. The pity may be cathartic, but the indignation is surely supposed to strengthen in the audience outraged opposition to tyranny.

Such indignation recurs in *The Mask of Anarchy*, inspired by the Peterloo massacre of 16 August 1819, but if indignation is aroused, Shelley brings his pacifism to bear as well; or rather, passive resistance. Anarchy is not the multitude who came to demonstrate peacefully, but the authority which forced them into resistance, and precipitated the chaos as it tried to break their resistance. Chaos is the forcible insistence of tyranny, and anarchy is clearly identified with the ruling class.

The enlisting cry for liberty again raises the problem of liberty for whom. Is it for a class, or for an as yet mandated but potentially autonomous nation, such as the Greeks were under Turkish rule? Shelley saw the interrelations of these two forces, but saw also their differences. Byron may also have seen the differences, but either he did not take this to be a problem, or he reduced it empirically. For instance his enlisting in the Greek cause tends to suggest a commitment to nationalist struggles, although some evidence in his work indicates that he sympathized with the oppressed section of the population, in his own country at least. See, for instance, 'Song for the Luddites', and, more substantially, the Venetian play *Marino Faliero*, part of which may fairly convincingly be read as demonstrating the need for class solidarity.

One further distinction between Shelley's and Byron's involvement with the struggle for liberty is the latter's recognition of it as

necessarily involving bloodshed, in that era at least. Whether the
revolutions then or since could have been achieved bloodlessly is
still a relevant question. One can only look at Shelley's ideas, on
the one hand, and at the bloodshed, on the other, and ask what
can be achieved if both sides are determined to avoid blood-letting.
The area between Shelley and Byron at least provides the question.
Although Byron admits the likelihood and apparent necessity of
revolution, he makes no distinction between the struggles of class
and radicalism on the one hand and nationalism on the other.

> But never mind;—'God save the king!' and *kings!*
>   For if *he* don't, I doubt if *men* will longer—. . .
> The people by and by will be the stronger: . . .
>
> At last it takes to weapons such as men
>   Snatch when despair makes human hearts less pliant.
> Then comes the 'tug of war';—'twill come again,
>   I rather doubt; and I would fain say 'fie on't,'
> If I had not perceived that revolution
> Alone can save the earth from hell's pollution.
>
> (Don Juan, VIII, l–li)

Byron's apparent levity may put in question the appropriateness of
verbal testing, but the ideas here still have to be questioned. The
'king' is presumably England's, and the 'kings' are all kings. These
lines imply, I think, both the social struggle inside England and
the nationalistic struggles in Germany, Italy, and Greece, where
one king or emperor is sovereign over several peoples. But by
putting the 'kings' in one line, together, Byron indicates that the
different struggles may be comprehended in the one idea of freedom. Thus 'the people', which ought to mean those who are hired
to labour, means surely in this context all those who make up the
nation-to-be. That the nation in the making will, like Italy in its
turn, raise the problem of a people tyrannized by its own sovereign
class is a problem by-passed in the passage. Perhaps Byron thought
that only one problem could be settled at a time, or that national
sovereignty should be settled before domestic tyranny. Either way,
Byron saw the nationalistic struggle as inevitably leading to war,
which, in *Don Juan*, occurs between two fully-fledged nations—
Russia and Ismail.

In cantos VII and VIII, war receives extended consideration, and

Byron ranges his powers of satiric bitterness and mockery against the wasteful barbarity; and, moreover, like Coleridge and Sassoon, against the callous civilian incomprehension of the suffering entailed. Of course, by implication he raises in the quotation above, and elsewhere, the question of a just or necessary war, but the barbarity of war is clinchingly condemned in the two cantos. As Byron suggests, war is waged not for the people but usually on behalf of an ambitious sovereign; if there are survivors they may, perhaps, share in a tithe of the spoils.

It has been contested that Byron's attack on war is part of his spoliation of society as a whole, and of no more significance than as part of his satire of society's hypocrisies; that his moral points are in any case subsumed under his enjoyment of the act of spoliation; that this view of war is simply another instance of 'the spoiler's art'—rather than Byron's diagnosis of a diseased society. It is suggested that, in any case, he does not think sequentially; his method being not analytic but accretive. There is some justification for this view, and it is interesting that Paul West in *Byron and the Spoiler's Art* offers no especial analysis of the two cantos in which Ismail is destroyed together with large portions of the Russian army. Even so, as an unspecific or rather unpointed ingredient in his general attack, war received from Byron enough attention for us to think that he regarded it as an emblem of society's follies, as well as an emblem of the Napoleonic struggle.

That Byron, with other whigs, was unappreciative of the struggle's outcome is indicated in the first ten stanzas of canto IX. However, for convenience perhaps we can put aside the overt political claims and consider the proposition that for Byron war is cruel and absurd. For him the two terms are inseparable, and at every instance of his indictment in *Don Juan*, he always points back to the civilian machinations which cause or implement the cruelty. This ranges from the egotistical aspirations of patriots and mercenaries, 'wishing to be one day brigadiers', to attacks on the false notion of *gloire* and the callous dismissal such notions receive in society: 'He fell, immortal in a bulletin.' The justification of total war—denied of course by Byron—receives its comment:

> . . . knock down
> The public buildings and the private too,
> No matter what poor souls might be undone.   (VII, xxiii)

The shoddy avarice of war profiteers is encapsuled in 'some con-
tractor's personal cupidity'. There is also the contrasting creativity
of God or Nature with that of man's destructiveness:[1]

> 'Let there be light!' said God, 'and there was light!'
> 'Let there be blood!' says man, and there's a sea!
>
> (VII, xli)

The scale of the destruction is implied in the non-contrasting entities
of light and sea. Byron is also concerned with the euphemistic
language in which society muffles its actions, either to avoid
unpleasantness or to give a false dignity to the act; in this case
nullifying it through the wrong kind of erudition:

> . . . blood and wounds . . .
> . . . as my true Muse expounds . . .
> So be they her inspirers! Call them Mars,
> Bellona, what you will—they mean but wars.   (VIII, i)

Connected with this is Byron's appreciation of how a certain kind
of history heartlessly incorporates the individual's suffering,
especially that of the non-aristocratic soldier, into its general
recital of 'deeds':[2]

> History can only take things in the gross; . . .
> The drying up a single tear has more
> Of honest fame, than shedding seas of gore.   (VIII, iii)

Byron could not tolerate euphemism, which for him amounted to
cant, and he criticizes Wordsworth's surprising lack of candour
(when one considers *The Prelude*) as it occurs in the Thanksgiving
Ode:

> 'Carnage, (so Wordsworth tells you) is God's daughter:'
> If *he* speak truth, she is Christ's sister, and
> Just now behaved as in the Holy Land.   (VIII, ix)

Byron repeatedly attacks the presumptions of rank, and indicates
that in war it is the common soldier who, because of his humble
status, receives scant attention:

[1] Compare with Wilfred Owen's 'Futility', p. 217.
[2] Consider also, in this context, Brecht's poem, 'A Worker reads History'.

Also the General Markow, Brigadier,
　　Insisting on removal of the *prince*
Amidst some groaning thousands dying near,—
　　All common fellows, who might writhe and wince,
And shriek for water into a deaf ear,—
　　The General Markow, who could thus evince
His sympathy for rank, by the same token,
To teach him greater, had his own leg broken. (VIII, xi)

Compounded in his consideration of war as an example of society's follies is his consideration of how man misuses his intellect and inventive powers:

> He rush'd, while earth and air were sadly shaken
> By thy humane discovery, Friar Bacon! (VIII, xxxiii)

He is aware, as Owen was to be in 'Arms and the Boy', that war corrupts and brings to the surface the innate savagery in men:

> He hated cruelty, as all men hate
> Blood, until heated—and even there his own
> At times would curdle o'er some heavy groan. (VIII, lv)

Finally, Byron's concern that the poet should tell the truth anticipates Owen's remark in the Preface to his *Poems* that: 'All a poet can do today is warn. That is why the true Poets must be truthful.' Byron remarks:

> But then the fact's a fact—and 'tis the part
> Of a true poet to escape from fiction. . . .
> (VIII, lxxxvi)

which may reflect the co-existing habit of the reading public to escape into the reading of fiction. These are a few of the many instances of brilliant conjunction of perception and condemnation to be found in these two cantos of his; as many instances could be cited of his compassion and of his honest recognition of courage. Perhaps one should add that such concentrated handling of war is of more significance than Byron's inability to distinguish between the two liberties I referred to on page 21.

On 8 August 1917 Owen wrote from Craiglockhart War Hospital:

I read a Biography of Tennyson, which says he was unhappy, even in
the midst of fame, wealth and domestic serenity. Divine discontent! . . .
But as for misery, was he ever frozen alive, with dead men for com-
forters? Did he hear the moaning at the bar, not at twilight and the
evening bell only, but at dawn, noon, and night, eating and sleeping,
walking and working, always the close moaning of the Bar; the thunder,
the hissing, and the whining of the Bar?—Tennyson, it seems, was always
a great child. So should I have been, but for Beaumont Hamel.[1]

The question and its honest answer dissolve I think the suggestion
of rhetoric here and lead us to consider the insight into Tennyson
himself. Owen is drawing on his experience of trench warfare, and
the criticism he makes of Tennyson's insufficient understanding of
misery is to be seen in relation to Owen's capacity, developed
through his experience of others' suffering, as well as his own.
Experience is not always necessary to understanding, as Coleridge's
'Fears in Solitude' and Hardy's *The Dynasts* instance, but Tennyson
is not after all a poet of great insight; his eloquence is best suited
to what he knows, and what he knows he obtains either through his
senses, or from what the age tells him. Officially, the age told him
little about war except that it was occasionally a national necessity,
and that therefore its cause was decorous. Thus the 'marine'
ballads, ostensibly pugnacious, are not about war in the proper
sense of the word, but are games in which there is no real suffering
and in which the stately English galleons are victorious, either in
the literal sense, or else in that the patriotic fortitude of the crews
remains intact whatever their loss.'The Charge of the Light Brigade'
purports to document an incident in the Crimean War, but it bears
as little relation to actuality as do the ballads; it tells us nothing
about the fears of the men, and nothing about their courage either.
It is a medal struck in defence of an official blunder. *Maud*, on
the other hand, although its subject is not war, conveys an interesting if disingenuous attitude to it. It may be objected that the poem
is, as Tennyson described it, a monodrama and that therefore the
poet is not expressing his own attitudes; but even if this were so
he has created *an* attitude, and one that is to be thought of as
representing a kind of thought then current. And since the mask is
itself unimpaired, handled without irony or double consciousness,

---

[1] *Wilfred Owen/Collected Letters*, ed. Harold Owen and John Bell (1967), p. 482.

one might imagine that it expressed ideas Tennyson felt no need to defect from. The attitudes I am concerned with occur in the first and last sections; in the first, Tennyson looks at the moral condition of the country and concludes that, if it can do no better than this, then it had better have war to purify itself of its moral sickness:

> And chalk and alum and plaster are sold to the poor for bread,
> And the spirit of murder works in the very means of life. . . .
>
> (*Maud*, I, i, x)

True. And thus he proposes:

> Is it peace or war? better, war! loud war by land and by sea,
> War with a thousand battles, and shaking a hundred thrones.
>
> (I, i, xii)

Rosenberg also felt that society suffered a sickness and hoped that war might cleanse it:

> O! ancient crimson curse!
> Corrode, consume.
> Give back this universe
> Its pristine bloom.

On the other hand, where Tennyson advises the remedy, Rosenberg only hopes that, if there must be war (which he deplores), then it will cleanse. Whereas Tennyson, in the last section, sees war as offering a personal solution to a private problem, as Brooke also seemed to see it:

> She seem'd to divide in a dream from a band of the blest,
> And spoke of a hope for the world in the coming wars— . . .
>
> (III, vi, i)
>
> And it was but a dream, yet it lightened my despair
> When I thought that a war would arise in defence of the right. . . .
>
> (III, vi, ii)

Rosenberg sees it, as curative perhaps, but as a 'curse'. Tennyson also confuses his metaphors in such a way as to indicate that he had never contemplated war except in melodramatic or romantic terms:

> And deathful-grinning mouths of the fortress, flames
> The blood-red blossom of war with a heart of fire.   (III, vi, iv)

For a major poet, 'blood-red blossom', subsuming blood within the image of blossom, is hardly the most credible, truthful image for a cannon's flame, or for war in general.

The poems of Swinburne are of direct relevance to the theme of this introductory chapter, because of their concern with (Italian) nationalism. His individualistic behaviour indicates that nationalism and not socialism was for him the more important concern; his rebelliousness, an ingredient in his eroticism, though not an integral one perhaps, has emotionally more in common with nationalism than with socialism, which requires a greater conscious merging of the individual with the community.

'*The Poems and Ballads* of 1866', E. K. Brown remarks in his reassessment of Swinburne's poetry, 'are dedicated not simply to the description of passion but to the praise of the idea of passion.' Every description, of course, is an idea of the thing described, but Swinburne is here characterized as representing passion as something so emblemized as to be representative of a range of responses; by implication therefore creating one that may take its place among the community of responses. Brown's quotation from Professor Beach, 'the worship of Venus . . . is but one article in the creed of naturalism', reinforces my sense of his meaning. Yet I do not consider that Swinburne's responses were so abstracted; he was sufficiently entangled with his own emotions to find their force a part of what shaped the poetry. The heavy tugging rhythms, the alliteration and assonance do not represent the idea of passion, but convey the passion itself—in, as it were, rhythmical and repetitive strokes of pain. Swinburne did not invite his readers to inspect his passion as one among many. He had, of course, to render very specialized sexual preferences in his poetry (although not as uncommon as we might imagine). The point about their being specialized is not simply that they are wilful—we do not choose our preferences at this level—but that they predominate over what is more habitually central to human sexuality. I am not here trying to diagram the abnormal and normal in sexuality in terms of the sexuality itself, but trying to place it as a performance to be defined by its relation to non-sexual activities. Normality is in relation to our capacity to act outside such compulsions. We do not have to look outside the poems, although the evidence is there, to see that what Swinburne expresses in the poems is a limited condition which excludes nearly everything but itself; and that the situations are frequently destructive of the agent and the sufferer. And that they admit nothing that changes the situation. This is the sense in which I use 'abnormal'.

That the poems permit few referents outside their own theme is, of course, a syndrome of the obsession, and I agree with Professor Brown's judgement that Swinburne's *Songs before Sunrise* is what his 'reputation as an intellectual poet . . . chiefly rests' on. Brown disposes of the idea, via M. Lafourcade, that Jowett converted Swinburne to healthier modes of behaviour by putting the poet in touch with Mazzini, and points out that immediately after the publication of *Poems and Ballads* Swinburne had written to W. M. Rossetti that he was tired of the poetry of passion, and that he was now, as he had always been, concerned with liberty and its cause in Italy.

Whatever he may have said, I think that here Swinburne was exerting the human capacity to choose, although one might also surmise that liberty had its echoes for him perhaps in an earlier permissiveness. It seems likely that the strength with which the sexualized feelings expressed themselves was now being re-harnessed in a change of direction. There were other pressures of course—notably his friends—but such a change can ultimately only be achieved alone, whatever the reasons for it may be. The strength of Swinburne is reflected in his ability, considering the force of the original obsession, to refashion a theme subsumed in his earlier work. The difficulty was that the theme and the means were one, as Swinburne indicated in 'Hertha', and that to change theme meant virtually to abandon the means of his work. Few poets can manage this kind of switch.

Ifor Evans indicates that Swinburne could not exclude from these later poems the earlier passions, and when they do recur, they are frequently, if ambivalently, some of the stronger parts of the poetry:

> And they slept and they rioted on their rose-hung beds,
>> With mouths on flame,
> And with love-locks vine-chapleted, and with rose-crowned heads
>> And robes of shame.

This stanza could have been taken from *Poems and Ballads*, but it comes from '*Super Flumina Babylonis*' (*Songs before Sunrise*) and represents the aristocratic youth of Italy in 'riot', where their behaviour is one of the causes to which Italy's failure to achieve independence is supposedly attributable. Once we realize that, we read 'shame' without any intentional, perverse ambiguity, and we see that the rioters' licence is held morally culpable by the poet. Whereas the characteristic complexity of such a stanza in *Poems and Ballads* would have been: how marvellous and exquisite is this behaviour I am indulging in and how my sense that it involves shame sharpens the pleasure. Thus, in *Poems and Ballads* 'shame' would have become sexualized by virtue of its context, its violation of admitted taboos, and would have acquired a localized and complex force of its own. Here, such intended complexity and ambiguity does not exist; 'shame' works against the sensuous direction of the stanza and purposefully but ineffectually condemns the behaviour it connotes. Any deprecating irony that 'rose-crowned' may have been intended to possess—crowned, that is, with shame since crowned with eroding pleasure—slips away. We can see but, like Coleridge, not feel the intention, and it seems to me irony of an almost tragic kind that is unintentionally involved. Despite his efforts Swinburne has not effectively changed direction with full emotional and sensuous accord. It is in this sense that I would agree with Professor Brown's word 'intellectual'.

Swinburne wrote:

> I cannot say that either ['Thanatopsis' or the 'Commemoration Ode'] leaves in my ear the echo of a single note of song. It is excellent good speech, but if given us as song its first and last duty is to sing. The one is most august meditation, the other a noble expression of deep and grave patriotic feeling . . . but the thing more necessary, though it may be less noble than these, is the pulse, the fire, the passion of music—the quality of a singer, not of . . . a patriotic orator.

In a sense, Swinburne is here reneging on his position in *Poems and Ballads*, although careful inspection of the statement shows that he considers the supreme attribute of the poet that of the capacity to sing. It may not be that nobility and song are fundamentally opposed attributes, but it is interesting to see how he sets them up against each other. It is in this sense perhaps that Wordsworth gives the poet back to Nature. With Swinburne it is more extreme; nobility may be lacking, but song, 'the pulse, the fire', must not be.

The difficulties of such separations, and inappropriatenesses, may be seen in the nationalistic 'songs'. The techniques are similar to those used in *Poems and Ballads*, but here they do not properly fit. Swinburne possessed strength but without deep or proper analytic power. The dedicatory poem to Mazzini in *Songs before Sunrise* contains the lines:

> I bring you the sword of a song. . . .
>
> It was wrought not with hands to smite, . . .
>   Nor tempered on anvil of steel;
> But with visions and dreams of the night,
>   But with hope, and the patience of passion,
>   And the signet of love for a seal.

Yet it was surely understood, it is in any case implicitly granted in 'not with hands to smite', that successful revolution and the independence of Italy from Austria would not be achieved without fighting. The poem is addressed as much to Italians as to the exiled Mazzini (whom Cavour put under death sentence). Education may have been what the Austrians needed before they would relinquish Italy; could they be directly educated into letting it go? The imagery of the poem invokes the sword, whatever Swinburne may say; the sword of passion, to conjunct his metaphors. Swinburne's 'song' could not, or at least did not, comprehend, as Shelley's did, that nationalism rarely satisfies itself within its originally named boundaries; that it was as Locke described sexuality—'Man is appetite in motion', and that the thing being fed, it will want more. It will clash and compete with other nationalisms. Thus in 1890, with Eritrea, Italy gave up her scruples about colonizing and, following the example that other European nations had long been offering, herself colonized where she had once been enslaved.

In later life, lacking his original preoccupations, or having at least separated them from his song, Swinburne fed increasingly on literature for his substance. He grew more nationalistic—anti-Irish, anti-Boer—and applauded the idea of a strong British navy. Perhaps, after all, the influence of Victorian morals was not subsequently as healthy as it was thought to have been, and it is an irony of the period that a man who once found himself so much at variance with the professed sexual morality subsequently moved with its official political currents.

CHAPTER TWO

THOMAS HARDY

I

Swinburne and Meredith both died in 1909, withdrawing as it were from the gathering tensions in Europe. The year was also, as C. K. Stead remarks in *The New Poetic*,

a year carrying the beginnings, unrecognized at the time, of what we now acknowledge to be a resurgence of poetry in the twentieth century. Yeats's collected poems of that year put an outworn style and restricted sensibility behind him, making way for the new, robust poetry that was soon to emerge. In the same year the Imagist movement was first formed, Pound's *Personae* appeared, and a valuable association between Pound and Yeats was formed.

Three years previously Hardy had published his 'epic-drama' *The Dynasts*, and this too marked some kind of unrecognized beginning in that a whole, sizeable work was devoted to the 'knowledge' that war brings. This is not the sole subject of *The Dynasts*, but the drama is concerned with war in the sense that war focuses the processes and effects of society's actions upon itself. This distinguishes the work from nearly all those poems considered in the first chapter; it concentrates on war as the others do not. Concentration may seem a peculiar description for a work of such size; but it is concentrated in its restriction of the reader's immediate attention to a knowledge of war's inflictions, even though the Spirits see war as merely the most destructive of society's operations. War is the most powerful metaphor used to encompass and focus society's actions, and, by implication, to indicate to it its need for a more developed and sympathetic consciousness.

The Dynasts differs also from the poems considered in the first chapter in that it is not only historical, but consciously so. By documenting a past era, Hardy seeks to make credible and applicable his conclusions to his (and our) situation. It documents in a way that *The Cenci*, for instance, does not attempt, despite its historical basis; although there can be no doubt that what Shelley was indicting in an earlier era he meant his readers to re-apply to their own. Shelley was drawing parallels, but one feels that Hardy was documenting his own age more immediately. Perhaps the difference lies in the fact that the Napoleonic era was closer to Hardy's age, and ours, than the Italian sixteenth century was to Shelley's. Certainly, in his preoccupation with the ten years of Napoleonic struggle (1805–15), Hardy was then still able to draw on people's memories of the precautions taken against a seemingly probable invasion, as well as on the songs and anecdotes of the people in the area, as they had been handed down.

Moreover, although Hardy had been making notes for the work since March 1874, and had started writing in 1897, consciousness of the Boer War (1899–1902) would almost certainly have helped to form the work's final didactic and anti-war emphases. War, Hardy seems to be saying, is not a distant historical phenomenon, but a present fact that will remain until society rejects it as a 'solution' to its problems. The consistency with which this idea is developed through the drama is further evidence of its concentration. As each group of conflicts is fought, the struggle becomes more excoriating; and more crucially, the spirit in which they are fought changes from a nominally 'civilized' code of war into one of desperate brutality and bitterness where, at last, most of the civilized decorums are thrust away. Finally, with regard to the concentrating shape of the work, while some of the characters employ what Yeats defined as 'an intricate psychology, action in character', they more usually work in the opposite way—'as in the ballads character in action'. ' "Tragedy is an imitation, not of men, but of actions", Aristotle says in the *Poetics*; "it is by [men's] actions that they are happy, or the contrary".' It is this subordination of the characters to their actions which concentrates meaning in *The Dynasts*.

At the close of the struggle only the most ruthless remain, to be slaughtered, defeated, or victorious. Those with more compunction have already passed from the stage. Villeneuve, for example, commits suicide in the first of the three plays, believing that he has failed Napoleon; 'An Emperor's chide is a command to die' (1, V, vi, p. 104).[1] Napoleon's rebuke results from Villeneuve's unsuccessful engagement with Nelson at Trafalgar. Villeneuve is later contrasted with his commander, whose equally critical self-appraisal (in Part 3) causes him to reject suicide when the means are offered

[1] Page references for *The Dynasts* are to the edition of 1930.

him. On the other hand, when he does subsequently make the attempt, his motives are quite unlike those of Villeneuve. For Napoleon, the failure is not a moral but a military and political one. When his friends and supporters fail him, he has nothing to fall back on except death. Napoleon in *The Dynasts* becomes increasingly indifferent to the expenditure of human life, as the opposition to him increases. Villeneuve, on the other hand, had concluded that to prolong his battle with Nelson would have entailed an entirely unprofitable waste of life and, incidentally, shamed the French fleet. Thus, the more humane are killed off at the onset of the struggle, leaving it to the ruthless, who can only complete the process by one side being annihilated, although not before their own has suffered immense casualties. This, of course, was the pattern of the First World War. Those who doubt the bitterness of the Napoleonic struggle, or who are inclined to sympathize with Napoleon the loser, should consult Goya's 'The Disasters of War'.

Hardy brings out Napoleon's increasing indifference to the suffering of others in his interview with Marie Louise after his defeat by the Russians and their winter:

MARIE LOUISE (simply)
But those six hundred thousand throbbing throats . . .
So full of youth and spirits—all bleached bones—
Ridiculous? Can it be so, dear, to—
Their mothers, say?

NAPOLÉON (with a twitch of displeasure)
            You scarcely understand.
I mean the enterprise, and not its stuff. . . .
I'll find a way to do a better thing. . . .

(3, I, xii, pp. 363–4)

The terms of his argument—'the enterprise, and not its stuff'—show how little he reckons the human cost.

If any sympathy is generated for Napoleon (and, to heighten the drama, some is), it is achieved through the reader's awareness that Napoleon is anything but a 'great' man, however fallen, and that his inflated attempts to view himself as such reduce his particular qualities. It is in a certain (partly spurious) sense of democratization that Napoleon makes his appeal. The kind of greatness he sometimes assumes clashes with his supposed hatred of kings; and he is at his best when he refutes the majestic gestures alien to his origins:

> ROUSTAN
> After this fall, your majesty, 'tis plain
> You will not choose to live; and knowing this
> I bring to you my sword.
> NAPOLÉON (with a nod)
>   I see you do,
> Roustan,
>   ROUSTAN
>   Will you, sire, use it on yourself,
> Or shall I pass it through you?
>   NAPOLÉON (coldly)
>   Neither plan
> Is quite expedient for the moment, man.
>   ROUSTAN
> Neither?   (3, IV, iv, p. 412)

The terse, comic effects are brilliantly informative. This is not pastiche of an earlier heroic style. Roustan's solicitousness is needlessly explanatory, as the phrase 'and knowing this' shows. By decorously placing it with 'to you', Hardy emphasizes the majestic but largely outdated code Roustan is pretentiously imitating, one suitable neither for Napoleon nor his personal attendant. They are manœuvring within a code of honour made anachronistic by, among other things, the revised character of the new warfare Napoleon himself is so much the exponent of. By 'new warfare' I mean not only the altered nature of the conflict, but also the new set of social assumptions with which the kings of the *ancien régime* were then being dislodged. Thus Napoleon's laconic *and* dignified knowingness, 'I see you do', fully characterizes the man. There are no noble refutations, but a terse acknowledgement of the suggestion, and its dismissal. The polite but horrific vacuity of 'Or shall I pass it through you' also effectively contrasts with Napoleon's rejoinder as much as it does with the real, if egocentric, despair which afterwards seizes him and prompts his own form of (attempted) suicide. The flat, undecorative vigour of the pentameter beautifully expresses the simplicity of Napoleon's own code.

However we may feel about Napoleon's emotional identification with his people (as assessed, somewhat dubiously, in Part 3, V, iv), we have to remember that such cordiality is followed by the carnage of Waterloo, which destroys the French nation and both morally and physically enervates Europe. Yet for the moment Napoleon's desertion of his troops in Russia after the failure of the campaign —agonizingly re-created by Hardy—is forgotten as Napoleon 'takes his turn with the rank and file in drinking sour wine provided by the peasantry'. This is no compensation, however, for the carnage of Waterloo, and Hardy, at pains to convey the massacre it becomes, undermines Napoleon's gesture by showing the deterioration of his democratic attitudes.[1] Hardy concentratedly conveys the reduction of the French army in this episode of the massacre:

The three or four heroic battalions of the Old and Middle Guard fall back step by step, halting to reform in square when they get badly broken and shrunk. At last they are surrounded by the English Guards and other foot, who keep firing on them and smiting them to smaller and smaller numbers. General Cambronne is inside the square.

> COLONEL HUGH HALKETT (shouting)
> Surrender! And preserve those heroes' lives!
>
> CAMBRONNE (with exasperation)
> Mer-r-r-rde!... You've to deal with desperates, man, today:
> Life is a byword here!

Hollow laughter, as from people in hell, comes approvingly from the remains of the Old Guard. The English proceed with their massacre, the devoted band thins and thins, and a ball strikes CAMBRONNE, who falls, and is trampled over.

$$(3, \text{VII}, \text{viii}, \text{pp. } 516\text{–}17)$$

That is as horrific and affecting as anything in the poetry of the First World War, and it spares neither the French nor the English. The brutality is immediately underlined by the Spirit of the Years:

> Nought remains
> But vindictiveness here amid the strong,
> And here amid the weak an impotent rage.

The victory of Waterloo marks the ultimate erosion not merely of civilized restraints, but any sense of humane behaviour.

One of the ways in which Hardy measures war's destructiveness is in its incidental spoliation of nature. Many of the poets of the First World War use this as a means of impelling the reader into an understanding of its horrors, yet none exceeds Hardy's pathos as he conveys the reduction of nature's minute, vulnerable creatures. The soldiers are unaware of what they are doing, so concerned are they with their own efforts. So, on the eve of Waterloo:

[1] See 3, V, iii, pp. 436–7.

CHORUS OF THE YEARS

The mole's tunnelled chambers are crushed by wheels,
The lark's eggs scattered, their owners fled;
And the hedgehog's household the sapper unseals.

The snail draws in at the terrible tread,
But in vain; he is crushed by the felloe-rim;
The worm asks what can be overhead,

And wriggles deep from a scene so grim,
And guesses him safe; for he does not know
What a foul red blood will be soaking him!

Beaten about by the heel and the toe
Are butterflies, sick of the day's long rheum,
To die of a worse than the weather-foe.

Trodden and bruised to a miry tomb
Are ears that have greened but will never be gold,
And flowers in the bud that will never bloom.

(3, VI, viii, p. 483)

The rhythms are as premonitory as the words. One senses that what is happening to the creatures today will happen to the soldiers tomorrow; they will be as much oppressed as 'The green seems opprest'. Thus, a hierarchy of destroyers is set up; as the creatures are destroyed by soldiers hardly aware of what they do, so the controlling mind of the universe is unconscious, as 'It' works its will, of who or what suffers. The frailty of nature's creatures is an exact emblem of human frailty and vulnerability, in war. When we come to examine, and censure, his poems about the First World War, we should remember this remarkable passage and recall also that Hardy never directly experienced war. This makes it the more surprising that he should have shown such perceptions in *The Dynasts* and 'Channel Firing' and should then have responded so inertly to the First World War.

H. D. F. Kitto suggests that in the Oresteian trilogy we are shown two entities, men and gods, evolving in separate but related ways. As the human beings evolve in relation to one another, there is an interacting change in their relationship with the gods. The difference between the Greek gods and Hardy's Spirits is that the former may act as he or she thinks best; whereas the Spirits act in obedience to 'Its' unconscious will. Yet Kitto's understanding of the interactions described above has relevance to Hardy's spirits in that some of them think that 'It' may in time become conscious. Becoming so, 'It' may reduce human suffering by choosing certain courses of action that do not lead to inevitable conflict, as they so disastrously do in *The Dynasts*. The question as to the Spirits' form of identity is given an answer of sorts in the Preface:

[The Spirits] are intended to be taken by the reader for what they may be worth as contrivances of the fancy merely. . . . The chief thing hoped for them is that they and their utterances may have dramatic plausibility enough to procure for them, in the words of Coleridge, 'that willing suspension of disbelief for the moment which constitutes poetic faith.'

This tells us little except that we do not have to believe in their literal (spiritual) existence, and that we may think of them, if we wish, as projections of human feelings and attitudes. 'These phantasmal Intelligences are divided into groups, of which only one, that of the Pities, approximates to "the Universal Sympathy of human nature—the spectator idealized" of the Greek Chorus.'

The Spirit of the Pities, which 'is impressionable and inconsistent in its views', is closer as well as more immediately sympathetic to human pain, and so is the most available possible mediator between sentient humanity and 'It'. The unconscious character of 'It' is stressed in the work's first lines:

SHADE OF THE EARTH
What of the Immanent Will and Its designs?

SPIRIT OF THE YEARS
It works unconsciously, as heretofore,
Eternal artistries in Circumstance,
Whose patterns, wrought by rapt aesthetic rote,
Seem in themselves Its single listless aim,
And not their consequence. . . .   (1, Fore Scene, p. 1)

The Immanent Will has hardly any consciousness, even of itself; in fulfilling its own 'patterns', it is only consummating its impulses.

CHORUS OF THE PITIES
Still thus? Still thus? . . .
An automatic sense. . . .
SPIRIT SINISTER (aside)

Good, as before.
My little engines, then, will still have play.

(1, Fore Scene, p. 1)

The Spirit Sinister reveals Hardy's strategy. The absolute power of the Will finds its consummation through those human beings most apt to *its* patterning. J. O. Bailey in *Thomas Hardy and the Cosmic Mind* (1956) speaks of the Will as operating 'in human beings as egotistic and selfish impulses'. Thus, the Prince of Wales and the doctors 'tending' the mad pitiful King are 'egotistical and selfish'; Bailey is referring, I think, to those men and women who ruthlessly struggle for power in *The Dynasts*, and as ruthlessly use it once it has been obtained. Napoleon, of course, fits this description, and it is through him that the Will most potently works; although from Napoleon's viewpoint it would have been better if the Will had worked even more potently, or not at all:

> ... 'tis true, I have ever known
> That such a Will I passively obeyed! ...
>   Why did the death-drops fail to bite me close
> I took at Fontainebleau? Had I then ceased,
> This deep had been unplumbed. ...

(3, VII, ix, p. 519)

The question of choice and responsibility is raised here, since it might be argued that, if Napoleon only ever 'passively obeyed' the Will (which in any case lacks consciousness), he cannot be held responsible for what he does; and the Will lacking consciousness cannot be judged either. There is, however, a different way of putting it. In some human beings the egoism is so strong and apt to the Will that 'It' finds in the character of that person nothing strong enough effectively to oppose its impulses—such as pity, for instance. In dramatic terms, the Will discovers its affinities in those most innately willing to work its egoistic impulses, as if these impulses were these people's alone. Napoleon is responsible in that he was by nature most apt to the Will's impulses. He would have obeyed such promptings in himself even though, without the Will's, he might have obeyed them less persistently. The problem then is how to change the unconsciousness of the Will, or its corresponding nature in human beings.

Hardy's view of the man-made horrors and absurdities of war is nowhere more finely shown than in the scene at Talavera where, significantly, the Spirit of the *Pities* says:

What do I see but thirsty, throbbing bands
From these inimic hosts defiling down
In homely need towards the little stream
That parts their enmities, and drinking there!
They get to grasping hands across the rill,
Sealing their sameness as earth's sojourners.—
What more could plead the wryness of the times
Than such unstudied piteous pantomimes!

(2, IV, v, p. 245)

Strangely similar is the episode in Blunden's *Undertones of War*:

. . . a German officer and perhaps twenty of his men . . . with friendly cries of 'Good morning, Tommy, have you any biscuits?' and the like, got out of their trench and invited our men to do the same. What their object was, beyond simple fraternizing, I cannot guess; it was afterwards argued that they wished to obtain identification of the unit opposite them. And yet I heard they had already addressed us as the 'bastard Sussek'. In any case, our men were told not to fire upon them, both by C. and the other company's officer on watch. . . . When this affair was reported to more senior members of the battalion, it took on rather a gloomy aspect; it appeared that the bounden duty of C. and R. had been to open fire on the enemy. . . . [subsequently] the unfortunate subalterns were reproved, and, what is more, placed under arrest.

Under arrest they marched towards the Somme battle of 1916.

The same compassion is implicit in Blunden's comments as in the Pities'; but, after compassion has had its say, it is usually left to the Spirit of the Years to qualify the Pities, or, as here, the Spirit Ironic:

The groping tentativeness [the Spirit Ironic says] *of an Immanent Will (as grey old Years describes it) cannot be asked to learn logic at this time of day! The spectacle of Its instruments, set to riddle one another through, and then to drink together in peace and concord is where the humour comes in. . . .*

SPIRIT SINISTER

Come, Sprite, don't carry your ironies too far, or you may wake up the Unconscious Itself, and tempt It to let all the gory clock-work of the show run down to spite me!　　　　　　　　　(2, IV, v, p. 245)

The contrast between the Spirit Ironic and Spirit Sinister is that, while the former understands the situation with a compassionate irony (ironic through its long witnessing of the Its unconscious impulses and its consequences), the Spirit Sinister has an egoistic if naïve cruel insensitivity; it has some of the aspects, one feels, that the It might have if It were made conscious of Its acts, and then, sadistically and consciously, continued in Its previous ways. The Spirit Sinister delights in human misery and is only afraid that the It will wake from Its unconsciousness and, waking, curtail those impulses which produce such devastation among the human beings. In this case, he need not fear. Bloodshed inevitably follows:

> *Opposed, opposers, in a common plight*
> *Are scorched together on the dusk champaign.*
>
> (2, IV, v, p. 246)

The word 'together' emphasizes the irony of their having hours before (as the Spirit Ironic observes) grasped hands in sympathetic friendship. As if to emphasize war's absurdity, cruelty, and irony, this scene of bloodshed is immediately followed by one of celebration for the British victory—the Prince of Wales's birthday party at the Royal Pavilion, Brighton.

The question of responsibility (as the Spirits Ironic and Sinister indicate) returns the reader to the Will and its agents. Bailey paraphrases Hartmann as surmising that the Will 'made conscious would relieve pain by ceasing to will and hence to exist—that is, by annihilation of the world'. This seems a gloomy assessment of what the prime unconsciousness would contrive if it were to develop consciousness, but in fact it is doubtful if, at the end of *The Dynasts*, the Will has become at all conscious. Such changes as mankind has undergone are in the direction of a greater brutality.

There are more hopeful changes among the Spirits: there is both a *general* heightening of human consciousness and understanding and, at the same time, the Spirits' recognition of the need to make conscious the Will and its impulses; which are perhaps one and the same thing. If the Spirit of the Pities has gained in balance and consistency—'There's logic in that', the Spirit of the Years at length says commendingly to it—the Spirit Ironic is, conversely, a little more open to compassion and to what the Spirit of the Pities has to say. A measure of interaction has taken place between them:

> SEMICHORUS I OF THE YEARS
> *O Immanence, That reasonest not*
> *In putting forth all things begot,*
> *Thou build'st Thy house in space—for what? . . .*

SPIRIT IRONIC

For one I cannot answer. But I know
'Tis handsome of our Pities so to sing
The praises of the dreaming, dark, dumb Thing
That turns the handle of this idle Show!

As once a Greek asked I would fain ask too,
Who knows if all this Spectacle be true,
Or an illusion of the gods (the Will,
To wit) some hocus-pocus to fulfil?

(3, After Scene, p. 524)

The logic of the Spirit Ironic is perhaps superior still to that of the Pities, but the former's sardonic character has been made more responsive by the compassion of the younger spirit, as well as by the latter's intellectual growth. That, at least, is how I read the Spirit Ironic's evaluation of It quoted above. In addition, the Spirit of the Pities has finally established some acknowledged rapport with the Spirit of the Years, with whom in any case he has as much in common as he has with the Spirit Ironic. Thus when, in constant dispute with the Spirit of the Years, the Pities says:

Thou arguest still the Inadvertent Mind.—
But, even so, shall blankness be for aye?

(3, After Scene, p. 522)

the Pities' careful questioning—made more careful not only by a developed logic but by a deepened power of sympathy—draws from the Spirit of the Years this response:

Something of difference animates your quiring,
O half-convinced Compassionates and fond,
From chords consistent with our spectacle!
You almost charm my long philosophy
Out of my strong-built thought, and bear me back
To when I thanksgave thus.... Ay, start not, Shades;
In the Foregone I knew what dreaming was,
And could let raptures rule! But not so now....

(3, After Scene, p. 524)

'Half-convinced' is what the Spirit of the Years is now, or rather, is again. The more powerful and coherent view of the Pities has elicited from the Years a confession of kinship. If the Spirit of the Years no longer lets 'raptures rule', this is partly because its experiences of the Will have eroded such apparently hopeful impulses, and is not merely the restraint resulting from a superior wisdom. Hardy carefully weighs and counts the costs of age against youth. The Pities had previously sung:

> *We hold that Thy unscanted scope*
> *Affords a food for final Hope,*
> *That mild-eyed Prescience ponders nigh*
> *Life's loom, to lull it by-and-by.*

(3, After Scene, p. 523)

Hardy shows the benign spirits inclining sympathetically towards the Pities' attitudes, among them, the recognition that some kind of meliorism is possible. The Pities believe that the Will may waken (be awakened?) and in so waking, become compassionate:

> *Nay;—shall not Its blindness break?*
> *Yea, must not Its heart awake, . . .*
> *In a genial germing purpose, and for loving-kindness' sake?*

(3, After Scene, p. 525)

If hope exists, it lies in awakening the Will to an amelioration of the condition of the creatures It has made. It was upon such meliorism, limited though it is, that the First World War made its impact.

2

> Trail all your pikes, dispirit every drum,
> March in a slow procession from afar,
> Ye silent, ye dejected men of war!
> Be still the hautboys, and the flute be dumb!
> Display no more, in vain, the lofty banner.
> For see! where on the bier before ye lies
> The pale, the fall'n, th'untimely sacrifice
> To your mistaken shrine, to your false idol Honour.

Anne, Countess of Winchilsea: 'The Soldier's Death'

The problem with Hardy's later poetry of war is not that it is constrained by facts, since all facts permit poetry. Setting aside for the moment the difficulty of appreciating a chauvinistic poem, our response to his poems about the First World War is complicated by his seemingly distorted response. In theory, one can conceive of a Hardyesque verse that sensuously responds to the suffering of the soldier, yet insists on the necessity of war.[1] This would at least fit

---

[1] See the discussion of Yeats on p. 177.

some of the facts of war, and at the same time postulate a belief in the necessity of one's culture surviving. Compare, for example, the position of the poet in the Second World War involved in the struggle with fascism. But Hardy's poems of the First War are neither indictments of war, nor, as is the case with certain poets of the Second War, tentative gropings for a position in which the demands of war and the compunctions at killing may be, if not reconciled, at least held in a tolerable equilibrium. Hardy's poems of this period are mainly distortions, unlike anything he had previously written about war, or afterwards wrote. This cannot be because they were concerned with a brutal struggle; Hardy could cope with brutality, as *The Dynasts* shows. The facts of the Napoleonic struggle do not overwhelm the poems; on the contrary (and here is an interesting affinity with Yeats), it is as though he chose to express as little of the nature of combat as possible. It is this exclusion, deliberate or otherwise, which seems to permit the rhetorical distortion and simplification of these poems. To argue from the other end, it is as though the exhortation to fight is pitched in such a way as to exclude any possibility of his responding—in the poems—to the brutalities of combat; as though, only by making such exclusions, would the exhortation not seem absurd. But the exclusion of the brutalities by necessity excludes also the recognition of the suffering, and the result is that such exclusion increases the hortatory nature of his appeals. This calls in question the honesty, or at least the validity, of such appeals. In both poetic and human terms, the heroic instructions sound thin and shrill.[1] They have the tones not of the human voice but of the megaphone; and they appear deceitful because we know from Hardy's earlier poetry that he recognized the facts of war. By omitting even a few telling, sensuous details, the verse becomes declamatory propaganda in the pejorative sense of the word.

One may feel that, where it is a question of producing efficient propaganda, most people are foolish, and that it is permissible to suppress the facts in a good cause.[2] Whether Hardy believed that he was turning out this kind of propaganda I do not know, but the strongest possible contrast exists between these First War poems and 'Channel Firing', written in April 1914. It is as though, when

---

[1] As Sorley noted. See below, p. 51.

[2] Raymond Williams has an interesting discussion of this in *Culture and Society* (pp. 292–4), and I share his view of such manipulation.

fighting broke out, he could no longer think in the mode of this poem and *The Dynasts*. There can be no doubt that the more complex and humane response produced the better poetry; witness the opening of 'Channel Firing':

> That night your great guns, unawares,
> Shook all our coffins as we lay,
> And broke the chancel window-squares,
> We thought it was the Judgement-day. . . .
>
> . . . Till God called, 'No;
> It's gunnery practice out at sea. . . .
>
> 'All nations striving strong to make
> Red war yet redder. Mad as hatters. . . .'

It is indeed Judgement Day, even though the dead have mistaken the nature of the sound that, ironically, wakes them. No such perception occurs, needless to say, in Hardy's First World War poems. There the words 'blood' and 'red' occur twice only ('In Time of Wars and Tumults' and, indirectly, in 'I met a Man'). In 'Channel Firing' the tetrameters gauge the strength of his convictions, the last stanza insisting on the malign and pervasive effects of war:

> Again the guns disturbed the hour,
> Roaring their readiness to avenge,
> As far inland as Stourton Tower,
> And Camelot, and starlit Stonehenge.

The encampment areas of Dorset, Wiltshire, and Hampshire were familiar enough to Hardy, and to the soldiers of the Napoleonic era, but he is not so much insisting on a historical topography as on a comparison between the two wars. He anticipates, in 'the coming fury', a greater involvement of the total population than ever before; a war fought not by relatively small professional and press-ganged armies, but by enlisted and recruited armies of millions. His dismay is brilliantly conveyed by the extra accented syllable at the end of that last line, and the disconcerting shift of stress from the second into the third foot of the tetrameter:

> Aňd Cámĕlŏt, aňd stárliť Stónehéňge.

'Channel Firing' sees war as an activity as mindless as that of the omnipotent It in *The Dynasts*. The attitudes in the Boer War poems, however, inasmuch as these poems form a whole, are at least more tentative in their evaluation. In his Preface to *Poems of the Past and the Present* (1902), Hardy seems content to let any emerging contradictions remain unresolved, speaking of

a series of feelings and fancies written down in widely differing moods and circumstances.... It will probably be found ... to possess little cohesion of thought or harmony of colouring. I do not greatly regret this. Unadjusted impressions have their value, and the road to a true philosophy of life seems to lie in humbly recording diverse readings of its phenomena as they are forced upon us by chance and change.

Which irony do we read there? Is it the irony in which (he is saying) there is no true comprehensive picture of life to which he can subscribe, and that the best he can do—unlike other more 'philosophic' writers—is to record what is forced on him 'by chance and change'? Or does he mean: there is a comprehensiveness that I have seen, but 'chance and change' disrupt it? Or is there no irony at all?

There are certainly contradictory elements in some of the poems. 'Embarkation', for instance, envisages not only the 'bands' that 'deckward tramp' with their vitality of youth 'alive as spring'; it sees also the likelihood of youth's death in 'yellow as autumn's leaves' which, as in nature, are an inescapable part of the 'tragical To-be'. The poem ends:

> None dubious of the cause, none murmuring,
>
> Wives, sisters, parents, wave white hands and smile,
> As if they knew not that they weep the while.

The first line of this quotation is ambiguous in that it does not reveal Hardy's attitude to the cause and its expenditure of life. We have the right to ask since he raises the issue in that line. Do the relatives endorse the sons' sacrifice, or admire it but question the cause? Each of these readings (and perhaps variants of them) is possible, but Hardy does not commit himself to any one, which is strange in that they tend to exclude each other. It is even stranger when we recall that he was still at this time writing *The Dynasts*, which is so much more specific in its attitudes to war. Is it possible that he could only condemn a war when its specific issues were 'safely' in the past? Did the present require a more philosophic/ stoical attitude, in which war was merely an item in the catalogue of life's 'moan', and therefore to be endured as a yet more diverse and chance event? Whatever one feels about the line in 'Embarkation', one should notice nevertheless the subtlety with which Hardy achieves his effects, a subtlety absent from his poems of the First World War. Little of this intimacy gets into the anti-Boer War poems either, for that matter, perhaps because feelings were so strong on either side of the pro/anti-war issue that any sense of intimacy, such as Hardy manages here, was erased from their possible responses. For instance, the white hand waving goodbye is a transferred image of the white handkerchief that will wipe away tears; thus, the image cleverly incorporates and anticipates the expression of hidden grief in the last line. 'White' may perhaps also be read as indicative of the purity of intention which the relatives see in the self-sacrifice of their young soldiers.[1]

In 'Departure', also dated 1899, Hardy reverts to the position held in *The Dynasts*:

'How long, O striving Teutons, Slavs, and Gaels

Must your wroth reasonings trade on lives like these,
That are as puppets in a playing hand?—
When shall the saner softer polities. . . .'

The appeal has the generalized directness of the orator, and while one may endorse *some* of the attitudes (he doesn't seem to question, for instance, why the Gaels/Irish were so agitated), the voice is dangerously near that of the self-appointed statesman of the First War poems. Hardy's professed attitudes are compelling only when they combine with his own genuine sensuous responses, experiential and not spokesmanlike.

Some of the Boer War poems exploit the ironies indirectly produced by war—ironies that seem almost too facile. In 'A Wife in London', the woman receives by telegram the news of her husband's death the day before a letter arrives in which he speaks 'of new love that they would learn'.

'Drummer Hodge' has two lines that anticipate the sentiment in Brooke's 'The Soldier'. Compare Brooke's

If I should die, think only this of me:
    That there's some corner of a foreign field
That is for ever England

[1] In contrast to this see 'The Souls of the Slain', p. 48.

with Hardy's

> Yet portion of that unknown plain
>   Will Hodge for ever be;
> His homely Northern breast and brain
>   Grow to some Southern tree,
> And strange-eyed constellations reign
>   His stars eternally.

There are differences. Hardy details his homely and star-lit prophecies: Brooke's perception is vague. Brooke's body is seen as contriving to remain in some mystical way English and separate from the foreign soil it is buried in, a curiously offensive inaccurate notion. Hardy, on the other hand, sees with ironic, perhaps too neatly ironic, foresight Hodge merging with the foreign context ('Northern breast/Southern tree'). There are also similarities, found I think in the tonal quality as well as in the overall idea, and focused on the phrases 'for ever/for ever'; although one should note the spiritualized connotations of the one and the materially based irony of the other. It is curious that Brooke should have become famous, partly as a result of his probably unconscious plagiarism.

In 'A Christmas Ghost Story' (1899), Hardy shares Blake's and Owen's version of the gentle, martyred Christ who redeems the world through his suffering, and his actions are contrasted with man's warring activities:

> 'I would know
> By whom, and when the All-Earth-gladdening Law
> Of Peace, brought in by that Man Crucified,
> Was ruled to be inept, and set aside?'

There is no ambiguity in this poem.

In 'The Souls of the Slain' (1899), the spirits of these dead revert to their original softness, and are indirectly compared with creatures more vulnerable and temporary than man:

> ... A whirr, as of wings
>   Waved by mighty-vanned flies,
>   Or by night-moths of measureless size,
> And in softness and smoothness well-nigh beyond hearing
>   Of corporal things.

The softness of the creatures is there, but they are also given a fearful dimension, which in turn suggests the intricacy of Hardy's attitudes. The slain are murdered killers, but if they are huge and predatory, they are also soft and vulnerable. Hardy departs from this central perception, as if he could not resist the opportunity of exploiting the possible ironies indirectly produced in war. The first irony, one should say, is very much central to a concern with the problem of war and its sacrifice. The slain are remembered by their 'kin' not for their 'glory and war-mightiness', but their 'dearer things', 'doings as boys', and 'babyhood's innocent days'. Very powerfully, Hardy subverts the popular heroic notion, showing that the patriotic cause for which the soldiers died is not the central concern of their kin, but rather their personal memories, many of them ironically inapt for soldiers. There are other, less central, ironies: 'Some pray that, ere dying, your faith had grown firmer', none of which is to the dead's purpose now; it is an incidental and possibly selfish desire of their kin to confirm their own religious beliefs. Finally there is Hardy's favourite irony; that of human frailty being tested and found wanting. This he introduces by showing how some of the relatives are, or are about to be, unfaithful; or are more concerned with vanity than grief:

> —'Many mourn; many think
> It is not unattractive to prink
> Them in sables for heroes. Some fickle and fleet hearts
> Have found them new loves.'

Such ironies are not confined to war, being negative distillations only to be expected within life's 'moan'.[1] Some of the souls learn that 'old kindness' is more to be prized than the fame which they expected to result from their death—certainly a more central perception. Some plunge into the 'fathomless regions/Of myriads forgot'. But the narrator is finally left without theme or commitment other than the irony of life's circumstances, in which war is seen as an exacerbator, but not as a factor qualitatively different from other experiences of 'chance and change'. Fate, as it were, lets Hardy off the hook. The total effect in this poem may be one of cumulative dismay, but the crucial point made in *The Dynasts*, that man is the self-enrolled victim of war, is an irony missed here. It is similarly neglected in his poems of the First World War.

[1] For a similar irony, concerning dress alone, consult 'At the Draper's', *Satires of Circumstance* (1914).

The war got off to a good start. In Paris, Berlin, and London, as photographs show, jubilant crowds cheered the news of its declaration, as if greeting news of some *universal* good. Thousands enlisted immediately, and these soldiers were cheered by the populace, as if they were departing to celebrate the rites of their fertility god. Simone Weil in 'The *Iliad*, or the Poem of Force'[1] wrote:

At the outset, at the embarkation, their hearts are light, as hearts always are if you have a large force on your side and nothing but space to oppose you. Their weapons are in their hands; the enemy is absent. Unless your spirit has been conquered in advance by the reputation of the enemy, you always feel yourself to be much stronger than anybody who is not there. An absent man does not impose the yoke of necessity. To the spirits of those embarking no necessity yet presents itself; consequently they go off as though to a game, as though on holiday from the confinement of daily life.

That last perception is telling. The enthusiasm, however, would seem to have been less universal than we, with our superior and ironic hindsight, have imagined it to be. In *The Last Sheaf* (1928) Edward Thomas reported:

Some of these recruits had enlisted for 'hunger', some for fun, not all to serve their country. So said the landlord, an old soldier. 'I wouldn't enlist for anything,' said a man with his cheese waiting on his knife-tip, 'not unless I was made. I would if it was a fair war. But it's not, it's murder. . . .' 'That's right,' said the postman. 'A man's only got seventy years to live, and ninety per cent don't get beyond fifty. I reckon we want a little peace. Twentieth century too.'

Such dissident accounts conflict with the contemporary historian's glib irony as he unfolds a picture of populations eagerly enlisting in a war that was to kill thirteen millions. Even so, it seems there was not a great deal of initial reluctance. How well Hardy catches the spirit of general festivity in his jaunty rhythms, although the words also simulate a martial sternness:

> Nay. We well see what we are doing,
>   Though some may not see—
>   Dalliers as they be—
>   England's need are we;
> Her distress would leave us rueing:
> Nay. We well see what we are doing,
>   Though some may not see!

[1] English translation by Mary McCarthy published in *Politics*, November 1945.

'Men who March Away' was first published in *The Times* of 5
September 1914. Hardy was quick off the mark, and the public
orientation of the poem does nothing to improve its sentiments—its
inspiriting reproaches directed at those who have not yet volunteered (conscription was not introduced until January 1916).
Simone Weil, in the passage quoted above, is paraphrasing Homer's
account of the festivities attendant on the outbreak of war. Both
use an insight that leads to an intense ironic bitterness:

> Where have they gone, those braggadocio boasts
> We proudly flung upon the air at Lemnos,
> Stuffing ourselves with flesh of horned steers,
> Drinking from cups brimming over with wine?
> As for Trojans—a hundred or two each man of us
> Could handle in battle. And now one is too much for us.

Where Homer and Weil perceive the wretched irony of the festivities
and the boasting, Hardy writes recruiting songs, but his confidence
in the cause does not compensate for the poverty of the sentiments
and the verse. Fortunately perhaps, he was a poor apologist for the
war; but this and other poems in the group illustrate the dictum
that 'in war truth is the first casualty'. Edward Thomas, surprisingly,
liked the poem; his biographer, William Cooke, quotes from a
letter to W. H. Hudson, in which Thomas wrote:

I thought Hardy's poem in *The Times*

> Ere the barn-cocks say
> Night is growing gray,

the only good one concerned with the war.

Criticism of this poem was to come from a much younger man
who, in fact, admired Hardy's work. He attacked him, not for his
belief that England was the just party, but for his unrealistic notion
that the just are always given the material rewards of victory.

Curiously enough, I think that 'Men who March Away' is the most
arid poem in the book, besides being untrue of the sentiments of the
ranksman going to war: 'Victory crowns the just' is the worst line he ever
wrote—filched from a leading article in *The Morning Post*, and unworthy
of him who had always previously disdained to insult Justice by offering
it a material crown like Victory.

This comes from a letter Charles Hamilton Sorley wrote as early as 30 November 1914, and it is no isolated flash of perception. Throughout this early pre-Somme period, and up to his death on 13 October 1915, Sorley's assessment of the war and the attitudes it engendered, and which produced it, remained intelligent and humane:

War in England only means putting all the men of 'military age' in England into a state of routinal coma, preparatory to getting them killed. You are being given six months to become conventional: your peace thus made with God, you will be sent out and killed. At least, if you aren't killed, you'll come back so unfitted for any other job that you'll have to stay in the Army. I should like so much to kill whoever was primarily responsible for the war. . . .

We don't seem to be winning, do we? It looks like an affair of years. If so, pray God for a nice little bullet wound (tidy and clean) in the shoulder. That's the place.

He was not that fortunate.

Hardy, by contrast, in March 1917 renews the call to action, when the spirit that launched the Somme offensive was a dead letter:

> Up and be doing, all who have a hand
> To lift, a back to bend. . . .
>
> —Say, then, 'I come!' and go, O women and men
> Of palace, ploughshare, easel, counter, pen;
> That scareless, scatheless, England still may stand.

This is dismayingly simplistic—even comic—and the poem, 'A Call to National Service', is not improved by Hardy's easy democratizing of Wordsworth's patriotic

> . . . altar, sword, and pen,
> Fireside, the heroic wealth of hall and bower. . . .

One has the sense of Hardy flattering the commoners by pointing out that, through association with Wordsworth's line, they are now as useful as their lords, and that their sacrifice is as valid as that of those who 'by chance' happen to be higher up the social register. But, because it is done so easily, one suspects that Hardy may merely be making this declaration to lubricate the war effort. Of course, in such combat, where numbers still count and superior equipment is not yet the only factor, every citizen is a democrat by virtue of his usefulness to the state. This was always so, but the cohesive force of nationalism was to ensure that each of its citizens proved a reliable soldier by offering a flat democratic utility in return for his service (life). Hardy's usually perceptive irony failed to make use of this opportunity for its operation, and thereby helped to confirm such nationalism. The easy enthusiasm of

> Would years but let me stir as once I stirred
> At many a dawn to take the forward track,
> And with a stride plunged on to enterprise . . .

(Hardy was then seventy-seven) rises to its rhythmical climax with the word 'plunged'. In physical terms the word is here inexactly linked with the adverbial preposition that follows it, and in being so used the meagre resources of the cliché itself are exposed. Consider also the inflated imprecision of the word 'enterprise'.[1]

There are, however, other attitudes expressed in *Poems of War and Patriotism*, and Hardy in his Preface himself noted the existence of contradiction in the Boer War poems. In 'Often When Warring' (1915) he speaks of the Sidney-like gesture of an 'enemy-soldier' who gives water to his adversary:

> . . . triumphing in the act
> Over the throes of artificial rage,
> Has thuswise muffled victory's peal of pride,
> Rended to ribbands policy's specious page
> That deals but with evasion, code, and pact,
> And war's apology wholly stultified.

Yet given Hardy's momentary defection here from blind patriotism, he does not make good verse out of good-hearted, although simplistic, politics (perhaps politics that ultimately flatter the English at the Germans' expense).

One other poem, 'In Time of "The Breaking of Nations"' (1915), should be considered in this group of non-aligned poems which declare the desirability of peace. Its 'eternal' ruralism has in its character something pantheistically English and optimistic. The affirmation of its conclusion, which is perhaps one reason for its popularity, is deliberately poised against the ominous title. Yet despite the admirable economy of its language and movement, the

---

[1] When compared, for example, with the precision of a poem like e. e. cummings's 'My Sweet Old Etcetera'.

rural affirmation and the vision of ideal human love hardly engage the context the title proposes. It does not, as Edward Thomas's 'As the Team's Head-Brass' does, show the incidence of war upon what is assumed natural and unchanging. One would have expected Hardy to have been among the first to see that despite love's eternal recurrence, war in many cases terminates the relationships which make up the total 'eternal' story. Seen in this light, the conclusion of Hardy's poem has a slightly facile ring. It does not, as recommended in 'In Tenebris', exact 'a full look at the Worst'.

In most of the *Poems of War and Patriotism* there is little of that 'exploration of reality' of which Hardy speaks in the Apology prefacing his *Late Lyrics and Earlier* (1922), and, in consequence, there can hardly be any 'evolutionary meliorism'. The terms of the war poems and the terms of *The Dynasts* are mutually exclusive.

The poem 'And There was a Great Calm', subtitled 'On the signing of the armistice, Nov. 11, 1918', recognizes the horror and pity of war. But why, one might ask, does this recognition come so late?

> And 'Hell!' and 'Shell!' were yapped at Lovingkindness. . . .

> . . . Out there men raised their glance. . .
> And murmured, 'Strange, this! How? All firing stopped?'

The poem also borrows some mechanism from *The Dynasts*:

> The Sinister Spirit sneered: 'It had to be!'
> And again the Spirit of Pity whispered, 'Why?'

After such a performance as the *Poems of Patriotism*, the whispering of the Pities sounds strangely sentimental, as it never does in *The Dynasts*.

Perhaps Hardy, in answer to the questions posed by his patriotic poems, would have cited the two lines last quoted. For him, evil and determinism seem to synchronize. The Immanent Will in *The Dynasts* is deterministic in that It is totally unconscious of the conflicts It initiates. Nevertheless, such determinism must also relate to the question the Pities ask. It could thus mean: I doubt if war really has to occur; or: tell me why war must be waged, because even if it must, I regret it. Even such a fatalist attitude as the latter reading supplies, however, is preferable to his prior patriot confidence. Even so, the shift from *The Dynasts* is disturbing, for

Hardy's modification of the attitudes in *The Dynasts* includes a recognition, or a belief, that war is unavoidable. It suggests that the area of human choice is so small as to be effectively non-existent in the important and collective matters, and that in consequence, our suffering, and perhaps our destruction, are inevitably sequential events. At least this is a more questioning conclusion than any reached in his poems of the First World War.

CHAPTER THREE

RUDYARD KIPLING AND RUPERT BROOKE

Hereditary bondsmen! know ye not
Who would be free themselves must strike the blow?
By their right arms the conquest must be wrought?
Will Gaul or Muscovite redress ye? no!
True, they may lay your proud despoilers low,
But not for you will Freedom's altars flame.
Shades of the Helots! triumph o'er your foe!
Greece! change thy lords, thy state is still the same;
Thy glorious day is o'er, but not thy years of shame.

Byron: Childe Harold

The transformation of a society is not likely to be achieved as a result of peaceful and intelligent *readjustment* on the part of literary men and politicians. But on the optimistic and romantic view of life this is quite possible. For the optimistic conception of man leads naturally to the characteristic democratic doctrine of inevitable *Progress*.

T. E. Hulme: Speculations

Freedom for Byron was a physical state, and he would almost certainly have agreed with Hulme that the 'transformation' of a society was more likely to be achieved through force, or the threat of it, than by peaceful means. Hence the assertion in *Childe Harold* that national freedom is only to be won through self-help—with 'the right arm'. The aid of allies inevitably more powerful than oneself results in a new tyranny.

Not apparently included in Byron's speculations, is the likelihood that the people of the liberated nation—in this case the Greeks—may find their own aristocracy or ruling or military class becoming at least as tyrannical as any foreign overlord had been. In the nineteenth century Italy was ruled by Austria; between the ends of the two World Wars by a military dictatorship drawn from her own people. In the nineteenth century Greece was an adjunct of the Ottoman empire; since the *coup* in 1969 she has been ruled by a military junta using brutal military methods to maintain its authority.

Force, however, is not the only reason for the survival of a government or group that would not for a moment be tolerated were it a foreign presence. The government can urge the threat of foreign invasion as a reason for national solidarity. A state, after all, has a territorial basis, and a threat to its integrity may be a means of persuading its people to obey conditions which, in other circumstances, they would regard as against their interests.

Although Byron's warning to the Greeks is sharp—'Shades of the Helots'—in that he is implying they resemble the former slaves of Sparta, he overlooks a crucial point. He forgets that those enslaved to the Greeks were as much entitled to rebel against their 'masters' as the Greeks were against the Turks. It is not to the point to say that the Greeks had their own slaves, whereas the Turks had *Greeks* as theirs. For this is merely to restrict the use of the word slave to your own interested domain. It confuses the issue by insisting that freedom is a word with only an inter-nation applicability. Here, once again, the two forces of nationalism and democracy are seen in competition, in that the nationalist struggle is organized by a ruling class that has more to gain from national freedom than its working class.[1] Of this conflict Bertrand Russell wrote in *Freedom versus Organization* (1935):

Economic nationalism, the dominant force in the modern world, derives its strength from the fact that it combines the motives of self-interest, to which Marx and the (Philosophical) Radicals appealed, with those less rational motives that inspire patriotism. Cool heads can be won over by dividends, hotheads by rhetorical appeals. By this means, a sinister synthesis is effected between the watchwords of different schools. Competition, yes, between nations; co-operation, yes, within the nation. Self-interest, yes, for the nation as a whole; sacrifice, yes, to the nation on the part of the individual who has no share in the plutocratic plunder. Wealth, yes, in the service of the national glory; money-grubbing, no, since the industrial magnate in all he does is helping to make his country great.

The injunctions of nationalist thinking rule out any democratic internationalism such as terrified the European monarchs into coalition against the French after the Revolution. Individual

---

[1] This was clearly not apparent in most of the nineteenth-century national struggles, though it was seen occasionally. See Lewis Namier, *1848: The Revolution of the Intellectuals* (1946).

responsibility is frontiered by the state and requires that individual conscience be orientated towards it. Criticism of the state is unpatriotic because it weakens, or could weaken, the national organism from which all individual and collective blessings flow. Once its people have been persuaded by these arguments, the state will have acquired the freedom to act collectively. Thus if a nation, or its rulers, believe that their culture must civilize other national and barbarian ones, or wish to extend its territorial domain, its citizens will obey because there is no higher court of appeal; individual conscience has already been invested in the state. And once within the competing capitalist system, one nation finds its resources limited by another, the outcome must be diplomatic bargaining, or a war in which its citizens are enrolled for the greater collective (and individual) good. So England gave up its 'Cobdenism', the idea that expansion abroad was expensive and unprofitable; Germany and France joined in the competition; and in 1890 Italy, which had previously demanded its freedom, annexed Eritrea. Africa had become the transfer-image of Europe.

Perhaps the most surprising fact in all this is that the working classes in each country should have not only sanctioned but supported the First World War. One searches for reasons. 'Hunger' is one, and Simone Weil's 'confinement of daily life' (see p. 50) another, but these hardly explain the initial commitment of millions. As for 'economic interest', many could have earned more than the infantryman's shilling a day. Russell again makes a useful point by asking the question in the terms he had used in the previous quotation: '[Marx] assumed that the proletariat, having no property, would have no patriotism, or at any rate not enough to stand in the way of opposition to capitalists. In this respect, he underrated the strength of non-economic motives.' With little property to lose, and only other people's to defend, the working class must appear the most selfless group within the national organism, unless other self-interested reasons can be found motivating their willingness to fight. But of course a culture is not made up only of economic motivation, and a man will fight for other reasons whether or not the economic structure is the principal qualification of his condition. Thus, what impairs the national demand for solidarity on the part of the working class is not, finally, the poor rewards, although this is certainly a strong and constant factor, but the unwillingness of a ruling class to allow its proletariat to share in the organization of the state.

Given the interests of the working class, this would amount to a restructuring of the whole economic and social system.

Ultimately, of course, only a very few benefit from war, but this is seldom evident in advance to either the government or the governed. Norman Angell's assertion that countries would in their best interests be reluctant to go to war was disproved in the event; the logic was not overthrown, but the forecast was. Either it was thought that benefits would accrue to the victor and that the gamble was worth the risk; or else economic competition had become so strained that only war could resolve it. There were of course many other factors, such as national pride, but at this point I am concerned merely to define the context in which men fought and poetry was written. Clearly, disinterested national pride was an important factor; so much so that before the war those people who had made investments abroad had in many cases made them with those nations to which they were professedly hostile in nationalistic terms. Whether their professions of patriotism were a façade merely, or whether they did not understand that to invest in a country is often to that country's benefit, we probably shall not discover.

The enthusiasm for the war remains the puzzle. Before it, England had many social and economic problems: the split between the Liberals and the Unionists over Ulster and home rule for Ireland; the suffragette dissent; and the strikes, which began in 1909 and would almost certainly have culminated in a general strike but for the war. Confronted with the 'national peril' the splits unaccountably healed, at least as far as fighting the war was concerned (although clearly party antagonisms remained). The force of nationalism must have seemed to the patriots to have been once more vindicated.

This preamble is intended to give some sense of the framework within which a number of poets were writing. Some, like Brooke (despite his Fabian socialism), hardly reacted to it consciously; others, like Kipling, responded to certain aspects of the situation with an extraordinary perception that has been largely underestimated, because the politics he seemed to stand for have become as despised as they were once approved.

Certain things have to be said about Kipling whether one likes his work or not, and the liking or not is itself, as we shall see, a considerable problem. Apart, ironically, from Hardy, Kipling was before the war the English poet most capable of visualizing and re-creating some of the conditions of both combat and army life. Many people, equipped with a hindsight that condemns war, and because they believe with Orwell that Kipling was 'a jingo imperialist . . . morally insensitive, and aesthetically disgusting', draw the faulty conclusion that he was *therefore* incapable of appreciating the nature of war. This argument is based on the assumption that anyone who understands the nature of war will condemn it, and that, conversely, those who do not oppose its waging are incapable of appreciating what it involves. It is an argument that solicits sympathy, but it must be said that, although Kipling's poems do not record the outrage and horror of Coleridge's 'Fears in Solitude' or Hardy's *The Dynasts*, they effectively dispute the charge of ignorance. What Kipling very well understood was that, given the necessity of national intransigence to preserve what he regarded as England's civilizing power, one had to appreciate that this often entailed war, in which case it must be waged effectively. Even so, his poems are permeated not so much with militarism—although that is also there—as with the atmosphere of army life, its endemic harshness and cruelty. This understanding he combines with an appreciation of how the dirty work of combat falls principally upon the private soldier. Wordsworth expressed an equivalent recognition of the hardships of the labourer (see Chapter One), but not of the soldier. Kipling recognized the hardships, sympathized with those who suffered them, frequently, like Sassoon, harassed the civilian who did not, and endorsed the necessity of which the hardships were compounded. It is this combination in Kipling of sympathetic evaluator and endorser of 'necessary' suffering which goads into stammering fury the average humane reader, for whom the idea of war is repugnant. We find it necessary to reject Kipling for ideological reasons, and all the more so because he recognizes war's brutalities. Why then, we are forced to ask, did he not reject the necessity of war? If we accept the idea that Kipling with us recognized its horror, we have either to divide our assent to his work (always a difficult process) or else assent to the argument of necessity. One can, like Herbert Read in 'To a Conscript of 1940', accept the necessity of this particular war, but deny that any glory is attached to its waging.

Kipling also encourages a divided criticism in that his poems are readily paraphraseable. As C. K. Stead remarked, they 'are "instruments" to serve a deliberate purpose. His only concern is to find the form which will serve that purpose.' The criticism that divides poems by form and content is the more encouraged to do so because the poems are already so divided. Therefore, setting aside for the moment the merits of the ideas, a consideration of the qualities of the verse—the kind of language and the extent to which his ideas are sifted into it—will show that Kipling's verse is hardly inferior to the stanza of *Childe Harold*, for instance, quoted at the head of this chapter. Compare that with these lines from Kipling's 'The Islanders':

> Men, not gods, devised it. Men, not gods, must keep.
> Men, not children, servants, or kinsfolk called from afar,
> But each man born in the Island broke to the matters of war.

The comparison is fair, I think, in that both passages are concerned with nationalism. If one allows that Byron is exhorting a group of people who want but have not yet got autonomy, whereas Kipling is haranguing the autonomous (and some would say, despotic) English, the feelings and arguments in each passage show a relatedness. Each claims that national aspiration and culture will be defended, with force if necessary. Although Byron identified 'Freedom's Flame' as a spiritual force, he knew precisely how that had to be implemented and, in that knowledge, died. Each poet lacks complexity, that sifting of experience into language, rhythm, and tone which conveys a sensuous as well as an intellectual impression of the original experience. Any objection to this particular parallel will be on ideological rather than literary grounds. Byron is seen as the defender of oppressed national aspirations; Kipling as one who represents nationalism in its imperialistic form, powerful enough to have, in other circumstances, oppressed that kind of patriotic desire for autonomy Byron was defending. That England was not in Byron's era markedly expanding its empire (and did not again start until 1870 in the European scramble for Africa) is immaterial. Had Byron wanted an example of British oppression he need have looked no further than Ireland. Byron is popularly associated with the idea of freedom, and Kipling with oppression. But these views ignore the disposition of Byron's support, and put the blame for all imperialist moves on to Kipling. A longer perspective, in which the issues of nationalism, *with all their implications*,

are taken into account, places Byron closer to Kipling than we have
previously supposed.

It must be said, however, that the best of Byron—*Don Juan*—is
more searching and honest, and more interesting as poetry, than
anything Kipling wrote. This is surely because of the greater
separation between Kipling's ideas and language, in which the
latter is merely the resonant vehicle of the former. If the ideas are
worth anything in such an unequal distribution, they must be the
most interesting part of such verse, and in 'The Islanders' they
are. He speaks of war realistically and candidly:

From the gusty, flickering gun-roll with viewless salvoes rent,
And the pitted hail of the bullets that tell not whence they were sent . . .

and

Ye pushed them raw to the battle as ye picked them raw from the street.

The first instance is of course rhetorical, but it does not pretend
that war is a game, and in this sense the reader would find it hard
to object to the lines on the grounds that they advocated war as an
ennobling activity. The second instance is even more interesting in
that 'raw', however patronizing, is sympathetic to the soldier.
Moreover, Kipling's target is Sassoon's, the civilian incapable of
understanding, or refusing to understand, the cost of war to the
soldiers. We sense a compassion in 'raw', until we realize that what
Kipling is deploring is not so much their sacrifice, as that they were
unfairly and, in the last resort, *uselessly* sacrificed, because they were
not properly taught how to fight, and were insufficiently armed.
The line 'Do ye wait for the spattered shrapnel ere ye learn how a
gun is laid' does not match the expectations roused by the lines
previously quoted. Again, 'They shall not return to us, the strong
men coldly slain' reads very much like a line deploring the slaughter
of men in the useless activity of combat, until it is qualified by 'In
sight of help denied from day to day'. 'Coldly' may mean the
(deplorable) coldness of their death, but, in the light of what follows,
it seems more likely to mean that inadequate training and equipment *coldly* leaves them to die a needless death. Kipling pursues
this relevant fact in 'Mesopotamia 1917':

But the slothfulness that wasted and the arrogance that slew,
Shall we leave it unabated in its place?

This is the slothfulness of government that expects soldiers to fight for the nation, but withholds the preparation due to them. The large omission, of course, in Kipling's argument is his exclusion of the 'enemies' ' suffering. He would have been incapable of writing 'I am the enemy you killed, my friend'—let alone 'I was a German conscript, and your friend'—not because he did not understand that the enemy also suffers, but because he was committed to upholding a cause in which you either lose or win. The possibility of reconciliation was not in Kipling's vocabulary. Thus, 'We have had an Imperial lesson' is not a crude rebuke for imperialism, but a reproof for past mistakes and a plea that the soldier should be better equipped in future to fight imperialism's wars: 'It may make us an Empire yet!' Kipling is not asking for an end to war, but that the cost of imperialism be recognized and our soldiers better equipped. Any feeling that he has taken us in may result from our expectations being disappointed. This is not Kipling's fault. The reader may dislike imperialism, but he has no right to complain that Kipling betrayed him because he misread certain initial assertions that seemed to promise a liberal position. Moreover, Kipling is fundamentally honest, with the exceptions noted above. What is distasteful is not even the postulate that war is necessary, but the confident assumption that nationalism is proper, where what is meant is English nationalism. Kipling does not choose to recognize the implications of this, or, if he does, he is careful to palliate the facts by infusing them with a moral justification, which most nations can produce. He may have believed that it was the moral duty of English nationalism to subsist, if necessary at the expense of other nationalisms, because the English brought their supreme civilization to such others. It was therefore the Englishman's duty to fight, if it came to that, for the civilizing destiny of his nation. The difficulty is obvious; each nation believes the same, but as far as Kipling was concerned this would have been a 'non-fact', as he indicates in 'The Veterans', 'Written for the gathering of survivors of the Indian Mutiny, Albert Hall, 1907':

> The remnant of that desperate host
> Which cleansed *our* East with steel [my italics].

He expresses a similar notion in the phrase from 'Recessional', 'Dominion over palm and pine', and receives perhaps unexpected support, or at least qualified defence, from Orwell, who says: 'The

whole poem [is] conventionally thought of as an orgy of boasting
[whereas it] is a denunciation of power politics, British as well as
German.'[1] Orwell continues by quoting the last two stanzas:

> If, drunk with sight of power, we loose
>   Wild tongues that have not Thee in awe,
> Such boastings as the Gentiles use,
>   Or lesser breeds without the Law—
> Lord God of Hosts, be with us yet,
> Lest we forget—lest we forget!

> For heathen heart that puts her trust
>   In reeking tube and iron shard,
> All valiant dust that builds on dust,
>   And guarding, calls not Thee to guard,
> For frantic boast and foolish word—
> Thy mercy on Thy people, Lord!

'Dominion over palm and pine' is certainly presumptuous, and
Kipling's whole ethic took for granted the British right not only to
lands they possessed (by force) but against all comers. Yet the
poem, if it expresses certain presumptions, is not boastful. The
Biblical message suffuses, as did all Kipling's messages, not only the
poem's tone but its language, which is as ever subservient to the
ideas—the ideas, as it were, colonize the language. Orwell suggests
that the 'lesser breeds' are not the African communities, and if this is
so, it is interesting that the common reading of the phrase has
usually taken it as meaning the colonized. The 'lesser breeds' are
those who put their 'trust in . . . tube and iron': the Germans as
they oppose British imperialism, or even the British themselves.
That may be a correct reading here, but since we are primarily
concerned with the full spectrum of Kipling's ideas, it must be
said that in most other places the ideas flout the profession of
distaste for the use of arms Orwell sees in this poem. Much depends,
of course, on how we take 'we' and 'Thy people'. These could
mean the British people, the 'Jews' of God entrusted with His
sacred civilizing mission; or, alternatively, 'all people' who obey
God's laws, which exclude (in this poem) any trust in force. The
'Law' is God's law, the law of morality and civilization. It is
difficult not to think, if Orwell is right, that Kipling has not contrived a *volte-face*. Apart from the discreet 'Dominion over palm

[1] 'Rudyard Kipling', by George Orwell, from *Kipling's Mind and Art*, ed. Andrew
Rutherford (1964), p. 71.

and pine', the tacit omission of the African from the poem suggests that he does not even qualify as a lesser breed. His status is perhaps not merely lower but qualitatively different. Yet in all this we must see the justice of what Orwell implies—that Kipling could not be accused of lightness. His sense of war's bitterness in 'The Islanders' —'When ye are ringed with iron'—contrasts with Newbolt's 'Play up, play up, and play the game.' The phrase 'Lest we forget' has been taken out of context (not that Kipling might have objected) when used to articulate the purpose of the war memorials on which it is inscribed. The sacrifice of the dead, whom their relatives are in any case unlikely to forget, was not, in 'Recessional' at least, a part of Kipling's specific allusion.

Yet with whatever care we read Kipling, we will surely feel not only that he excludes the larger sense of Europe's pre-war tensions, but that his story is essentially one-sided. There is no deep anticipation of how bloody the combat of the First World War would be, no sense of how long it would last. Perhaps this is more inexcusable if we take into account that he knew something of what war involved; what he left out of his calculations was the willing persistence of the 'lesser breeds' to struggle, and the immoral causes of the tensions themselves. Even so, before the war few English poets —Imagists or Georgians—had anything approaching Kipling's sense of the realities of combat.

The Georgian sensibility was insular, complacent, and not at all exploratory, but one must agree with C. K. Stead's view that

the fashion of treating [the Georgians] as representatives of reaction in poetry has obscured the good service their appearance did. . . . many of the younger Georgian poets were considered dangerous literary revolutionaries. Edward Marsh in fact turned his back on the established names of the day in an attempt to show the reading public that a more genuine poetry [existed].

Much of this seems to be confirmed both by Christopher Hassall's account of the origins of Georgian poetry in his biography of Rupert Brooke, and by a reading of what Brooke called the 'great slabs of minor verse' that he was reviewing for the *Cambridge Review*. Yet to value the Georgian opposition to the received poetic modes is not to say much for Georgian poetry itself. The achievement is slight. Geoffrey Matthews has suggested that the value of these poets lies principally in their response to objects, and that their moderate demands on the reader's attention were in contrast to the 'messy' (Hulme's word) abstractions and languid self-regard which characterized much poetry at that time. Matthews cites Brooke's poem 'The Great Lover' in support of his view:

> These I have loved:
> > White plates and cups, clean-gleaming,
> Ringed with blue lines; and feathery, faery dust;
> Wet roofs, beneath the lamp-light; the strong crust
> Of friendly bread; and many-tasting food;
> Rainbows; and the blue bitter smoke of wood;
> And radiant raindrops couching in cool flowers;
> And flowers themselves, that sway through sunny hours,
> Dreaming of moths that drink them under the moon;
> Then, the cool kindliness of sheets, that soon
> Smooth away trouble; and the rough male kiss
> Of blankets. . . .

The passage is in a sense 'accurate', but the perceptions do not sufficiently fix the objects, because they do not relate them to anyone (the poet, for instance) except in a mode of easy kindliness. The 'thingness' of them does not emerge, either through strenuous definition or in relationship to the writer. The objects are used, self-comfortingly, to 'smooth away trouble', but the poet's attention is not focused outwards, or in any real sense upon himself. The passage says mellifluously something we may have at various moments felt, but it does not crystallize our responses beyond acknowledging that something like these moments exists. It answers to Orwell's description of not very 'good bad poetry'. And since we are now touching on an aspect of his work which has biographical equivalents available to us, we take up the point that both Marsh and Hassall make; which is that Brooke, after his relationship with Ka, having 'done with love', moved into the more convivial, more public 'radiance' of 'goodness' and friendship. He became increasingly committed, if that is the correct word, to a public and vacant attitude. The two are not necessarily synonymous, but where the poetry is void of personal conviction, it is unlikely to be more than oratory. Brooke's output became poetic oratory, and the more that Hassall writes of Brooke's tortured relationship with Ka, the more one has the sense that he avoided a personal committedness in his life and his writing alike. If Brooke chose to restrict his responses in this way, we have no right to complain, except in so far as it affected his work. With less fluency, not less talent, he might have been luckier; lacking a ready currency, he might have been forced into a more substantial mode. Unfortunately, his skills and his public voice confirmed each other and hardened together; and his connections with highly placed people gave to this formation a final emphasis.

He would be [Geoffrey Matthews argues] a kind of repository of English holiness, which in the physical sense would fertilize un-English soil and in the spiritual sense would discharge its home-produced contents purely into the Eternal Mind. . . . This is really what the five famous 'war sonnets' are about—they are not war poems at all, except in the most accidental sense, but—to put it crudely—poems celebrating the export of English goods. . . . Everyone knew Brooke had written *1914*, and whether he liked it or not he was committed to the cause of the ruling classes and surrounded by their watchful care.[1]

Brooke's sonnets are 'war poems'—'The Soldier', especially—in the sense that they are vehicles for imperialist attitudes. But to see how little they are to do with war in the overt sense one might compare 'If I should die, think only this of me', not with any of Sassoon's or Owen's war poems,[2] which is too easy a comparison, but with Kipling's 'The Islanders'. It is fair to say that this is, as Brooke's sonnets purport to be, a defence of war's necessity, or at least a plea for the waging of efficient war, given its necessity. The contrast is significant. Brooke's poems begin with the context of war, but move into a peaceful idealization of the sacrifice pending its immortality. Death in an aura of public sympathy, but underlying approval, provides the ennobling quality that was privately satisfying. Any conscience or pain he may be caused by having ceased to be a poet is equalized by his ennobling example and by his preparedness for death. When Brooke learned he was being sent with the Royal Naval Division to Gallipoli, he wrote to Violet Asquith: 'I've never been quite so happy in my life, I think. Not quite so *pervasively* happy; like a stream flowing entirely to one end.' The tragic meaning possible here is of an unconscious adherence to public service and death, used to dissolve those personal problems with which he had been racked.

---

[1] *Stand*, IV, No. 3.
[2] But see Owen's 'Ballad of Purchase Money' quoted in Jon Stallworthy, *Wilfred Owen* (1971), pp. 17–18.

This may be read as selflessness, but it is an abnegation in which personal responsibility has been dissolved. And perhaps this is what the argument over Brooke is about. In a sense it was not his fault, since however much one detests the chauvinistic angelicizing of the soldier killed in battle, it was never his intention to send millions to their death. His mission may have been to make such a death seem more noble, but not to bring about wholesale slaughter; Brooke was far too kind a man for that. He was perhaps not intelligent enough to have grasped the possible dimensions of the struggle, and probably too enfolded in his own sensations to learn from the experience, even when immersed in it. In the middle of the chaos of the Belgian retreat he is able to speak of it as 'an extraordinary and thrilling confusion'.[1] This was not war-mongering, but, unfortunately for him and for other victims of the war, cleverer and more adroit persons capitalized both on his published sentiments (which in any case expressed the feelings of a good many people) and then his example; and used them as instruments for 'speeding glum heroes up the line to death'. One might consider the sequence of events. Brooke saw little action; with a now easily perceived irony he died, on 23 April 1915, from a mosquito bite that developed into septicaemia. The sonnets had been published in the December 1914 issue of *New Numbers*.[2] On 5 April 1915, Easter Sunday, the Dean of St. Paul's preached to a

congregation [consisting] of widows, parents, and orphans in their hundreds. As the Dean reached the pulpit, a man jumped to his feet and began a loud harangue against the war. When he was removed, Dean Inge gave as his text, Isaiah XXVI, 19. *The dead shall live, my dead bodies shall arise. Awake and sing, ye that dwell in the dust.* He had just read

---

[1] This letter of 17 October 1914 to Cathleen Nesbitt should be read in full in *Letters of Rupert Brooke*, edited by Geoffrey Keynes (1968), p. 622.

[2] In letters to Robert Frost, Edward Thomas had written that he had not dared say that

[Brooke's] sonnets about him enlisting are probably not very personal but a nervous attempt to connect with himself the very widespread idea that self-sacrifice is the highest self-indulgence. You know. And I don't dispute it. Only I doubt if he knew it or would he have troubled to drag in the fact that enlisting cleared him of 'All the little emptiness of love'? [13 June 1915]

I think he succeeded in being youthful and yet intelligible and interesting (not only pathologically) more than most poets since Shelley. But thought gave him (and me) indigestion. He couldn't mix his thought or the result of it with his feeling. He could only think about his feeling. Radically, I think he lacked power of expression. He was a rhetorician, dressing things up better than they needed. And I suspect he knew only too well both what he was after and what he achieved. [19 October 1916]

['The Soldier'] . . . and remarked that 'the enthusiasm of a pure and elevated patriotism had never found a nobler expression'.[1]

At once, with the help of the war, Dean Inge, and even the man who had made his protest, Brooke became famous; and in a way that not all the combined publicity of Marsh and the Georgian anthologies had managed. There are several ironies here, but the principal one is that despite his flair for publicity, nothing of this, except the writing of the poems, was Brooke's doing. With the Church's erastian complicity he was canonized for the 'needs of the nation', and used as an instrument to promote further slaughter.

[1] Christopher Hassall, *Rupert Brooke/A Biography* (1964), p. 502

CHAPTER FOUR

CHARLES SORLEY AND OTHERS

In September 1916 Galloway Kyle's anthology, *Soldier Poets: Songs of the Fighting Men*, was published. His Preface declared that the poems

define, record and illustrate the aspirations, emotions, impressions and experiences of men of all ranks ... and they reveal a unity of spirit, of exultant sincerity and unconquerable idealism that makes the reader very proud and very humble. ... The note of pessimism and decadence is absent, together with the flamboyant and hectic, the morose and mawkish. The soldier poets leave the maudlin and the mock-heroic, the gruesome and fearful handling of Death ... to the neurotic civilian who stayed behind to gloat on imagined horrors and conveniences and anticipate the uncomfortable demise of friends. ... It is not a new spirit, but a new bright efflorescence—a survival and a revival. 'The half-men, with their dirty songs and dreary' were stricken dumb by the storm—at the most, they whimpered in safety with none to heed them: the braver spirits were shocked into poetry and like the larks are heard between the roaring of the guns—the articulate voices of millions of fighting men, giving to poetry a new value and significance.

The assertion that the poems 'define [the] experiences of men of all ranks' is misleading in the sense that we might suppose a proportionate representation of contributors. This of course is not so: of the twenty-four contributors, fifteen are officers (in this stage of the war, men drawn from the middle and upper classes), nine are non-commissioned officers and other ranks. The anthology contains seventy-two poems, of which forty-four are by people of probable middle-class background, and twenty-eight by men of working-class and petit-bourgeois upbringing. One's unease about Kyle's use of the phrase 'all ranks' comes from one's sense of democracy being extended (and being *shown* to extend) to the working class now that it was useful to have this class actively participating in the war. Other objections to the Preface emerge.

Such a passage as 'leave the gruesome and fearful handling of death to the neurotic civilian who stayed behind to gloat on imagined horrors' is naïve and inconsistent. Kyle admits death as a part of war, but declares its horror a civilian manufacture. Nevertheless, the 'braver spirits [are] shocked into poetry'. Why 'shocked' if there was no horror? By September 1916 the Somme offensive had been under way for two months. Allowance must, of course, be made for the time it took to print the anthology, although Kyle did not alter his Preface in later editions. A. J. P. Taylor, in *The First World War* (1963), writes that 'On 1 July the British sustained 60,000 casualties, 20,000 of them killed—the heaviest loss ever suffered in a single day by a British army or by any army in the First World War'—and of the total figures, 'The British lost some 420,000 casualties: the French nearly 200,000. The Germans lost about 450,000.' One does not know how much information Kyle had, either through (distorted) newspaper reports, or hearsay, but it seems unlikely that he would be ignorant of the failure of the Somme offensive, its cost, and the subsequent revisions of attitude towards combat, even at home. The ruthless idealism of the Preface remains.

Yet even if his own idealism remained untested by combat, it could have been tested by the contributions to the anthology itself. A certain ambivalence and even hostility to war and the heroic-glorious attitudes to it, are beginning to emerge, as in 'The Counter-Attack' by H.D'A.B.:

> . . . Shouts exultant, harsh,
>   A mêlée of cold steel colliding,
> Gaunt shadows grappling in a bloody marsh,
>   And low moans rising and subsiding.

The exultant shouts (of those successfully grappling?) are there, but mixed with 'low moans'. How do we read this passage? As instructions on how to keep up one's courage, or as realistic, horror-struck information? Is it documentation simply, or is there the didactic intent of showing how fearful war is? Whatever the intention, what comes through is not idealism or 'song', and it does not fulfil any part of Kyle's formula. Many of the poems indicate that the original idealism was being qualified by experience of combat, and that experience and idealism were conflicting in such a way as to force a reinterpretation of the writer's values. For instance, one way of squaring knowledge of combat with chauvinist idealism was to merge the death of the soldier with nature, thus vaguely associating the need for survival (immortality) with nature's recurrent life. The sweetness of nature bestows itself upon the dead man no matter how terrible his death had been. Nature thus joins with man as the principal mourner, and in such a way that, whether you hated your living enemy or not, you could respect his dead by bringing his and yours together in an elegiac image of nature.

The inconsistent figure in this anthology is Julian Grenfell. One might loosely associate pleasure in combat with some form of patriotism, but in fact he emerges from his verse as neither patriot nor disaffected. Although the popularity of 'Into Battle' was due to its coincidence with patriot fervour, it is not properly speaking a 'war poem' but a release in verse of Grenfell's predatoriness. War is central for the enactment of the predatoriness, but where in the poem he comes closer to expressing his feelings, war is an incidental component fortuitously providing the arena in which these feelings and their concomitant actions are re-created. T. Sturge Moore, in *Some Soldier Poets* (1920), wrote:

At last [Grenfell] feels free to be what instinct and capacity make him; general consent and his own conscience permit him to kill and to die. The ecstasy is like that of married love: a fundamental instinct can be gratified untaxed by inward loss or damage and with the approval of mankind. Harmony between impulse and circumstance creates this joy; but not only is it more complex than that of the young male stag who attacks the leader of the herd, there is in it an element of quite a different order, a sense that wrong within can be defeated by braving evil abroad. The strain between worldly custom and that passion for good which begets spiritual insight, finds relief in fighting, looks for peace in death.

By joining the Royal Dragoons in 1910, Grenfell set up those conditions in which he could fulfil the instincts so clearly realized in the poem; although when the war came it must have arrived with greater intensity than he had expected. He was killed in May 1915. For him, however, the war can hardly have provided a qualitative difference, but an intensification merely of terms he had already created for himself. Thus, in his poem there is no recognition of war as an event crucial to society, and hardly any recognition of society's needs. He writes in a letter that 'One loves one's fellow-man so much more when one is bent on killing him.' The only way to read this is (for once) with ironic detachment; Grenfell is not, I think, expressing a perceptive paradox, but naïvely recording a truthful apprehension of his emotional state which finds active corroboration in his poem. More interestingly for us, what it creates, it finds a social acceptance of, mirrored in the poem's popularity.

The word 'loves', in the sentence just quoted, would seem to mean a kind of self-love in which the foe both mirrors and provides for the appetites of the predator. If this is the meaning, then his version of life, 'And he is dead who will not fight', is a parasitism feeding on the life of the hunted, 'And who dies fighting has increase'; where 'fighting' defines the nature of the appetite. These attitudes may seem to have something in common with those of the German officer in Herbert Read's 'The End of a War':

> I was blooded then, but the wound
> seared in the burning circlet of my spirit
> served only to temper courage. . . .
> I have lived in the ecstasy of battle.

The feeling in that last line comes close to Grenfell's 'brazen frenzy' and 'Joy of battle'. Yet there are differing emphases; given that, in any case, Grenfell is directly expressing his feelings, whereas Read is ostensibly recreating those of another—moreover, those of a type of man, rather than of a specific individual. For Grenfell, the war is as incidental as for the German officer it is the means of helping to forge the fatherland. The latter finds ecstasy in battle, it is true, but even this must be controlled by the ultimate needs and purposes of the nation. Grenfell, however, was among the last of the amateur warriors, and remained up to his death largely un-moulded by the demands of the war. Even the way in which he fought suggests this. In the end Grenfell probably felt he needed some kind of approval—as opposed to sanction—for his behaviour. He contrives to find this in nature, which is itself unmodified by humane restrictions and provides many satisfactory parallels which can be 'converted' into human justifications:

> The woodland trees that stand together,
>   They stand to him each one a friend. . . .

> The kestrel hovering by day
>   And the little owls that call by night,
> Bid him be swift and keen as they. . . .

> The black bird sings to him, 'Brother, brother,
>   If this be the last song you shall sing
> Sing well, for you may not sing another;
>   Brother, sing.'

Clearly, nature is used here not to provide exact parallels, but because, in its asserted corroboration of his activity, it cannot answer back. The various creatures who approve his spirit may some of them be predators, but they enact nothing here and have no proper life of their own in the poem, and therefore do not demonstrably corroborate his 'natural' instincts. What might have been a precise congruity between these instincts and the creatures' remains a generalized, supportive comradeliness, invented for the purpose of providing approval. 'Song' and 'sing' remain counters, expressing the joyful marriage between love of combat, its fruition ('increase') in death, and finally, peace. If he has fear, he learns to conquer this in the example set by nature:

> The horses show him nobler powers;
> O patient eyes, courageous hearts!

The last line shows again the inadequacy of the poetic equipment. 'Patient' and 'courageous' are not various, precise, or unanthropomorphic enough to establish the qualities of the animals themselves, so that he loses the strength of an independent corroborating agent.

Charles Hamilton Sorley was born on 19 May 1895 and killed in the battle of Loos on 13 October 1915. He was the most interesting of the poets killed in the early part of the war, and from his letters seems to have had a more acute intelligence than any in that period. He has been neglected, except by Robert Nichols, and it is only with the revived interest in the war and its poets that he has again been noticed. John H. Johnston, and Bernard Bergonzi in *Heroes' Twilight*, give him sympathetic attention, and John Press has written a disturbing although perhaps imprecise essay on him. He is also represented in Brian Gardner's anthology *Up the Line to Death* and Ian Parsons's *Men Who March Away*.

Sorley's *Marlborough and Other Poems*—an indication of his neglect—is still available in a reprint of what is virtually a sixth edition (1932, first published in 1916); and his letters are also available in the original 1919 edition. He was educated at Marlborough, left at the end of 1913, won a scholarship to Oxford, and went to live in Germany in January 1914. For approximately half the year he studied German language and literature, and then, in April, began studying philosophy and economics at the University of Jena. He was on a walking tour when war was declared, and after a brief imprisonment at Trier on 2 August, was released and ordered to leave the country. On arriving in England, he applied immediately for a commission, an action that accords oddly with his attitude towards the war and its patriotism. In a letter of 14 November 1914 he wrote:

England—I am sick of the sound of the word. In training to fight for England, I am training to fight for that deliberate hypocrisy, that terrible middle-class sloth of outlook and appalling 'imaginative indolence' that has marked us out from generation to generation. . . . And yet we have the impudence to write down Germany (who with all their bigotry are at least seekers) as 'Huns', because they are doing what every brave man ought to do and making experiments in morality. Not that I approve of the experiment in this *particular* case. Indeed I think that *after* the war [my italics] all brave men will renounce their country and confess that they are strangers and pilgrims on earth. . . . But all these convictions are useless for me to state since I have not had the courage for them. What a worm one is under the cart-wheels—big clumsy careless lumbering cart-wheels—of public opinion. I might have been giving my mind to fight against Sloth and Stupidity: instead, I am giving my body (by a refinement of cowardice) to fight against the most enterprising nation in the world.

This is a courageous expression of some of the pressures under which he enlisted, although it disposes of any patriotic reasons to which his enlisting may at the time have been attributed. What Sorley is committed to is a scrupulous honesty; and this same attribute that gives rise to these comments on Brooke and his 'patriotism' evaluated his own actions:

I saw Rupert Brooke's death in *The Morning Post* . . . which has always hitherto disapproved of him . . . now loud in his praises because he has conformed to their stupid axiom of literary criticism that the only stuff of poetry is violent physical experience, by dying on active service. I think Brooke's earlier poems—especially notably *The Fish* and *Grant-chester* . . . are his best. That last sonnet-sequence of his [*The Soldier*] which has been so praised, I find (with the exception of that beginning 'These hearts were woven of human joys and cares . . .' which is not about himself) overpraised. He is far too obsessed with his own sacrifice, regarding the going to war of himself (and others) as a highly intense, remarkable and sacrificial exploit, whereas it is merely the conduct demanded of him (and others) by the turn of circumstances, *where*

non-compliance with this demand would have made life intolerable[my italics].
It was not that 'they' gave up anything of that list he gives in one sonnet:
but that the essence of these things had been endangered by circumstances over which he had no control, and he must fight to recapture
them. He has clothed his attitude in fine words: but he has taken the
sentimental attitude.

Sorley was not yet in the trenches in April 1915 when he wrote
this, so one may claim that, like Rosenberg, he possessed attitudes
to nationalism and war that were not transformed abruptly by
experience of combat. He brought to war attitudes that were
already formed. That he was capable of distinguishing the good
aspects of Germany's social life from the militaristic is evidenced
by a letter dated July 1914:

> You say that the 'corps' aren't bad really. But they are! Black-rotten!
> The sooner one dispels the libel on German Universities that the corps
> student is the typical student, the better. They comprise only a third of
> the total number of students at Jena: and Jena is the most traditional of all
> German Universities. . . . A peculiarly offensive form of 'fagging' for the
> six youngest students in each corps: compulsory drunkenness; com-
> pulsory development of offensive and aggressive behaviour to the out-
> sider; and a peculiarly sickening anti-Semitism are their chief features.
> The students with whom I mostly go about are Jews, and so perhaps I
> see, from their accounts of the insults they've to stand, the worst side of
> these many-coloured reeling creatures.

Sorley underestimated the rapidity with which the 'Sedanish spirit'
would evaporate, but he does put his finger on that sense of
superiority which Heine had remarked on (in 1834):

> The two great sins people impute to Germany are that she says that
> might is right and bullies the little dogs. But I don't think that she means
> might *qua* might is right, but that confidence of superiority is right, and
> by superiority she means spiritual superiority. . . . We are not fighting a
> bully, but a bigot.

A month earlier, on 20 September 1914, he had identified the lie
of expediency which equates justice with victory:

> For the joke of seeing an obviously just cause defeated, I hope Germany
> will win. It would do the world good and show that real faith is not that

which says 'we *must* win for our cause is just', but that which says 'our cause is just: therefore we can disregard defeat'. All outlooks are at present material, and the unseen value of justice as justice, independent entirely of results, is forgotten. It is looked upon merely as an agent for winning battles.

It seems that Sorley had not recognized the enormity of the war in the sense of how large such a defeat would be were it to occur; but the central point in this passage is the assertion of Britain's cause being just. This assertion is made without patriotic attachment. As he remarks on his poem 'Whom Therefore We Ignorantly Worship' (September 1914): 'I think it should get a prize for being the first poem written since August 4th that isn't patriotic.' And in connection with the insensitivity invariably concomitant with patriotism, he wrote to his mother on 10 July 1915, having recently gone out to France: '[I deplore] the growing tendency to think that every man drops overboard his individuality between Folkestone and Boulogne.' Of course, in a way that Sorley does not here imagine, war did thrust anonymity on to the soldier, but this he perceives in 'A Hundred Thousand Million Mites We Go'.

'Whom Therefore We Ignorantly Worship' stems from Sorley's ideas concerning justice; there are warrior-like apprehensions,

> Strong sounding actions with broad minstrelsy
> Of praise, strange hazards and adventures bold,

but these contrast with what 'we hold to' and a stoic sense of identity with the victims: 'We, the blind weavers of an intense fate. . . .' One supposes that Sorley was temperamentally and intellectually unsympathetic to the 'broad minstrelsy' and all it connotes, but the tone of the poem is not fully dissociated from the heroics it apparently disclaims.

> Wé, the blind wéavĕrs ŏf ăn inténse fáte

has its own rhetoric, although the disturbed metrical emphasis in 'intense' institutes an unexpected, querulous feeling.

'To Poets', written in September 1914, is concerned like Owen's 'The Calls' with the soldier's inarticulate distress, but where Owen deals with this alone, Sorley turns the situation into a dispute in which the inarticulate point to the advantage of the poet, who can express his feelings:

We have no comeliness like you.
We toil, unlovely, and we spin. . . .

We have the evil spirits too . . .
But we have an eviller spirit than you,
We have a dumb spirit within:
The exceeding bitter agony
But not the exceeding bitter cry.

Written in the same month, 'A Hundred Thousand Million Mites
We Go' shows Sorley's growing awareness of the increasing
numbers the war would involve and destroy:

> . . . some
> Step forth and challenge blind Vicissitude
> Who tramples on them: so that fewer come. . . .

With ironic bitterness he indicates his understanding of the destructive strength of modern war's instruments. 'Ankle-deep in love
or hate'—'ankle-deep' with its associations of mud and blood—shows
a tentative realism, but this was not apparently what Sorley was
after. In certain poems, he seems to have been trying to resolve the
question of his faith, which he examines in '*Deus Loquitur*',
'*Expectans Expectavi*', and more obliquely in 'Two Sonnets'. These,
written in 1915 after he had *experienced* trench fighting, question
the idea of an afterlife and seem to reject it. The relation of faith
(involving a perhaps compensatory afterlife) to the experience of
war was of course a problem crucial to many, and the war either
destroyed belief or intensified it. The question of whether an early
death—in a sacrificial context—would be correspondingly rewarded
in heaven is not one that Owen entertained, and it seems doubtful
if Sorley did either. Death is

> Only an empty pail, a slate rubbed clean, . . .

> Death is not life effete,
> Life crushed, the broken pail. . . .
> Victor and vanquished are a-one in death.

The 'bright promise', which 'Is touched, stirs, rises, opens',
continues, but without fulfilment: 'And blossoms and is you, when
you are dead'. The 'promise' remains something that might have
been, and 'blossoms' only in others' minds. The actual achievements
of youth, its fulfilled potential, receive a Rosenberg-like immortality,

only through the suspension of its actual promise. It is the *promise*
that blossoms, and not its achievement; and in the third of these
sonnets, 'When You See Millions of the Mouthless Dead', Sorley
writes: 'Say not soft things as other men have said.' This, perhaps
a reference to Brooke, is followed by:

> Give them not praise. For, deaf, how should they know
> It is not curses heaped on each gashed head?

with the suggestion both that their death is probably acknowledged
with as little concern, and that the praise could as easily become
condemnation. 'Gashed' is intensely physical and counterpoints the
civilian's hypocritical praise. The idea and the language are far
removed from

> Blow, bugles, blow! They brought us, for our dearth,
> Holiness, lacked so long.

In his implied didacticism Sorley stands closer to Owen than to
Brooke.

John Press argues that Sonnet I, and II especially, mark a
'willing acceptance of death, both as a great leveller, and as the
prelude to a richer life'.[1] This is the standard Christian viewpoint,
and it is interesting to see this attitude as Press expresses it clashing
with the anti-war one, which is often agnostic, or atheist. Yet
although Sorley indicates in Sonnet I that death is

> a land
> I did not know and that I wished to know

he expresses something more like curiosity than acceptance. Nor
do I think Press's view that the afterlife was for Sorley a 'richer
life' is supported by the line 'Where the mists swim and the winds
shriek and blow'. Though it is true that he loved nature, the verbs
'shriek and blow' suggest a harsher state than the conventional
heaven. We must be cautious, as Press indicates, of seeing Sorley
in an Owen-like position, or as 'a stepping-stone from Brooke to
Sassoon'. In the second sonnet, perhaps the 'bright Promise,
withered and long sped' is in fact blossomed by death; as with
Brooke, for whom 'a world grown old and cold and weary' ('Peace')
blossomed as a result of sacrificial death. Yet the 'blot' of death,
in line 10 of Sorley's poem, does not support Press's contention

---

[1] 'Charles Sorley', *Review of English Literature*, III, No. 2, pp. 43–60.

that the poet saw this as fruitful. One might argue that the last
three lines are ambiguous, but I prefer to think that 'bright' refers
to the potential of the living, which 'withered' in death, but remains
'sweet' for those surviving you who may speculate on what might
have been achieved. As with Keats, the promise itself cannot wither.
Thus, although Sorley thought of himself as a Christian, referring
in a letter of 20 September 1914 to 'my ultra-strong religious
instincts', I do not see either of these sonnets as expressing a
Christian belief in an afterlife. Death is only 'like' the nature in
his land; he can draw on its aspects to express what he feels about
death, but external evidence may be misleadingly *unlike* what he
wrote in his poems. Moreover, the sonnet that follows these and is
akin to them in tone and feeling, ends in a denial of afterlife: 'Great
death has made all his for ever more'.

In warning us not to read into these poems the attitudes of
Owen and Rosenberg, Press quotes from Sorley's letters, in one
of which is a reference to 'false pity'. Remembering Yeats's dislike
of Owen, and his rejection of 'passive suffering' as a theme for
poetry, we come to Press's argument that 'even on the battlefield
[Sorley] retained what his house-master called "an extraordinary
thrust of life" '. The phrase is quoted as though that thrust were a
corroboration of Yeats's view that 'tragedy is joy', a response alien
to Owen's (and Rosenberg's) pity. Press supports his reading with
the reminder that Sorley's war was not as embittered as Owen's
was to become. He suggests, quoting again from Sorley's letters,
that he marched to the Front with exhilaration. I read Sorley's
remarks as more jocular, even wryly self-conscious, than exhilarated;
an interpretation supported by fuller quotation from the letters
than Press offers. To make my point I italicize the extracts quoted
in his article:

> Drink its cider . . . It brings out a new part of one's self . . . beautiful
> and calm without mental fear. And in four-score hours we will pull up our
> braces and fight. These hours will have slipt over me, and *I shall march
> hotly to the firing-line, by turn critic, actor, hero, coward and soldier of
> fortune: perhaps even for a moment Christian, humble, with 'Thy will be
> done'*. Then shock, combustion, the emergence of one of these: death and
> life: and then return to the old rigmarole.

Such a statement as 'we shall pull up our braces and fight' is wryly
jocular, and shows Sorley attempting to control something that
would otherwise force very different responses from him.

Press quotes from another letter, dated fifteen days later (16 June 1915) to indicate 'how, in some ways, the war had liberated' Sorley. I make the same use of italics:

So one lives in a year ago—and a year hence ... but where, while riding in your Kentish lanes, are you riding twelve months hence? I am sometimes in Mexico, selling cloth: or in Russia, doing Lord knows what: in Serbia or the Balkans: in England, never. England remains the dream, the background: at once the memory and the ideal. *Sorley is the Gaelic for wanderer. I have had a conventional education: Oxford would have corked it. But this has freed the spirit, glory be. Give me The Odyssey, and I return the New Testament to store. Physically as well as spiritually, give me the road.*

Only sometimes the horrible question of bread and butter shadows the dream: it has shadowed many, I should think.

The word 'liberated' must be used with caution in this context. Sorley is speaking of travel—'the road'—and not the war as such. It is true the war contrasted with much of his 'conventional educa-tion', although this had included work in Germany; yet given this 'liberation' into a new experience, Sorley seems to be stressing the release *from* the conventionality of his experience rather than the liberation of the war itself. It is significant that he does not mention the war. And qualifying all is the last sentence, which is colder, less fanciful than the preceding italicized quotation. Sorley recog-nizes that part of this freedom is illusory.

Finally, Press quotes from a letter of 26 August 1915 to indicate not only how Sorley's attitude to pity differed from Owen's, but also I think to question whether Sorley was not moving further from the anti-war, anti-heroic mode that most of the post-Somme 'war poets' endorsed:

On the whole—except for the subtle distinction that I *am* at the front, you not ... I am disposed to envy you. ... But out in front at night in that no-man's land and long graveyard there is a freedom and a spur. Rustling of the grasses and grave tap-tapping of distant workers: the ten-sion and silence of encounter, when one struggles in the dark for moral victory over the enemy patrol: the wail of the exploded bomb and the animal cries of wounded men. Then death and the horrible thankfulness when one sees that the next man is dead: 'We won't have to *carry* him in under fire, thank God; dragging will do': hauling in of the great resist-less body in the dark, the smashed head rattling: the relief, the relief that the thing has ceased to groan: that the bullet or bomb that made the man an animal has now made the animal a corpse. One is hardened by now: purged of all false pity: perhaps more selfish than before. The spiritual and the animal get so much more sharply divided in hours of encounter, taking possession of the body by swift turns.

Of this passage, Press writes:

It is arguable that Sorley, having been purged of all false pity, would have discovered the true pity of war and, like Owen, would have made it the theme of his poetry. Yet this letter suggests that Sorley was near to embracing the joyous, tragic, heroic mood which Yeats advocates as the proper temper for poets writing of war.

'Joyous, tragic, heroic' are the key words here, and there is certainly the suggestion of his 'being spurred' by the experience. The first sentence quoted from Sorley's letter (and not by Press) would seem to confirm this, but the part concerning the cries of the wounded men and the relief at being able to drag rather than carry the body does not suggest that he regarded the experience as enviable. The truth is surely that Sorley was responding in two ways to the experience of war. It seems likely that, had he lived, the spur would have diminished as the suffering—his own and others'—intensified. It is hard to know how to interpret 'false pity': is pity something it is useless to waste on the dead? Is Sorley, in honesty, contrasting it with fear and self-preservation and implying that these override pity? I think so, and though *this* is hardly heroic, in a sense his honesty *is*. Moreover, his reference to the dead not needing to be carried implies a compassionate assumption that the wounded did.

To return to Sorley's poems; 'When You See Millions of the Mouthless Dead', for example, has something of Owen's tragic apprehension of war. The magniloquence, from which Sorley was slowly breaking free, is well qualified by 'Say only this, "They are dead" ', which I read as a comment on Brooke's 'If I should die, think only this of me'. In contrast to Press, I imagine Sorley developing some form of didactic protest. Like Owen, he reveals a didactic and analytical strength in his letters; and I believe that his awareness of suffering would have produced a lean, spare poetry no less condemnatory than Owen's, with perhaps more analytic force. He might also have developed the conflict between his response to others' pain and his natural desire for survival. He was, however, only twenty when he was killed, and just beginning to emerge as a poet. The incompleteness of his attitudes is revealed in 'All the Hills and Vales Along', which Bernard Bergonzi, in *Heroes' Twilight*, regards as one of Sorley's best poems. Press rightly remarks that it owes 'much to Housman's concept of Nature as hostile or indifferent to man':

> Earth that blossomed and was glad
> 'Neath the cross that Christ had,
> Shall rejoice and blossom too
> When the bullet reaches you. . . .
>
> Strew your gladness on earth's bed,
> So be merry, so be dead.

This poem was written, of course, before Sorley had experienced the trenches, a fact that serves only to emphasize that his attitude to combat had not been worked out in relation to his other (poetic) preoccupations. Johnston points to the difficulty of deciding whether to read it as a conventional patriotic lyric or as an ironic poem. Thus,

> All the hills and vales along
> Earth is bursting into song,
> And the singers are the chaps
> Who are going to die perhaps.

That last 'perhaps' adds an ironic touch absent from Grenfell's 'Into Battle', for instance; but the ambiguity of the poem as a whole lies in the relation between man and nature, or rather, in the absence of any human attitude towards the soldiers' probable death. In Owen's 'Exposure' and 'Spring Offensive', nature is also alien to man, but this by way of judgement on man as killer. To Sorley, nature in its joyful hostility is seemingly indifferent to the dying men and whether or not they were culpable in that they had killed others. War is merely one agent that destroys men and which in consequence causes nature to rejoice. The poem derives ironic force from the men's cheerfulness in the face of nature's even more joyful knowledge that they are going to die. Nature does not condemn war, and makes use of it in the way that the Spirit Sinister in *The Dynasts* does, feeding on war's carnage. Nature and man are seen as unrelated components; nature does not actively contribute to man's death, and on the contrary permitted him pleasure when he was alive. Yet the proper focus in a poem about war is on man as man's victim; only indirectly—and then because of war—is man nature's victim. Thus, nature's rejoicing is irrelevant to the central question of what we are to think of men killing each other. The poem is awry because it postulates a nature–man antagonism in the context of an antagonism between men, in which nature is at best incidental. Nature has something of the malign but passive role of Hardy's Spirit Sinister, but is also presented as though it had an active role in man's destruction. Such inconsistencies indicate that Sorley was finding the *experience* of war more difficult to evaluate than he found an expression of attitudes *towards* it and its related problem of chauvinism. He knew what he thought on questions that confused people much older than himself, but his experience of war was changing his understanding of human relations, and of man's relations with his environment, when the war killed him.

CHAPTER FIVE

EDWARD THOMAS

Born of predominantly Welsh parentage in 1878, Edward Thomas read history at Oxford and married while still an undergraduate. There were three children, and a constant shortage of money, largely the result of his decision to live by his writing. He produced thirty books of prose between 1897 and 1915, quite apart from his poems, innumerable book reviews, and various editions and anthologies. William Cooke gives a painful account of Thomas's drab, unremitting labour in *Edward Thomas: A Critical Biography* (1970). There is a good examination of the prose in this book, and in H. H. Coombes's *Edward Thomas* (1956). Comparisons are invidious, but Cooke's work especially shows the relationship, in all its inequality, between the prose and the poetry, and the growth of the one from the other. For Thomas, the prose was a testing ground and a filter through which the poems came. While, on the one hand, it is surprising that he survived the labour of his prose to write his poetry, on the other, he was in a sense preparing himself for his poetry.

Cooke is at pains to show that, contrary to most critics' assertions, Thomas did not wait to be urged by Frost before starting to write poetry; other friends had made this suggestion before. The turning point, Cooke maintains, occurred in November 1914, when Thomas was writing the prose of *The White House* (which was never published) and *In Pursuit of Spring*. Even so, Frost's encouragement was important, though not perhaps crucial, in making Thomas a poet. He had favourably reviewed Frost's *A Boy's Will* (1913) and *North of Boston* (1914), and they first met on 5 October 1913. Frost summed up the help he had given Thomas in this way:

> Right at that moment he was writing as good poetry as anybody alive, but in prose form where it did not declare itself and gain him recognition. I referred him to paragraphs in his book *In Pursuit of Spring* and told him to write it in verse form in exactly the same cadence. That's all there was to it. His poetry declared itself in verse form. . . .

Clearly this is an over-modest account, and no doubt Frost helped Thomas the man, as perhaps Thomas also helped Frost. Yet the critics too often forget that no man can make a poet of another; help may be important, but a man's talent is his own. Frost acted catalytically, but he was not the only catalyst, and he did not make Thomas's poems. Indeed, Thomas was in a sense his own catalyst. The wheels took fire, eventually, by the laboriousness of their own motion, and ironically the war also helped him in that, after enlisting in the Artists' Rifles in July 1915, three months before Owen, he got some leisure for his poetry before he sailed to France in January 1917. His first poem, 'Up in the Wind', was written on 3 December 1914 and many others were to follow in rapid succession. Yet the war cannot be said to have helped Thomas in any active sense. Lloyd George's assertion that it was the war that released the poetic flow; 'all was well from then on . . . the winning through of an obscure youth to triumph and renown', would have a little more substance had Thomas had a book of his poems published in his lifetime. Only a few appeared before his death, and the sixty-four poems he had arranged for publication early in 1917 were published posthumously.

Lloyd George was not alone in seeing the war as a blessing in disguise for Thomas. R. P. Eckert, for example, wrote: 'With regular army life his melancholy and dark agonies disappeared for ever.' John Moore, in his *Life and Letters of Edward Thomas*, similarly maintained that 'He had changed his whole attitude to life, shaken hands with the past and shut his eyes to the future, so that he was troubled neither with regrets nor apprehensions.' Confidence of this sort was as alien to Thomas's poetry as to his nature. These comments share a belief that Thomas was not only able to enlist with comparative ease of mind, but that, having done so, his melancholy was dispersed for ever. That it was not so erased is shown in the poems. But finally what is distorting in these statements is that the war and his so-called patriotism are both given the credit for his poetry.

Of the hundred and forty-one poems in his *Collected Poems*, twelve are explicitly impinged on by the war, and many others have a particular relationship with the war, quite apart from the fact that all were written during it. Few can be identified as 'war poems', in the way that most of Owen's can, but on the other hand there are more subtle, indirect ways of reflecting the nature of war. All Thomas's poems were written before he sailed for

France in January 1917, but according to Cooke's dating he was
writing almost up to the moment of his departure: 'Out in the
Dark' is dated 24 December 1916. In the sense that Lloyd George
and perhaps Eckert and Moore might have understood the term,
Thomas was not a 'war poet' at all, although he edited, with a
certain kind of love of his country, the anthology *This England*
(1915). Yet even 'This is no Case of Petty Right or Wrong'
(December 1915) evidences an awareness far removed from Grenfell's 'Into Battle' or Brooke's '1914'. The difference is important,
because the version of patriotism here offered—although the word
'patriotism' does not fit Brooke's sonnets well, and Thomas's poem
even less—is organized in relation to the countryside he observed,
knew, and felt. Cooke writes that

> The distinction between subtle (private) patriotism and deliberate
> (public) patriotism was one that Thomas himself drew several times. In a
> second review of [*War Poetry*] 1914 he wrote:
> '. . . The worst of the poetry being written today is that it is too deli-
> berately, and not inevitably, English. It is for an audience: there is more
> in it of the shouting of the rhetorician, reciter, or politician than of the
> talk of friends and lovers.'

Although this is one distinction, another can be seen through
Eleanor Farjeon's comment on the poem in *The Last Four Years*
(1958):

> Edward's first poem in 1916 [actually it was the last of 1915] is the
> complete expression of his feelings about the war. For love of the dust
> of his country he cried 'God save England!' in 1915, as in 1415 he might
> have cried it at Agincourt. His hate-feelings were reserved for the Jingo
> Press and those who used its jargon in argument. His father was among
> them. . . . Edward had to write this war-poem, but having written it he
> did not include it in his book, when the time for choosing came later in
> the year. [It *was* included in *Six Poems*, 1916.]

Eleanor Farjeon also records an incident which emphasizes the
difference in attitude not merely between Brooke and Thomas, but
between the latter's patriotism and the chauvinism which abstractly
endorses its country. It forms, I think, the germ of her perception
quoted above—'For love of the dust of his country'. She asked
Thomas if he knew what he was fighting for: 'He stopped, and
picked up a pinch of earth. "Literally, for this." He crumbled it

4

between finger and thumb, and let it fall.' Thomas believed he
would be fighting not so much for the nation as for the land, a
territory with a culture and way of life which, ironically, he knew
was disappearing, even before the war.

> But with the best and meanest Englishmen
> I am one in crying, God save England, lest
> We lose what never slaves and cattle blessed.
> The ages made her that made us from dust:
> She is all we know and live by. . . .

The last but one line indicates, however slightly, the rhetorical
position that any patrotism, no matter how moderately expressed,
tends to lead one into. But the modesty of the last line above,
remarking merely on the debt of nourishment, indicates the extent
to which Thomas differed from the patriots:

> . . . I hate not Germans, nor grow hot
> With love of Englishmen, to please newspapers.
> Beside my hate for one fat patriot
> My hatred of the Kaiser is love true:—
> A kind of god he is, banging a gong.
> But I have not to choose between the two,
> Or between justice and injustice.

In the sense that he believed he was fighting for the land, his
'patriotism' might be said to spring from an accident of birth;
and in this his feeling for his country has some kinship with
Blunden's love of nature and a particular, known territory.

Certainly, it is clear in this poem that Thomas did not discard
either his own or a collective past, and it is therefore all the more
ironic that he should have fought for a territorial, physical entity
which Moore would also have supported, but for different reasons
and with different emphases. It was because Thomas could not
reject his land and the past (and leave, on Frost's invitation, for
America) that he enlisted. Yet, in assessing the influence of the
past, and of nature, we cannot discount the war's effect on him and
his poetry. The difficulty is to determine to what extent and in
what way it affected him, and to gauge how he would have written
had there been no war.

With most writers there are clues to be obtained by comparing the writing before a particular experience, such as the war, with the writing during it. But Thomas had not written any poetry before the war, although he had written a great deal of prose, much of it concerned with nature and his responses to it, either for its own sake or as it provided a screen on to which he could project his own feelings. When Thomas came to write his poetry he—as it were—repeated his past, already contained in his prose, in the sense that the themes, or at least the subject-matter, of his prose became that of his poetry (see Frost's suggestion on p. 85). For such a conscious and experienced writer, the past was not merely his long apprehension of nature but, mixed with it, his own self-perceived melancholy and darkness, his apprehension of the past itself, and what it must certainly lead to: 'Only an avenue, dark, nameless, without end'. This theme (partly that of 'Old Man') is the theme of many of the poems in that it colours his apprehension of nature; and I think that war confirmed the brooding, melancholy, painful, and sometimes despairing impulses found in his poetry. Thus, he is not a poet 'made' by the war, one whose theme is its horror and pity; but a poet who found the war an objective corroboration of some of his earlier less identifiable feelings. In this sense only is he a 'war poet'. The 'patriot' poem is a complex instance of this, because as well as being a record of his attitude to the war, as he expresses it through nature, it is also an evaluation of his past and a collective one, seen in terms of nature and the countryside.

Thomas and his family lived in south and south-eastern England for most of their adult lives, and as a child in London he had had access to the surrounding country. He also stayed frequently with his aunt or grandmother in Swindon.

Leavis remarks in *New Bearings* (1963 edition) that the 'outward scene is accessory to an inward theatre. . . . the end of the poem ['October'] is not description', and other poems such as 'Old Man', 'Aspens', and 'Wind and Mist' bear this out. What helps to maintain the intensity of the theatre in these poems is the unforced presence of physical detail.

> The shell of a little snail bleached
> In the grass; chip of flint, and mite
> Of chalk; and the small bird's dung
> In splashes of purest white. . . .

His apprehension of nature springs from small things observed and recognized. Known, they re-impinge on the mind as memories, introducing other associations:

> I, too, often shrivel the grey shreds,
> Sniff them and think and sniff again and try
> Once more to think what it is I am remembering. . . .

The disturbed, hastening movement of the line—located precisely and with some anxiety in the forgotten object, 'what it is'— indicates a mind disturbed, and conscious of its own disturbance. And this image of the conscious mind is also an emblem of the relationship between the experience, the prose, and the poetry. The poetry often, and perhaps at its best, conveys the impression of a mind thinking about itself, and its responses to its past experience. The prose is less conscious of itself and more concerned with the mood it evokes. This is hardly surprising, because the prose came first, and because the poetry then drew on the material of the prose, subtly altering the responses to objects that often provoked the day-dreaming nostalgia of the prose. A painful honesty subsequently corrects in the poetry the indulgence and nostalgic dislocation of some of the prose.

If we have an approximate model of his self-insight, which helps us to understand what it was he was trying to re-create, we can more exactly get at the presence of the war in his poems, and understand what he felt about it. He was in most respects mature when, at the age of thirty-six, he enlisted; and he had already been writing poetry for about seven months. Given the intensity of his self-absorption (not to be confused with egocentricity), it might seem that the war was unlikely to make a great impression on his poetry, which must have been one of his most absorbing activities. In fact the war is present in quite a few of the poems; and present not only, as in Blunden's poems, as an undertone to his apprehension of nature or as an almost overwhelming presence. It enters the very structure of the way of life Thomas was re-creating, but is thoroughly absorbed, even in the most 'direct' of the 'war poems', into the natural context which is his 'theatre'.

The relation between the prose and the poetry is worth considering in some detail, because their differences illustrate my thesis. Conveniently, as Vernon Scannell indicates in his pamphlet, *Edward*

Thomas, a passage from *The Icknield Way* (1913) was re-worked in the poem 'Rain':

everything was embedded in rain. Every sound was the rain. For example, I thought I heard bacon frying in a room near by, with a noise almost as loud as the pig made when it was stuck; but it was the rain pouring steadily off the inn roof.

This passage is interesting in that the 'natural' rain and the pig are easily linked with the domestic 'bacon frying'. The link provides an awareness that the pig must be killed to provide the human being with food; but the ease of association is qualified by the facts. Thomas manages to keep everything within the context of the rain—'everything was embedded in it'—and so keeps its pervasiveness. Good though the passage is, it leads nowhere, or only into this very different, melancholy sense of self-erosion and futility:

I lay awake listening to the rain, and at first it was as pleasant to my ear and my mind as it had long been desired; but before I fell asleep it had become a majestic and finally a terrible thing, instead of a sweet sound and symbol. It was accusing and trying me and passing judgment. Long I lay still under the sentence, listening to the rain, and then at last listening to words which seemed to be spoken by a ghostly double beside me. He was muttering: The all-night rain puts out summer like a torch.

From something benign, almost parental, it becomes terrible, and in psychological terms, castrating. The rain answers to two sides in him:

the heat of summer is annihilated, the splendour is dead, the summer is gone. The midnight rain buries it away where it has buried all sound but its own. I am alone in the dark still night, and my ear listens to the rain. . . . Even so will the rain fall darkly upon the grass over the grave when my ears can hear it no more. . . . Now there is neither life nor death, but only the rain.

This passage and the opening lines of 'Rain' have in common certain qualities of misery and despair, and the similarities indicate I think how little Thomas either could or cared to reject his past, but, on

the contrary, worked through it to apprehend more deeply his
present:

> Rain, midnight rain, nothing but the wild rain
> On this bleak hut, and solitude, and me
> Remembering again that I shall die
> And neither hear the rain nor give it thanks
> For washing me cleaner than I have been
> Since I was born into this solitude.

Apart from the concentration, one considerable difference between
the prose and the poem is the focus upon the self, and upon that
self in relation to a universal condition of life. It is the relationship
that has been intensified. Compare 'Even so will the rain fall
darkly upon the grass over the grave when my ears can hear it no
more' with

> . . . and me
> Remembering again that I shall die . . .

In the verse he is aware—'remembering'—that he is thinking about
himself and the condition of death; one additional layer of awareness
has been added, or perhaps defined. In the prose the awareness of
death is a passing one, however painful; it is floating, idle, passive,
an intermittent consciousness no *more* painful than any of the
other miseries. In the poem it is an insistence, and related to the
war. There is no specific indication that his death is thought of as
in battle, but the very insistence on the approaching apprehension
of death indicates a response intensified by war. One might compare
these lines with the opening lines of Brooke's 'The Soldier' to get
the full force of Thomas's apprehension.

In Thomas's poem the elements of misery, self-consciousness, and
half-ironic self-accusation are closely related; they are much more
a part of a closely seen situation, in which he is more positively
present, than they are in the prose. There, the elements anthropo-
morphize nature and give it a day-dreaming ambiance. When these
elements are closely focused in the poem, complex meanings
emerge:

> Remembering again that I shall die
> And neither hear the rain nor give it thanks
> For washing me cleaner. . . .

The weight of meaning falls on 'cleaner' for, although it may be
desirable to be purified, it is of little use when one is dead which,

it seems to follow, is the only condition in which such purity may be obtained. And yet, clearly, at least some of the misery and anguish are related to an apprehension of death. Or rather, these are more strongly related to his *own* death in the prose than in the poem. In the poem, the misery of anticipating death in war is something shared; but that is premature. For the moment, the elements of self-criticism which consciousness brings him are present, but these are ultimately formed into a different set of apprehensions more concerned with a sympathetic sharing of this misery, of which his own is a part. In the prose, the accusation (whatever it is directed against) is expressed, but remains somewhat dangling, although clearly directed, a little indulgently, upon himself. It is tinged with masochism:

I am weary of everything. I stay because I am too weak to go. I crawl on because it is easier than to stop. . . . Once I heard through the rain a bird's questioning watery cry—once only and suddenly. It seemed content, and the solitary note brought up against me the order of nature, all its beauty, exuberance, and everlastingness like an accusation. I am not a part of nature. I am alone. . . . Once there was summer, and a great heat and splendour over the earth terrified me and asked me what I could show that was worthy of such an earth. It smote me and humiliated me. . . . I have done evilly and weakly, and I have left undone.

The predominant feeling here is of a certain indulgence, and in this it contrasts, I think, with a similar passage in Wordsworth's 'Resolution and Independence' (stanzas 3–6 especially). Ostensibly they are saying the same thing, but in Thomas's *poem* the consciousness plays upon what is absent in the prose—an awareness of others' misery and isolation, in which he shares. Here, as in 'The Owl', there is an increase in awareness of himself—over the prose, but it now indicates how well qualified he is to feel and share others' misery. Thomas makes the transition from self to others in the line 'Blessed are the dead that the rain rains upon'. The seeming quotation (which I have been unable to identify), which in almost identical form ends the prose passage, conveys a feeling of thankfulness and relief. In the poem, where the transition occurs, the intensified awareness of death as an inevitable and not entirely welcome event qualifies and balances the thankfulness. Death is more clearly apprehended, as a doubtful relief, and the rain is a doubly doubtful benediction in that it also falls upon the dead who can feel nothing. The ironic doubt in this line increases subsequently his sense of pity in that it fully exposes his own position, which is that of others:

> But here I pray that none whom once I loved
> Is dying to-night or lying still awake
> Solitary, listening to the rain,
> Either in pain or thus in sympathy
> Helpless among the living and the dead. . . .

He too is 'in pain. . .in sympathy/Helpless'. The syntactical placing of 'Helpless' is especially telling because he is not only, like the others, helpless in his own passive suffering, but also helpless in his active sympathy to relieve their suffering. He prays that none is in his position, knowing that there must be many. The misery and the sympathy is shared and re-shared. The word 'among' is also suggestive, in that it conveys a physical sense of sharing with those living and dead on the battlefield. The fact that he was not at the front and had not yet experienced combat shows how Thomas could sympathetically project his imagination into the condition of front-line soldiers, a sense of whose annihilation is to be found in the prose: 'Everything is drowned and dead, all that was once lovely and alive in the world, all that had once been alive and was memorable though dead is now dung for a future that is infinitely less than the falling dark rain'. But in the poem the tragic sense of mortality is sharpened by being directed towards living individuals, rather than an abstract Mankind:

> Helpless among the living and the dead,
> Like a cold water among broken reeds,
> Myriads of broken reeds all still and stiff,
> Like me who have no love which this wild rain
> Has not dissolved except the love of death. . . .

The 'cold water' is unable to succour the 'reeds' because they are 'broken'. His sympathy (cold comfort) can do nothing for the dead, and little more for the living, such is their miserable condition; the human suffering and sympathy are almost equally helpless. This is a fine and accurate image, in that just as the water cannot succour the reeds that are broken, water-logged, so sympathy cannot hearten the living, who are not in a position to be helped. 'Still and stiff' strongly suggests the stretched-out human corpses, and 'Myriads' of reeds and humans (such was the slaughter) are imaged.

The poem ends by returning syntactically to its beginning, with Thomas expressing an awareness of his own responses; again, a fine movement, because it suggests to the reader that he too should now become aware of his responses:

> Like me who have no love which this wild rain
> Has not dissolved except the love of death,
> If love it be for what is perfect and
> Cannot, the tempest tells me, disappoint.

The prose passage ends with the paradoxically benedictory 'rain' quotation, but the poem finishes with the rain beating on the dead and on the living alike. In the poem, the rain dissolves an active love and not a passive, debilitating misery. What it cannot dissolve, a love of death, a partial love, is thus judged here. It is done with honesty, since what is left, Thomas tells us, is the 'love of death' which, because of the war, is more likely to find its actual realization.[1] The seeking of perfection in nature finds its partly ironic fulfilment in death, but such a consummation is not devoutly to be wished. It is conceivable that, having found the proper outlet for his creativity, he was no longer as haunted by death. The parenthetical sentence, 'the tempest tells me', supports this, suggesting that it is not Thomas who seeks (in himself) a perfection, least of all in death. The tempest offers him the idea, but in this dialogue it is by no means clear that he welcomes or even accepts the tempest's suggestion. Nor does he at all seem to accept this form of perfection as a solution for those he pities. Thomas has moved on from the melancholy of the prose passage, but hardly in the way that Eckert, Moore, and Lloyd George seem to have thought.

Eleanor Farjeon writes of Thomas as 'so excellent and so contented and so greatly liked a soldier'.[2] He may have been the last, but it is less certain that he was the first and second. It is true that he wrote in a letter of 10 February 1917: 'I enjoyed the exercise, the work with map and fieldglass, the scene, the weather, and the sense of being able to do a new job.' But he also wrote several times in 1917 of how he thought it would be impossible to write poetry and to read under trench conditions. His letters of this period, in fact, show him as far from contented, and they also show something else. On 27 March 1917 he writes to Eleanor Farjeon:

[1] See John Burrow, 'Keats and Edward Thomas', *Essays in Criticism*, VII, No. 4 (1957).
[2] Helen Thomas did not appear to think her husband was 'so contented . . . a soldier'. See *As It Was . . . World Without End* (1935), ch. XV, especially pp. 278–80.

It is walking up to or among ruined houses—gable ends all big holes
and piles of masonry round and splintered walnut—that I dislike most,
with a lowering sky like this evening's. I keep feeling that I should enjoy
it more if I knew I would survive it. I can't help allowing it to trouble
me, but it doesn't prey on me and I have no real foreboding, only occa-
sional trepidation and anxiety. The men are better but then they are
comrades and I am usually alone or with them. I wish that what is coming
would be more than an incident—the battle of— Still I can't wait a great
while, though of course what is coming is to be far worse than anything
I know so far. It is worse for you and for Helen and Mother, I know.

That last generous sentence evidences Thomas's concern for others
in the midst of his own anxieties. Its compassion resembles that in
'Rain' and 'The Owl'. In this latter poem he is 'hungry', 'cold',
'tired'. Yet, in his own deprivation seeing the deprivation of others,
he never loses sight of his own. At the inn he satisfies his needs,
and as he does so, hears

> An owl's cry, a most melancholy cry
>
> Shaken out long and clear upon the hill,
> No merry note, nor cause of merriment,
> But one telling me plain what I escaped
> And others could not, that night, as in I went.

That familiar melancholy condition of which he is reminded, not
by identification with the owl, but by its hostile warning cry, also
reminds him now of his own comfortable condition and the discomfort of others. There is also an element of irrational, perhaps,
but understandable guilt—Thomas had not yet enlisted—which
emerges in the last stanza:

> And salted was my food, and my repose,
> Salted and sobered, too, by the bird's voice
> Speaking for all who lay under the stars,
> Soldiers and poor, unable to rejoice.

'Salted' is first used to mean tasty, but then, qualified by 'sobered',
it suggests, as Scannell says, 'the harshness of salt, the salt in the
wound, the taste of bitterness, and of tears'. Possibly, as Scannell
goes on to say, Thomas's enjoyment is increased by his awareness
of the deprivation of the 'Soldiers and poor', or, as I should prefer
to put it, by his sense of enjoying something special and privileged.
The honesty acknowledges the guilt, both of them necessary not
only as qualifying factors of his conscience but as factors in his

relish. This kind of conscience Wilfred Owen also possessed. Mrs. Mary Gray, who knew him well when he was at Craiglockhart, wrote that 'His sensitiveness, his sympathy were so acute, so profound, that direct personal experience and individual development can hardly be said to have existed for him. He could only suffer or rejoice vicariously.' Thomas was slightly more 'opaque', more conscious of others' suffering in relation to his own—or perhaps, originally, through his own—but Mrs. Gray's description of Owen's responses fits very well *some* of those in 'The Owl' and 'Rain'. But just as it would be fair to say that what gives Thomas his special kinship with Owen is this compassion, what marks him off from Owen is his realistic assessment of his own suffering in a situation in which he is also aware of the suffering of others.

Thomas's debt to Frost is well known, but the extent to which other poets of his time influenced his work is insufficiently recognized. 'In Memoriam (Easter, 1915)' and 'A Private', for example, have the tone and trick of Housman—the poignant grief supposedly withheld both internally and from outside view, but signified by the extent that it is compressed into *almost* impersonal and epigrammatic sharpness. 'In Memoriam', however, has something which Housman had not:

> The flowers left thick at nightfall in the wood
> This Eastertide call into mind the men,
> Now far from home, who, with their sweethearts, should
> Have gathered them and will do never again.

'Should' reveals a knowledge of how war destroys the basic human relationship. Where Housman uses the death of youth, or (more commonly) a youth as an occasion for private grief, Thomas is concerned with death only as something which destroys life. Death for Housman is pervasive, the cause of a continuous, private grief; Thomas, on the other hand, sees death as an intruder, not as life's central event. Housman saw death as the eclipsing irony of living.

'A Private' has less of Housman's tone, but the method owes much to him. The secret, the source of the irony, a joke made out of death, shows how well Thomas understood Housman:

> 'I slept'. None knew which bush. Above the town,
> Beyond 'The Drover', a hundred spot the down
> In Wiltshire. And where now at last he sleeps
> More sound in France—that, too, he secret keeps.

'More sound' is effectively Housmanesque in its irony although, as in Housman, the irony is so evident that it covers up the elements of the situation that are potentially stronger than irony. The 'joke' depends on the discrepancy between sleep and death; and a further, slighter joke is that which exploits sleep as the euphemism for death, 'sound' as it were rounding it off. The point Thomas fails to make, and cannot while he uses Housmanesque irony, is that the actual discrepancy between sleep and death *is* the man's death; the irony is unnecessary since the difference between the two makes its own point.

In the sonnet 'February Afternoon' he creates, I think, an image for his atheism; certainly the cycle of life and death in nature seems to be self-perpetuating, and without a God:

> So that the first are last until a caw
> Commands that last are first again,—a law
> Which was of old. . . .

In the sestet, a millennium of this is concerted to a day

> while the broad ploughland oak
> Roars mill-like and men strike and bear the stroke
> Of war as ever, audacious or resigned. . . .

The poem broaches adequately what might be described as Thomas's war theme—the impact of war on nature (and man with nature) and its disturbing of the outward semblances of the natural rhythm and cycle. Man's mortality, especially in war, is contrasted both with the ageless (but not perhaps entirely unchanging) cycle of nature, and with the longevity of the oak. This is emphasized by the rhyme 'oak/stroke', but something more subtle occurs—in the nature of a pun—since the stroke of war suggests the stroke of the axe and the tree's fall. As the one foreshortens men's lives so the other does the tree's. In the last two lines of the sestet Thomas seems to want two different ideas to bear equal weight:

> And God still sits aloft in the array
> That we have wrought him, stone-deaf and stone-blind.

God, who has been made by man ('in the array/That we have wrought him'), seems as indifferent to man's carnage and suffering as men are to each other's suffering.

'Fifty Faggots' delicately interleaves the impingement of war on two processes connected with nature. These are shown to be in a positive/negative relation to each other by the war which, however, changes round their values so that what was positive becomes negative and vice versa. The thicket can provide wood for 'Winters' fires', but if not gathered it provides effective cover for the birds to nest there:

> This Spring it is too late; the swift has come.
> 'Twas a hot day for carrying them up:

but the second line refers to the taking in of the faggots, which he in fact did not do:

> . . . though they must
> Light several Winters' fires. Before they are done
> The war will have ended, many other things
> Have ended, maybe, that I can no more
> Foresee or more control than robin and wren.

'Before they are done' refers perhaps to the gathering of the faggots, but it also perhaps refers to the birds' nesting. By syntactically, simultaneously referring to the two activities, Thomas conveys not merely the relatedness between man's and nature's activity, but the effect of war upon the latter. By telling us that no one individual can control the war, as the creatures cannot prevent men from taking away the wood they are nesting among, Thomas shows the effect of the war upon nature. The poem's structure is ironic since, but for the war, the birds would be without the shelter for their nests which they now have. The war tarnishes. In 'Gone, Gone Again' the young men are turned to dung. Nature also tarnishes:

> The Blenheim oranges
> Fall grubby from the trees.

The adjective is ugly, as are the reasons for the trees' neglect.

'As the Team's Head-Brass' opens with an allusion to nature's regenerative life. The ploughman, who has remained on the land, and the soldier, perhaps on leave but with no experience yet of fighting, assess the war and their situations. The war is introduced with typical obliqueness:

> Every time the horses turned
> Instead of treading me down, . . .

which ominously suggests war's treading down. Nature has also destroyed something of herself: 'The blizzard felled the elm', but,

as in 'Fifty Faggots', the war has interfered with man's care of
nature; the removal of the elm is indefinitely delayed because the
men who would have done the work have gone:

> 'When will they take it away?'
> 'When the war's over.' So the talk began—
> One minute and an interval of ten,
> A minute more and the same interval.

The movement of the conversation, dictated by the coming and
going of the plough and the ploughman, imitates the recurring
cycle of nature. The speakers' wit and wisdom convey a realistic
assessment of the likely costs of war. Acknowledging human
vulnerability, they waste no time on cant: 'Have you been out?' the
ploughman asks the soldier. 'No.' 'And don't want to, perhaps?'
The soldier replies: 'If I could only come back again, I should.' The
canny, unemotional sizing of the odds is coupled with a humour
that sees the war as a creditor, the job of whose debtors is to give
to its destructiveness as little as possible. The humour reminds
one of Hood's 'Faithless Nellie Gray', although Thomas is not
facetious as he underlines the real cost of the war:

> 'I could spare an arm. I shouldn't want to lose
> A leg. If I should lose my head, why, so,
> I should want nothing more'. . . .

The last line seems to play on the idea that the patriot's supposedly
highest desire is to lay down his life for the cause. The ploughman
reports on the war's decimation of local men, and reiterates the
point that, as a result, nature is left untended:

> 'Now if
> He had stayed here we should have moved the tree.'

The Hardyesque statement, 'If we could see all all might seem
good,' is highly complex in that the good, the final good when all
is added and subtracted, is both confirmed and denied as a possibility. This final score includes not only the war but the generative
processes of nature as well. The war prevents any certainty on these
questions. But as though to begin an answer to them

> The lovers came out of the woods again:
> The horses started and for the last time
> I watched the clods crumble. . . .

That phrase 'for the last time', pointed subtly at his seeing the crumbling of the clods but aimed in a different and negative sense at the lovers, indicates Thomas's doubts as to the continuing harmonious and productive relationship between nature and man and between human beings which, he seems to feel, the war will inevitably disrupt. It also, of course, points to the soldier's uncertain fate.

Philip Hobsbaum makes a comparison between Hardy's 'In Time of "The Breaking of Nations" ' (1915) and this poem of Thomas's.[1] However, Thomas's pessimistic 'for the last time' is not consonant with Hardy's confidence:

> Only a man harrowing clods. . . .
>
> Yet this will go onward the same
>   Though Dynasties pass.
>
> Yonder a maid and her wight
>   Come whispering by:
> War's annals will cloud into night
>   Ere their story die.

Curiously, Thomas is much more in agreement with the verses of Jeremiah from which the title of Hardy's poem is taken:

Thou art my battle axe and weapons of war: for thee will I break in pieces the nations, and with thee will I destroy kingdoms. . . .

I will also break in pieces with thee the shepherd and his flock; and with thee will I break in pieces the husbandman and his yoke of oxen; and with thee will I break in pieces captains and rulers.

One might add that the verses read like a text for *The Dynasts*.

[1] 'The Road not Taken', *The Listener*, 23 November 1961.

CHAPTER SIX

EDMUND BLUNDEN AND
IVOR GURNEY

I

Edmund Blunden enlisted in 1914. His war poetry is hard to characterize in that like his poetry as a whole it does not have cohering themes, in the strict sense, so much as contexts and specific experiences. He writes of nature and war, or rather, of events within a rural pattern. Nature is made to contain war, as best it can, as the sanative framework of an otherwise disrupting experience. War impinges on him in a more specific way than nature does and, to this extent, it is more deliberately examined. He sees it as a disrupting force, not merely because it is so intrinsically, but because it interferes with his fruitful contact with nature. Nature provides that kind of assuring context that religion provides for some. In answer to Faustus's question 'How comes it, then, that thou art out of hell?' Mephistophilis replies, 'Why, this is hell, nor am I out of it.' Absence from 'the face of God' is hell and only an experience such as war could exile the poet from nature as Mephistophilis is exiled from God.

Siegfried Sassoon maintained in conversation that Blunden is the surviving poet of the war most lastingly obsessed by it; a fact perhaps anticipated by Blunden himself in his epigraph to *Undertones of War* (1928). He quotes Bunyan: 'Yea, how they set themselves in battle-array I shall remember to my dying day.' On the other hand, Blunden had seen even before the war a haunted and fearful aspect in nature. The war intensified this awareness and made more complex the relation between war and malign nature.

Leavis, in the chapter of *New Bearings* (1932) entitled 'The Situation at the End of the First World War', writes that

The Shepherd, Mr Blunden's first mature book of verse, marked him out from the crowd as a poet who, though he wrote about the country, drew neither upon *The Shropshire Lad* nor upon the common stock of Georgian country sentiment. There was also in his poems, for all their rich rusticity, the home-spun texture that is their warrant, a frank literary quality. . . . out of the traditional life of the English countryside, especially as relived in memories of childhood, Mr Blunden was creating a world—a world in which to find refuge from adult distresses; above all, one guessed, from memories of the war. . . . There [is] something satisfying about the dense richness of his pastoral world. . . . He was able to be, to some purpose, conservative in technique, and to draw upon the eighteenth century, because the immemorial rural order that is doomed was real to him.

Leavis of course brings to sight not merely the relation between rurality and war, as Blunden used it, but the relation of the rural order to urban civilization. To assess accurately the war's impact upon him and his poems, we must first establish what the country meant to him.

Blunden's 'country' was the South. He was born in London in 1896, but the family moved subsequently to Yalding in Kent. Kent and Sussex are his counties, an area of few dramatic contours and a quietness matched by that of his poems. The 'frank literary quality' that Leavis detects in his poems is perhaps related to the encroaching urbanization, more advanced in the South than in the North. Despite the industrialization of the last hundred and fifty years, the North retains a stronger hold on the doomed rural order.

Poets without Blunden's solidity tend to draw a false antithesis between urban evil and rural innocence—both distortions—adopting a crude version of Darwinism which they invert by asserting that, despite the claims of utilitarianism, the more society becomes industrialized the further it regresses. Clearly, neither this 'golden age' syndrome nor its opposite is true, since progress, if we can at all speak of it, consists in our development in human relations which technology may or may not serve, but which in any case has no absolute or necessary connection with them. I do not mean to imply that all we associate with the rise of capitalism has not a fundamental connection with social relationships; but I do mean that our formularization of social relations, our moral beliefs, are not dependent on our technological expertise.

The millennium, however, is always elsewhere. Such debased and materialistic Darwinism is essentially prospective, pastoralism retrospective. And pastoralism is an earlier ruralism peopled with deities and pietistic shepherds; the society itself innocent of evil. The pre-lapsarian state is reset to pre-date the Industrial Revolution, which pastoralism, at its most extreme, sees as both the fruit of its own evil and a punishment of future societies. Of course, neither pastoralism nor utilitarianism apprehends the present except as corroborative evidence for its own case, and such prejudices drastically limit a serious understanding of the present and its relation to rural life. Blunden himself identifies the problem of rural life in its relations with an urban society in his essay 'Country Poets' (1954): 'But to many of us the ultimate question is whether or not the tradition (of country poets) is dead. . . . The verse is the thing, not the circumstances of its production.' Not quite so, surely, for the circumstances of its production would be bound up with the kind of relations a man has with rural life. Seamus Heaney's first book, *Death of a Naturalist* (1966), makes precisely the right point in that, whereas his father's generation was connected with the land because they farmed it, he has a naturalist's concern; he is an observer of, and perhaps an inquirer into, nature, but he does not depend on it for his livelihood. His connection with it is less intimate. Blunden's difficulty as a poet, inasmuch as he is a poet of nature or uses nature as the propulsion for his feelings, lies precisely here. And this may provide an even more profound reason for the literary quality in some of his perceptions of nature. The difficulty works in two directions. It is not merely *his* connection that is not vital, as a farmer's is. The audience he could count on to read his poetry was also either urban or composed mainly of people who had a 'naturalist's' connection with nature. Even in his own youth rural society was in decay, and urban society could at best only 'see' nature. If Edward Thomas's remarks about contemporary nature verse are taken in conjunction with the verse itself, it may more clearly be seen that the customary response to nature was one of civilized euphoria, in that the pleasures of nature confirmed the agreeable notion that here at least was something that gave man innocent pleasure. It was not until the middle classes and working classes had been thoroughly urbanized that the 'stripes on the tulip' were once again 'numbered'. Although the meticulous detail in Thomas's poems and some of Blunden's is perhaps in part a result of the urbanizing process.

The subject cannot even be left there, for one aspect of Blunden's rurality employs not the observer but the eye of the distant urban society, as it derived its rural joy through the filter of a taste that edited its sensuous responses into some form of decorative painting before these responses could be more freshly and directly made. Thus, in 'The Gods of the Earth Beneath', written when Blunden was already on the Western Front, the nature of observed detail co-exists with this stylized and partly even eighteenth-century version of nature:

> Emmets and lizards, hollow-haunting toads,
> Adders and effets, groundwasps ravenous. . . .

Blunden has here woven the 'agreeable' and the melancholic grotesque together into a complex structure. And even if it is nature selected into a particular kind of picture, 'groundwasps ravenous' feels observed—despite the inversion. The creatures are not described merely for what they can contribute to pictorial artifice, but lend verisimilitude to an image of nature, here, one divided and ruled by seven deities. This kind of conjunction, where folklore and concrete detail fuse, occurs when a poet is thinking carefully. But the frequent appearance (in this quite early poem) of stylized passages shows how Blunden could be drawn aside by the taste of the sophisticated eye:

> He thins frail gold for crowns of daffodil,
> And inlays silver leaves for ladysmocks.
> With rubies in his palace underground
> Windowed, to let the cavern's twilight in;
> Of alabaster are his buttresses,
> Of pallid mica are his little doors. . . .

'Of alabaster are . . .' has the tone of a Shakespearian song articulated, in this instance, for the purpose of inducing a belief or response to the fanciful; nature has here become the ornament of the wealthy collector. On the other hand, only a sophisticated mind could take the fancy but drop the factual basis of 'Of his bones are coral made'. Blunden's lines are inlaid with a Pre-Raphaelite liking for simple colours and a decorative strangeness.

The section in Blunden's *Poems 1914–30* called 'War: Impacts and Delayed Actions', which is perhaps a reference to delayed shock from the experience, contains most of his war poems. Yet, describing them as 'war poems', one thinks of them as different from Sassoon's. Blunden seems to need to keep nature present, which inevitably produces some distortions. But the war is equally omnipresent, and we may see how he evaluates it by seeing how he evaluates the—for him—contrasting context of nature, in three extracts from *Undertones of War*:

Was it on this visit to Etaples that some of us explored the church—a fishing-village church—and took tea comfortably in an inn? Those tendernesses ought not to come, however dimly, in my notion of Etaples. I associate it, as millions do, with 'The Bull-ring', that thirsty, savage, interminable training-ground.

The tender rural memory is interleaved with the experience of war, and the whole is held together in a questioning retrospective gentleness. In Blunden's mind the two seem inalienable from each other, linked not merely by place, but also perhaps because the emotional extremity of the one recalls the contrasting gentleness of the other. Other simpler contrasts emerge: 'On the blue and lulling mist of evening, proper to the nightingale, the sheepbell and the falling water, the strangest phenomena of fire inflicted themselves.' The contrast between the gentle fall of the three natural agencies and the 'fire' is emphasized by the rhythmical differences. Elsewhere, Blunden uses a device similar to Owen's use of 'red' in 'Greater Love'.[1] The frogs' cries and the sound of bullets both seem natural sounds—a kind of audible pun: 'the frogs in their fens were uttering their long-drawn *co-ash, co-ash*; and from the line the popping of rifles grew more and more threatening.' Experience tells us that the lesser sound of the bullets appears harmless in the natural setting, through the expectation of the senses *only*; our intelligence tells us otherwise. Similarly, in the phrase 'whizzing like gnats', it is only the intelligence, basing itself on experience, that distinguishes between the harmfulness of the one and the innocuousness of the other. The difference is pointed to by the use of 'like'—the very sound of gnats it is so (un)like. In all three instances nature is used by way of contrast and as the basis for all judgements. In such contrasts it is the troubled intelligence that communicates its message to the senses, and causes a seemingly permanent distress, as it is apprehended emotionally:

> And yet its stream ran through my heart;
>   I heard it grieve and pine,
> As if its rainy tortured blood
>   Had swirled into my own,
> When by its battered bank I stood
>   And shared its wounded moan.

[1] See p. 234 below.

Blunden is able to speak of his own pain without sentimentality because he genuinely and without artifice speaks for the river; its flood runs through his heart as though it were his own blood, which in a sense it is. 'Shared' is the crucial word.

In the section 'The English Scene', the poem 'Malefactors' (1919) describes those foxes who, 'Hovering among the miller's chicks', were caught and 'Nailed to those green laths'. But the killing of the fox is one in a hierarchy of deaths which includes man's:

> There's your [the fox's] revenge, the wheel at tether,
> The miller gone, the white planks rotten, . . .
> Felons of fur and feather, can
>   There lurk some crime in man,
>
> In man your executioner,
> Whom here Fate's cudgel battered down?

Though written after the war, the poem shows the way in which the war undertoned so much of Blunden's subsequent writing. He does not transform nature as Owen did, for instance, in his use of the flowers as chalices for the soldiers' blood in 'Spring Offensive';[1] he is concerned with his sanative relationship with nature.

The poems concerning war seem to have a deliberate sequence. The first group deals with the impact of war on a countryman fresh to the trenches, and is succeeded by a group that articulates the horror of war, and contains one of Blunden's central war poems, 'Third Ypres'. The poems that follow record the effects of war, principally on the mind. Lastly, there are poems of retrospection, which relate the soldiers' courage to the waste of war. Many of these are elegaic.

The poems concerned with the horror of war form a crucial group and should be seen as a whole. 'Two Voices' makes the familiar conjunction of nature and war:

> 'We're going South, man'; as he spoke. . . .
> The death-news, bright the skylarks sang. . . .

The Hardyesque coinage 'death-news' does not bring with it any of Hardy's ironic double structure. Its appearance here is literary; nature and war ironically co-exist, thus emphasizing the disparity between them. In 'Thiepval Wood and All its Worst', however,

[1] See p. 215 below.

war absorbs nature until it only exists for the poet as an image remembered.

In the ironically entitled 'Preparations for Victory' (preparations entailing more fruitless slaughter), one part of the man tries to buoy up another part that is dismayed and afraid. In the second stanza the mind marks those relics of rural life still intact after battle but inwardly 'fouled with war'. The soldier's mind, wracked by battle, cannot see them except through the filter of such spoliation:

> 'And I will mark the yet unmurdered tree,
> The relics of dear homes that court the eye,
> And yet I see them not as I would see.
> Hovering between, a ghostly enemy
> Sickens the light, and poisoned, withered, wan,
> The least defiled turns desperate to me.'
> The body, poor unpitied Caliban,
> Parches and sweats and grunts to win the name of Man.

As Leavis indicated, it is the quality of indirectness which works so finely, in this instance in 'unmurdered tree'. Arrested by the conjunction of those two words, we are forced to assent to the justice of the conjunction, and thus bring a freshly sensitized mind to bear on the murdered soldiers. 'Unpitied' shows Blunden's understanding of the soldiers' predicament and accompanies his condemnation of what they are exposed to. The earlier lines

> Manly move among
> These ruins, and what you must do, do well . . .

have a stoic impersonality, but although they have the same tone as 'Parches and sweats and grunts to win the name of Man', they are by implication heavily qualified by it. One wonders, in fact, if perhaps the earlier lines with their exhortation to manliness are not in some sense ironic, but I think they are not. What the last line does is to show what man has to do to win his name, and the question implicit in the statement is whether or not the burden put on the soldier can in any sense be justified; particularly when the human beings are reduced to the animal 'grunts' of Blunden's Caliban. In the 'Manly move among' passage there is no indication that Blunden distinguishes between the demands put on the soldiers and the cost involved; whereas 'to win the name of Man' has implicit in it a just evaluation of the cost. Man is there not an approximation to an ideal but a sentient suffering creature, a soldier-slave condemned to drudgery or extinction. The poem's end has a startling resemblance to Owen's 'Exposure' in that, for once, Blunden transforms nature not only to indicate its disapproval of man's activity, but to show by how much man is the loser:

> Look, we lose;
> The sky is gone, the lightless drenching haze
> Of rainstorm chills the bone; earth, air are foes. . . .

In 'Zero' the irony and anguish are combined in the word 'red', which draws on its associations with nature, the colours of dawn, shed blood, and fire:

> O celestial work of wonder—
> A million mornings in one bloom!

The poem narrows down its ironic rhetoric until the reader is forced to make a direct comparison between the redness of dawn and the soldier's blood:

> The dawn but hangs behind the goal.
> What is that artist's joy to me?
> Here limps poor Jock with a gash in the poll,
> His red blood now is the red I see. . . .

Compare this with Owen's Preface, 'Above all I am not concerned with poetry', and the lines from 'Insensibility':

> But they are troops who fade, not flowers
> For poets' tearful fooling. . . .

Between the idea of red and the colour of blood exists the man's wounds and his suffering. Similar is Blunden's use of the obsolete word 'poll' which, in its drollness, suggests tonally the drifting conjunction of madness and clown-like insight we experience in the relationship between Lear and his Fool. The slightly comic quality also indicates a severe exercise of control, which finally demonstrates itself in the stark simplicity of 'It's plain we were born for this, naught else.' The dismaying nature of the poet's perception of doom recalls Owen's 'Exposure': 'Therefore, not loath, we lie out here; therefore were born'.

In 'The Zonnebeke Road' Blunden creates a brilliantly knowing and bitter facetiousness:

> Why, see old Stevens there, that iron man,
> Melting the ice to shave his grotesque chin!
> Go ask him, shall we win?

The humour is shared between the poet and reader, in that Blunden knows the question is inane, and readily imagines the kind of reception it would get were Stevens asked it. The affection consciously given in that passage contrasts with the in-drawing isolation, which each man experiences as he steels himself against danger with the one remedy left—disdain of it:

> Watch as you will, men clench their chattering teeth
> And freeze you back with that one hope, disdain.

'Vlamertinghe: Passing the Château, July 1917'—a title that indicates the contrast between the earlier 'aristocratic' tour of Europe and the soldiers' experience of it—opens with a quotation from Keats's 'Ode on a Grecian Urn': 'And all her silken flanks with garlands drest'. The sedate beauty of this immediately contrasts with the next line: 'But we are coming to the sacrifice.' Blunden is questioning the moral basis of such sacrifice. He not only indicates the horror of the soldiers' experience but, by placing the lines together, questions the blandness with which the civilians (the other nation) accept such sacrifice. He makes the connection explicit by the verbal sharing of 'sacrifice', and draws attention to the decorousness of the one and its contrast with the other. But the real weight of Blunden's objection consists in the implication that the pastoral image created by Keats is, more or less, projected unrealistically on to the soldiers:

> Must those have flowers who are not yet gone West?
> May those have flowers who live with death and lice?

The conventional and decorous gift of flowers (given as if the wounded were dead already) is skilfully juxtaposed with the actuality of the soldiers' living 'death and lice'. Blunden the countryman courageously perceives that the pastoral tradition is weakened, and uses that weakness in a self-revealing way to point at the unreality with which it had helped to obscure a culture.

This ability to locate, zeugmatically, the contrasting modes of

nature and war in a word (or its synonym), 'vermillion', again occurs
in the poem:

> Such a gay carpet! poppies by the million;
> Such a damask! such vermillion!
> But if you ask me, mate, the choice of colour
> Is scarcely right; this red should have been duller.

Shed blood dulls, and the soldier's criticism of 'damask/vermillion'
is based on his experience of war, which eschews poetic rhetoric.
Thus, 'scarcely right' is not merely the correction of inaccurate
observation but carries with it the sense of fairly good-humoured
moral disagreement: 'It isn't right or proper to dress suffering up in
such bright colours.'

This kind of scrupulous precision also appears in 'The Welcome':

> The shell had struck right into the doorway,
> The smoke lazily floated away;
> There were six men in that concrete doorway,
> Now a black muckheap blocked the way.

'Lazily' draws on associations of a pleasurable sensuousness, but
the smoke is malign that drifts off to reveal the men's violent
transformation. 'Muckheap' is a good country word, whose use
points up the difference between the slow natural decay of manure
and this sudden reduction of human flesh. It suggests that it is all
one and the same to nature. There is a Hardyesque irony in the
poem, in that a man newly arrived from leave escapes this shelling
with his life, albeit

> With nerves that seldom ceased to wince
> Past war had long preyed on his nature,
> And war had doubled in horror since.

The attempt to re-create the horror of war is more successfully
made in 'Pillbox', perhaps because Blunden concentrates his
expression narrowly within a specific situation:

> And out burst terrors that he'd striven to tame,
> A good man, Hoad, for weeks. *I'm blown to bits*,
> He groans, he screams. *Come, Bluffer, where's your wits?*

The use of the colloquial here is more complex in that it not only
represents Blunden's reportage of actual conversation, but at the

same time marks an attempt to provide some compassionate comfort through a familiar diction. As for the facts of the poem, the man's slight wound is the means by which the hysteria (?) 'spirited away' his life. Blunden's placing of this incident next to the equally unlikely survival of the man in 'The Welcome' effectively illustrates what Owen, in 'Insensibility', called 'Chance's strange arithmetic'.

In 'Gouzeaucourt: The Deceitful Calm', there is a comparative mildness, a lull between periods of combat, which resembles the mildness of the guide-book writer in the poem following it ,'The Prophet'. In reality, however, this is a different mildness, since such lulls came to be interpreted as a prelude to the fury of combat:

> There it was, my dears, that I departed,
> Scarce a plainer traitor ever! There too
>   Many of you soon paid for
>   That false mildness.

The motivation in this passage is extremely complex, but I sense an element of guilt at being absent—and gladly absent—from comrades subsequently killed. Perhaps the guilt is resented and aggressively turned back on those who are seen as its unwitting cause. There might even be an element of *schadenfreude* comparable with that acknowledged with scrupulous honesty in Read's 'My Company'.[1]

'Third Ypres' is Blunden's longest, most sustained, and perhaps central war poem, although Cecil Day Lewis thinks '1916 Seen from 1921' is his finest. It opens with an obsessive and painfully irreconcilable contrast between war and nature:

> Triumph! How strange, how strong had triumph come
> On weary hate of foul and endless war
> When from its grey graveclothes awoke anew
>   The summer day.

Reason has lost some of its power. There are sudden reversals of feeling as irrational as faith, or its waning. There would be, for instance, an irresistible advance:

> The War would end, the Line was on the move,
> And at a bound the impassable was passed.
> We lay and waited with extravagant joy.

[1] See p. 175 below.

The joy is 'extravagant' both because it is in its nature to be so and because it is unrealistic. In their reversals, the despair is equally as uninformed:

> ... 'They're done, and they'll none of them get through,
> They're done, they've all died on the entanglements,
> The wire stood up like an unplashed hedge and thorned
> With giant spikes—and there they've paid the bill.'

The misery and fear reasserted by having to wait for the news are increased by the ominous weather:

> Then comes the black assurance, then the sky's
> Mute misery lapses into trickling rain. . . .

Personal discomfort, honestly admitted, obtrudes upon what ought to be 'unselfish concern for his comrades'; but Blunden is here concerned with 'what was'. The shelling starts:

> ... He's gone,
> Falls on a knee, and his right hand uplifted
> Claws his last message from his ghostly enemy. . . .

The messenger dies as if, emblematically, in the act of conveying a message, and this image of him is uncannily set within the remoteness of the battlefield. The imaginative transcription is abruptly interrupted—as if there were no time for it then—by the terse message of affection:

> Well I liked him, that young runner,
> But there's no time for that.

Affection is suppressed by the demands of battle. The enjambments and the sparse punctuation convey, with the expanded pentameter, the surging violence of the activity under the bombardment's violence:

> Bŭt thére's nŏ tíme fŏr thát. Ŏ nów fŏr thĕ wórd
> Tŏ órdĕr ŭš flásh frŏm thĕse drówniňg róariňg tráps
> Aňd éveň húrl ŭpón that sńarliňg wiře?

which is followed by an almost tearful dismay and chagrin:

> Whý aře oŭr gúns sŏ ímpŏteňt?
>   Thĕ gréy ráin . . .

The clumping rhythm of the last phrase contrasts with the movement of the lines before. This scene is succeeded by a calm on the
'second night' (notice the duration of the ordeal) and the survivors
of the attack reappear. Then the enemy bombardment is renewed,
and the mind begins to lose its already eroded control:

> And flaming burst and sour gas we are huddled
> Into the ditches where they bawl sense awake
> And in a frenzy that none could reason calm,
> (Whimpering some, and calling on the dead),
> They turn away. . . .

Significantly, the poem's only controlling *emotion* is pity. The
whole poem then rises to its climax, with the effect of the shelling
upon four soldiers who find momentary refuge in a pillbox. The
enjambments and the break-up of the syntax express a corresponding disintegration of the mind's control:

> The demon grins to see the game, a moment
> Passes, and—still the drum-tap dongs my brain
> To a whirring void—through the great breach above me
> The light comes in with icy shock and the rain
> Horridly drips. Doctor, talk, talk! if dead
> Or stunned I know not; the stinking powdered concrete,
> The lyddite turns me sick—my hair's all full
> Of this smashed concrete. O, I'll drag you, friends,
> Out of the sepulchre into the light of day,
> For this is day, the pure and sacred day.
> And while I squeak and gibber over you,
> Look, from the wreck a score of field-mice nimble,
> And tame and curious look about them; (these
> Calmed me, on these depended my salvation).

Blunden uses all the means at his disposal both to express the
terror and control it. The call for the doctor is more than the
summoning of a healer of the flesh; but in the midst of such appeal
the narrator becomes conscious of his own nausea. This is followed
by the Marlovian 'O, I'll drag you, friends'. The pentameter,
beautifully rounded and regular, which follows, makes both a
positive statement and an attempt at reassurance: 'For this is day,
the pure and sacred day.' It is the day, and it is sacred; and yet in
it there is destruction and everything that profanes life. This is a
statement of a position, beyond irony, in which two irreconcilable

opposites must be conveyed simultaneously without either excluding the other. At this point the poem produces a further surprise of a fine and tender kind, a moment that seems as crucial to Blunden as those other 'spots of time' were to Wordsworth. The field-mice save him, even though, a line previously, his own 'squeak and gibber' had so affectingly conveyed the idea that man is to war, as mice are usually to human beings. The calm fearlessness of the mice subdues his own 'squeak and gibber' and, recalling nature and all that is benign, restores a mind fast losing sanative control over itself. The very word 'salvation' suggests just how near such an extremity was. At this point a message from headquarters tells of similar carnage there, but by now he is past his own disintegration and able to promise help. As the poem ends, it gradually distances the reader with the despoliation of the country: 'A whole sweet countryside amuck with murder', and concludes with play on the word 'relieve'.

Alec Hardie maintains that it was after Blunden's discharge in 1919 that the real impact of the war slowly and insidiously made itself felt. There is no way of telling. But 'Third Ypres' suggests not merely an ingraining of the memory with the experience, but the experience immediately impacting itself; we should not perhaps be too willing to distance that. The remaining poems in this section relate to 'Delayed Actions', as they recollect the war, the courage, the suffering and the death of those in it. They also, of course, convey the personal stress. '1916 Seen from 1921' opens

> Tired with dull grief, grown old before my day,
> I sit in solitude and only hear
> Long silent laughters, murmurings of dismay,
> The lost intensities of hope and fear;
> In those old marshes yet the rifles lie, . . .
>   and I
> Dead as the men I loved, wait while life drags
>
> Its wounded length from those sad streets of war
> Into green places here, that were my own. . . .

It is the nakedness of the grief, in these heavy rhythms, that forces the reader to ask what the nature of the sickness is. The experience that has prematurely aged him binds him not only with its insistent fears but also with its ties of love. This is the force of 'green places . . . that were my own'. But where nature has made 'green' again the hideousness of a mutilated territory and should offer benign comfort, the very terms of his previous life so lovingly and fearfully bound together have been eradicated; and not merely in that many of the men he knew are dead, but by the force of nature. Thus what should succour him does not; it exiles him from the area to which he was committed, and its now sanative character is no consolation to him. Nature fails him and this failure increases his desolation, in that it was nature that he had always relied on before, and through, the war, to provide a comfort that he could find nowhere else. It is, of course, memory which exiles him from a developing present, but he feels betrayed, although nature cannot be blamed for restoring itself. Implicated in this isolation is perhaps the feeling of guilt at survival, which is explicit in 'War Autobiography':

> Then down and down I sunk from joy
> To shrivelled age, though scarce a boy,
> And knew for all my fear to die
> That I with those lost friends should lie.

There is some sense of wishing for death here, or, to put it less crudely, of weariness at being deprived of those relationships which the war made and destroyed, and which, destroyed, leave nothing. The same kind of complexity is expressed in '11th R.S.R.':

> What mercy is it I should live and move,
> If haunted ever by war's agony...?
> Let me not ever think of you as dead....

In 'A.G.A.V.' a particular man, now dead, is remembered:

> Sleep—bless you, that would not please you, gallantest dear.
> Should I find you beneath yew trees? better to look for you here.
> With those others whom well we knew, who went so early away....

The language, the rhythms, the note of affectionate recollection, derive from Hardy, but whereas he would so distance the dead person that the mourning would suffer ironic failure, Blunden seems at one and the same time to be trying to distance the war and to restore a comrade killed in it and thus inseparable from it. To remember the man as courageous gives his death some meaning in terms generally accepted:

> ... where you so nobly stood....

> Well shone you then, and I would will you freedom eternal there,
> Vast trial past, and the proud sense still of vast to-morrows to dare.

Yet what meaning are we to give 'shone'? It depends on the kind of evaluation society puts upon his courage. What meaning for that matter do we give 'freedom eternal'—a phrase with a Roll-of-Honour ring? Would Blunden wish him that kind of shrine? The same problem underlies 'where you so nobly stood'. It is not that the man lacked courage, but that the adverb 'nobly' links his courage with the cause it was *supposed* to serve, and blurs the fact that courage was found not because of, but often despite, the cause for which he was killed. This man and many others (who may or may not have held his attitudes—we are not told what these were) are made into willing martyrs instead of brave, but probably unwilling, victims. By enshrining these victims in such heroic and distant clichés, their sacrifice is distorted by a poet who knew so well, and so sensitively and powerfully expressed, the agonies of war. Enshrining them, he unwittingly permits those authorities who set up monuments to the dead to offer a palliative to the surviving relatives, and an example to the next generation, pending their sacrifice. Joseph Cohen writes of this 'stellarification' of the dead:

Let us remember them, but simply as poets. There is more honour and more truth in that designation than in making of them archetypal spokesmen and happy warriors which at best is now a contradiction in terms and at worst a form of sacrificial preparation for the next generation.[1]

This is, of course, valid not for the poets only. One feels that Blunden would agree, for in 'War's People' (Ypres, 1919), the personifying rhetoric of

Go forth, you marching Seasons, horsemen Hours;
Blow silver triumphs, Joy, and knell, grey grief

is undermined by

These after-pieces will not now dispel
The scene and action that was learned in hell.

The last poem in this section is 'Return of the Native' (Ypres, 1929). As its title implies, some kind of Hardyesque irony is employed, where the irony and the pathos are inextricable. Blunden, that is, remains an exile to peace and to his former life as much as he

remains a native of Ypres and the war. What should now be a
peaceful home ('the summer night/Cast a soft veil') is charged with
violent and tragic memories. The poem's complex ending indicates
the incapacity of the youthfully slain to 'stir a weed or moth'
(except by helping to nourish the former). 'Time's vast compulsion'
(the reason for that particular war) is now dissipated with the flesh
of the dead. Blunden's use of Hardyesque pastiche is a kind of
metaphor, bringing to his service Hardy's sense of time-spaces
that cannot be bridged because the point of departure for the new
epoch bears no kinship with a past alienated from it.

The accuracy of Sassoon's assertion that Blunden remains the
poet most obsessed with the war is beyond dispute, and is evidenced
by a poem like 'The Pike' (1919), which concentrates an image of the
predatory:

> While in the shallow some doomed bulrush swings
> At whose hid root the diver vole's teeth gnash.

We see not only Blunden's recognition of nature's 'concealed
violence', but also the sunken and inextractable memories of war's
gnawing, as if at his mind's peaceful roots. Not only is this violence
emphasized by his making it occur within a supposedly peaceful
context; it is added to by the bulrush itself being 'unsuspecting'.
Yet these are only intimations of a larger violence to follow, which
disturbs the 'broad pool's hush':

> Intense terror wakens around him, the shoals scud awry, but there chances
> A chub unsuspecting; the prowling fins quicken, in a fury he lances. . . .

The images of sudden violence and terror might easily correspond
with the mind's terror being suddenly quickened by war's violence.
The image of the unsuspecting chub has sufficient resemblance to,
say, new recruits fresh to the Western Front, for some kind of
comparison to be made.

'The Midnight Skaters' records the same terror, but more
explicitly. Death hates through the ice and, although the depth of
his home is unfathomable and his size and power thus incalculable,
he is held behind it—but not for ever. The ice, moreover, like the
mind's barriers to terror, is chill, and only by its rigidity is death
and the fear of death disdainfully held in check. This situation
elicits from Blunden the almost flirtatious tactics of daring, in

which the skater approaches death as nearly as possible, not merely
to enrage him but to assert a defiant courage:

> Then on, blood shouts, on, on,
>   Twirl, wheel and whip above him,
> Dance on this ball-floor thin and wan,
>   Use him as though you love him;
> Court him, elude him, reel and pass,
> And let him hate you through the glass.[1]

'Report on Experience' has a tentative movement in which the
self-perception of being disillusioned is cautiously advanced: 'I
have been young, and now am not too old.' Even where the assertions are verbally forthright, the rhythms are tentative and thus
weaken the assertiveness. The last line of each stanza shows the
discrepancy between what had formerly been thought true and
what experience now seems to show to be the case. What he once
regarded as inalienably benign, things sacred in nature, the woman-
ness of woman, became distorted: 'I saw her smile warp, heard her
lyric deaden.' 'Warp' suggests a smile distorted by corruption, or
else a smile that is seen as corrupt through the perceiver's distorted
senses. I think the former more likely. There is an acute criticism
implicit in these lines, for the woman has the pastoral name of
Seraphina. This suggests not merely a corruption that eats at the
pure lyric force, but also a revaluation of the pastoralism itself. The
two re-estimations may confirm the report that the 'lyric strength'
is enervated (the feminine ending of the line culminating in
'deaden' expresses this), but they have not sufficiently modified
each other to let Blunden offer any final conclusion. The most he can
report is an ambiguity and a questioning:

> These disillusions are His curious proving
> That He loves humanity. . . .

God's benignity is also in doubt. Does God scourge those he loves?
Is this love? And if it is, can the result of such an infliction as war
(his scourging) be thought of as beneficial, if what it produces is a
warping? What are we then to think of such scourging, and its
value? If this is love, Blunden suggests, he has not been able to
verify it from his experience: 'Over there are faith, life, virtue in
the sun.' With the stress falling on 'there' and on the distant 'sun',

---

[1] Compare with the ending of 'The Zonnebeke Road' quoted on p. 110.

I understand this as meaning 'impossible, here'; and that we understand these idealized abstractions only in that they are transmitted to us from an area we do not live in. We may see these virtues, if that is what they are, but even that may be illusory. The report is honest and ends there.

Blunden has tentatively confirmed in conversation that 'The Sunlit Vale'—a similarly tentative report—glosses 'Report on Experience':

> And never have I seen such a bright bewildering green,
>> But it looked like a lie,
>> Like a kindly meant lie.

A belief in nature as a permanent repository of goodness cannot be fully recovered. A kind of religious disillusioning remains. If the 'green' is a lie, it may be God's 'kindly' invention, but we cannot make do with untruths. A belief in nature as an antidote for what men inflict upon one another is no longer tenable. It is the best nature can offer, but it is not enough. Other facts undermine her. The pastoral framework has been shattered by contemporary experience. Nature may be consolatory now, but she is no longer man's preceptress.

2

Ivor Gurney was born in Gloucester on 28 August 1890, the year of Rosenberg's birth, and three years before Owen's. Unlike Owen and Rosenberg (who, prior to the invention of wireless, had little opportunity of listening to music), Gurney's preoccupation with music pre-dates his concern with poetry. He began by writing conventional pastoral poetry but in 1919 his friend John Haines lent him Bridges's edition of Hopkins's *Poems* (1918). He was already interested in Whitman.

If there is some development, an uneven one, in Gurney's first two books, *Severn and Somme* (1917) and *War's Embers* (1919), it is in the selection of what are mostly post-war poems, edited by Blunden and published as late as 1954, that an interesting and original poet is seen. Blunden maintains, in his Introduction to this edition, that

he possessed from early days a peculiar unconventionality, yet not hostile to traditions, of his own; and in poetics the masters of remote date or recent did not supply him with what he had not got, but energized his use of innate and personal strength. Gurney's 'gnarled' style was not that of Hopkins or of Bridges (who did not always write translucencies), but, when he found such poets achieving their victories over the flying moment with strenuous remodellings of language, he was reassured and newly animated in his own search for the shrewdly different in phrasing and metring.

This last comment may be just, but there are echoes of Hopkins in some of his unpublished poems. 'Gold-fretted' in 'Half Dead', for instance, is a Hopkins-like coinage.

> And I love men should achieve to surpass the first
> Beauty. . . .

Here, the enjambment ends on a stressed word which is not the last of the syntactical unit, an effect reminiscent of Hopkins's 'God's Grandeur', for instance:

> It gathers to a greatness, like the ooze of oil
> Crushed.

But while Hopkins's 'Crushed' acts as a powerful afterthought, Gurney merely breaks up his unit by means of enjambment.

Gurney's poem 'To God' has the confessional rage and pathos of Hopkins's six 'terrible' sonnets, in particular 'Thou art indeed just, Lord, if I contend'. Perhaps a further kinship between the two may be identified in their concern with prosody (Hopkins was also interested in music); prosody being the instrument that would wrest from language an almost absolute expressiveness.

Both poets were preoccupied with nature, but where with Hopkins it was a detailed concern with the energies inherent in it, with Gurney (and with Blunden, to a much lesser extent) it was localized and named. Even so, this aspect of Gurney's work almost certainly appealed to Blunden, who does not however underestimate its dangers: this 'immense love of his country . . . was to act almost as a tyranny over his poetical character'. There was another obstacle, which Blunden describes:

His delusions, not (it is believed) dangerous to others but imperilling him, led to his being confined from September 1922, first at Barnwood House, Gloucester, and later—when his recovery was felt to be extremely improbable—in the City of London Mental Hospital at Dartford. . . . In many [of his] letters to all sorts of people—but the letters were not posted—he appealed for 'rescue'; and even in these queerly phrased

petitions there was no mistaking the derangement which kept him
where he was. . . . He saw himself as 'the first war poet', and as one who
had been shamelessly and cruelly treated; the obsession needs little comment except that, so far as his reading went, and in the notion that he was
a complete writer, Gurney might fairly claim to be writing in verse of the
soldier on the Western Front with a curious originality. He described the
life of the infantryman, as the examples of a host of poems given in this
book will show, in a subtle series of reminiscences, catching many details
and tones which had combined in the quality of seasons and moments,
anguish and relief never again to occur.

On 7 April 1917, two days before Edward Thomas was killed in
the battle of Arras, Gurney was wounded. He recuperated in time
to take part in Passchendaele (near Ypres, during the Allied offensive,
begun 31 July 1917), but on 22 August he was gassed. He was taken
to a mental hospital at Warrington where, Blunden records, he
'passed through a period of exceptional misery'. He was discharged
from the army a month before fighting stopped but was again, as
Blunden says, confined in 1922.

C. Day Lewis has maintained, in conversation, that Gurney's
derangement was incipient before the war, and progressive, and
that it would probably have developed without his war experience.
That may be. The certificate describing his illness speaks of
'manic/depressive psychosis, aggravated but not caused by War
Service'. This is of course as accurate as a document can be. In its
terseness it gives the verdict to both parties—the man or the war—
and denies neither. On the other hand, as William Curtis-Hayward
has indicated, another interpretation is possible: 'This [diagnosis]
seems to me the guilty conscience of society refusing to acknowledge
its responsibility. . . . Gurney persisted in living for some time, a
silent witness to the hideous crime perpetrated upon the spirit of
man by modern war.' We can be fairly sure that his trench experience
aggravated his condition beyond control; but, in any case, the
diagnosis is suspect, not because it suggests that the war was not the
cause, but because it categorically denies that it was.

Gurney's first two books contain few poems that wholly, and from
the then current and official viewpoint, tell the truth about war.
The poems themselves differ, and there are even conflicting
attitudes within the one poem. For example, in 'To His Love', one

of three poems by Gurney included in Ian Parsons's anthology *Men Who March Away* (1965), a noticeable hesitation between contradicting attitudes occurs:

> You would not know him now . . .
>   But still he died
> Nobly, so cover him over
>   With violets of pride
>   Purple from Severn side.

The first line suggests that had you known the man, you would hardly, because of his mutilations, recognize him. It also suggests that hardly anyone else would recognize him, for the same reasons, as human. The line derives its force not merely from these ideas but by contrasting them with the conventional expressions of sorrow that those related to the man would feel, either as their own expressions of grief, or else as those which they had been taught to feel. They would naturally feel sorrow, but the conventional idea consists in their feeling an inextricable pride also. The tone undermines this idea as doing no justice to the man's suffering, yet the stanza as a whole is ambivalent in that it also hesitates between acceptance and rejection of the pride. Enormous social forces would quite naturally cause such hesitations. Gurney is, of course, sympathizing with the bereaved, but he had to hold in relation to it the idea that the sentimental consolations of pride not only 'harmed' the man's sacrifice, but perpetuated the sacrificing of others. Thus, he here seems to be saying: 'Your grief would be all the more terrible in that you would be shocked to see the state he is in, but you do not see him, and therefore do not comprehend the nature of his death. I am glad that you cannot be so shocked, but I am sorry, for all the other soldiers' sakes, that you do not know the facts of warfare'. Other hesitations accumulate. What right has he to oppose what is a time-honoured consolation of pride in the sacrifice? 'Nobly' covers a number of related difficulties; and Gurney sees the problems, as Blunden also did (in part) in 'A.G.A.V.' (see p. 116 above). 'Nobly' is not merely the individual soldier's attribute; it is the propagandistic aura that the state awards the dead in an effort to persuade the living to continue their efforts.

After hesitating between these conflicting attitudes, Gurney, disappointingly, moves the stanza in the aureate direction by forcing an anthropomorphic change on his native Gloucestershire.

Patriotic tradition and local pastoral were, after all, what he began with. Thus, Gloucestershire mourns one of its sons and sheds its blood in sympathy (having already shed it in the death of the man)—in sympathy, but also in pride. The resulting sentimentality is the product both of the anthropomorphism and the abstractions thus entailed. The poem, however, ends on a different note:

> Cover him, cover him soon!
> And with thick-set
> Masses of memoried flowers—
> Hide that red wet
> Thing I must somehow forget.

'Red wet' expresses with raw precision the response of horror and nausea that shed blood elicits, and by ending the line on the adjective 'wet' he transforms it momentarily into a noun, which reinforces the rawness. The man is no longer a person but a 'wet thing'. This is what Gurney must—and because must, cannot—forget. The 'Masses of memoried flowers' is also complex—the flowers suggesting the conventional symbol of grief and respect, but the 'Masses' suggesting by how much the corpse needs to be buried from sight, and memory.

'The Silent One' presents its problem with a more overall precision because, partly, it is less sensuous and requires therefore less complex attention. But Gurney has now more clarified objectives and to express them a greater linguistic precision.

> Who died on the wires, and hung there, . . .
> Yet faced unbroken wires; stepped over, and went
> A noble fool, faithful to his stripes—and ended.

Although this was apparently written in the period of madness, it shares an experience of reality, which is lucid in the interrelation of its parts, and acceptable in the version of reality it offers. 'Noble' in this poem is carefully qualified and the two representative judgements on this man, and many others, are made in such a way as to qualify each other. By letting the man's courage into the poem, we are made to feel compassion, but this comes through because the courage and the foolishness hold each other in check. The victim's vitality is uncannily expressed in

> . . . had chattered through
> Infinite lovely chatter of Bucks accent. . . .

Gurney uses similar devices to express the absurdity and waste of combat. The politeness of the upper-class voice is made to sound absurd by making it articulate fearful demands, and by placing alongside these a parallel and polite refusal by the man to obey his officer's lethal demands:

> Till the politest voice—a finicking accent, said:
> 'Do you think you might crawl through, there: there's a hole'
> Darkness, shot at: I smiled, as politely replied—
> 'I'm afraid not, Sir.' There was no hole no way to be seen
> Nothing but chance of death. . . .

The 'finicking' accent of the controlling class is contrasted with the 'lovely chatter of Bucks accent'. Anger is certainly somewhere present in this poem, but it is explicit in 'What's in Time':

> God curse for cowards; take honour and all damn
> For bastards out of good blood, last leaving of diseases,
> The rulers of England, lost in corruptions and increases
> All mean, foul things they lap up like (powderless) jam—
> While the cheated dead cry, unknowing, 'Eadem Semper'.

Resentment is as explicit—and more coherent—in the poem Blunden cites in his introduction:

> . . . who have let destroy
> A servant of yours, by evil men birth better at once had slain.
>
> And for my Country, God knows my heart, and men to me
> Were dear there, I was friend also of every look of sun or rain;
> It has betrayed as evil women wantonly a man their toy.

Had Gurney not become intermittently mad, would anybody have thought to say that this was the expression of someone deranged? Blunden writes:

even in these queerly phrased petitions (for 'rescue') there was no mistaking the derangement which kept him where he was. He was aflame with anger which had for him the clear and undeniable cause that he, a lover of England if ever one existed, had been flung into a trap by England the beloved. 'The earth opened.'

From the syntax it is not clear if the additional evidence of derangement is the accusation made against England; but if it is, I can only disagree with Blunden's contention that this is a sign of madness. Gurney's accusation may be unreasonable in that England did not deliberately sacrifice him in the way a woman may play with a man; but that he felt betrayed by his love for his country, casually betrayed as millions, he would have felt, were, is hardly madness. Gurney was struggling to articulate a real grievance in which he felt men were unnecessarily sacrificed through their attachment, and he had to filter this through what was intermittently a deranged mind. But does this invalidate the grievance? Gurney wrote, in the same poem:

> Soldier's praise I had earned having suffered soldier's pain,
> And the great honour of song in the battle's first gray show—
> Honour was bound to me save—mine most dreadfully slain.

'Honour' is especially hard to paraphrase: does it mean 'privilege of being a poet+due recognition'? Gurney seems to be saying that, as a soldier, he had earned the right to speak of his suffering in poetry, and that this poetry alone could save him from the effects of the war on his mind; but at the same time the war had mutilated his capacity to write. It is perhaps the most bitter and personal accusation he could make, but it seems to have substance to it.

Indignation of a similar kind, but explicitly on behalf of those who suffered, is at the heart of 'Mist on Meadows':

> Dreadful green light baring the ruined trees,
> Stakes, pools, lostness, better hidden dreadful in dark
> And not ever reminding of these other fields. . . .
>
> But they honour not—and salute not those boys who saw a terror
> Of waste, endured horror, and were not fearer, . . .
> But could not guess, but could not guess, alas!
> How England should take as common their vast endurance
> And let them be but boys having served time Over-seas.

That 'take as common' is surely the ubiquitous complaint of Sassoon and Owen, and may, in Gurney's instance, help to counterbalance the personal resentment so frequent in his poetry:

> But the body hurt, spirit is hindered and slow,
> And evil hurts me past my maker's right.

This, from 'The Bronze Sounding', is of course an expression of self-pity, but I have never fully understood the stoic form of objection to it. If it is that the self-pitier is withholding pity from others by focusing on his own pain, there is a double objection to this criticism. One is that the self-pitier is as valid an object of compassion as anyone else, and the other is that those who condemn

are themselves withholding the very pity the man may need.
Gurney, in any case, is not selfishly withholding his compassion for
others, but complaining of his own suffering as one among many.
There is nothing solipsistic in it.

'War Books' takes the complaint a stage further:

> What did they expect of our toil and extreme
> Hunger—the perfect drawing of a heart's dream?
> Did they look for a book of wrought art's perfection,
> Who promised no reading, nor praise, nor publication?
> Out of the heart's sickness the spirit wrote
> For delight, or to escape hunger, or of war's worst anger. . . .

Gurney's objections are to a philistine community unprepared to
pay (in every sense of this word) for the kind of art that would
emerge from war's experience. What was wanted, it seemed, was a
perfectly 'wrought' art impossible under the circumstances and
inappropriate to the experience. He objects to an involuted 'art for
art's sake' style divorced from substance, the falsely decorative
which Pound locates in '*E.P. Ode pour L'Election de son Sepulchre*':

> The 'age demanded' chiefly a mould in plaster, . . .
>   not, not assuredly, alabaster
> Or the 'sculpture' of rhyme.

Gurney also seems to be implying that what the public wanted was
not an honest response to the war but a distortion implicit in
those 'tales' from which they might obtain a vicarious sense of
excitement. Thus Owen in 'Dulce et Decorum Est':

> you would not tell with such high zest
> To children ardent for some desperate glory,
> The old Lie. . . .

Nature, for Gurney, remained part of another era and another
poetic, a refuge and a touchstone. It could not be handled with
developing delicacy and understanding, because to disturb the
relationship between himself and nature, as he understood it,
would have meant destroying those springs with which he was intermittently but surely in touch. If Gurney was mad, his incompleteness has nevertheless some completely sane limitations, and it
is this that makes him a tragic figure ('mine most dreadfully slain')
as much as his madness. If the madness in some way helped him
to discard his earlier conventional poeticisms (and he may have

done this in perfect sanity), it also prevented him from merging the newly wrought components of his art as deliberately as he might have done, and from merging them with his apprehensions of nature in such a way as to transform these. Blunden deliberately chose the traditional order and has maintained a conscious relationship with it, but we do not know if the word 'deliberately' is applicable to Gurney.

In the Introduction to his edition of *Poems of John Clare's Madness*, Geoffrey Grigson has written:

> [Clare's] biographers have suggested that, at times, he was actually sane. 'To be sane, even for short periods, while confined within a madhouse, is perhaps one of the most exquisite horrors which can be imagined for any man; and Clare, in the years to come, must have endured this often.' That is a dangerous attitude. It belongs more perhaps to the romanticism of the eighteen-thirties than to a justifiable estimate of Clare's case. One must guard oneself against such a romantic view. . . .

Equally, one must guard oneself against counter-reaction; for, if I understand Grigson correctly, he is suggesting that the insane do not suffer during their sane periods from a lucid realization of where they are, and why they are so confined. If one cannot say that Gurney was *definitely* tormented by a knowledge that at times he was mad, he was undoubtedly tormented by his confinement, and it would be correct to hear what he writes of this:

> Why have you made life so intolerable
> And set me between four walls, where I am able
> Not to escape meals without prayer, for that is possible
> Only by annoying an attendant. And tonight a sensual
> Hell has been put upon me, so that all has deserted me
> And I am merely crying and trembling in heart
> For death, and cannot get it, and gone out is part
> Of sanity. And there is dreadful hell within me
> And nothing helps, forced meals there have been and electricity
> And weakening of sanity by influence
> That's dreadful to endure, and there is orders
> And I'm praying for death, death, death
> And dreadful is the indrawing and out-drawing of breath
> Because of the intolerable insults put on my whole soul
> Of the soul loathed, loathed, loathed of the sun.[1]

---

[1] This poem, not previously published, was quoted in a letter to me by William Curtis-Hayward.

Gurney endured this until his death on 26 December 1937. In a letter of 3 June 1964 Curtis-Hayward wrote to me:

Although I am in favour of any attempts to get Gurney into print, I think it will be doing him a disservice if he is presented as a good minor poet who happened to be mad. I believe that what we have is the ruins of a major poet, and that his madness is of the essence of the fragments of really original poetry he left.

I am unsure of even this assessment and only feel certain that he is a considerable poet, fragmented by the war as well as by his own disabilities.

CHAPTER SEVEN

SIEGFRIED SASSOON

Robert Graves has indicated in *Goodbye to All That* (1929) that Sassoon's first poems about the war were not in opposition to it:

At this time I was getting my first book of poems, *Over the Brazier*, ready. . . . I had one or two drafts in my pocket-book and showed them to Siegfried. He frowned and said that war should not be written about in such a realistic way. In return, he showed me some of his own poems. One of them ('To Victory') began

> Return to greet me, colours that were my joy,
> Not in the woeful crimson of men slain. . . .

Siegfried had not yet been in the trenches. I told him, in my old-soldier manner, that he would soon change his style.

Of the thirty-five poems in 'War Poems: 1915–1917' (one section of *The Old Huntsman and other Poems* (1917)), twenty-one fulfil Graves's prediction, being poems written against war. His testimony is interesting because it emphasizes how much Sassoon's earlier attitude to the war changed, and how dramatically, when seen in relation to a background that seemed unlikely to equip him to deal with war and to make a sustained protest against it.

This is one of many points that emerges from a comparison between *Memoirs of a Fox-hunting Man* (1928) and the other two books which together comprise the trilogy *The Complete Memoirs of George Sherston*: *Memoirs of an Infantry Officer* (1930) and *Sherston's Progress* (1936). The retrospective ease with which they are written (the first was begun in 1926) tells us something of the background in which he grew up as well as of the one he re-settled into. This retrospective ease may be understood by comparing the prose of the trilogy generally with that of Sherston's diary (*Sherston's Progress*, Part 3), which consists of extracts from a diary that Sassoon kept during some of his time in the trenches. But even allowing for the abbreviated character that diaristic prose, especially under such conditions, must have, a plainness emerges, a harshness absent from the prose of the trilogy. This absence has to do with the tolerant but not uncritical evaluation the older Sassoon makes of Sherston and his actions; needless to say, this gently critical tone implies that some of the depth and wisdom lacking in the younger man have subsequently been acquired. But apart from a gathering self-assurance which this retrospective ease has, it contains also a knowing melancholy and regret merged with some pleasure, the whole seeming to stem from a nostalgic memory of the pre-war past. Sassoon has idealized this past, it has been said, and this is true, perhaps. His wealthy country upbringing must have been idyllic in many ways. He writes his first *Memoir* with no attempt to pronounce on, for instance, the troubles in Ulster, the suffragettes, the social condition of the workers, and the series of increasingly bitter strikes which before the war were beginning to fracture the country's social patterns. Still less, had it then been known to him, was he concerned with the increasingly competitive dismemberment of Africa by Europe. So that, although Sassoon may have idealized his early youth and manhood (he was twenty-eight when he enlisted), he has shown us, with full self-awareness, that his background was not one to prepare him for either the war or for strenuous emotional and intellectual activity.

He allowed himself little time to think over his enlistment 'two days before the declaration of war', and gives the impression that he enlisted without questioning either his own patriotism or any contingent issues. This sets him apart from Rosenberg who, in letters prior to his enlistment in November/December 1915, writes at length about his hesitations and makes it clear that he joined without patriotic motive. Harold Owen, in the third volume of *Journey from Obscurity* (1965), establishes that his brother hesitated for some time before enlisting on 21 October 1915.

Before the war Sassoon, unlike Rosenberg, had not discovered much of his poetic equipment or ideas, and *The Old Huntsman*, written in 1915 in the interim period between enlistment and the trenches, has some colloquial ease (via the Masefield of 'Dauber'), some shrewd insight into country wisdom, but has none of the clarity, passion, and commitment of the war poems. This can be seen in his re-working of 'But now I'm old and bald and serious-minded', which in 'Base Details' becomes

> If I were fierce, and bald, and short of breath,
>   I'd live with scarlet Majors at the Base,
> And speed glum heroes up the line to death.

The difference is immediately apparent.

Unlike the pre-war Owen, there is little to indicate that Sassoon had much social awareness; and unlike Sorley he had not, prior to the war, developed an analytical capacity able to foresee how the war would develop, and the patriotic cant that would be used. His *Memoirs of a Fox-hunting Man* does not pin-point any finely felt anxiety when he is given news of embarkation—'An uncertain but unceasing disquiet', as Blunden puts it in *Undertones of War*. He differed from Herbert Read in that, before the war, he had little curiosity about ideas and aesthetics and, although he was in contact before and during the war with Edward Marsh and the Georgians, nothing in his *Memoirs* indicates either contact with, or interest in, the Imagists. Indeed, although I suspect Sassoon of playing up this side of Sherston, the *Memoirs* record almost comic bafflement on Sherston's part when confronted by new ideas. He abandoned his study of law at Cambridge, and gives no indication that his Jewishness in any way impinged on his consciousness—either before the war or during it. During his months in Palestine in 1918, he even speaks of the Jews there patronizingly as Hebrews. Thus, with many of the disabilities of his class, he enlisted in August 1914 and sailed for France in November 1915.

There he joined the first battalion of the Royal Welch Fusiliers, encamped near Festubert, and first met Robert Graves (referred to in the *Memoirs* as David Cromlech). The initial impact of the war affected Sassoon much the more violently. Conversely, the violence of Sassoon's subsequent writing about the war, and his hostility towards the generalized class of people supposedly responsible for its continuance, testify to the impact of it on him as well as to the suddenness of his development. The violence has immediacy, and the abruptness entails a desire to communicate swiftly and widely. His message is 'burningly' direct.

But this simplicity of expression is accompanied by a disinclination—of which Sassoon was aware—to explore and experiment with language. He seems to treat this limitation with a scepticism almost philistine, writing in *The Old Century* (1938):

> From my earliest years I was interested in words, but their effect on my mind was mainly visual. In a muddled way I knew they had derivations, but my spontaneous assumption was that a mouse was called a mouse because it was mouse-like.

In his lecture 'On Poetry' he expands slightly on the visual element in his make-up: 'Thinking in pictures is my natural method of self-expression. I have always been a submissively visual writer.' That he was not much concerned with 'ideas for their own sake' would naturally follow from this, the strength and serious weakness of British pragmatism. The 'submissively visual' attribute yields immediate but short-term results: directness, clarity, and even a ferocious sharpness. But it limits the poet's exploration of language, and perhaps therefore an exploration through language of his feelings. Once the poet has worn through his language-mode he is, without an interest in language and ideas, wanting the means to renew the mode or find a related or new one; he cannot regenerate himself, and this, I feel, remained Sassoon's problem. The later poems may gain in conciseness, and new areas of thought and apprehension (the religious for instance) are explored, but the poems remain the same; there is no development in expressive understanding. Sassoon, of course, adds what he thinks to what he sees, but this is a fairly accurate description of what his war poetry is like, and what its limitations consist of. Like Tennyson, but to a greater extent, he cannot feelingly think or reason sensuously; thought and response suffer in isolation from each other, and the poem therefore suffers. One feels that the sharpness of the visual quality is perhaps the result of some desperation, in that his techniques are pushed to their very limits by what he wishes to say about this suffering, that cruelty, or that injustice. The observed event and the commentary on it are only just held together by the language. A fraction more stress, one feels, and they would surely fall apart.

The war poems in *The Old Huntsman* were written between the spring of 1915—his officer-training period—and early 1917, when he returned to France. This volume, *Picture-Show*, privately printed in June 1919, and *Counter-Attack and other Poems* (1918), contain the majority of the poems I am concerned with, although of course Sassoon published much after these three. The pastoral elegies, which sanctified and idealized the soldiers so far sacrificed, were fairly general practice, as Graves implies, in the early stages of the war.[1] Thus Sassoon in 'Absolution' apostrophizes war as the agent of nobility:

> War is our scourge; yet war has made us wise,
> And, fighting for our freedom, we are free.

[1] See p. 130.

Contrast this with Rosenberg's 'Break of Day', but compare it with the life-through-death paradoxes in Brooke's 'Soldier' sonnets:

> War knows no power. Safe shall be my going,
>   Secretly armed against all death's endeavour;
> Safe though all safety's lost; safe where men fall;
> And if these poor limbs die, safest of all.

This kind of paradox derives, especially in its religious pointing, from the metaphysicals, but where for the seventeenth-century poet the still currently viable belief in an afterlife and its heavenly rewards offered an ambivalent counter-tension to earthly suffering, one questions in Brooke whether the belief is strong enough to do this. I feel, rather, that it has degenerated into a current piece of shared 'knowledge' conveniently at hand for the paradox but informed by no genuine belief; or, if there is an element of belief, the paradox is more important than the relationship of the life before death to that after it. Thus, the argument in the paradox is ultimately circular.

The convention, however, of noble death and the immortality derived from it was so strong that it even depersonalizes Sassoon's responses to his brother's death at Gallipoli (August 1915)—at least in his poem 'To my Brother'. The aura of comradely heroism remains innocent of any physical detail of war:

> For we have made an end of all things base. . . .
> And I am in the field where men must fight.
> But in the gloom I see your laurell'd head
> And through your victory I shall win the light.

Brooke had again been first here:

> These laid the world away; poured out the red
> Sweet wine of youth; gave up the years to be. . . .
>   . . . They brought us, for our dearth,
> Holiness, lacked so long, and Love, and Pain.

Few *offer* their lives to war so much as *risk* them; life, moreover, is taken from a man and it is not within another's mandate to offer it on the other's behalf, and the euphemistic language hinders the emergence of these distinctions. Indeed, it is a necessary part of the convention that patriotism and its contingent sacrifice be accepted without questioning. The argument for consigning people to death, either in practice or within the metaphor, is related to the generalized social demands on individual responsibility. In the anti-war poems that follow, Sassoon moves sharply away from this towards individual responsibility and the right of the individual to dissent.

Concerning *honour* in relation to one's country—the public and social virtue as against the individual's self-interest—many arguments exist, and Lady Winchilsea's fine poem, 'The Soldier's Death' (quoted on page 43 above), takes up some of them. Did Villeneuve (in Hardy's *Dynasts*, at least) kill himself because he had failed Napoleon, retracting his earlier humane considerations that prompted him to break off his engagement with Nelson? Modern generals (in the West) do not often commit suicide as a point of honour if their campaigns fail, although some are executed by the state—'*pour encourager les autres*', as Voltaire put it on the execution of Admiral Byng. A practical objection to Brooke's and Sassoon's *honour* is that it only partly serves the needs of nationalism. Nationalism requires the concept as an aid to persuading its subjects that its cause wants of them the highest possible sacrifice, but it also needs to control wasteful sacrifice as long as the conservation of man-power remains a crucial logistical factor. Modern warfare is democratic and knows the value of the individual and his specialism.

Sassoon's 'France' expresses however the convention of honour found in his early war poems:

> And they are fortunate, who fight
> For gleaming landscapes swept and shafted
> And crowned by cloud pavilions white. . . .

It has echoes of Grenfell, but it transforms Grenfell's motivation.[1] An interesting contrast emerges with Edward Thomas's 'This is no Case of Petty Right or Wrong' in that, where Thomas speaks of a concrete love for the actual land,[2] Sassoon's projections are abstractly visionary—'gleaming landscapes', clouds.

A little more candour emerges in 'To Victory':

> I am not sad; only I long for lustre.
> I am tired of the greys and browns and the leafless ash.
> I would have hours that move like a glitter of dancers
> Far from the angry guns that boom and flash.

In the last line the actual—if distant—prospect of war occurs; yet

[1] See p. 72 above.   [2] See p. 87 above.

perhaps the measure of the realism is obtained more by contrast with nature, which is used not as an actual context so much as a reflection of his mood. He wants the hours to move as glitteringly as dancers (Marsh's education in ballet-going?), but knows they cannot. We are left uncertain whether the poem is meant to convey disillusionment or the beginnings of confused realization.

At some point in this period Sassoon changed his attitude to the war and thus to what poetry should be about. David Jones in his Preface to *In Parenthesis* (1937)[1] writes, 'so did we in 1916 sense a change', meaning just such a change in attitude to the war. Sassoon's change was perhaps quickened by his experience of the Somme[2] and perhaps also by his experience of the Fourth Army School at Flixécourt in spring 1916, where he attended lectures on 'The spirit of the bayonet'.[3] Certainly, his expression of feelings has greater verisimilitude in 'When I'm among a Blaze of Lights', and noticeable too is a change in the kind of subject admitted into his poetry. In 1916 Sassoon began writing what he thought were 'genuine trench poems'.[4] Although it cannot be dated with certainty, 'Golgotha' contains the beginnings of realistic observation:

> The huddled sentry stares
> On gloom at war with white,

where the language, at least, is plain and the phrase 'mimic thunder' begins to assemble that mixture of realism and qualified pastoral convention which he later used with such effect. 'The Kiss', however, gets and merits (*as a poem*) this from Graves:

while in France, I had never seen such a fire-eater as [Sassoon]—the number of Germans whom I killed or caused to be killed could hardly be compared with his wholesale slaughter. In fact, Siegfried's unconquerable idealism changed direction with his environment: he varied between happy warrior and bitter pacifist. His poem:

> To these I turn, in these I trust—
> Brother Lead and Sister Steel.
> To his blind power I make appeal,
> I guard her beauty clean from rust.

---

[1] See p. 327 below.

[2] See *Memoirs of an Infantry Officer*, pp. 321–62.

[3] This sadistic piece of instruction seems to have been universally hated. See, for example, *Memoirs of an Infantry Officer*, pp. 289–90; David Jones, *In Parenthesis*, p. 222, notes to pt. 7, no. 18; Edmund Blunden, *Undertones of War*, p. 17; Robert Graves, *Goodbye to All That*, pp. 195–6 and 226.

[4] *Siegfried's Journey*, p.14.

had originally been inspired by Colonel Campbell, V.C.'s blood-thirsty 'Spirit of the Bayonet' address at an army school. Later, Siegfried offered it as a satire [in what context, one asks, did he do this; to Graves, privately?]; and it certainly comes off, whichever way you read it. I was both more consistent and less heroic than Siegfried.

This is perceptive but also perhaps unfair, in that the phrase 'changed direction' implies a continuous oscillation in both life and poetry, whereas I understand only the one change—from a Brooke-like idealism to angry satire. The change in later life noticeable in, say, 'The English Spirit' and 'Silent Service' (both published in the *Observer*, May 1940) is disturbing; yet such poems should also be seen in the context of his reaction to Nazi Germany. It is, however, the 'positive' expressiveness that I cannot accommodate. Sassoon's remark, ' "pacifism is not enough", against the powers of evil—as I'd realized fully before 1938', may be just, but the pietistic language of 'A kneeling angel holding faith's front line' surely abandons, in language and attitude, all he had painfully achieved in his later poems of the First World War. But the line, once taken during that war, seems unwavering. And on the whole there is little wavering in either his conduct or attitude to the war once this is established, unless one considers Sassoon's intermittent ferocity in the trenches themselves. There seems more inconsistency between the intermittent ferocity and the *poems* than in either the poems or the action taken separately. But perhaps the truth is that internal conflict under the stress of combat cannot always be rationalized into consistent behaviour. And when, in 1917, Sassoon did try to behave consistently he was foiled, even if out of kindness, by Graves himself. Finally, however ambiguous 'The Kiss' may seem (and I think of it as a ferocious poem), Sassoon's purpose in retaining it is perhaps to complete the record of his responses to the war.

'The Redeemer' represents a further shift towards the anti-war mode, identifying the soldier and his suffering with Christ:

> I say that He was Christ; stiff in the glare,
> And leaning forward from His burdening task. . . .

Owen makes a similar identification in 'For 14 hours yesterday I was at work—teaching Christ to lift his cross by numbers . . . . and not to imagine he thirst till after the last halt.' Individual suffering stands out in contrast with the general sacrifice, un-itemized and anonymous, demanded by the national cause. Sassoon, at this stage, still feels compelled to explain why such sacrifices are being made; the alternative to such explanation being the conclusion that the sacrifices were futile—a conclusion he was not yet ready to make, and never absolutely settled on. In 'The Redeemer', the soldier can willingly

> endure
> Horror and pain, not uncontent to die
> That Lancaster on Lune may stand secure.

This is much more like Thomas's 'She is all we know' and his 'pinch of earth', and has also some kinship with Owen's 'kind fires'. The patriotic mode at first assumed a sacred cause and sacred sacrifice. The change came when sacred duty was discarded as an acceptable creed. The sacred cause was then discarded, which left one (when one had extracted duty from sacrifice) with the latter. Sacrifice was harder to do away with, inasmuch as the individual who made the sacrifice remained (or became) sacred; but through his own efforts and despite—not because of—the by now discarded demands of the cause. Sacredness is the most difficult element to discard, even assuming it ought to be; it is the last refuge before bitterness, in that if a comrade dies you feel he has contributed something; when that sense goes, nothing remains. The image of sacredness is hinged in the middle.

In Sassoon's poem, the traditional emphasis on the things to be valued and defended indicates some lingering association with the appeals the patriots were making. These appeals being made were via traditional and rural concerns, which by 1914 were of little or no relevance to the bulk of an urbanized population, driven into the towns by the enclosure acts and industrialization; except that they could be hoodwinked by authority to believe that the countryside was an integral part of their actual fruitful experience. A cursory glance at the industrial slums of Manchester, Leeds, and Newcastle, even today, fifty-five years later, will quickly show what a contemptible lie this was. The 1911 Census for England and Wales shows that out of a total population of thirty-six million, twenty-eight are classed as Urban and less than eight as Rural. A labourer in Birmingham, a miner in the Rhondda, a riveter from Wallsend, even a *farmer* in Sutherland might be excused for feeling little commitment to the traditional rural England, which had probably shared little of its wealth or *concern*, either with him or his ancestors. The patriotic appeal, in any case, is made in impersonal terms that disguise the fact that what is to be defended are the interests of the landowners. Sassoon's poem hesitates between the generalized appeal of tradition and the revelation of individual suffering, but it also makes another appeal, by the merging of blasphemy and invocation:

> And someone flung his burden in the muck,
> Mumbling: 'O Christ Almighty, now I'm stuck!'

The upper case reinforces this double intention.

'A Working Party' develops the techniques that characterize the majority of the poems in *Counter-Attack*: the edgy, colloquial realism, a choice of language that reflects not merely an immersion in the daily routine, but selects from it responses to its most wearying recalcitrant aspects:

> he stooped and swore
> Because a sagging wire had caught his neck.

The objects in this routine are not, in the poem, used as symbols or as emblematic equivalents of some psychological condition or impulse; they are part of the soldiers' material experience. Yet Sassoon's use of language is more subtle than he suggests, describing himself as a 'visually submissive writer'. 'Glimmering sandbags' develops the technique, perhaps consciously initiated in 'Golgotha', of juxtaposing the pastoral with the harshly realistic. A moment of romantic illusion, introduced by the flares' slow silver movement, is brutally dispelled by the realities of the trenches. And, as sometimes with the several voices in the *Memoirs*, we have a sense of one era being despoiled by another.

'They' is one of Sassoon's most sustained and powerful anti-war poems, certainly the most concentrated in this volume. D. J. Enright, in a disappointing essay, 'The Literature of the First World War' (1961), remarks of it that 'Sassoon has shot, right through the heart, a sitting duck—a too-amenable Bishop'. Strangely, though, in this same essay, Enright had occupied a seemingly different position in asserting that '*Counter-Attack* is first-class propaganda and rather more. . . . Not poetry, perhaps? But did that matter? The poetry—to adapt a phrase from Owen—is in the anger.' This ambivalent defence ('is it poetry? It is at any rate good propaganda; it may be poetry by virtue of its *anger*') is retracted when Enright considers 'They', which in the end is treated not for its positive anger, spelling out the message of the casualty lists, but instead impugned for its over-obvious attack. Even so, elsewhere in his essay Enright presents the necessity of such attack at that time. Moreover, the 'sitting duck' might not then have appeared such an easy target as it now seems to be, and perhaps Sassoon's early attack helped to make the target vulnerable. Whether or not one agrees with Enright's strictures, the concerns of the poem are not so much with the Bishop as with the Church's failure to cope with the situation. Owen makes similar reservations about the Church in his letter concerning pacifism as well as in his two poems 'At a Calvary near the Ancre' and 'Le Christianisme'. Both poets appear to think that the Church was acting in an erastian way, in that not only did some army padres and civilian clergymen seem to have little idea of the barbarity of combat, but also in that they unthinkingly complied with the nationalistic demands of the State. The Church has, after all, a position of moral leadership. It is not enough, in such contexts as war and poverty, to say like Sassoon's Bishop: 'The ways of God are strange!' That last line does not indict the Bishop for his lack of intelligence—he cannot altogether be blamed for this (although morality and intelligence are surely closely co-operative)—but for his lack of feeling, to which neither man nor religion should be immune. Thus the Church, as surely as the State, speeds 'glum heroes up the line to death', but in the name of God. J. C. Squire neatly encapsulated God's divided position:

> God heard the embattled nations sing and shout:
> 'Gott strafe England'—'God save the King'—
> 'God this'—'God that'—and 'God the other thing'.
> 'My God', said God, 'I've got my work cut out.'

This is implied in Sassoon's

> The Bishop tells us: 'When the boys come back
> 'They will not be the same; for they'll have fought
> 'In a just cause: they lead the last attack
> 'On anti-Christ. . . .

'Will not be the same' is of course a bluntly ironic pun, reflecting the unthinking phrases of the Bishop. They will not be the same

physically; but, he implies, a 'just' war develops man's moral
condition. The Church's doubtful moral position is skilfully im-
peached through the Bishop's ignorant rhetoric, and the 'boy's'
reply to it:

> 'We're none of us the same!' the boys reply.
> 'For George lost both his legs; and Bill's stone blind;
> 'Poor Jim's shot through the lungs and like to die;
> 'And Bert's gone syphilitic: you'll not find
> 'A chap who's served that hasn't found *some* change.'
> And the Bishop said: 'The ways of God are strange!'

One might object that the attack on the Bishop is misplaced, in that
he is being brought to account for damage already inflicted. On the
other hand, the Bishop has, wittingly or not, contributed to the
damage; and one might add that Sassoon's strictures were meant
prophylactically in the sense that he wanted truth from the Church
in future, in some co-operative effort to make another war impossible.

The reductive irony of 'The ways of God are strange' works
through several layers of meaning, all of them organized so as to
indicate that the Bishop, the Church and its religion are unable to
find meaning or consolation for those—now dead or wounded—they
urged into the war. The poem's last line suggests that the Church,
confronted with the men's 'changes', saves its face by taking refuge
behind God's inscrutability. The earthly doings of the Church
(encouraging enlistment) may bring earthly consequences, but the
responsibility for them is passed on to God who, as most sceptics
know (the Bishop perhaps among them), can be relied on to keep
his mouth shut.

'Stand-to: Good Friday Morning', one of Sassoon's weakest
satirical poems, was on publication attacked for its blasphemy. It
deserves criticism, but for different reasons. Its metrics are crude,
and, even more, its antitheses:

> Larks were singing, discordant, shrill;
> *They* seemed happy; but *I* felt ill.

The poem expresses a desire for a wound that will make the soldier
unfit for further war service, that being the greatest gift that the
(crucified) Christ could bestow on the day of His crucifixion. In
return, the soldier promises belief. His promise is unlikely to be

fulfilled, but the point of alluding to his disbelief (the poem draws on this question without in any way sufficiently exploring it) is not so much to reject religion as affirm the actuality of war that cannot be modified by religious miracles. Thus the invocation, 'O Jesus', is partly exclamatory, but it represents a proper cry for help, with the contingent faith wanting. The language of the poem is however weak, and its irony never serious enough to engage the real problems in the situation it clumsily raises.

The same area of meaning is more skilfully explored in 'The Tombstone-Maker'. The profit-motive of the craftsman, disguised in hypocritical, chauvinist piety, is set against the supposed materialistic economy of the Germans:

> I told him with a sympathetic grin,
> That Germans boil dead soldiers down for fat;
> And he was horrified. 'What shameful sin!
> 'O sir, that Christian souls should come to that!'

All 'souls', even good Christian ones, are similarly rendered down, reduced neither to heavenly nor diabolic shades, but to matter.[1] The implication is that men are to be evaluated in terms of their earthly actions, and in this instance the war shows up the man's profits in terms of the soldiers' pains. Like 'The Tombstone-Maker', 'The Hero' is also a criticism of civilian ignorance of the war, although in this instance the ignorance is treated, uncharacteristically but justifiably, with sympathy. Or rather, the dead soldier's mother is given sympathy although, like Swift, the civilian population *in general* is condemned for projecting onto their soldiers, universally, the image of hero. Sassoon, brutally I think, *re*tells the actual story, making good use of this current notion of hero by deliberately contrasting it with how

> . . . 'Jack', cold-footed, useless swine,
> Had panicked down the trench that night. . . .

We have no sense of Sassoon understanding the man's panic, although one cannot help but feel that the animosity implied towards civilian ignorance has been transferred in its fury to Jack, whose cowardice suffers perhaps harsher treatment than it merits (in the poem) and who, in any case, is 'blown to small bits'. The direct, almost formal use of dramatic irony is obtained, finally, in

[1] Compare this with Owen's ' "Pushing up daisies" ' in 'A Terre'.

the officer's telling the mother 'some gallant lies'. ('Gallant' is perhaps fair in that, to argue the other way, 'panic' robs one's comrades of what little comfort they would otherwise have in combat.) The irony is pressed home by the mother's being genuinely consoled that her son died bravely. The poem is more complex than it at first appears because, with this irony, we are caught in the now familiar situation of thinking that the mother's being glad of her son's supposed courage helps to entrap more soldiers in further suffering; and that she ought therefore not to feel this. Consolation quenches bitterness, which in turn quenches a desire to end the war. Yet who would grudge her consolation? Finally, the ubiquitous and complex problem of courage emerges—but is not explored—in the poem. The courage, for instance, required to kill one's enemies in desperate hand-to-hand fighting, and that needed for rescuing a wounded comrade while you and he are exposed to rifle-fire, are perhaps not only different in kind but may also need different evaluations.

Whatever inconclusiveness one may complain of in Sassoon's poems, it must be said that *The Old Huntsman* and *Counter-Attack* both raise most of the principal problems made active by war. One of these is the selectivity of war in which the fittest, the young, are its principal victims. This is a theme that is common to nearly every writer of the period concerned with war. It occurs directly in Rosenberg's 'Dead Man's Dump', and more especially in 'Daughters of War'; it is the theme of F. S. Flint's fine 'Lament', and of Owen's 'The Parable of the Old Men and the Young'; it occurs in his 'Exposure', in Blunden's 'War Autobiography', Read's 'Kneeshaw Goes to War', and in 'The Execution of Cornelius Vane'. It occurs in Sassoon's 'Suicide in the Trenches' and also 'The Death-Bed':

> He's young; he hated War; how should he die
> When cruel old campaigners win safe through?
>
> But death replied: 'I choose him.' So he went. . . .

It occurs again in Sassoon's 'The Last Meeting' (Flixécourt, May 1916), but in this instance Sassoon attempts something more than the comparatively uncomplicated assertion of youth bearing the principal inflictions of war. He attempts to compound for the slain friend some kind of immortality by working through his friend's affections, and by moulding with nature, in his imagination, the essence or spirit of his friend, as that spirit might appear in nature's benign manifestations.

> Ah! but there was no need to call his name.
> He was beside me now, as swift as light.
> I knew him crushed to earth in scentless flowers,
> And lifted in the rapture of dark pines.

This is a slightly dramatized restatement of the idea and method found in *Adonais*, a method that permits Sassoon to immortalize his friend, and to provide himself (and others) with a consolation that no other kind of earthly activity can:

> He is made one with Nature; there is heard
> His voice in all her music, from the moan
> Of thunder, to the song of night's sweet bird. . . .

The crucial difference between Sassoon's and Shelley's assertions is that, while Sassoon uses a sense of nature's cyclic fecundity for his own purposes, as they relate to his friend and his feelings for him, Shelley is at least as much concerned with saying something about nature itself. Shelley of course was not the first to use nature in this way, but the method by which the poet's responses are balanced between the friend's death and nature's recurrent 'immortality' produces an effect of freshness, as though the complexity were something he had found for himself. This is not the case with Sassoon. Moreover, Shelley's identifying of Keats with nature is not only a comment on Keats's double attitude to death, but on the latter's articulated relationship with nature, in which Keats has immortalized himself. It is therefore fitting that in death Keats should continue to live through nature:

> He is a portion of the loveliness
> Which once he made more lovely. . . .[1]

There is an irony here, however, in that Keats, being mortal, cannot continue to 'shape' nature or any image of it, and this elegaic, regretful irony which qualifies the above assertion is confirmed not only in the careful word 'portion', but by a subsequent phrase 'he doth bear/His part' with the metrical stress falling on 'bear'. Shelley acknowledges these conscious adjustments, which

---

[1] Consider also Hardy's 'Drummer Hodge' and Brooke's 'The Soldier', pp. 47–8 above.

are so much a part of his total meaning, in his Preface to *Adonais*: 'John Keats died at Rome. . . . The cemetery is an open space among the ruins, covered in winter with violets and daisies. It might make one in love with death, to think one buried in so sweet a place.' He says 'might make one' and stresses the living perception of nature.

In the passage quoted from 'The Last Meeting', however, one loses the fruitful sense of tension obtained through the interfusing of a portion of nature with Keats's perception of nature, with Keats being reproduced through nature's manifesting itself. In the second section of the poem Sassoon almost loses the elegaic quest to be found in the first section. And by *insisting* that his lost friend is to be found in nature, he not only loses sight of his human identity but also loses him in that medium through which he was to be resurrected. The metaphysics of the poem are thin.

Thus when, in section III, Sassoon wishes to remember his friend's death again, 'Men may not speak with [nature's] stillness', the effect of this truthful denial is not so much to qualify the earlier resurrection motif in a balancing way, as to obliterate it. And when he once more returns to this 'found in sweet nature' idea, the result is one of flat contradiction and bewilderment, instead of qualification or ambiguity. He cannot integrate the ideas of death and nature, as the greater poet does. He fails to show, or even recognize—as Owen did in 'A Terre'—that death in war is different from death through disease or age, and does not as easily lend itself to this idea of metamorphosis by nature. Sassoon's difficulties here point to those of a more general kind—those of synthesizing conflicting or differing ideas into some form of equilibrium and concentration. This perhaps explains why, despite the continuous presence of specific objects, the total impression of his poems is blurred. It may also help to account for the seeming thinness of some of the poetry. Sassoon frequently fixes single targets in his sights, but forgets that his own responses to these targets, as well as the targets themselves, are incorporated into the poem, and that therefore his own responses need to be more deliberately a part of the poem. That is why 'visually submissive' may be an accurate assessment of an aspect of his work, but why the limitation needed to be overcome. It is possible, of course, that Sassoon wished to exclude complexity and concentrate on specific objectives. The prolongation of the war through 1916–17 may have convinced him that he should produce direct, simple work, as the best way of marshalling opinion against the war's continuation. It may also be that the shock of the war made him self-censoring, as far as revealing his personal responses were concerned. One remembers the numbness with which Graves describes casualties in *Goodbye to All That*. Similarly, in *Memoirs of an Infantry Officer*, Sassoon writes:

> It was queer how the men seemed to take their victimization for granted. In and out; in and out; singing and whistling. . . . A London editor driving along the road in a Staff car would have remarked that the spirit of the troops was amazing. And so it was. But somehow the newspaper men always kept the horrifying realities of the War out of their articles, for it was unpatriotic to be bitter, and the dead were assumed to be gloriously happy.

This is strangely dissonant with the ending of 'The Last Meeting':

> . . . his name shall be
> Wonder awaking in a summer dawn,
> And youth, that dying, touched my lips to song.

It is not, of course, directly stated that the dead man is now happy, but there is a hint of this in the last line. Such inconsistency indicates uncertainty, the presence of a conflict acknowledged in his *Memoirs*: 'Arriving at my bed [the doctor] asked how I was feeling. I stared up at him, incapable of asserting that I felt ill and unwilling to admit that I felt well.' This was the dilemma of many who, in hospital, felt the tug of guilty self-preservation in conflict with the solidarity they felt for their comrades at the front.

Sassoon was at this time becoming conscious of other conflicts in his position. Convalescing in England after a severe attack of gastric fever contracted during the battle of the Somme, he met Lady Ottoline Morrell and her husband, an M.P. who held a pacifist position. In February 1917, on his return to France, Sassoon records that he 'was losing his belief in the war'. He was now attached to the Second Battalion of the Flintshire Fusiliers and in April, taking part in the battle of Arras (in which Edward Thomas was killed), he was wounded with a 'bullet-hole through my lung'. 'I felt a stupendous blow in the back between my shoulders', he records. Contrast this brute, physical fact with the incident on his way to hospital: 'At Charing Cross a woman handed me a bunch of flowers and a leaflet by the Bishop of London who earnestly advised me to lead a clean life and attend Holy Communion.' The pointedness of this conjunction of events (whether intended or not) indicates the extent to which Sassoon became alienated from the war and its aims, or rather, its lack of aims—as he was to point out in his 'statement' made later on the same year.

In May, he was transferred from hospital to 'Nutwood Manor' (Craiglockhart) for convalescence. Here he found himself increasingly hostile to the newspapers' misleading articles, and to some of those attitudes held by civilians, Lady X, for instance, who

symbolized the patrician privileges for whose preservation I had chucked bombs at Germans and carelessly offered myself as a target for a sniper. When I had blurted out my opinion that life was preferable to the Roll of Honour she put aside her reticence like a rich cloak. 'But death is nothing', she said. . . . 'And those who are killed in the War—they help us from up there. They are helping us to win.'

David Jones in *In Parenthesis* makes a similar point:

and into it [the Somme battle] they slide . . . of the admirable salads of Mrs. Curtis-Smythe: they fall for her in Poona, and it's worth one's while—but the comrade close next you screamed so after the last salvo that it was impossible to catch any more the burthen of this white-man talk.

That last phrase saves one from thinking that Jones is merely creating a kind of reportage of different soldiers' feelings; the narrator, John Ball, is in a position to know rather than merely report, as the end of the poem makes clear.

In July 1917 Sassoon was clarifying his ideas concerning the war, up to the point where he drafted his courageous statement indicting the war leaders. Two copies were to be made public; one he posted to his commanding officer at 'Clitherland', and one he arranged to get into the hands of an M.P., intending it to be read out in Parliament. Yet even at this crucial point in Sherston's narrative, when he is clearly undergoing an emotional and intellectual crisis, the older, retrospecting Sassoon injects into the narration a simplistic and deflating humour. This has the effect of encompassing Sherston, and may even be intended as a kind of modesty; the insight that it projects is of a still naïve and blundering young man embarking on a massive crusade, not single-handed but, so far as he was concerned, alone. Yet whatever the motives that authorize the tone, apart from casting slight dubiety on Sherston, Sassoon tampers with the seriousness, not only of Sherston's intentions but of the issues themselves, which seem both to be played down and treated with less concern than they deserve.

And now Markington had gloomily informed me that our Aims were essentially acquisitive, what we were fighting for was the Mesopotamian Oil Wells. A jolly fine swindle it would have been for me, if I'd been killed in April for an Oil Well! But I soon forgot that I'd been unaware of the existence of the Oil Wells before Markington mentioned them, and I conveniently assimilated them as part of my evidential repertoire.

But whatever reservations one may have about Sassoon's affectionate distancing of his younger self, he reproduces what he must surely have felt was still an important statement:

I am making this statement as an act of wilful defiance of military authority, because I believe that the War is being deliberately prolonged by those who have the power to end it. I am a soldier, convinced that I am acting on behalf of soldiers. I believe that this War, upon which I entered as a war of defence and liberation, has now become a war of aggression and conquest. I believe that the purposes for which I and my fellow soldiers entered upon this War should have been so clearly stated as to have made it impossible to change them, and that, had this been done, the objects which actuated us would now be attainable by negotiation. I have seen and endured the sufferings of the troops, and I can no longer be a party to prolong these sufferings for ends which I believe to be evil and unjust. I am not protesting against the conduct of the War, but against the political errors and insincerities for which the fighting men are being sacrificed. On behalf of those who are suffering now I make this protest against the deception which is being practised on them; also I believe that I may help to destroy the callous complacency with which the majority of those at home regard the continuance of agonies which they do not share, and which they have not sufficient imagination to realize.

As if to add a slightly wiser 'frame', the older Sassoon makes Sherston add, 'It certainly sounds a bit pompous, I thought, and God only knows what the colonel will think of it.' There is a touch of the 'spoiler's art' in Sassoon, but perhaps a more helpful comparison would be between Sassoon's *Memoirs* and Wordsworth's *Prelude*. Both are not only autobiographical but retrospectively evaluative, while at the same time both remain concerned with the part that each took within the wider, highly disturbed and disturbing social context. And yet the interesting difference is that, while Wordsworth gradually withdrew from his earlier political allegiances, the frames he puts round his recorded feelings and activities undermine them less than do Sassoon's.[1] The later Sassoon was perhaps less earnest and egotistical than Wordsworth, but I believe that the subsequent ambiguity in the *Memoirs* (which may arise from Sassoon having no subsequent satisfactory position) recoils on Sassoon rather than Sherston.

Sherston was courageous. In issuing and adhering to his statement, with all its implications, his actions amounted to military defection. And although he was not of the military caste, he came from a class of similar pretensions that mingled with those who retained their military status. It often requires more courage to defect from one's own group than to attack another. This can be seen for instance in Sassoon's interview with an officer at 'Clitherland' who (officially) tried to persuade him to retract his statement. Sassoon conscientiously records that his refusal to do so constituted 'committing a breach, not so much of discipline as of decorum'. Thus, he sympathizes with his superior's difficult position, both as a member of his own class and as an individual; recognizing the latter's restraint, while at the same time refusing to attend a medical board that had been arranged for him. This would have given both parties the possibility of compromise. A medical board pronouncing Sherston as medically unfit—suffering from shell-shock, as they would put it—would have permitted a fellow-officer a tactful last-minute solution to a situation that they would not have understood, but nevertheless a situation compromising an individual who had up to now fought with courage and been decorated for it. It would also enable the military and higher echelons of civil authority to avoid any embarrassing discussion of the issues in question. It could all, if Sherston took the opportunity offered him, be explained as neurasthenia. In the frustration resulting from much waiting, Sassoon flung his military cross 'into the mouth of the Mersey'.

At this stage David Cromlech (Robert Graves) enters the narrative and, if one compares Sassoon's account of what followed with Graves's, the two will be found to differ in important respects. According to Graves, for instance, Sassoon sent him a news-cutting containing his statement; the likely consequences of Sassoon's

---

[1] See p. 11 above.

defection gave Graves 'anxiety and unhappiness' on his friend's behalf, who, he felt, was not in good enough physical condition 'to be court-martialled, cashiered, and imprisoned. I found myself most bitter with the pacifists who had encouraged him to make this gesture. I felt that, not being soldiers, they could not understand what it cost Siegfried emotionally.' Trench warfare (the alternative to imprisonment) was hardly good for one's health either. Graves further maintained that he, Graves, 'realized the inadequacy of the gesture. Nobody would follow [Sassoon's] example, either in England or Germany. The war would inevitably go on and on until one side or the other cracked.' Two World Wars have proved the truth of this, although they have also shown that defeat is eventually followed by retaliation. And on the other hand, Graves's argument rests too strongly on alternative action not having been fully tried. Rosenberg, for instance, mentions in a letter that 'One reg close by did break out and some men got bayoneted'; and this in England, probably before the men had even seen the trenches. Graves proceeded to annul Sassoon's actions by writing to the Hon. Evan Morgan, whom he knew, asking that Sassoon's letter be given as little publicity as possible when 'Mr. Lees-Smith, the leading pacifist M.P.' raised a question about it in the House.

I explained to Evan that I was on Siegfried's side really, but that he should not be allowed to become a martyr to a hopeless cause in his present physical condition. Finally, I wrote to the Third Battalion. I knew that Colonel Jones-Williams was narrowly patriotic. . . . But the second-in-command, Major Macartney-Filgate, was humane; so I pleaded with him to make the colonel see the affair in a reasonable light.

Graves was taking no chances and had indirectly got 'Evan's Minister [to persuade] the War Office not to press the matter as a disciplinary case, but to give Siegfried a medical board'. This suggests, I think, that if both military and civil authorities were going to take the case seriously, and one presumes they were, then they were faced with either awarding punishment, or incarceration in a hospital for neurasthenics. Would Sassoon have been understood by the civilians if his case had been made public? Graves had one further argument to use against Sassoon's persisting with his refusal to see a medical board: he 'made it plain that his letter had not been given, and would not be given, the publicity he intended.

At last, unable to deny how ill he was, Siegfried consented to appear before a medical board.' Graves then proceeded to 'rig' the board:

> Much against my will, I had to appear in the role of patriot distressed by the mental collapse of a brother-in-arms—a collapse directly due to his magnificent exploits in the trenches . . . [although] I entirely agreed with Siegfried about the 'political errors and insincerities' and thought his action magnificently courageous.

Sassoon records their discussion as follows:

> 'I'm not going to be talked out of it just when I'm forcing them to make a martyr of me.' 'They won't make a martyr of you,' he replied. 'How do you know that?' I asked. He said that the colonel at Clitherland had told him to tell me that if I continued to refuse to be 'medically-boarded' they would shut me up in a lunatic asylum for the rest of the War. Nothing would induce them to court martial me. It had all been arranged with some big bug in the War Office.

This last assertion was true, of course, although not in the sense that Sassoon would have understood it; that is, it was a decision made by the W.O. through Graves and via Morgan, provided that Sassoon consented to the medical board. Sassoon thought that the W.O. had themselves decided to resist a court-martial, publicity, and prison. It seems by no means certain, however, that the W.O. would have been content to have had him even incarcerated in a 'lunatic asylum', from which in any case he would eventually have been released. Even so, what is interesting is the comparatively gentlemanly treatment that Sassoon received. By the end of the First World War the concept of gentlemanly treatment for gentlemen had been eroded for ever. Graves finally prevailed on Sassoon to attend the medical board. Sassoon wrote: 'I was unaware that [Graves] had, probably, saved me from being sent to prison by telling me a very successful lie. No doubt I should have done the same for him if our positions had been reversed.' Thus, despite Graves's contention that he 'entirely agreed with Siegfried about the "political errors and insincerities"', it seems that he was to a large extent responsible for Sassoon's neutralizing confinement in Craiglockhart hospital for shell-shocked cases. Thus, the de-fusing of the letter in Parliament[1] was not difficult once he had entered

---

[1] See Hansard, 30 July 1917, pp. 1798–9 and 1805.

Craiglockhart, since it could be said that he was not altogether in his right mind, if that in fact even needed saying.

Sassoon arrived there in July 1917, and his *Counter-Attack* poems were published in July 1918. The volume is prefaced by a quotation from Barbusse's *Under Fire* (1916):

> In the troubled truce of the morning, these men whom fatigue had tormented, whom rain had scourged, whom nightlong lightning had convulsed, these survivors of volcanoes and flood began not only to see dimly how war, as hideous morally and physically, outrages common sense, debases noble ideas and dictates all kind of crime, but they remembered how it had enlarged in them and about them every evil instinct save none, mischief developed into lustful cruelty, selfishness into ferocity, the hunger of enjoyment into a mania.

The passage might well serve as a preparatory text for Herbert Read's 'The Happy Warrior', and it is certainly an apt introduction to Sassoon's volume. The quotation is also valuable in that it contradicts the popular notion of how the evils of war are to some extent counterbalanced by the manly virtues produced amid the stresses of war. On the contrary, Barbusse insists that the primary effects of war, outweighing others, are those of depravity. He indicates that the men were at the time only hazily conscious of their depravity, and also suggests that this insight into their recent actions was not one they might necessarily be able to keep and use.

In *Counter-Attack*, Sassoon's targets are clearer than in his earlier poems and the tone, an important ingredient in his poetry, is buoyed up by the metronomic regularity of metres running in already established and familiar forms. As before, what he loses in lack of complexity, he gains, to some extent, in simplicity and directness. This directness is not a literary device, but the result of his responses to war. The stronger these become, the clearer his aims, and the more the poems are composed into direct, compact units. For Sassoon, the strong, superficially simple response to combat may have been the only possible one, because of a context that was becoming more than ever destructive. In his poems, as in his prose, he rarely abstracts his experience of war into a theory concerning it, but re-creates his sensuous responses to it which are joined to his anger and indignation. John H. Johnston regards this as a weakness in his verse and thinks that, had Sassoon possessed more facts, he might have abstracted and concluded differently. Johnston, however, sees Sassoon's problem not merely in terms of particular facts but in relation to abstract principles: 'he could hardly portray a soldier mastering his own emotional turmoil and responding to the imperatives of duty. To write such things would have been to grant that the war had some positive moral or historical significance.'[1] 'Duty' is oddly propelled into the argument. It prevents one from examining closely what 'moral and historical significance' the war might have had, because it sets up existing principles which have prior and primary claims, and which then make legalistic any debate about the merits of such moral and historical factors as existed. In making his plea for the epic and heroic poem, Johnston seems to align himself with the idea of duty no matter what it may consist of, and his appeals to its moral significance are never in fact debated in his book. He might say that his real question is whether Sassoon was not in some position to weigh what facts he had at his disposal, but that is never a question he considers; the imperatives of duty intervene. It never enters his consideration that Sassoon, and similarly aligned poets, could have been in possession of enough facts and experience to conclude differently from him. More facts, he seems to imply, would *per se* have led to an even more developed sense of duty. I, on the other hand, believe that with more facts, and more time perhaps, Sassoon would have gone even further than he did.

Some of Johnston's arguments are obscure. He implies that only those poets who adhered to his premise were capable of making significant poetry, and that, conversely, those whose poetry was deficient (whose judgements concerning the war do not correspond with his own) wrote no better because of their inability to perceive the war's moral and historical significance. And, as a rider, with more facts, they would have responded oppositely to the way they did. This is an adroit but circular argument, the effectiveness of which depends on the reader's accepting that good poets conceptualize, not just locally, in metaphors, but throughout a whole poem; and that doing so they would have made the only possible abstraction (enunciated throughout Johnston's book). Making this abstraction, they would have accepted their clear duty, although for many duty meant, in an almost tautological way, the continuation

[1] *English Poetry of the First World War* (1964), p. 102.

of fighting without even as many facts as Sassoon had. Without assent, duty is surely empty and tyrannical, and without facts you have submission rather than assent. As Herbert Read suggests in his 'Kneeshaw' poem, to persist in action to which one gives no assent is to be culpable. To make judgements of this kind, however, is at best factitious; lacking the skill and experience to organize, the soldiers fought because they had to; but patriotism, if one is speaking in terms of duty, eroded as the combat was prolonged and embittered, and to judge evidence such as this as inferior because it did not measure up to the imperatives of duty is to complain that reality was inferior to the imposed abstraction.

Sassoon's reasons for wanting the war discontinued are never seriously challenged by Johnston; Sassoon's whole attempt in *Counter-Attack* is, after all, to convey the suffering of the men to an ignorant and often apathetic populace.

His pre-war life, as *Memoirs of a Fox-hunting Man* testifies, was easeful. He describes it in terms often child-like, even pre-lapsarian. The copiousness of his lyrical response to nature can be seen in the poems of 1908–16. In his war poems, he frequently juxtaposes this pastoral lyricism (or concomitant images of complacent civilian ease) with the horror of war; a juxtaposition that produces the implicit comment both on the nature of war and on the kind of life lived at home which, in its assumptions, takes into account little of the soldiers' privations. Another version of this technique is to juxtapose the language, or even the word, of common speech with the word of a previous, romanticized poetic diction, exposing thereby how much this diction and its underlying attitudes conflicted with the facts of mundane existence in general, but the war in particular. Even the traditional metrical forms filled with unexpectedly horrific material provided the same kind of shock and implicit criticism. 'Glum heroes' is a fair example of this technique, where 'glum' subverts 'heroes'. The method employs something like zeugma, one of the few devices that has moral energy built into it. Sassoon may not necessarily have thought out this technique, but given his background and then his sudden and shocking experience of war, it would seem a natural development. Whichever version of the technique he uses, he constantly exploits the discrepancy between civilian apathy and the suffering of the soldiers. Thus the gap between the accepted or acceptable poetic norm and the facts themselves provides the energy with which his satire operates. Indeed, the gap is almost one that self-converts into satiric energy. The method is the meaning, which perhaps explains why the poems seem so relatively uncomplex. The meaning is also the purpose, in which he wanted to shame those at home into an awareness of the realities of trench warfare—in the hope that they would be so appalled as to make public protest against the war's continuance. The method, meaning, and purpose are anything but imposed; they have each of them grown out of an awareness that the civilian life and its attitudes, and the soldiers', are irreconcilable so long as the war continues and the civilian continues to endorse its continuation—whether from apathy or ignorance. The implicit comment that such an avowed purpose makes is that this complacency is not especially a product of the war but something revealed by it.

As with Owen and Blunden, Sassoon's principal poetic patrimony was a pre-lapsarian pastoralism, expressed in sub-Keatsian diction and shared with many other writers in this period. Thus, although modified slightly, in the first of the *Counter-Attack* poems, 'Prelude: The Troops', nature is deployed in the kind of sanative and pleasure-affording mode found in Blunden; it is the repository of goodness and peace, and in the greatest contrast to war:

> They march from safety, and the bird-sung joy
> Of grass-green thickets, to the land where all
> Is ruin. . . .

Consonant with such a prelude to *Counter-Attack*, is the reference to 'The unreturning army that was youth', although even the tone of this permits ambiguity. It could be read as the elegaics of an anti-war humanist, but it could also be the expression of a regretful but decided militarist at an anniversary service for the 'slain'.

In 'Counter-Attack' itself, one of Sassoon's most relentless poems, the language is as dense and rich as anything in his work, and in noting the horrific quality of the sensuousness one sees by how much he has inverted his habitual pastoralism to express his image of war. Here, nature is compared to the face of a fatigued soldier, appropriate in that the soldiers are subject to the conditions of nature; in trench warfare it was often the decisive component. It is certainly the omnipresent factor for him and thus images *him* in detail:

> While dawn broke like a face with blinking eyes,
> Pallid, unshaved and thirsty, blind with smoke.

The harsh but not detached observer/narrator notes that the soldiers, having gained their 'first objective' (the detached military diction taking no cognizance of the cost), were free, as they deepened the shallow trench, to notice what they were clearing away:

> The place was rotten with dead; green clumsy legs
> High-booted, sprawled and grovelled along the saps
> And trunks, face downward, in the sucking mud,
> Wallowed like trodden sand-bags loosely filled;
> And naked sodden buttocks, mats of hair,
> Bulged, clotted heads slept in the plastering slime.

Nature has certainly been transformed, and it is this transformation that finally makes the passage allusively rich and dense. Johnston grants its 'graphic intensity', but argues that in Sassoon's desire 'to communicate the shock . . . he forgets his obligations to the action he has initiated and resorts to the dubious techniques of photographic realism'. In fairness, this statement should be compared with Sassoon's view of himself as a 'visually submissive' writer. Johnston goes on to quote Middleton Murry—'is horrible, but it does not produce the impression of horror'—and himself adds: 'The appeal is to the senses and not to the imagination.' The distinction is too insistent, I think, for it to be ultimately acceptable, since it is in any case through the senses that the imagination operates, having embedded in its recreation their responses. Moreover, the registration of shock forms a part of the loathing and anger with which the whole scene has been recreated.

There are several pointers to the shaping intention of Sassoon's imagination. 'Green' suggests gangrene, while at the same time setting up the green of nature, as a possibility which he dismisses. The word 'clumsy' suggests that the legs are not merely swollen but useless in death. It also emphasizes the detachment of the limb from its body and points to the violence that accomplished this. 'High-booted' is also doubly suggestive—of the arrogance of those who wore the boots when alive, but now pathetic and beyond vulnerability, yet revealing in their postures how vulnerable they had in fact been. Portions of the body, by being compared to 'trodden sand-bags', are shown to be no more animate, no higher up the scale of objective phenomena than what they are likened to; 'loosely' emphasizes the similarity but points also to the difference. What is effectually different, however, has been erased by war; though, if anything, the torn limbs are of even less *use* for the purpose of the survivors (to build a trench). Finally, but with more directness than Owen's 'Futility', the passage tells us that all this debris which was once alive is in the 'act' of coagulation, of sinking into the mud from which life once emerged, and this is pointed by the ironic 'slept'. The word itself is less explored than it is in Owen's poem. Sassoon is saying: if we are honest we shall not be able to afford the euphemism for death of 'slept'; the contrast is between the potential life, which slept before emerging, and death (its euphemism in 'sleep' exposing, in this context, the wastefulness of war). Finally, 'slept' is too dignified a word for the corpse that is not merely dead, but dismembered.

This notation is abruptly broken off with the living response to the rain: 'And then the rain began,—the jolly old rain!' This line makes an interesting contrast with the previous six (quoted above) in which recognition of barely human remains is made; in this line there is an animating human response, with some relief, to a non-human phenomenon. The phrase 'the jolly old rain', however, has something of a sting to it, verbalizing the back-slapping camaraderie not of the trenches but of the cricket-ground, and representing a class whose clichés have become insensitive, enervated, and which have little place here. This is also a way of reminding us that with the soldiers the phrase would be used ironically.

In the next stanza the Germans begin their counter-attack. The narrator observes a soldier who had once relaxed into yawning now alert with fear. Curiously, some of the aggression to be directed against the war has in some malign way rubbed off onto one of war's victims (as it more deliberately has in 'To any Dead Officer', and 'Glory of Women'). In the third stanza, 'An officer came blundering down the trench', and he is I think caricatured slightly by 'blundering'. The panic-stricken figure of authority announces what must be evident to anyone who was wondering when 'the Allemands would get busy'. The enemy move into attack and are repulsed, but not before the perception of the once yawning

soldier has been cut by death. Their counter-attack, like so many
of ours, 'had failed'. The undistinguished line of the last stanza,
'Down, and down, and down, he sank and drowned', crudely
attempts to convey sensations of dying, the diminishing of consciousness, through the analogy of drowning—itself tautological,
since drowning is also death. But since we also know little of what
it feels like to drown, and since moreover the diminishing of
consciousness by drowning is unsatisfactorily conveyed, we gain
little from the analogy. The failure is not merely one of inadequate
representation but of unclear thinking, and this is emphasized by
Sassoon's recourse to repetition; as though by reiteration the
idea would finally prove adequate. The difficulty is perhaps that at
this point Sassoon is not much concerned with recreating a sense
of individual death, but with using the man to represent the absurdity
and futility of the situation. *His* death is juxtaposed with the failure
of *their* counter-attack, and it is this perception that finally works.

'Wirers' picks up the same kind of perceptive bitterness:

> Young Hughes was badly hit; I heard him carried away,
> Moaning at every lurch; no doubt he'll die today.
> But *we* can say the front-line wire's been safely mended.

The matter-of-fact 'no doubt' reproduces the depreciation of
feeling that war entails (which is not to deny that it also provokes
extremes of compassion). The casual attitude to suffering and loss
is, on the surface at least, an infection necessary perhaps for our
immediate survival. The tone of voice becomes merged I think with
that of authority and its complacent boast, 'safely mended'. But
whatever the tone of voice is identified with, Sassoon shows that
the war damaged the mind as well as the flesh.[1]

One of the advantages of his ability to focus precisely on a
particular situation is his capacity to build up the outcry of the
human being under extreme pressure, as for instance in the last two
clinching lines of 'Attack':

> And hope, with furtive eyes and grappling fists,
> Flounders in mud. O Jesus, make it stop!

Noticeable here (and in contrast to 'Stand-to') is the controlled
use of religious exclamation and/or blasphemy, for the phrase here
is both an appeal and an expression of anguish.

---

[1] 'Damage inflicted on the mind did not count as illness' (*Sherston's Progress*, p. 523).

On the other hand, Sassoon has small regard for the civilized and enervated version of Christianity which, in polite society, glides over the surface of human suffering without a tremor of concern except that all be done with decorum:

> The dying soldier shifts his head
>   To watch the glory that returns;
> He lifts his fingers toward the skies. . . .
>
> But they've been taught the way to do it
>   Like Christian soldiers; not with haste
> And shuddering groans; but passing through it
>   With due regard for decent taste.

'Base Details' and 'The General', two of Sassoon's most anthologized poems, have as theme incompetent and callous military authority. The first poem, with its pun on 'base', parades the 'fierce' but incompetent middle-aged men, 'scarlet' in their uniform as in their over-dined complexions, who 'speed glum heroes up the line to death'. I have already suggested the ironic and compassionate juxtaposition of 'glum' with 'heroes' and would add only that this kind of clarity and anger in Sassoon's writing represents him, I think, at his best. The poem as a whole is built out of contradictions such as those present in this phrase. The actual fighting in the trenches is implicitly contrasted with the 'guzzling and gulping' of the armchair officers, who seem to have no comprehension of what the war entails. These, in the poem, are blown up with food, their gluttony an index of their indifference to 'their' men's suffering, and in contrast to the sparse rations of the soldier. The alert inserting of the detached manner in which the two men discuss the casualties, referring to combat in terms of a fierce game—'scrap'— is perhaps the most damaging way in which Sassoon could have exposed their insensitivity. The soldiers themselves might have used the word, but as a way of minimizing the terror of the experience, whereas in the mouths of the staff officers it is a figure of speech that terminates in its own verbal understatement without reference to the real situation.[1] There is also the suggestion that these men considered themselves to be in control of events,[2] as

[1] Newbolt inadvertently used the same kind of non-referential language, with perfect sobriety, in his poem 'The Best School of All'.

[2] The question of men's ability to control such events is of course one of Tolstoy's preoccupations in *War and Peace*.

though, being officers, the threads of destiny ran through their hands.

'The General' is a slighter poem with the same concerns. It works by placing before the reader two elements: firstly, the General who, it is hinted, once more misjudges his campaign and incurs large casualties; and, secondly, the two soldiers who, by their almost affectionate comments, reveal their trust in the General. This trust is not precisely betrayed since in war all generals will lose some men, but in this as in so many instances, the trust is frittered away in pointless offensives: 'he did for them both by his plan of attack'. The emphasis, I think, falls with ironic calm on 'plan'. The men's trust and acquiescence makes their sacrifice more possible. One might link these two poems with 'The Fathers' and note in both the brilliant juxtaposition of brutal facts with an elderly insensibility and bewildered ignorance.

'Fight to a Finish' is the poem that comes nearest to envisaging a revolutionary change. (One remembers that Sassoon held briefly a socialist position after the war, when he was literary editor of the *Daily Herald*.) The first stanza evidences his characteristic equipment—brisk scene-setting with ironic commentary built adjectivally into the situation:

> The boys came back. Bands played and flags were flying,
>   And Yellow-Pressmen thronged the sunlit street
> To cheer the soldiers who'd refrained from dying. . . .

How indecorous—Sassoon suggests—these surviving soldiers are, their survival arguing a lack of patriotism. Thus far the situation is seen from the 'Yellow' (not merely gutter press, but also cowardly?) Pressmen's, and civilians' position, but in the last two stanzas the emphasis shifts abruptly to the soldiers, who, having purposefully retained their weapons, at last release their aggression on those who have kept them fighting:

> I heard the Yellow-Pressmen grunt and squeal;
> And with my trusty bombers turned and went
> To clear those Junkers out of Parliament.

'Junkers' implies how much the ruling class on both sides had in common, as much as the soldiers fighting each other. Sassoon is indicating where he thought the natural alliances lay, and suggests that these should be formed. Needless to say, apart from brief mentions of the 'two nations', little of this gets into the *Memoirs*;

instead we have this sad admission, made approximately twelve years later in *Sherston's Progress*:

Yes; my mind was in a muddle; and it seemed that I had learned but one thing from being a soldier—that if we continue to accept war as a social institution we must also recognize that the Prussian system is the best, and Prussian militarism must be taught to children in schools. They must be taught to offer their finest instincts for exploitation by the unpitying machinery of scientific warfare. And they must not be allowed to ask why they are doing it.

Sassoon is not endorsing such a situation, naturally enough, but there is enough quietness in the tone of voice for us to suppose that he is not dismissing it as a possibility. What is unclear is whether this is merely a temporary conclusion reached by the younger Sherston under the stress of depression, or whether this is the older Sassoon inserting later conclusions, or clarifications.

There are further poems within the civilian target-area, and 'Glory of Women' and 'Their Frailty' should be taken together as assaults on those false appreciations of war which Sassoon, unfairly, suggests are the especial prerogative of women:

> . . . you believe
> That chivalry redeems the war's disgrace.
> You make us shells. You listen with delight,
> By tales of dirt and danger fondly thrilled.

'Fondly thrilled', however, seems uncannily accurate, locating how notions of honour and courage become thoughtlessly transmuted into a version of sexualized male glamour. Such a transmutation permits—if it does not augment—the possibility of further suffering.[1] Consider also the endless knitting by the womenfolk which, kind though it may have been, through its incessant activity suggests itself as not only a distraction from personal anxiety but a substitute for imagination:

> O German mother dreaming by the fire,
> While you are knitting socks to send your son
> His face is trodden deeper in the mud.

That last line seems unnecessarily brutal, however; aimed, it seems to me, at the mother, who is also a victim of war, although a lesser one than both her son and the other soldiers. The proper target

---

[1] Compare this with Owen's 'Dulce et Decorum Est'.

for Sassoon would again have been those who 'By choice . . .
made themselves immune/To pity'. Strangely enough, the very
directness of his treatment of the theme indicates how complex it
is and how it deserves more than the brisk, efficient treatment
Sassoon gives it.

A special problem is posed by the poem, 'To any Dead Officer'.
Although he is as much a victim of war as the private soldier,
Sassoon's attitude to him is not wholly sympathetic. The problem
is not that the victim forfeits his sympathy, but that he gets it
ambivalently. Yet if the crux is that officers were comparatively
privileged, this should surely not preclude sympathy for them. The
opening stanza unfolds an exaggerated mockery which is turned
partly upon the man, but mainly upon the sanctimoniousness that
surrounds those ideas concerning a 'compensatory' afterlife:

> Tell me, have you found everlasting day,
>   Or been sucked in by everlasting night?

The repetition of 'everlasting' initiates a conflict of attitudes within
two differing applications. 'Everlasting day' would imply an infinite
span of heavenly glory; 'everlasting night' suggests that the notions
concerning an afterlife compound a fiction, which in its turn mocks
the man, in that what he has found is nothingness. The next line
blends anguish and compassion:

> For when I shut my eyes your face shows plain;
>   I hear you make some cheery old remark—

The slightly disbelieving tone of 'cheery' is almost immediately
deepened by the recollection of the man: 'I can rebuild you in my
brain'. This switching of sympathy and alienation continues until,
in the last two stanzas, the poem begins to expand its focus to
include the suffering of all soldiers:

> 'Wounded and missing'—(That's the thing to do
> When lads are left in shell-holes dying slow,
>   With nothing but blank sky and wounds that ache,
> Moaning for water till they know
>   It's night, and then it's not worth while to wake!)

This expanded focus releases its anger on the negligent euphemism
'wounded and missing'. The rest of the stanza, however, is notable
for its *explicit* compassion, a response rather more rare in Sassoon

than anger. The poems ends with a complex blending of responses, and if the dominant one is an anguished irony, there is also a certain belied, ironic jauntiness:

> Goodbye, old lad! Remember me to God,
>   And tell Him that our politicians swear
> They won't give in till Prussian Rule's been trod
>   Under the Heel of England. . . .

Here a neat reversal is effected of the roles Prussia and England have traditionally—according to England—held. This jauntiness gives way to:

> Yes . . . and the War won't end for at least two years;
> But we've got stacks of men . . . I'm blind with tears,
>   Staring into the dark. Cheero!
> I wish they'd killed you in a decent show.

The dominating anxiety and despair have finally and clearly emerged, partly through the preparatory revelation of how false is the notion that the 'Heel of England' is the instrument of powerful and correct retribution. The inability to see clearly into the situation (Sassoon is implicitly claiming) is yet another apparently irremovable obstacle to the war's ending. The complex of points is thrust home by Sassoon's demonstration of the futility of the man's sacrifice in yet another 'hopeless dud-attack', a sacrifice that is merely one in an endless series of sacrifices. The strength of this assertion lies in its directness, as in his direct and moving response to the facts—'I'm blind with tears'. Nothing more subtle would have sufficed. But what solicits our responses so expertly are the sudden alterations of tone in this passage, together with the pastiches of official confident optimism—'But we've got stacks of men'—which is immediately undermined and made to give way to a glimpse of the men themselves. 'Stacks', in any case, not only incorporates the mindless cliché but emphasizes its vacuity by applying it, as perhaps the patriot mind did, to the numbers of lives available as war-fodder; lives as numerous as stacked shells, and as expendable.

The last of Sassoon's poems I want to consider is 'Repression of War Experience', and it is one that most nearly, I think, grasps a tragic vision. It does not reach it because of its concentration on the victim's anxiety as produced by war experience. Such concentration need not rob a poem of wholeness, but I think that Sassoon's effort to keep the reader's consciousness on the causes of the man's disturbance deprives the poem of its potential, by stimulating undue interest in the narrative and tendentious facts rather than in the man as he is, representative and yet unique. It is as though the poem has become a breathless sequence of anguished events. The danger with the 'tragic vision', on the other hand, is that it too easily contemplates the impulses in all human beings which create their unhappiness and reduction, and forgets in its cataclysmic intellectuality that it is human beings who comprise such a totality. This is all the more important in that the tragedy is democratically shared by millions; the danger would thus be to produce a simple diagram that enunciates the universal terror.

Sassoon's tendency is two-fold in that, on the one hand, he transcendentalizes (as in 'The Last Meeting') and, on the other, he must keep rigidly to the facts, the situation, the truth, with puritanical conviction. He is willing to relinquish the poetry as long as the truth remains. To some extent this helped him in that he was able to relinquish what *he* at one time regarded as poetry—the pastoral mode—in order to speak the truth about war. On the other hand, able to see only these two modes, the truth-telling 'visually submissive' mode was robbed of its potential which, had it been permitted to develop, might have fused fruitfully with the pastoral mode. I think this dilemma is the result of sensing the inappropriateness of his own pastoralism, but of being unable to assess in what ways it was inadequate, not only with regard to war, but as an instrument of expression. Thus I suspect Sassoon's practice, especially in this poem, of deliberately withholding poetic possibilities, while no less deliberately dissolving his ego in the truth-telling the war demanded of him. To see if these suppositions in any way correspond with the poem, we should look at it in some detail.

The moth that blunders into the flame suggests to the man the scorching experience of war:

> What silly beggars they are to blunder in
> And scorch their wings with glory, liquid flame—
> No, no, not that,—it's bad to think of war,
> When thoughts you've gagged all day come back to scare you. . . .

The connection Sassoon makes between glory (a kind of incandescence) and fire is tragically apt, and yet in this instance not full or felt enough. It might be objected that, for the sake of realism, he did not want yet to make the impact powerful until, that is, the man can no longer contain his fears. But it is also as though he had censored a metaphoric insight for the sake of verisimilitude; since, for instance, the man in the poem is not a poet and would not be as articulate as the metaphor would seem to make him had it been denser and more allusively complex. Even so, it is hard to tell how much the naïve pathos, obtained by the man's reliance on popular notions of how mental stability is maintained ('and it's been proved'), is character building, how much Sassoon's own ideas. Probably the poet is deliberately exploiting these popular notions, one of which is that a steady hand, the physical equivalent of a steady mind, demonstrates control over 'nerves':

> Now light your pipe; look, what a steady hand.
> Draw a deep breath; stop thinking; count fifteen,
> And you're as right as rain. . .
> > Why won't it rain? . . .

The sharp wandering of the mind back to the obsessive anxiety indicates the persistence of the shock. The desired release is expressed in

> I wish there'd be a thunderstorm to-night,
> With bucketsful of water to sluice the dark. . . .

The mind woefully tries to distract itself: 'Books; what a jolly company they are', but 'jolly', the companionable, gay word, shows the man's inability to break through the isolating effect of his experiences. 'Come on; O *do* read something; they're so wise.' More than wisdom is needed to release these memories of fear and guilt. 'So' is too pointed and directive, but the reappearance of the moth later shows what Sassoon can do by way of dramatically enacting a monologued situation:

> There's one big, dizzy moth that bumps and flutters;
> And in the breathless air outside the house
> The garden waits for something that delays.

This is genuinely frightening, and moving; the ominous recall—of stealthy combat perhaps—but of something else too, is retributively uncertain. The clumsiness of the moth suggests the man's emotional helplessness, and its movement parallels the movement of his hysteria nearly now beyond control. Catharsis must involve breaking the controls that hold back the painful memories. The breathless air conveys precisely his tension, partly a result of the effort for control. Then the memories refuse altogether to be excluded from his consciousness, and in the silence he hallucinatedly listens to the noise of the guns: 'Hark! Thud, thud, thud,—quite soft . . . they never cease'. It is not merely the noise, but the knowledge that it is hallucinatory, which finally makes him feel he is at the verges of madness, and breaks his control:

> Those whispering guns—O Christ, I want to go out
> And screech at them to stop—I'm going crazy;
> I'm going stark, staring mad because of the guns.

The man's helplessness is conveyed in several ways; perhaps the most moving one is implied in his need for that catharsis which entails a breakdown of those formal controls by which he consciously recognizes himself.

This is a fine poem, but it is marred, not so much by the headlong expression of the feeling as by the failure of those last lines to convey finely enough the sense of hysteria. This is involved with the failure to integrate the hysteria with the man; it is too frequently asserted by the narrator to exist, and this assertiveness is the result of the narrator/poet either not being completely merged with the man or else not being separate from him. 'Crazy . . . stark, staring mad' attempts to force by verisimilitude the man's fear of madness into existence, a force that perhaps derives from the confusion I have been describing.

There are perhaps other reasons for this failure. Sassoon was not only attempting to convey the torment suffered, but to use the cruel, seemingly limitless effect it had on those who endured it, as evidence; that is, as a weapon with which to awaken society's conscience. The impatience that such a desired objective must have produced in him—an objective only to be achieved by further insights—mars certain poems and shows a serious limitation in him as a poet. The size of the limitation is, however, an index of the achievement and the scope of the attempt. Yet Sassoon seems often to refuse to recognize that bald refutation and assertive description are not always adequate, especially if one is at the same time to persuade sensuously and experientially.

His poetic achievement is an external one; it is with events (and responses to them) to which he submits visually, whose effects are in their turn made submissive to his purposes. Within these qualifications, his poetry is concise and demanding. It fastens in the mind what Rosenberg called an 'impression', and very frequently, an 'idea'.

Fifty years have passed since he wrote these poems and their force has hardly diminished. This is not merely because society is still warring, although the poems I have been discussing are relevant in this, too. Analogues of conflict and suffering not only survive their original context, but keep the context in more general reapplicability after the original immediate effects of the context have gone. The verse itself, belonging as it does to the mode of commentary, and standing often in sharp distinction to the poetry of individualized and enacted response, retains its didactic feeling and interrelatedness with society compacted together, filling a verse form, keeping it live and insistent.

CHAPTER EIGHT

HERBERT READ, RICHARD ALDINGTON, AND FORD MADOX FORD

I

Read was born in 1893, the same year as Owen, near Kirbymoorside, Yorkshire. The vale in which he lived as a child had once been a lake and was 'flat as once the surface of the lake had been'. In *The Innocent Eye* he refers to the stillness of the rural world which in early years had helped nurture his mind's innocence. His father, who had been a farmer, died in 1903, and his next five years were spent in Crossley's boarding school, Halifax. Subsequently, he earned his living as a bank clerk in Leeds until, when he was eighteen, he entered the University; although, as he writes in *The Contrary Experience*, 'what basis of disciplined education had been devised by the university authorities was completely swamped' by his own voracious reading. He speaks of his education by contrasting 'Character' with 'Personality', observing the connection between 'the force, the steadiness, the comprehensiveness and the versatility of intellect, the command over our own powers' with 'the normal process of university education, in other words, the release from the older universities of men apt for the "Civil Service or business" '. To the building of 'character' and this 'disciplined education' with its closing of the mind and the senses, he opposes 'personality', which 'is distinguished by immediacy and what I would call lability, or the capacity to change without loss of integrity'. Where 'character' is built through 'limitation', 'personality' has 'the senses . . . open to every impression which falls upon them, and the mind surrenders to its environment'. This important contrast indicates the desirability of growth as a part of personality, and the likelihood of little growth resulting from the formation of 'character'; this formation being 'moral . . . its "taste" . . . rational rather than aesthetic . . . historical rather than experimental'. Although in implying a distinction between rational and moral on the one hand, and aesthetic and labile on the other, it would *seem* that personality is to exclude morality. Yet the important ingredient of growth may perhaps for Read be taken to assume morality, growth of each individual achieved by education through art (and art perhaps through an apprehension of nature). His opposing of 'free sensibility' to 'academic sterilization' is a part of this complex.

In his note 'What is a Poem?' (*Collected Poems*, 1966) Read makes clear how important Imagism was, not only in the development of his own poetry, but also in the poetry of England and America in the twentieth century. The Imagist principles were:

1. To use the language of common speech, but to employ always the *exact* word, not the nearly exact, nor the merely decorative word.
2. To create new rhythms—as the expression of new moods. . . .
3. To allow absolute freedom in choice of subject. . . .
4. To present an image. . . . We are not a school of painters, but we believe that poetry should render particulars exactly and not deal in vague generalities. . . .
5. To produce poetry that is hard and clear, never blurred nor indefinite.
6. Finally, most of us believe that concentration is of the very essence of poetry.

In 1918 Read published his own 'definitions' in *Art and Letters*:

1. Form is determined by the emotion which requires expression. *Corollary:* Form is not an unchanging mould into which any emotion can be poured.
2. The poem is an artistic whole demanding strict unity.
3. The criterion of the poem is the quality of the vision expressed, granted that the expression is adequate. *Corollary:* Rhyme, metre, cadence, alliteration, are various decorative devices to be used as the vision demands, and are not formal qualities pre-ordained.

The suggestion perhaps is that the formal demands of Imagism were shown to be inadequate by the experiences of the war. Thus, the idea of form being determined both by the emotion and 'the quality of the vision' (rather than by the image) is now the crucial principle. Read in fact makes specific objections to Imagism in *The Contrary Experience*:

I criticized them because 'in their manifestoes they had renounced the decorative word, but their sea-violets and wild hyacinths tend to become as decorative as the beryls and jades of Oscar Wilde'. . . . We were trying to maintain an abstract aesthetic ideal in the midst of terroful and inhuman events. In my own case I am certain that this devotion to abstract notions and intellectual reveries saved me from a raw reaction to these events. But as the war went on, year after year, some compromise between dream and reality became necessary. The only worthy compromise, I even then dimly realized, was a synthesis—some higher reality in which the freedom of the mind and the necessity of experience became reconciled.

Read's own poems reveal the justice of this, if one compares, for instance, *Eclogues* (*1914–18*) with *War Poems* (*1916–32*).[1] The poems of the former are imagistic, and only one or two show the influence of the war. 'Appeal' is a good example of his early manner:

> O dark eyes, I am weary
> Of the white wrath of the sea.
>
> O come with me to the vernal woods
> The green sap and the fragrant
> White violets.

Compare that with 'The Happy Warrior':

> His wild heart beats with painful sobs
> His strain'd hands clench an ice-cold rifle
> His aching jaws grip a hot parch'd tongue
> His wide eyes search unconsciously.
>
> He cannot shriek.
>
> Bloody saliva
> Dribbles down his shapeless jacket.
>
> I saw him stab
> And stab again
> A well-killed Boche.
>
> This is the happy warrior.
> This is he. . . .

[1] One senses that Read regrouped his poems in the most recent edition of the *Collected Poems* (1966) with this distinction in mind. Thus, the dates quoted above are taken from the earlier *Collected Poems* (1953). But in the 1966 edition, *Eclogues* is dated 1919 (the publication date: Notes p. 277); and the earlier group *War Poems* (*1916–1932*) is regrouped, making *Naked Warriors* (*1919*) (the publication date) a unit on its own. There is also a note (p. 278) to the effect that 'The poems in *Naked Warriors* were written some time before the date of publication, most of them in the years 1916–17'. There follow in the 1966 edition four 'hitherto uncollected poems . . . written in 1915–16' (Notes p. 278): 'Aeroplanes', 'Ypres', 'The Autumn of the World', and 'Auguries of Life and Death' (this last in memory of his brother Charles Read, killed in action on 5 October 1918). These four all date from the period of the First War. 'The End of a War', which in the earlier edition was grouped with *War Poems* (*1916–1932*), is, in the 1966 edition, given as a separate unit, on its own, and is dated 1933 (its publication date). The regroupings in the 1966 edition indicate, I think, a literary and historical distinction; whereas the 1953 (or '46) groupings of the 'war poems' indicate experiential units. In other words, the war as the sole or main grouping principle has been partly displaced in the 1966 edition by the claims of 'style' and literary history as an at least comparably important principle.

Johnston dismisses this poem, saying that

[it] attempt[s] to portray the psychological effects of warfare, but both amount to little more than abbreviated notations. . . . the realistic and satiric impulse is not much different from Sassoon's; it has merely been compressed to conform to the *Imagist* principle of verbal economy [my italics].

Certainly the similarity between the two poems above is marked, as far as *structure* is concerned. The lineation is governed by an image or an idea, and a new line adds an image or an idea; if it does not it (usually) breaks the syntax at the line-ending for some deliberate effect. For, as Read himself suggested:

The war came, but that did not make any essential difference to our poetry. I myself wrote imagist poems in the trenches, and did not see or feel any inconsistency in the act. War was one thing, and poetry was another; and if war was to be expressed in poetry, the imagist technique was as adequate as any other.[1]

Yet if war and poetry were isolated phenomena apprehended by one mind, in what sense could the two be fruitfully kept apart?

There are three distinct problems here, two of them related to each other. The first is Read's growing awareness, immediately subsequent to the war, that the imagist technique, whatever it maintained about 'absolute freedom in the choice of subject', was nevertheless inadequate to cope with a re-creation of war's experiences. The other problem is, as Read expresses it in the above quotation, that the imagist demands had that quality of hermeticism which enabled those who used or were governed by them to take them as if they were both the means and the ends of their poetry. They permitted, and perhaps even partially entailed, a reduction of or even a separation between the experiences of war and the writing of imagist poetry.[2] The third problem is that raised by Johnston's strictures on 'The Happy Warrior'. Clearly, this poem is imagistic and would therefore seem to belie the problem as to whether imagism could adequately accommodate war's experiences; but my suggestion is that this is an exceptional case; that on one level it is a poem concerned with reproducing an incisive experience, and that for once the imagist demands and the war's coincide.

[1] *Kenyon Review*, I, No. 4 (Autumn 1939).
[2] But see Ungaretti's poems of this period.

Clearly, too, it has much in common with Sassoon's poetry, in
that it shocks the reader into recognition of the true nature of war.
So that, despite the imagistic concealment of the idea in the lines
'This is the happy warrior,/This is he', the poem nevertheless
manages to make its reference to Wordsworth's poem 'Character of
the Happy Warrior', and it is upon this reference that it mounts
a criticism of Wordsworth's ideas and thus initiates its own.

> Who is the happy Warrior? Who is he
> That every man in arms should wish to be?
> —It is the generous Spirit, . . .
> Whose high endeavours are an inward light . . .
> Who, with a natural instinct to discern
> What knowledge can perform, is diligent to learn; . . .
> . . . rendered more compassionate; . . .
> He labours good on good to fix, and owes
> To virtue every triumph that he knows: . . .
> And, through the heat of conflict, keeps the law
> In calmness made, . . .
> —He who, though thus endued as with a sense
> And faculty for storm and turbulence,
> Is yet a Soul whose master-bias leans
> To home-felt pleasures and to gentle scenes; . . .
> More brave for this, that he hath much to love. . . .

Wordsworth's key evaluative words—'generous', 'moral', 'gentle',
'compassionate'—contrast with the image of Read's warrior. He
has no 'high endeavours'; his actions do not show us 'his moral
being as his prime care'; he cannot, in war, retain laws 'in calmness
made'. We have no sense of his 'master-bias' leaning 'to home-felt
pleasures and to gentle scenes', no sense of self-possession, but
only hysteria and blood lust:

> I saw him stab
> And stab again
> A well-killed Boche.

'Bloody saliva dribbles' materializes our sense of the man's hysteria:
he is not even properly aware that his enemy is dead.
    Read's terms not only refute those of Wordsworth (who had, in
any case, no direct understanding of combat) but correct our notion
of what men are, or become, in the stress of combat. In Read's

poem the antique word 'warrior', with its aura of heroism, is doubtfully used. Perhaps the poem was additionally aimed at Yeats (as was 'Naked Warriors') and his concern with heroic ideals. But above all, Read stresses here the impossibility of a soldier fulfilling Wordsworth's idealism. He is expressing, as Owen did in 'Arms and the Boy', man's corruption under the duress of war; that is, the unleashing of instincts which destroy the fabric of what little civilized behaviour we have acquired. By forcing upon us this realization, Read indicates that compassion between enemies (in action, at least) must be almost non-existent, and directs a further criticism at Wordsworth. At the same time he offers a realistic alternative to those who imagine that society will remain unaffected and uncorrupted by war.

'The Happy Warrior' is a central poem in the group entitled 'The Scene of War'. Some of its rhythmical movements occur in other poems, 'The Refugees', for example:

> They do not weep:
> their eyes are too raw for tears.

And one of its ideas finds expansion in 'Fear'. A further adaptation of imagist technique, for the purposes of sharp narrative information, is made in 'Leidholz'—a poem whose source is to be found in *A War Diary*. The laconic absurdity of the situation is well within the range of imagism's detachment and hardness:

> We met in the night at half-past one
> between the lines.
> Leidholz shot at me
> And I at him.

The three longer poems in *Naked Warriors* incorporate something of Read's shift in attitudes. 'Kneeshaw Goes to War' describes a man unable to assert his will, even though creative forces are slowly wakening in him:

> But even when his body burned and urged
> Like the buds and roots around him,
> Abash'd by the will-less promptings of his flesh. . . .

At Boulogne he is touched by the strength, variousness, and heroic sense of venture felt at seeing the assembled ships; but the 'romantic fringes' of his fantasies are brutally invaded by trench warfare. A man sinks into the mud:

> They could not dig him out—
> The oozing mud would flow back again. . . .
> An officer shot him through the head:
> Not a neat job—the revolver
> Was too close.

In all three situations, even the last, the 'labile' possibility of growth with its subsequent formation of will (choice, belief, action) confronts Kneeshaw. Of course, the first two situations of sexuality and venture contrast with the third one of horror, but all three imply the possibility of choice. How shall he behave? What shall he feel? Kneeshaw does not choose; he passively undergoes. The imagist forms are more noticeably used in the second quotation, but something new has crept into both—an emotion, and an idea—which is perhaps not easily integrated with imagistic writing. Moreover, both are deployed in what is essentially a narrative structure, which is again subservient to the poem's overall idea. In addition, each stage in the narrative is what now governs the lineation, and the flow of images is largely pictorial of the narrative unfolding.

Subsequently Kneeshaw is wounded, but not before he has become more actively conscious of war. Finally his 'war-song' expresses an insight into himself in which he recognizes that he had not enough will to defect from a war to which his humanity and sensuousness were opposed:

> *Judas no doubt was right*
> *In a mental sort of way:*
> *For he betrayed another and so*
> *With purpose was self-justified.*
> *But I delivered my body to fear—*
> *I was a bloodier fool than he.*

Which is to say: Judas did what he willed, but though I killed with my hands (as Judas did not) I lacked the will to do otherwise. Hence 'bloodier'. Now he can respond to the 'Beauty of the still tarn' and aligned with such active response is the recognition of these essentials:

> *To speak truth and so rule oneself*
> *That other folk may rede.*

That others may understand. And like Owen's 'Strange Meeting',
the truth they are to understand is the truth concerning war—as
Read speaks of it in 'Ode' (1940):

> —only a resolve
> to tell the truth without rhetoric
> the truth about war and about men
> involved in the indignities of war.

'My Company' records the experience of a captain who becomes
absorbed into the communal life of the company he commands:[1]

> In many acts and quiet observances
> you absorbed me. . . .

In their joint experience it seems to him as though the company
developed in unison a sacred quality, a 'radiance', which in its
turn becomes allusive:

> They bear wooden planks . . .
> through the area of death

and explicitly so:

> My men, my modern Christs
> your bloody agony confronts the world.

There is a strange interlude:

> In godlike mood
> I laugh till space is filled
> with hellish merriment.

This is hard to characterize, but it is as though his men's vulnerability provokes a *schadenfreude* that obtains from his sense of
responsibility for them. It also implies a shedding of that responsibility. When this delight in others' pain passes, responsibility
for them returns:

> Then again I assume
> my human docility
> bow my head
> and share their doom.

---

[1] Here again there is an interesting shift of emphasis in Read's regroupings. In the
1953 edition, 'My Company' and 'Cornelius Vane' are un-numbered poems, therefore
not part of a group; whereas in the 1966 edition these are numbered and thus aligned
with their more imagistic neighbours.

His principal responsibility is to share their afflictions, and in that way engender a true compassion.

'The Execution of Cornelius Vane' examines the problem of courage and cowardice. Like 'Kneeshaw', it plots a man's internal dislocation from an external situation. The two poems may be read as mutually supporting explorations of one predicament:

> 'I, Cornelius Vane,
> A fly in the sticky web of life,
> Shot away my right index finger.'

This, so that he would be unable to use his rifle, and face

> ... their hosts spread over the plains
> Like unleash'd beads.

The comic relegation of Vane to the cookhouse is skilfully achieved:

> For nearly a year Cornelius peeled potatoes
> And his life was full of serenity.

When, however, everyone is suddenly needed to fight, Cornelius indicates 'his fingerless hand'. The sergeant bluntly observes, 'But you can stab.' This has the abrupt movement of imagist poetry, but in its context it achieves a different effect by directing attention not on, but rather, through, the image and on to the central character. Pathos and the comic element in the situation check any impulse we may feel to condemn Vane for betraying his comrades—through fear. It is checked again when, after running away, he is caught. About to be executed, he says to those who are to kill him:

> 'What wrong have I done that I should leave these:
> The bright sun rising
> And the birds that sing?'

As with Kneeshaw, nature is brought in at a crucial moment and used to convey and evaluate the man's sense of life's worth. Nature, forgetting the mud and rain that made such havoc of the trenches, is always, in these instants, beneficent and used as a touchstone to contrast with the hideousness of war. One further contrast emerges between Kneeshaw and Vane. Kneeshaw was not in the obvious sense a coward, and like many, one supposes, fought in the end because he had to. Vane defected, through fear; but he had also the will to defect. If we put the two poems together, we are finally left with the alienation that both men experience in relation to their context:

> I did not discover I was brave
> until I had sheltered in a ditch with a coward.

Unlike the poems so far considered, 'The End of a War' was (according to Read) written between 1931 and 1932—that is, long after the war. In 1933 it was published and was the only 'war poem' Yeats wished to include in *The Oxford Book of Modern Verse* (1936). Yeats's reasons for the other exclusions—and they are numerous—are well known, but since the reasons perhaps provide some oblique criticism of Read's poem, they should be cited:

I have a distaste for certain poems written in the midst of the great war . . . but I have substituted Herbert Read's *The End of a War* written long after. . . . I have rejected these poems for the same reason that made Arnold withdraw his *Empedocles on Etna* from circulation;[1] passive suffering is not a theme for poetry. In all great tragedies, tragedy is a joy to the man who dies. . . . When man has withdrawn into the quicksilver at the back of the mirror no great event becomes luminous in his mind; it is no longer possible to write *The Persians, Agincourt, Chevy Chase*: some blunderer has driven his car on to the wrong side of the road—that is all.

If war is necessary, or necessary in our time and place, it is best to forget its suffering as we do the discomfort of fever. . . . (pp. xxxiv–xxxv.)

Read, in *The Contrary Experience*, questions Yeats's judgement on passive suffering and its relation to poetry: 'Even passive suffering can be a fit theme for poetry if seen objectively enough. . . . The direct expression of suffering is an animal cry; poetry, too, is an animal cry, but of another kind.' One might add an overall comment on Read's poetry to the effect that sometimes the difference between these two cries is excessive in that the one has lost touch with the other.

Yet 'The End of a War' is a remarkable poem. It sets out passive suffering, nationalism, righteousness, and faith in a context where they qualify each other until some kind of conclusion is obtained.

---

[1] Arnold restored it in the 1867 edition of his *New Poems*.

Of Read's two prose accounts of the war, *In Retreat* (1925) and *Ambush* (1930), Francis Berry writes:

> There remains to note the enduring effects, after it is over, of an experience, so central and deep in a man's life, which remains for him an enigma. To go on living, during the height of one's intellectual powers, without being able to assimilate one's chief emotional and nervous experience to the pattern of the entire rest of one's knowledge and feeling, is a frustrating burden for anyone to carry.[1]

The question of assimilation is a crucial one. Of the one hundred and eighty pages of Read's *Collected Poems* (1953) eighty are devoted to 'war poems', and many of the other poems carry references to war. 'The End of a War' was written twelve years after the armistice, while the poems of the Spanish Civil War and Second World War still contain references to the First War, or are in other ways spectred by it. Yet Berry's remark about Read being unable 'to assimilate [his] chief emotional and nervous experience' raises a number of questions. As I understand it, his meaning is that Read's poetry *suffers* from the experience of war in that it remains unassimilated. The judgement partly depends on whether one believes that such an experience should be assimilated; that whether, as the principal experience of our century so far, it ought not to remain the constant reference point (implicit or not) by which other events in other poems are validated. It is, in any case, arguable whether poetry should be consolatory. 'Assimilate' also hinges on whether the war's presence in Read's poetry displaces everything else. Far from doing this, it remains, I think, a constant evaluating factor in his work.

Johnston maintains that Read 'excluded adequate realization of the sensuous levels of experience'; and it should be admitted that, in attempting to objectify his experience in a form that would encompass universal and particular truths, Read does not solve his equation. The sensuousness is of a particular kind, and there is little narrative element in 'The End of a War'. On the other hand, one takes the prose argument with one's reading of the poem; and certainly, its incidents are unforgettably brutal. The three principal characters in the argument correspond to the three sections of the poem, and the sections are, in a sense, interpretations of the events in the argument. Conversely, the prose narration qualifies the meditative quality of the poetry, and prevents the reader from

[1] Francis Berry, *Herbert Read* (1961).

entirely withdrawing into the meditative ambiance the poem
induces.

Yet it is not entirely true to say the poem lacks sensuousness.
Thinking has its own form of this, and so has the poem. In addition,
certain of the images have interlocking sensuous associations with
war, and such sensuousness acts as a link between the experience
of war and the thinking of it. To complain, therefore, that the
poem lacks sensuousness—because its responsiveness is different
from other poems—is unreasonable. Nor am I entirely sure with
Berry that 'Read's interests and achievements were, from the start,
primarily formal', whether this applies to 'The End of a War' or
not. The firmness of surface, the uniting (in both senses) of idea
and image, the distancing of the poem from the reader—these are
more controlled by the events from which the poem issues than they
were in the earlier poems, where considerable attention was paid
to 'objective' formulae governing their structure.

In the 'Meditation of the Dying German Officer' one crucial
'fact' in his life is obtained through glimpsing his relationship with
the Christian, Heinrich. This 'Nothing' is what 'Heinrich made
his argument for God's existence'. But for the officer 'The void is
icy', and he employs a scepticism that hides perhaps the fears and
the faith he rejects—'a concept beyond mind's reach'. For him
faith consists of a nationalism in which men are drawn together:

> The world is full of solid creatures—these
> are the mind's material, these we must mould
> into images, idols to worship and obey:
> The Father and the Flag. . . .

When death and chaos intervene, crumbling the empire (but not
his faith), nothing remains, for the world in 'folly' has rejected all
of this. To the Christian faith is opposed a faith in the supremacy
of a particular sovereign state (presumably triumphant at least as
early as Bismark's victory over the Austrians in 1866).

> When the last jump comes
> and the axe-head bláckness slíps through flésh
> that wélcomes it with ópen but unquívering líps
> thén Í shall be óne with the Unknown. . . .

The 'axe-head blackness' expresses not only decapitation (and the
officer's oncoming death) but the empire's extinction. The rhythmical movement of these lines is unquestionably sensuous—the

heavy strokes of the second leading into the fluttering movement in the first part of the third, and followed by a steadying stoic reassertion of calmness in the face of death. It is beautifully managed and, although one may feel that the poem needs perhaps more of such intensifying movements and imagery, the passage effectively demonstrates Read's especial sensuousness, inward, firm, and quiet.

The question of the man's ecstasy in battle—'I fought with gladness'—is neither shirked nor over-emphasized by Read:

> ... the wound
> seared in the burning circlet of my spirit
> served only to temper courage. ...

Without accepting the ecstasy, one should couple it with the cause to which he is devoted; the ecstasy is compounded of zealousness and an active rage in combat. This is not mitigation, even if it is in contrast to the happy warrior, who is entirely mindless in his 'activity'. And if one admires the man's courage, one must notice that fear does exist for him in the Christian 'abstraction' which 'freezes the blood at death'. It is the void which terrifies. Heinrich's Christian conception of love is too stark and isolated for him. His love may involve a form of renunciation, but it is essentially a link with other human beings. His personal responses and his nationalism are of a piece. 'Faith in self comes first', but this faith is built up into a complex of human beings whose ultimate focus and authority is the state, whose 'web' is made durable through the 'weft'. The 'weft' is all things made by, and which body forth, the Fatherland —the landscape, the town, the language, the songs—which, in a maundering sentimentality, get caught up in the 'music ... of our Fatherland'. The glib association of heard music with the outworn metaphor for the state's spiritual cohesion works against the would-be enriching metaphor the man is trying to construct. It impairs the register of his faith which, ironically, is in tangible things that are destroyed in death. The destruction of the empire and its rejection by the rest of the world is the destruction of that faith. It is perhaps because such recognitions are implicitly acknowledged that, in an effort to assert a permanence for his faith comparable to Christianity's, he asserts, as he is dying, the mind's idealism. It is an idealism aristocratically abstracted from the empire's creed, which demands a certain stoic and individual

purity. The mind 'rises like a crystal sphere above the rigid wreck'.
What remains

> is petulant scorn, implanted passions,
> everything not tensely ideal.

'Courage is not born in men, but born of love' is an important
line because it implies that the differing idealisms of the German
soldier and the murdered French girl have a shared component;
and it is more than an irony that these idealisms are opposed to
each other. The question of faith is delicate in that evaluation of it
depends not only on what its demands consist of, but also on the
nature of the resulting actions issuing from these demands. But it
could be said that the tendency of faith is towards autonomy, and
thus the exclusion of those for whom the faith is not operative; it
may be more binding than the assumptions of the human contract.
The German soldier's faith led him into a violation of the trust his
enemies extended to him. Such trust means little to him, and his
own words are dictated by faith that excludes everything which
does not serve the 'flag'. Trust does not mean universal trust but
only between the citizens of the empire. On the other hand, because
the German soldier was wounded and defenceless, his enemies did
not, at first, kill him; some form of trust was unilaterally employed.
'We will not kill you,' they seem to say, 'but we do not expect
deception from you, because we have renewed a binding and
universal human contract.' The German's betrayal is if possible
worsened by the fact that the machine guns open fire 'chiefly from
the tower of a church'. The so-called universal implications of
Christianity are deliberately, or casually, disregarded. This fact
underlines the extreme exclusivity of the German soldier's faith.
Yet in considering trust we should notice that it works in the poem
in both directions. The French girl had previously betrayed those
who had permitted her to live after they had occupied her village:

> My sacrifice was made to gain
> the secrets of these hostile men.

The trust put upon her is of course less direct and demanding, but
in both cases it should be seen that it is a trust extended to the
weaker by the stronger. In both cases the trust is betrayed. The

vengence rendered on each of them is blood-thirsty, but it would
be unjust to suggest that the German soldier was the more especially
deserving of it. The girl acted out of her sense that God and France
were equally worthy of being served. Yet in that case her faith,
within the terms on which the German's faith was evaluated, must
also be questioned; the debate between the girl's body and the soul
is an examination of her motives in which the purity of her faith is
questioned, partly with these qualifications in mind. The *body*,
accounting for its actions, explains that the body's innocence was
capacitated by the soul to 'love and hate'; and this dual capacity
(the suspension of which is innocence) is excited to action by the
occupation of enemy soldiers, 'swift, grim, scorning, exulting'. This
hate for her enemies and love for her motherland is increased, as I
sense it, by her loss of sexual innocence—a hate based in as spiritual
a love for France as is the German's for his country. The difference
between them is that whereas her final appeal was to Christ,

> But still I swear
> Christ was my only King

his was to his nation. It is a difference of dubious validity, since the
faith of both leads to betrayal and bloodshed. With France for her
motherland and Christ for her King, her cause was for her sanctified
by the ultimate spiritual authority of Christ. Or, more subtly, once
the purity of her cause had been established in her mind, then the
purity of Christ could be made subservient to her cause by seeing
Him as endorsing it. Of course, the equation can work the other
way, and in reality no doubt such a situation would circuit in either
and in both directions. But this is to say little more than that her
justifying of her cause, through Christ, was no more superior
than the German's regard for his. It is by their fruits you shall
know them; and by their motives you may evaluate them. The girl's
actions are at least as animated by hatred for her enemy as by love
of her cause; so the German is animated by the ecstasy of battle as
well as by his cause. The ecstasy of battle may be dubious, but the
girl's motivation is open to question too.

In the debate between the body and the soul, partly formalized
into two-line stanzas, disagreement emerges, which the stichomythia emphasizes. One cause for disagreement occurs within the
context of the girl's conscious martyrdom:

BODY

I died for France.

SOUL

A bright mantle fell across your bleeding limbs.
Your face averted shone with sacred fire.
So be content. In this war
many men have perished not bless'd
with faith in a cause, a country or a God
not less martyrs than Herod's victims. . . .

The girl's sense of her sacred dedication contrasts with those who perish in war without the sustaining belief in a cause or centre of spiritual rightness, such as she feels herself to possess. People therefore have nothing to comfort themselves with. They too, the soul asserts, are martyrs. In its pride the body answers:

Such men give themselves not to their God but to their fate
die thinking the face of God not love but hate.

Recalling Kneeshaw's inability to choose, one may feel traces of justice here, but the defensiveness of the body indicates the impurities of pride in its motivation. Moreover, it has itself forgotten how its 'seedling hate' grew. Her self-love, with its unremitting sense of superiority over those who die without sacred attachment to a cause, distorts her actions, and her assessment of them. The soul offers its rebuke:

Those who die for a cause die comforted and coy;
believing their cause God's cause they die with joy.

The extent of belief in the sacredness of one's actions is neither a measure of those actions, nor of the cause, nor of the cost to others who have no cause. 'Comforted and coy/joy' with its rhyme disconcerts the self-sanctification, and points to the narcissism. 'Coy' indicates withdrawal into self-admiration, and its rhyme with 'joy' asks us to question the appropriateness of the self-celebration of the martyrdom. The cause, that is, was not exclusively this one person's, but the country's, and was moreover supposed, ultimately, to be God's. The pride is shown as gathering to itself a triumph it is incapable of sharing, not least with those who died causeless. This is quite apart from whether one can be sure that one's country's cause is God's.

7

The third Meditation opens with the English officer waking to the beginning of peace. The peasants stirring behind the screen 'intone a litany', which at first seems concordant with the officer's incredulity at having survived the war; but this gives way to the realization that 'In excess of horror/war died' and that 'fray'd men fought obscenely'. In contrast to the German officer, for him

> . . . there was no fair joy
> no glory in the strife. . . .

Unlike the French girl, he felt 'no blessed wrath', 'no hate', and more like Kneeshaw than the German officer, he 'answered no call'. Like Kneeshaw he felt 'the storm' about him, and like Kneeshaw and Vane, experienced some identity with beneficent nature, but he is more conscious and articulate than either man. He relates, in sensuous terms, his individual helplessness to a young tree 'toss'd' in the storms. In such a context the hearts of men were no more than 'insentient engines pumping blood'. In such a destructive situation, the only evaluation he can make is that

> . . . the infinite is all
> and I, a finite speck, no essence even
> of the life that falls like dew. . . .

Life evanesces more rapidly than dew—where life is seen as the dew breathed on to matter:

> . . . the life that falls like dew
> from the spirit breathed on the fine edge
> of matter. . . .

This sensuous delicacy is finely conceived and serves to convey the ephemeral quality of life, in war especially. The thinking and the sensuousness of the thought are each a part of the other. The sensuousness, however, has no meaningfulness for him within the system he has so far evolved:

> Where all must be, there is no God
> for God can only be the God of prayer
> an infinitely kind Father whose will
> can mould the world. . . .

Yet if this is so, why does God not mould the world into peaceableness; and since He does not, can we believe in the existence of such a will? Unable to pray he

> . . . can't believe
> but in this frame of machine necessity
> must renounce not only God, but self.
> For what is the self without God?

What is God without His creation? Like the German, the French girl was absorbed into a 'greater good'; the English officer suffers no absorption of this kind (although absorbed into the war itself) but exists without a sense of self, God, or faith, and as within the 'frame of machine necessity'. Loss of belief is concomitant with participation in the 'deathly offices' of war; 'Fate is in facts', and the facts appear to militate against God's existence. Hell's ringing bells are perhaps sounding for the German, who had a faith of a kind, but not for the English officer who has none. The implication is that he would prefer the faith of the former (with hell) to his present position. Thus, ironically, the German feared the void of the after-life, which void the English officer feels in his mortal life. Yet it is a void he suffers from his lack of belief. He perceives a kind of visionary quality in the German's face:

> Your fair face was noble of its kind
> some visionary purpose cut the lines
> clearly on that countenance.

The 'meek' have defeated this 'visionary purpose', but their early 'devotion to the rights of men' has died. The choices seem to be these: either the life-force is 'mechanic', bringing the inevitable consequence of human primitivity and violence; or God's obscure purpose in trying us is to temper us and produce some 'finer stock'. Without either believing or denying the possibility of this latter idea, the English officer opens to it, and joins his prayers with those of the country people:

> doubting till the final grace a dove
> from Heaven descends and wakes the mind . . .
> in light celestial
> infinite and still
> eternal
> bright

Yet the praying signifies for him a defeat of a kind—an erosion of
his idealism (although perhaps leaving him with an openness
tempered through experience). For if he rejects war's 'mechanic
force' (fatality), there remains to him the idea of God as a Tambur-
laine-like power tempering the soldier through suffering. This is,
in effect, a version of conservative fatality and is in contrast to his
earlier 'devotion to the rights of men', for here man's choosing for
man has reverted to a schemata in which God has absolute jurisdiction. The fatality may be more acceptable than that of blind
chance since God is sentient and his design has intent (unlike
Hardy's It in *The Dynasts*). But the jurisdiction deprives man of
his small but crucial area of choice and responsibility, and puts
him once more into the position of a trusting child. If this is what
the English officer's prayer implies, as it seems to, then the war
has destroyed even for the quite 'humble' man the chance of trying
to implement his ideals and make choices. He is at most 'labile',
open to the possibility of constructive ends, but the means are
God's and not his. In this he contrasts with the German officer,
who dies with his will intact yet believing in the ultimate *dis*harmony
of things:

> no music of the spheres—and so break with a sigh
> against the ultimate
> shores of this world
> so finite
> so small
> Nichts

In his final note to this poem Read remarks: 'It is not my business
as a poet to condemn war. . . . I only wish to present the universal
aspects of a particular event. Judgement may follow, but should
never precede or become embroiled with the act of poetry.' It is
difficult to see how judgement (evaluation) of some kind did not
precede the poem. The selection of events itself implies a predeter-
mining evaluative act; but perhaps what Read means is that it is
the poet's business to keep the *reader's* evaluative faculties open for
as long as possible until the whole experience has been rendered.
In this sense, Read's poem forms the strongest possible contrast
with Sassoon's war poetry and perhaps, finally, produces a stronger
effect through its culminative nature. It is certainly concerned with
evaluating the war in relation to the framework of peace.

2

Inasmuch as Aldington's and Read's literary and historical contexts have much in common, I consider them in the same chapter, although the collocation does not imply great similarity between them as poets. It is more for the convenience of pointing to the war and to Imagism that they are so placed. Both draw attention to the fact that they shared alike the war *and* Imagism; that in such a dual context each contained in himself the possibility of integrating the two experiences of literary and social upheaval, assuming that such an integration was possible.

Richard Aldington was born in Hampshire in 1892, the year of Pound's birth, and one associates some of his earlier published verse with the Imagist movement. His contribution to the anthology *Des Imagistes* (1914) was larger than that of any other poet—ten poems, nine of which he re-published in the section 'Images' in the *Complete Poems* (1948). In his Introduction to that book he remarks:

The beginning of the 'new poetry' or of 'modernist poetry' . . . is generally placed in . . . 1912. . . . I claim no share . . . in the so-called 'revolution of 1912'. It was mere accident that what I was writing then chanced to meet with the approval of the verse revolutionaries. . . . Willy-nilly I have been associated with the 'revolt of 1912', and I think it appropriate to say a few words to dissociate myself from attitudes towards poetry which are not mine.

Aldington's wishes are reasonable in that they warn us off making a value judgement on his poems merely in terms of Imagist verse; although I suspect his dissociation may be designed to imply his own originality. But of course a poet has the right to have his work evaluated in relation to a variety of poets rather than made to compete inside one inclusive and limiting norm.

Aldington enlisted as a private in 1916, the year that Rosenberg sailed for France, and something of the quality of such choice emerges, I think, from a passage in *Death of a Hero* (1928). Winterbourne, the central figure in the novel, is asked by his officer if he would volunteer for a commission:

Winterbourne hesitated. He didn't want the responsibility; it was contrary to his notion that he ought to stay in the ranks and in the line, take the worst and humblest jobs, share the common fate of common men. But then, he had consented to be a runner. And then, he was sorely tempted. It meant several months in England, it meant seeing Fanny and Elizabeth again, it meant a respite.

Winterbourne volunteers and, passed for officers' training, returns to England only to find that both Elizabeth and Fanny have abandoned him. More wounding even than their reluctance to be honest with him is his sense of the alienation which he feels to be caused partly by their civilian indifference to the majority of soldiers. This rejection underlies his subsequent virtual suicide at the front.

This resentment, generated not so much by women as by civilian indifference, but certainly amply represented by women, finds expression in 'The Blood of the Young Men':

> The horror of it!
> When a woman holds out a white hand
> Suddenly to know it drops black putrid blood;
> When an old man sits, serene and healthy,
> In clean white linen, with clean white hair,
> Suddenly to know the linen foully spotted,
> To see the white hair streaked with dripping blood.

The two figures define the missing figure present in almost all poetry of the First World War—the slain youth. The 'dripping blood' is not only the guilty blood of those complacent onlookers, but the blood of the soldiers themselves, guiltily irremovable from the flesh of the two civilians. Yet frequently, when confronted with the need to speak directly, Aldington melodramatizes his assertions. This does not indicate that assertion is the wrong way of presenting what he has to say but, rather, shows that he has not properly valued it. He melodramatizes, it would seem, because he distrusts the power of the image to express his responses. And in this instance, one feels that resentment thus gets the better of his aesthetics.

Resentment is Aldington's most powerful mode and he seems to have half-grasped, somewhat ashamedly, the idea that poetry is not especially concerned with the fine expression of the 'finer feelings' but with a delicate organization of (perhaps powerful) responses, of which resentment is clearly one. The question of a demand for the 'finer feelings' has clearly to be faced here, and at his best, Aldington unflinchingly rejects such a demand in his desire to articulate his responses. Thus, in the poem 'Childhood':

> I've seen people put
> A chrysalis in a match-box,
> 'To see', they told me, 'what sort of moth would come.'
> But when it broke its shell
> It slipped and stumbled and fell about its prison
> And tried to climb to the light
> For space to dry its wings.
>
> That's how I was.
> Somebody found my chrysalis
> And shut it in a match-box.
> My shrivelled wings were beaten,
> Shed their colour in dusty scales
> Before the box was opened
> For the moth to fly.
> And then it was too late,
> Because the beauty a child has,
> And the beautiful things it learns before its birth,
> Were shed, like moth scales, from me. . . .
>
> I don't believe in God.
> I do believe in avenging gods. . . .

The resentment is natural and ample; the hatred for the 'interesting' experiment justified. It could equally apply to the civilian ignorance of war. Such truculence as

> That's how I was.
> Somebody found my chrysalis. . . .

finds one source of its power in an untampered-with directness. But, despite indications in *Images of War* (1919) that he is fusing imagist techniques with his experience of war, Aldington rarely achieves this concentration of direct anger and resentment. One finds, for example, in 'In the Trenches', a strong if overstated metaphor,

> Sever and rend the fine fabric
> Of the wings of our frail souls,

but inflated language too often distorts the experience it is trying to recreate. His frequent use of Greek mythological imagery (used with no great intrinsic depth) adds little to our understanding of men in combat, building up, rather, decorative metaphors of superhuman-ness precisely contrary to the experience of vulnerability in war. Aldington seems to have anticipated objections to such mythology, saying in his Introduction: 'when I use the word "god" or "gods" or the name of some Hellenic deity, I am not indulging in a mythological flourish but refer to the actual experience of some "potency".' Such a 'potency' does not easily fit with a re-creation of combat; one thinks of David Jones's exacting interfusion of ancient with contemporary matter in *In Parenthesis* (see Chapter Eleven), and one sees that Aldington did little of Jones's patient interweaving of contrasts and similarities.

The more interesting poems in *Images of War* are 'Field Manoeuvres', 'Trench Idyll', 'On the March', 'Machine Guns', and 'Bombardment and Resentment'. In the first of these, what one responds to is not sensuous description,

> Through the great bronze pine trunks
> Glitters a silver segment of road. . . .

but the flat, impersonal language of command. This is evaluatively measured against the spirit's sensuous contact with nature:

> I am 'to fire at the enemy column
> After it has passed'—
> But my obsolete rifle, loaded with 'blank',
> Lies untouched before me,
> My spirit follows after the gliding clouds. . . .

Henry Reed, in the Second World War, created the same kind of contrasting dissociativeness with 'Naming of Parts'. Like Reed, Aldington, by placing two elements together, makes them comment on each other and point to the man trapped in the man-made activity of war. It is an effective poem (marred, however, by the phrase 'mother of beauty') and Aldington expresses this theoretical set of alternative conditions through the use of quotation marks. Thus the figure in the poem is led by the quotation marks out-wardly into the command, but the syntactical flow ensures that the reader understands that emotionally the figure inwardly rejects all war's paraphernalia.

In 'Trench Idyll', the meaning is reached by moving from the external, bodily 'frozen' to the internal 'cold' of fear and horror:

> 'The worst of all was
> They fell to pieces at a touch.
> Thank God we couldn't see their faces;
> They had gas helmets on. . . .'

Aldington seems to be adapting the 'hard and clear' image to an expression of war experience; yet, interestingly, he has this information transmitted in conversation—as though to distance it. What he achieves by way of balance he loses in another way in that the speech lacks, not clarity, but tautness. And such loss can be more easily seen if one compares this with the passages quoted above from 'Childhood'. It is as though imagism was more viable to synoptic uses than in a re-creation of close, localized experience.

The components of Aldington's verse then are already at odds, and one sees that some crucial resolution of these was necessary if his poetry as a serious instrument of expression was not to be endangered. One's sense of Aldington's indecision is increased by passages of unimagistic garrulousness (and much pronounced in poems subsequent to the war), by irrelevant mythology, and by visual patterning. As he wrote in the 'Proem' to *Images of War*:

> Each day I grow more restless,
> See the austere shape elude me,
> Gaze impotently upon a thousand miseries
> And still am dumb.

That surely was his exact predicament. As a poet he grew more restless, incapable of deeply sustaining his attention upon anything. Even in the war poems, which are in the main his best work, the austere shape of Imagism eluded him, or permitted his weaknesses to operate. And in 'gaze impotently' we have an indication of the degree to which he failed to develop his mode, and to integrate the war into his poetry as perhaps one of his most crucial experiences. Understanding this permanent fragmentation, we can understand a particular, individual tragedy, in which the war played its part.

3

When Ford fell in love, not far from the end of his life, properly and deeply, he wrote some slightly haunted, rejoicing poetry. These love poems comprise the last section of his *Selected Poems* (1971) and are called 'Buckshee'. To rejoice in later life in the central human experience is to rejoice with the blade facing you. Such love is unexpected—buckshee—an outright gift requiring of an older man the sustained attention and nurture which a younger man gives without such sense of limitation in time. He rejoices in his fortune but wishes that it had come sooner.

> Because God was a stupid man and threw
> Into our outstretched palms, Haïtchka, you!

he writes in 'Buckshee'. Such a poem as 'Champêtre' relies on tonal accuracy to render the complexity of the experience:

Then one of us would find a bee orchid. . . .
And God promised us the Kingdoms of Earth and a corner in France
And the heart of an Oriental woman!

Well, here is the corner in France;
The Kingdoms of the Earth are now rather at a discount:
We should not know what to do with them if we had them!
And you—you have no heart!

The lineation has in common with imagism and some Hebrew poetry the making the idea, or some part of it, originate the line-length:

> We shall have to give up watering the land
> Almost altogether.
> The maize must go.
> But the chilis and tomatoes may still have
> A little water. The gourds must go.
> We must begin to give a little to the mandarines
> And the lemon-trees.

There is concentration in the sensuousness:

[grapes] will shrink and grow sweeter till honey is acid beside them.

And, from 'Coda',

> Two harsh, suspended, iron tocsin notes
> Reverberate panic from that clock of Richelieu's.

The war is occasionally admitted into these poems. Of the war and Ford, Bernard Bergonzi says in *Heroes' Twilight* that '*Parade's End* . . . is the greatest English novel to come out of the war'.

Certainly the character of Tietjens's patriotism is unrecognizably more subtle than anything in the 'patriot poems' Ford was commissioned to write. And in noticing that his patriotism (in the novel) has something in common with Edward Thomas's 'This is no Case of Petty Right or Wrong' (see p. 88 above)—love of the land—one sees that Tietjens is among the few remaining aristocrats, a landed man, as opposed to his steel-owning Middlesbrough neighbours. One crucial difference between the novels and these patriot poems is that in the former the debate concerning patriotism is sincere. Ford may have thought he knew the answers, but the problem is thoroughly explored, and such answers as are returned are qualified and doubtful; although one must add that Tietjens's patriotism is never entirely rejected. Its consequences are voluntarily suffered and one acknowledges the sobriety of his decision. Such acceptance, however, is in its turn balanced by his infinitely greater reluctance to accept—as he does—his wife's unfaithfulness. These two themes are interwoven in such a way that, when his wife finally leaves him, the evaluation of his suffering at her hands is made in relation to an evaluation of his patriotism and its contingent suffering. Such a scrupulous investigation at last forces one to ask what Ford could have imagined he was doing in the patriot poems, and whether or not the *ultimate* rejection of patriotism was not perhaps a slight over-compensation for the forced—as it seems—patriotism of the poems. It is not of course a question that can be answered, but it is none the less one that should be asked.

This patriotism in the war poems comes with an almost blatant insistence, which, apart from its intrinsic unpleasantness, is also surprisingly propagandistic, in the bad sense. Compared with the love poems, they are so assertive, so much of the will. Bergonzi comments on this:

Despite his partly German origins, and the fact that a few years earlier he had made an attempt to claim German nationality in order to obtain a divorce in Germany, Ford responded to the war in a whole-heartedly patriotic fashion; indeed, there may have been an element of compensation for his previous inclinations towards Germany. Under the auspices of a Government propaganda scheme Ford produced two books of a somewhat didactic kind, one attacking Prussia and the other praising France. . . . In 1915, Ford, though over military age, volunteered for the Army and was commissioned as a subaltern in the Welch Regiment. He had a simple patriotic motive in doing so, but, as his biographer, Douglas Goldring, admits, Ford may have also had a secondary motive in wishing to get away from his entanglement with the novelist, Violet Hunt.

He seems to have had absolute trust in his and everyone else's 'love of the land':

> How could they do it?
> Those souls that usually dived
> Into the dirty caverns of mines; . . .
> What the devil will he gain by it?
> Digging a hole in the mud and standing all day in the rain by it
> Waiting his doom, . . .

he asks in 'Antwerp'. He pretends to no illusions and does not pass off the *experience* of combat as intrinsically fine. The man 'meets his doom':

> He finds that in a sudden scrimmage,
> And lies, an unsightly lump on the sodden grass . . .
> An image that shall take long to pass!

The last line shows that, unlike those war poets for whom the brutality of war proved the desirability of stopping it, Ford treats the experience as proof of the depth and propriety of patriotic feeling. He cleverly manipulates the debate by suggesting that, if the experiences are brutal, this must demonstrate the worth of patriotism whose demands are so exacting. Or, to put it the other way, only such terrible sacrifices can meet the exclusive demands of patriotism.

There are other aspects of his poetry, which in themselves are ideologically neutral:

> This is Charing Cross;
> It is midnight;
> There is a great crowd
> And no light.
> A great crowd, all black that hardly whispers aloud.
> Surely, that is a dead woman—a dead mother!
> She had a dead face;
> She is dressed all in black;
> She wanders to the bookstall and back,
> At the back of the crowd;
> And back again and again back,
> She sways and wanders.

Taken from its context the passage is not chauvinistic; it acquires this tincture only within its frame. Separated from it, the passage shows concentration of a kind, and vividness. Something like imagism seems to originate the verse but again, interestingly, the woman's grief is neither evidence for nor against war; or rather, it could be used in either role. It lacks almost entirely that kind of partiality intrinsic to Owen and Sassoon and, in the long run, to Rosenberg. It is imagism of a kind, argumentatively neutral and susceptible to any moral framework it is placed in.

A patriotism similar to that of 'Antwerp' can be found in 'Foot-sloggers' from *Poems Written on Active Service*:

> What is love of one's land?...
> I don't know very well.

The sense of 'I am inarticulate but my feelings are the deeper for that' which he uses here is gratuitously humble.

> It is omnipotent like love;
> It is deep and quiet as the grave....

Ford in his love poems knew better than to summarize love, and this gnomic authority should make us suspicious. He adroitly uses some of the arguments used against patriotism:

> Vile alcoholic voices in the ear, vile fumes
> From the filthy pavements ... vileness!
> And one thought:
> 'In three days' time we enter the unknown:
> And this is what we die for!'

The question of whether the sacrifice is worthwhile must surely have occurred to every soldier; to make his argument stronger Ford rehearses the counter-argument as strongly as he can. But as a protest against patriotism the expression is inadequate; one would hardly dismiss patriotism, any more than one would endorse it, on account of 'Vile alcoholic voices'. Drunkenness is meant to have representative force in that one is being asked to think of what one most detests in one's country and then test it against one's patriotism. Clearly, patriotism is going to survive this kind of test, and the argument as well as the instance of it is so enfeebled as to make one doubt Ford's sincerity. Characteristically, 'love of one's land' gets its positive expression in nature imagery (of a not too detailed kind):

> It is because our land is beautiful and green and comely,
> Because our farms are quiet and thatched and homely,
> Because the trout stream dimples by the willow,
> Because the water-lilies float upon the ponds. . . .

Is this what the soldiers were fighting for, when the majority were, in any case, from urban backgrounds?

In only one poem, as Bergonzi indicates, does Ford contrive insight of a kind contrary to that of the poems so far discussed. In 'That Exploit of Yours' he projects the irony of three patriots, all concerned with a dutiful patriotism, whose attitudes, when autonomously extended until they meet, can end only in collision and death:

> 'I at least have done my duty to Society and the Fatherland!'
> It is strange how the cliché prevails . . .
> For I will bet my hat that you who sent me here to Hell
> Are saying the selfsame words at this very moment
> Concerning that exploit of yours.

One wonders if the poem seems more valuable than the others because of the ideas it expresses. That query might more precisely be asked if one questioned whether the expression were not more satisfactory because it was originated by more insightful and selective meanings. Valid or not, Ford's patriotism admitted some proper counter-arguments and some doubt.

CHAPTER NINE

WILFRED OWEN

The poetry of modern warfare may be in the pity, but neither pity nor
self-pity in themselves can inspire great poetry.

John H. Johnston: *English Poetry of the First World War*

See the great bards of elder time, who quelled

The passions which they sung, as by their strain
May well be known: their living melody
Tempers its own contagion to the vein

Of those who are infected with it—I
Have suffered what I wrote, or viler pain!
And so my words have seeds of misery—

Shelley: *The Triumph of Life*

Wilfred Owen was born, on 18 March 1893, into a background one
constituent of which was the Evangelical wing of the Church of
England. The eldest of four children, he entered the Birkenhead
Institute on 11 June 1901. In October 1911 he matriculated at
London University, and from later that month until the early spring
of 1913 he was the pupil and lay assistant of the Reverend Herbert
Wigan at Dunsden Vicarage, Oxfordshire. Some prior indication of
that alert conscience in his war poetry emerges in this period, through
his prolonged contact with others' suffering in a society he could
exert little influence over, and which produced in him that peacetime equivalent of pity and indignation, the two principal impulses
in his war poetry:

a gentle little girl of five, fast sinking under Consumption—contracted
after chickenpox. Isn't it pitiable. . . . the Father is perennially out of
work, and the Mother I fancy half-starving for the sake of four children.
This, I suppose is only a typical *case*; one of many *Cases*! O hard word!
How it savours of rigid, frigid professionalism! How it suggests smooth
and polished, formal, labelled, mechanical callousness![1]

The over-literate alliteration indicates the self-conscious attempt to
press his points, but the seriousness is there. It is also present in a

---

[1] All quotations from Owen's correspondence are taken from *Wilfred Owen/Collected
Letters*, ed. Harold Owen and John Bell (1967).

further letter, and the reference to the rebelliousness inherent in the situation reflects much dissatisfaction with his own position, and his incapacity to change the conditions of the men's lives. The fires of revolt may have died down, he writes, 'in the bosoms of the muses, but not in my breast. I am increasingly liberalising and liberating my thought. . . . From what I hear straight from the tight-pursed lips of wolfish ploughmen in their cottages, I might say there is material here for another revolution.' This early social awareness suggests that Owen was not, as is often implied, a man for whom the war worked a miraculous and beneficial awakening, and without which there would have been no conscience-bearing poet. What the war did, if it can be claimed it did anything, was to increase the pressure under which the responsive conscience quickened, and to hasten the fusing of the lyrical poet with the socially responsive man. Evidence for this is provided by a comparison between his verse and letters prior to the war with those written during it. Before it, the letters do not carry their concerns into the verse; whereas during the war the social responses of the letters and the poetry have one originating impulse. In the meantime, Owen himself revolted, to the extent of leaving Dunsden in February 1913 and rejecting the earlier plan of his taking orders. With such a rejection goes his putting aside of an orthodox, or at least institutionalized Christianity, and he expresses this in a letter to his mother earlier that year: 'I have murdered my false creed. If a truer one exists, I shall find it. If not adieu to the still falser creeds that hold the hearts of nearly all my fellow men.'

In September 1913, he started teaching at the Berlitz School of Languages in Bordeaux, and in August 1914 he met Laurent Tailhade of whom F. S. Flint wrote so glowingly in his account of contemporary French poetry.[1] Owen's mind, in its growth, shows an interesting kinship with the older man's in that, for instance, he had also 'been intended for the church', but had lost his faith. More significantly, Tailhade's pacifist tracts, *Lettre aux Conscrits* (1903) and *Pour la Paix* (1908), would almost certainly have been read by Owen and, with hindsight, one feels that the older man's ideas awoke or at least strengthened in Owen a similar set of responses (see p. 232 below). But Owen's ideas were also strengthened by experience. For instance in this letter of 28 August 1941,

---

[1] *The Poetry Review*, I, No. 8 (August 1912).

almost a month after the opening of war, Owen can callously consider the unselective decimation of combat:

I feel my own life all the more precious and more dear in the presence of this deflowering of Europe. While it is true that the guns will effect a little useful weeding [*sic*], I am furious with chagrin to think that the Minds which were to have excelled the civilization of ten thousand years, are being annihilated—and bodies, the products of aeons of Natural Selection, melted down to pay for political statues.

One month later, after having witnessed post-combat operations at Bordeaux hospital, it is not the cultural loss that he is counting but the human suffering:

One poor devil had his shin-bone crushed by a gun-carriage-wheel, and the doctor had to twist it about and push it like a piston to get out the pus. . . . I deliberately tell you all this to educate you to the actualities of the war.

The didactic impulse is very evident, and however over-modestly Sassoon may tentatively claim (in *Siegfried's Journey*) to have influenced Owen, as a war poet Owen was making his own isolated development (apart that is from whatever contact with Tailhade may have brought about).

In September 1915 he returned to England and on 21 October enlisted in the Artists' Rifles. His brother Harold, in *Journey from Obscurity*, gives an account of his hesitations concerning enlistment, which is confirmed by a letter to his mother dated 6 November 1914:

I heard that Tailhade, together with Anatole France, is shouldering a rifle! <u>Now I *may* be led into enlisting when I get home</u>: so familiarize <u>yourself with the idea! It is a sad sign if *I do:*</u> for it means that I shall consider the continuation of my life of no use to England. And if once my fears are roused for the perpetuity and supremacy of my mother-tongue, in the world—I would not hesitate, as I hesitate now—to enlist.

Considerations of the supremacy of the English language are hardly the moral objections one would look for in Owen, who writes to his mother again on 6 February 1915: 'I could not bear to draw comparisons with the life of the trenches and mine; unless I felt in a manner to have suffered my share of life. . . . I have not abandoned all idea of enlisting.' His father was at this time pointing out that his 'present life [was] not leading to anywhere in particular' and that perhaps he might enlist. In June that year he told his mother: 'I *now do* most *intensely want to fight*.' Harold Owen's account of his brother's change of heart begins:

His immediate reaction [to the war] was, I am certain, his usual one when any disrupting influence threatened his absorption with his poetry— one of exasperated nervous intolerance. . . .

It is manifest from the letters he wrote to my mother during these first few months of the war that the declaration of war . . . did not stir in him any patriotic ardour . . . did not present itself to him as a personal challenge. . . . If a war was likely to destroy or even retard his poetry, he would have nothing to do with a war. . . .

Wilfred in those first months was never troubled in himself about NOT enlisting.[1]

This chapter of Harold Owen's 'Memoirs of the Owen Family' should be read in full for its insight into Wilfred's mood at this time.

On 4 June 1916, Owen was commissioned into the Manchester Regiment and at the end of December sailed to France where he was attached to the Lancashire Fusiliers. In January 1917, he joined the second battalion of his former regiment located, as Blunden observes in his 'Memoir' of Owen, 'on the Somme battle-field, where the last sharp fighting was in progress'. Before leaving the base he wrote to his mother:

This morning I was hit! We were bombing and a fragment from somewhere hit my thumb knuckle. I coaxed out 1 drop of blood. Alas! no more!! There is a fine heroic feeling about being in France . . . but excitement is always necessary to my happiness.

Something of Sassoon's early euphoria (and even Brooke's) emerges here, but it is qualified in such a way as to indicate that he is aware of himself and by no means absorbed by the idealistic cant. Never-theless by 16 January, only a few weeks later, he has changed. He sees the war clearly, and can assess himself as one item in the total wreckage, yet do this without diminishing the validity of his own responses:

I can see no excuse for deceiving you about these last 4 days. I have suffered seventh hell. I have not been at the front. I have been in front of it. I held an advanced post, that is, a 'dug-out' in the middle of No Man's Land. We had a march of 3 miles over shelled road then nearly 3 along a flooded trench. After that we came to where the trenches had

been blown flat out and had to go over the top. It was of course dark, too
dark, and the ground was not mud, not sloppy mud, but an octopus of
sucking clay, 3, 4, and 5 feet deep, relieved only by craters full of water.
Men have been known to drown in them. Many stuck in the mud & only
got on by leaving their waders, equipment, and in some cases their
clothes. High explosives were dropping all around out, and machine guns
spluttered every few minutes. But it was so dark that even the German
flares did not reveal us. Three quarters dead, I mean each of us ¾ dead,
we reached the dug-out, and relieved the wretches therein. I then had
to go forth and find another dug-out for a still more advanced post where
I left 18 bombers. I was responsible for other posts on the left but there
was a junior officer in charge. My dug-out held 25 men tight packed.
Water filled it to a depth of 1 or 2 feet, leaving say 4 feet of air. One
entrance had been blown in & blocked. So far, the other remained. The
Germans knew we were staying there and decided we shouldn't. Those
fifty hours were the agony of my happy life. Every ten minutes on Sunday
afternoon seemed an hour. I nearly broke down and let myself drown in
the water that was now slowly rising over my knees. Towards 6 o'clock,
when, I suppose, you would be going to church, the shelling grew less
intense and less accurate: so that I was mercifully helped to do my duty
and crawl, wade, climb and flounder over No Man's Land to visit my
other post. It took me half an hour to move about 150 yards. I was
chiefly annoyed by our own machine guns from behind. The seeng-
seeng-seeng of the bullets reminded me of Mary's canary. On the whole
I can support the canary better. In the Platoon on my left the sentries
over the dug-out were blown to nothing. One of these poor fellows was
my first servant whom I rejected. If I had kept him he would have lived,
for servants don't do Sentry Duty. I kept my own sentries half way
down the stairs during the more terrific bombardment. In spite of this
one lad was blown down and, I am afraid, blinded. This was my only
casualty.[1] The officer of the left Platoon has come out completely prostrated and is in hospital. I am now as well, I suppose, as ever. I allow
myself to tell you all these things because *I am never going back to this
awful post*. It is the worst the Manchesters have ever held; and we are
going back for a rest. I hear that the officer who relieved me left his 3
Lewis Guns behind when he came out. (He had only 24 hours in). He
will be court-martialled.

And on 19 January:

They want to call No Man's Land 'England' because we keep supremacy there. It is like the eternal place of gnashing of teeth; the Slough of
Despond could be contained in one of its crater-holes; the fires of Sodom

[1] See 'The Sentry'.

and Gomorrah could not light a candle to it—to find the way to Babylon the Fallen. It is pock-marked like a body of foulest disease and its odour is the breath of cancer.[1] I have not seen any dead. I have done worse. In the dank air I have *perceived* it, and in the darkness, *felt*. Those 'Somme Pictures' are the laughing stock of the army—like the trenches on exhibition in Kensington. No Man's Land under snow is like the face of the moon chaotic, crater-ridden, uninhabitable, awful, the abode of madness. To call it 'England'! I would as soon call my House (!) Krupp Villa, or my child Chlorina-Phosgena. . . . The people of England needn't hope. They must agitate. But they are not yet agitated even.

Many of the constituents of his poetry are here: the detailed description of war's effects; the outrage and indignation; the Biblical references, and the pity. Finally, there is that crucial contrast between the uninformed civilian attitude to the war and the actual conditions the soldiers endure. The discrepancy between the two produces, as in Sassoon, the sardonic but furious sarcasm of 'Krupp Villa . . . Chlorina-Phosgena', which leads into his political recognition of the need for civilian agitation such as would help to bring a negotiated peace.

We cannot know, of course, if these responses in the letters were partly conscious preparations for the writing of the poems, but it appears that Owen had by February 1917 produced a version of 'Exposure' which, Sassoon believed, he revised at Craiglockhart after reading Barbusse's *Le Feu* (lent him by Sassoon). If this dating is correct, then Owen's writing of 'Exposure' is almost simultaneous with the events his letters describe.

The poem opens with a description of the tense weariness that characterized life in the trenches. The 'merciless iced east winds . . . knive us', Owen writes, and the tension of waiting in the silence seems to intensify the cold. Men are 'nervous' and, in creating the half-rhyme 'knive us/nervous', Owen points to the interrelation between bodily and spiritual freezing. The first verse establishes the (end) refrain, 'But nothing happens', yet something is constantly happening to the soldiers' minds. In the second stanza he opens out the relationship between the dissimilar entities of nature and war, which he explores in many of his poems. 'Wire', for instance, may be said to have 'brambles', but it is also a comparison used to point the actual, fearful dissimilarities. Thus, the comparatively harmless vicissitudes of the brambled are countered by the 'twitch-

---

[1] See 'The Show'.

ing agonies of men' hooked, wounded, and dying on the wire. This interrelation between war and nature is continued in the third stanza:

> The poignant misery of dawn begins to grow . . .
> We only know war lasts, rain soaks, and clouds sag stormy.
> Dawn massing in the east her melancholy army
> Attacks once more in ranks on shivering ranks of gray. . . .

'Dawn' is 'poignant' in that it evokes a boundless sense of potential in a context where that potential may never be realized. 'Poignant' receives a double emphasis from the certain knowledge that the day will terminate some people's potential. In the third and fourth lines Owen introduces a new idea which substantially alters the course of the poem, for here, against our expectations of nature poetry, with nature—despite Wordsworth—as the invariably friendly presence, 'Dawn' is seen as hostile to man, 'massing . . . her melancholy army'. In the next stanza this idea is extended: 'Sudden successive flights of bullets streak the silence', and are said to be 'Less deathly than the air that shudders black with snow'. 'The wind's nonchalance' is such that it is indifferent to human suffering both at its 'hands' and those of war. In the fifth stanza nature makes even more malignly intimate contact: 'Pale flakes with fingering stealth come feeling for our faces—' prompting the question that strikes all the more sharply and poignantly in that it replaces the expected refrain: 'Is it that we are dying?'

In stanza six nature functions differently, but although Owen recalls an earlier romanticism, he qualifies its received sensibility by here inverting it. Thus 'our ghosts' glimpse 'the sunk fires, glozed/With crusted dark-red jewels'. 'Glozed' here means a deception practised. As soldiers, says the poet, we cannot any more believe in such a mode of nature, and with such a sensibility as sees fires as having 'dark-red jewels'. Such sensuousness is no longer viable; the force of 'glozed' offers to dispel such a sensibility. Instead, nature is seen as harsh, and we therefore withdraw those acts of fancy we had before committed upon her. The remainder of the stanza introduces a further torment, which deeply affects our understanding:

> For hours the innocent mice rejoice: the house is theirs;
> Shutters and doors, all closed: on us the doors are closed,—
>   We turn back to our dying.

The delicate Keatsian perceiving of the mice in their rejoicing—for
the unlooker initially also a rejoicing—is all the more painful as he
realizes that their joyful activity is possible only in his absence. It
is not a simple contrast between the innocent small creatures and
the larger human ones; nor is it merely that the mice rejoice as the
humans cannot. The crucial distinction is that these creatures are
innocent by virtue of their inability to inflict harm, whereas we
fulfil our opposite capacities. Their rejoicing is in contrast to our
misery and savagery. Thus, even nature's most vulnerable creatures
are, by implication, judgementally hostile to man. He is excluded
from the scene of their rejoicing and can only turn to his dying.

In the next verse an extremely complex set of ideas is explored:

> Since we believe not otherwise can kind fires burn;
> Nor ever suns smile true on child, or field, or fruit.
> For God's invincible spring our love is made afraid;
> Therefore, not loath, we lie out here; therefore were born,
>   For love of God seems dying.

The first line contains two readings: we turn back to the war,
which is our dying, and we choose to do this so that what we
value—our homes and spiritual values—may be preserved. A
second reading takes 'since we believe' as a separate unit. The
line would then read: because we believe in God, we therefore
believe that it is God who has given us these good things and their
contingent values ('kind fires') and, being sacred, they must be
preserved. Or, as a second alternative within this second idea,
'kind fires' can burn only if we believe in God, the 'if' possibility
centring on 'not otherwise'. But believing in God we believe in the
'kind fires', attributes of His by virtue of His having given them to
us, and we must therefore defend them. Thus, the war becomes a
partly religious struggle. Of course these last two suggestions are
intensifications of the first reading, which is however mainly
secular in character. Whichever meaning is preferred—and all
could be carried together without any contradiction—we may think
of our fighting as an activity on behalf of the benign aspect of
nature (and man)—making its first appearance in this poem. And
believing in God or His intrinsic values, fruit and children become
valuable in the sense that, tautologically, these are valuable because
they are the issue of attributes which we value.

The stanza now becomes even more complex. 'For God's

invincible spring . . .' could mean we are afraid, on spring's behalf, that this war is so destructive as to confound all we had before regarded as indestructible. The possibilities of life's renewal are, for all this, nevertheless threatened by man's activity. Another reading of 'for', however, could be 'because of': because God's 'spring' is invincible, our fighting over it and for it incurs his wrath. It is invincible, indivisible, and must be shared. Thus, our love (fighting for) is itself made afraid. The next (fourth) line suggests that, because we value the 'kind fires', therefore 'not loath, we lie out here', and must suffer. We have accepted the idea that these values must be defended, and the consequences are inextricable from the decision. But the bitterness of the last phrase in the line, 'therefore were born', qualifies the uplifted offering of the previous phrases, in that it partly retracts the offering, partly resents the consequences even though it does not retract the original decision. The phrase suggests that, for the soldier, it is as though his generation was born to be sacrificed. 'Were we not born for anything else?' The ironic answer implicit in the line seems to be an acquiescing 'no'. We (had to) choose this; we are morally obliged to; our fate is self-sealed, although we have not wished this. Compare this with what Harold Owen says of his brother's attitudes to enlisting prior to his doing so.

But if our fate—to continue—is self-sealed, it is also differently sealed. Line 5, 'For love of God seems dying', could mean either 'God's love for us seems to be ebbing' or 'combat inevitably erodes our best values, one of which is our belief in God'. The latter possibility is especially hurtful because it reveals the unevadable impasse; we are fighting to preserve those values which are embodied in a belief in God or goodness, but the action itself at the same time destroys a response to those values on whose behalf we are struggling. The bitterness is given final emphasis as we recall that we accepted the seeming necessity of the struggle. Yet now, as it seems, we have alienated God, from whose values our own spring, or, if the reader rejects the religious version, we have made ourselves unresponsive to those very values we are supposedly defending. The tautological bitterness completes its own circle. Finally, this sense of alienation deepens in the last verse into an apprehension of retribution: 'To-night, His frost will fasten on this mud and us.' If we choose to destroy not only nature but also each other, who are a part of nature and thus His handiwork, we must expect to be treated no

better than as if we were mud as it is visited with frost. The frost
is 'His' and He punishes us with it. We had originally, but mis-
takenly, thought that war was a moral act because it was committed
to moral objectives, but it is immoral and we must now bear God's
retributive wrath in the form of hostile nature.

I have discussed 'Exposure' at length because I believe its process
represents a crucial stage in Owen's thought and its sensuous
expression. The use of half-rhyme and internal assonance—'Flakes
that flock'—constitute important, discordant, and ironic ingredients
in the poem. The rhythms are strong and supple, the ideas complex, honest, and questioning, and the analytic impulse persistent
throughout. Everything is compactly worked together. Finally,
Owen uses nature in a way that is new, not only for him, but in
relation to the generally accepted romantic view of nature, which
is the view he inherited.

His use of nature is in fact so persistent, but various, that it may
be helpful to trace its course, linking it as a theme with others, and
compacting these interrelations into an overall interpretation of his
attitude to war and its effect, as he saw it, not only upon the doomed
generation of which he was a representative, but on the society
that survived him.

Owen's crucial poems—those concerned with war, and two or
three others—can be grouped under three headings, without
violating their complexity. Firstly, poems in which nature, if one
excludes war, is the principal element: 'Exposure' (Feb. 1917),
'Anthem for Doomed Youth' (Sept. 1917), 'Miners' (Oct. 1917),
'Asleep' (Nov. 1917), 'The Show' (Nov. 1917), 'Hospital Barge at
Cérisy' (Dec. 1917), 'Futility' (June 1918), 'Spring Offensive' (Sept.
1918). Also, I would add 'The Last Laugh' (Feb. 1918) for its last
two lines which are, in this context, important. Secondly, come the
Sassoon-like poems protesting against the war, in which anger, satire,
or irony is especially directed against its continuation: and thus,
directed also at the civilian who seems to have little understanding
of war's horrors. Also included here are the poems which recreate
such horror: 'Le Christianisme' (April 1917), 'The Dead-Beat'
(Aug. 1917), 'Dulce et Decorum Est' (Oct. 1917), 'Soldier's Dream'
(Oct. 1917), 'Wild with all Regrets' (Dec. 1917), 'The Last Laugh'
(Feb. 1918), 'A Terre' (April 1918), 'Mental Cases' (May 1918),
'Arms and the Boy' (June 1918), 'The Sentry' (Sept. 1918), 'Spring
Offensive' (Sept. 1918), 'Smile, Smile, Smile' (Sept. 1918). The

following poems are also grouped here, but apart from the above because their dating is problematic: 'The Letter', 'Conscious' (? May 1917), 'Disabled' (? Oct. 1917), 'The Chances', 'S.I.W.', 'Inspection', 'The Parable of the Old Man and the Young', 'At a Calvary near the Ancre', 'On Seeing a Piece of our Artillery Brought into Action', 'The Next War'. Thirdly, poems whose originating impulse is compassion or pity: 'Anthem for Doomed Youth' (Sept. 1917), 'Miners' (Oct. 1917), 'Asleep' (Nov. 1917), 'The Calls' (June 1918). And also here, poems whose dating is problematic: 'The Send-Off',[1] 'Greater Love', 'Strange Meeting'. A fourth category contains poems which do not fit any of the others: 'Apologia pro Poemate Meo' (Nov. 1917), 'Insensibility' (March 1918), 'Futility' (June 1918). Needless to say, these headings are to be taken as no more than ways in which the poems may be helpfully explored. D. S. R. Welland has observed that 'Owen's poetry may come to be of increasing value as a bridge between the poetry of the nineteenth century and that of the twentieth.' Certainly his use of nature is a pertinent instance of such a bridge. On the other hand, the Sassoon-like mode of anger and satire is very unlike anything in nineteenth-century poetry, apart from Byron.

Owen's meeting with Sassoon in 1917 at Craiglockhart War Hospital is well described in Edmund Blunden's 'Memoir':

About the beginning of August, Captain Siegfried Sassoon arrived. Owen had been reading his *Old Huntsman*. 'Nothing like his trench-life sketches has ever been written or ever will be written.' One day he ventured to call at his hero's room and to show him some poems, which received some praise and some blame. On the evening of September 7, again, 'Sassoon called me in to him; and having condemned some of my poems, amended others, and rejoiced over a few, he read me his very last works, which are superb beyond anything in his book. . . .'

Clearly there is some hero-worship in excess of admiration in these responses, and evidence exists to suggest that Sassoon was directly responsible for certain changes in 'Anthem for Doomed Youth', if no other poem (see *Collected Poems*, pp. 185–8). On the other hand, nothing emerges so clearly as Owen's spontaneous perception of himself as an independent man and poet. He writes to Sassoon in November 1917: 'And you have *fixed* my Life—however short. You did not light me: I was always a mad comet; but you have fixed me. I spun round you a satellite for a month, but I shall

---

[1] *Collected Letters* dates 'The Send-Off' May 1918.

swing out soon, a dark star in the orbit where you will blaze.' Certainly, Sassoon's modest account of his possible influence on Owen, in *Siegfried's Journey*, confirms the above independence.

What Sassoon did for him perhaps was to give him the confidence to draw into his work a greater realism, a more stringent anger and satire, which in their turn may have helped him more fully to realize his compassion. The colloquial element present in Sassoon's work would also have constituted a learning point for Owen, as much as *Le Feu*, 'which set him alight as no other war book had done'. Yet what is interesting, if the classifications I have attempted are at least temporarily granted, is that the largest number of poems comes under the second heading of anger and satire. This would seem to refute the commonplace assertion that Owen was overwhelmingly the poet of compassion. I am not suggesting, of course, that he was not, but I am indicating a large body of work that gets ignored, or is at least not accommodated in the popular image of him, an image which in its turn forces upon the poems a reading that emphasizes the very weaknesses that Owen I think was partly aware of. That is, anger and compassion are complementary elements in his work, and exclusion of the former throws the latter into radical weakness of quite the wrong kind. The weakness itself amounts to a certain 'haloesque' quality, which can obscure the horror of war that Owen in other poems was committed to recounting, but which pity is always I believe held in right concord and activity by the simultaneous presence (when it occurs) of anger.

The poems subsumed under the heading of compassion can be considered as being in some senses versions of Owen's responses to nature. They are composed partly of what he inherited, from Keats, Shelley, and Tennyson, for instance, and from the versions of pastoral current through Arnold and the whole of the nineteenth century. The pacific and the pastoral are closely interrelated syndromes, but what is interesting about Owen's use of the pastoral as a pacific attribute is that with a poet's proper intensity he proceeds to make literal a conversion which lesser, more immediately sophisticated writers would have seen as metaphor. He is deeply and directly in touch with a fundamental constituent or reflecting image in nature, and which is basically important to human concerns. Wrath of course has its ample counterpart in nature and he clearly incorporated this aspect in such poems as 'Exposure' and 'Spring Offensive'. But to repeat what might risk becoming a formula, to be angry at destruction is to put a value on what is destroyed; thus, the richest response of compassion is one that also contains anger. It is an anger that includes those who have been corrupted by war, the anger directed not at these but at those in society who are in a position so to expose human beings to such corruption:

> some for love of slaughter, in imagination,
> learning later . . .
> some in fear, learning love of slaughter. . . .

That Owen attributed responsibility to the civilians more than to the soldiers (of either side) is confirmed not only by his earlier version of 'I am the enemy you killed, my friend', which read 'I was a German conscript, and your friend', but also by a letter written in August 1918 from Scarborough:

this morning at 8.20 we heard a boat torpedoed in the bay about a mile out, they say who saw it. I think only 10 lives were saved. I wish the Bosche would have the pluck to come right in & make a clean sweep of the Pleasure Boats, and the promenaders on the Spa, and all the stinking Leeds & Bradford War-profiteers now reading *John Bull* on Scarborough Sands.

This passage has a political perceptiveness, which Welland is inclined to deny Owen, who admittedly lacked Sassoon's ability to translate it into action. In this respect, one might compare Sassoon and Owen with Byron and Wordsworth. Byron criticized Wordsworth for writing but not joining action to it. Wordsworth's intelligence and imagination, however, were richer on the whole than Byron's, as Owen's were richer than Sassoon's. To Sassoon's anger, Owen added compassion, and advances a further term into the perspective on war. In so doing, he also qualified his version of pastoral, as Wordsworth had done before him, 'fostered alike by beauty and by fear'. Nevertheless, Owen often kept his compassion and anger in separate poems, and to my mind this is his principal weakness. Nevertheless, his complex consciousness was an advance on Sassoon's and permitted a more flexible understanding of war.

Owen was discharged from Craiglockhart in November 1917 and posted then to the Northern Cavalry Barracks, Scarborough. In the spring and early summer of 1918 he worked as an instructor where, as Johnston observes, he felt 'his conflicting roles of leader and betrayer': 'For 14 hours yesterday I was at work—teaching Christ to lift his cross by numbers'. At the end of August he returned to his old battalion in France. Blunden records that C. K. Scott-Moncrieff, 'then at the War Office, endeavoured to find some post for Owen which would mean that he would be kept in England'. And on 21 May Owen wrote that, although it seemed he had some opportunity 'of becoming Instructing Staff Officer to a Cadet Battalion[,] I would *rather* work in the War Office itself, and that seems not impossible either. Really I would *like most* to go to Egypt or Italy, but that is not entertained by Scott-Moncrieff.' But none of these possibilities occurred and in July, preparing for the Western Front, he wrote, 'Now must I throw my little candle on [Sassoon's] torch and go out again' and 'I am glad. That is I am much gladder to be going out again than afraid. I shall be better able to cry my outcry, playing my part.' I imagine that Owen's prior reluctance to return was partly caused by the anxiety he must surely have felt that the war might cut short his realizing his full potential as a poet; and, if this is so, it is not completely consonant with his brother's comment on the poet's attitudes subsequent to his enlistment: 'Wilfred having given himself that first year to make his own decision was content with [its] rightness ... he never wavered in this and never looked back with regret.' Yet such natural dismay as returning to the front must have produced, is turned to remarkable account in 'able to cry my outcry, playing my part'. Owen was not unaware of the double-edgedness of the situation; from the front he wrote to Sassoon on 22 September: 'You said it would be a good thing for my poetry if I went back. That is my consolation for feeling a fool. This is what shells scream at me every time: Haven't you got the wits to keep out of this?' But in all this ambiguity he is determined that his poetry shall plead for those who suffer and are inarticulate—to those who are ignorant of, or apathetic to, this suffering.

'Anthem for Doomed Youth' makes this plea by comparing the soldiers' peremptory treatment with that which cattle receive prior to their slaughter. The consolatory and decorous ceremonies of religious and institutional mourning contrast with the brutal nature of their deaths. Yet there is ambiguity in the poem in that Owen seems to be caught in the very act of consolatory mourning he condemns in 'What passing-bells for these who die as cattle?'—a consolation that permits the war's continuation by civilian assent, and which is found ambiguously in the last line of the octet: 'And bugles calling for them from sad shires.' Is 'sad shires' ironic, or consolatory (for Benjamin Britten in the *War Requiem* the line has no ambiguity; the interpretive music is sweetly elegaic). Geoffrey Hill, in a review of Keith Douglas's *Selected Poems*,[1] writes: 'The fact that Owen employs irony in this poem cannot alter the fact that he takes thirteen lines to retreat from the position maintained by [the first].' The first line of the sestet may question what kind of cheer may be wished the embarking soldiers, but 'candle', already in an antique mode, steadily leads to pastoral elegy that so falsifies their actual deaths:

> Their flowers the tenderness of patient minds,
> And each slow dusk a drawing-down of blinds.

The sorrowing patient minds of the women in mourning are no different from the sorrowful religious consolation we have been taught to accept in exchange for human lives, and the sanctified nature of the soldiers' deaths found in grieving 'shires' and 'flowers' excludes the horror of war as effectively as if Owen had been propagandizing for the war. The pun of 'pallor' with 'pall' is consonant with this kind of elegizing, but he misses the perhaps better pun more consonant with his later poems in 'pall' 'appal'. Peter Dale has also remarked on the weakness of the poem which 'sets up memory as an equalizer of the suffering on the field and in the home and makes some sort of compensation out of it'.[2]

In 'Asleep', the opposite of consolation is conveyed in the tone of 'took'—

> And in the happy no-time of his sleeping,
> Death took him by the heart.

There is a concealed pun of a kind in Owen's variation of the phrase 'take by the hand' that has gentle beneficent associations. The contrast with the echoed cliché undercuts any possible sentimentality.

> There was a quaking
> Of the aborted life within him leaping. . . .

The brutal verb 'aborted' qualifies the romanticized vitality of 'leaping' (compare with Brooke's 'swimmers into cleanness leaping'),

---

[1] *Stand*, VI, No. 4.   [2] *Agenda*, III, No. 3.

but qualifies it in such a way as to stress what has been lost. And by means of the rhyme 'sleeping/leaping' he criticizes the euphemism 'sleep', but also contrasts the natural remedial sleep with death. Yet Owen is not consistent in this poem in that, although his use of physical detail marks him off in the main from Brooke, some of the latter's sacred euphoria is present in the lines:

> Whether his deeper sleep lie shaded by the shaking
> Of great wings, and the thoughts that hung the stars,
> High pillowed on calm pillows of God's making. . . .

Owen's pastoral is rendered in consolatory religious terms, despite the ironic intent of 'deeper sleep'.[1] There are, in fact, several attitudes vying for predominance in this poem. The version of hostile nature found in 'Exposure' occurs in the next line, 'Above these clouds, these rains, these sleets of lead', and contradicts the sacred version of nature in the lines just quoted. It seems as though Owen was working through unintendedly conflicting attitudes, which leave the reader in some confusion. Gradually, however, one attitude predominates, and persists to the poem's conclusion:

> —Or whether yet his thin and sodden head
> Confuses more and more with the low mould,
> His hair being one with the grey grass. . . .

'Confuses' is the telling word, for at this stage the attitudes are richer and no longer unintentionally conflicting. Man is seen as soluble in nature. So much for the supposed sympathy of nature for the slain (see 'A Terre') and its consolatory sweetness (see Gurney, p. 124 above). This neutral attitude of nature is, however, slightly qualified in the next line, 'And finished fields of nature that are old', in that where before the man was seen to be absorbed by nature, here nature is again manipulated, although this time to reinforce a sense of the war's lethal horror. Nature ages, as perhaps society does, through the experience of war; and it ages through its incorporation of the slain. This is 'the winter of the world'. As in 'Futility', though not as emphatically, some comparison between nature's and man's death is made, both poems exploiting the euphemism and the resemblance between sleep and death, any

---

[1] For a more ironic reading of this poem, see Jon Stallworthy, *Wilfred Owen*, p. 21.

resolution possible being made in the pity. It is Owen's conclusion, and surely the right one.

Nature is given a different dimension in 'The Show', and, as Geoffrey Matthews has suggested, the poem echoes the visionary horror of *The Triumph of Life*.

> And others, as with steps towards the tomb,
> Pored on the trodden worms that crawled beneath. . . .

> '. . . The old anatomies
> Sate hatching their bare broods under the shade

> Of daemon wings, and laughed from their dead eyes
> To reassume the delegated power,
> Arrayed in which those worms did monarchize. . . .'

Compare these lines of Shelley's with Owen's:

> Across its beard, that horror of harsh wire,
> There moved thin caterpillars, slowly uncoiled. . . .

> And Death fell with me, like a deepening moan.
> And He, picking a manner of worm. . . .

Owen's soul, here glimpsing earth as 'cratered like the moon with hollow woe,/And pitted with great pocks and scabs of plagues', recalls his letter of 19 January 1917, describing No Man's Land:

the Slough of Despond could be contained in one of its crater-holes. . . . It is pock-marked like a body of foulest disease and its odour is the breath of cancer. . . . No Man's Land under snow is like the face of the moon, chaotic, crater-ridden, uninhabitable, awful, the abode of madness.

There is too much genuine horror here for one to think of these responses as of a Georgian idealist's revulsion from the horrific. The transcription from the letter into the poem's more violent imagery shows a mind contemplating the unpleasantness, but also circumscribing and naming it. We find in Pope's *Dunciad* images of diseased and distorted nature which correspond to a moral disease in society. In Owen, the decay of the slain constitutes a similar perception. The caterpillars, nourished on such decay,

> . . . pushed themselves to be as plugs
> Of ditches, where they writhed and shrivelled, killed.

What most increases the horror is the uncontrollable proliferation
of decay, which has its own form of generation, and unlike anything
in nature as we know it in its reproductive sense:

> On dithering feet upgathered, more and more,
> Brown strings, towards strings of gray, with bristling spines. . . .

Owen might well have wished this malignant version of nature could
be controlled, but the only form of control it submits to is of its
own (and not man's) devising:

> Those that were gray, of more abundant spawns,
> Ramped on the rest and ate them and were eaten.

Control is exercised through cannibalism resulting from there being
insufficient food for the creatures in their adult stage, although
presumably there had once been enough dead for them to hatch
out of. The cannibals produce more of their species, which in turn
devour their progenitors; thus, a kind of world is emblematically
envisaged to which man has contributed but over which he has
now no control. This is literally how war escalates; the dead demand
more deaths. The image is also an image of nature in that its
malignant aspects are evidently always present, but through man's
destructiveness magnify themselves upon their own predatoriness.
The creatures are seen through a magnifying naturalism:

> I saw their bitten backs curve, loop, and straighten, . . .
> Whereat, in terror what that sight might mean,
> I reeled and shivered earthward like a feather.

These lines give the sense of a mind struggling for control of itself,
partly through its attempt to understand the meaning of the image.
Death shows him its meaning:

> And He, picking a manner of worm, which half had hid
> Its bruises in the earth, but crawled no further,
> Showed me its feet, the feet of many men,
> And the fresh-severed head of it, my head.

Owen perceives that he is part of the decay, both through his being
killed and through his killing. With others, he is both 'severed' by
war, and severs—'the feet of many men'. The dead feed on the
living, which, politically, is what they were made to do: and this

perhaps is what Owen's creature ultimately signifies. It is the guilt and the suffering at what has been done. He creates one image from opposed and irreconcilable ideas. As he expressed his own position, 'And am I not myself a conscientious objector with a very seared conscience?' It is this involvement in the image of the worm that *meaningfully* completes its horror. Nothing in Owen's work exceeds the horror of this poem, and it is interesting that the resolving irony which he employs elsewhere is absent here.

'Spring Offensive' expresses the hostility of nature to warring man found in 'Exposure' and 'The Last Laugh':

> The Bullets chirped—In vain! vain! vain!...
>
> And the lofty Shrapnel-cloud
> Leisurely gestured,—Fool!

There is a reciprocity in 'Spring Offensive' in nature's hostility to man, in that it varies with man's destructiveness. Thus, at first nature is beneficent, as long as the soldiers permit her to offer her gifts:

> Marvelling they stood, and watched the long grass swirled
> By the May breeze, murmurous with wasp and midge,
> For though the summer oozed into their veins
> Like an injected drug for their bodies' pains....

Nature heals. She anaesthetizes the past horrors of war, although she cannot annul the knowledge of the future, which in fact warningly clashes with the soldiers' present deep enjoyment:

> Sharp on their souls hung the imminent line of grass,
> Fearfully flashed the sky's mysterious glass.

The soldiers ignore the warnings—in 'the imminent line' and 'fearfully flashed'—and in doing so reject the beneficent aspects of nature:

> O larger shone that smile against the sun,—
> Mightier than his whose bounty these have spurned.

The hugeness of the crime they are about to commit is magnified for us by the poet's making it appear larger than the huge sun that they spurn, with all its beneficence. In one sense only are they 'mightier' than the sun; in that, while the sun's power in the poem is

8

restricted to helping creation, they can destroy. They have ignored nature's warning, and all nature is in arms against them:

> And instantly the whole sky burned
> With fury against them; earth set sudden cups
> In thousands for their blood. . . .

The benign flower becomes a chalice expectant for their sacrificed blood. God in his mercy may catch some of them as they fall, but the hostility of nature confirms the guilt, which is compounded into the survivors' silence:

> Long-famous glories, immemorial shames—
> And crawling slowly back, have by degrees
> Regained cool peaceful air in wonder—
> Why speak not they of comrades that went under?

These lines again raise the problem (involuntarily emphasized perhaps by the differing tones of the two dictions in the last line) of the men having courage, deserving compassion, but still being a part of war's evil. Owen condemns war, but does not discount the courage, although this in its turn is qualified by its context. Perhaps his greatest virtue is to present an unresolved problem in no way mitigated (as Leavis observed of Rosenberg) by irony.

'Miners', one of four poems published in Owen's lifetime, refers to the colliery explosion at Halmerend on 12 January 1918. The first two verses animate the coal—in the first it is said to whisper and sigh, and this anthropomorphism is strengthened in the second, where the coal is said to originate from ferns and forest. Owen's sensitivity apprehends plant as well as human life, and in doing so enriches his responses to both; for although 'smothered ferns' is an analogue for the suffocated miners, 'men/Writhing for air', there is sensuous indication that his *feelings* fix also upon the plant life, 'the low, sly lives' which are given a place, if a humbler one, in the community of creatures. There is also a contrast as well as a similarity, reinforced by the dexterous slow-moving internal rhyme—both of 'sly' with 'lives' and of the whole phrase with that of 'wry sleep', further reinforced by 'Writhing for air'. 'Sly' suggests some active sense in which the plants are at least able to struggle for life, whereas 'wry' suggests a situation in which the miners can do nothing, a situation ultimately made by other men. This is not the only place in which such an idea occurs, but in stanza five the poem makes a characteristic turn. The miners' suffering is contrasted with those consumers who, through insensitivity or ignorance, do not associate with their burning of the coal the labour (and, in this instance, the sacrifice) of the men who hack it out of the earth:

> And I saw white bones in the cinder-shard.
>   Bones without number;
> For many hearts with coal are charred
>   And few remember.

This may have its meaningful antecedent in Shelley's refrain in *The Mask of Anarchy*: 'Ye are many—they are few.' Owen's lines very closely parallel his attitude to war and its constantly forgotten victims; as he said of the poem, 'I get mixed up with the War at the end.' The miners' dark pits become fused with the soldiers' saps and trenches:

> I thought of some who worked dark pits
>   Of war, and died. . . .

The miners are bound by their need for hire as much as the soldiers are compelled to fight. And in this interfusing of civilian and military contexts Owen shows the beginnings of a political consciousness. It is not that he gets 'mixed up' with the war, but that the inevitable and right sharing of contexts is only gropingly realized. But all the implications of the analogue are present, where, in similar sets of coercions, men are forced to labour and to fight and derive little if any tangible benefit. This kind of consciousness in Owen was, however intermittently, formulating itself, and in a thoroughly international way. He wrote on 29 October 1918:

The civilians here are a wretched, dirty crawling community, afraid of *us*, some of them, and no wonder after the shelling we gave them three weeks ago. Did I tell you that five healthy girls died of fright in one night at the last village? The people in England and France who thwarted a peaceable retirement of the enemy from these areas are therefore now sacrificing aged French peasants and charming French children to our guns. Shells made by women in Birmingham are at this moment burying little children alive not very far from here.

In 'Futility', the last of the poems in my 'nature' category (although clearly this admits of more and more themes), Earth may be thought of as one of man's progenitors. 'She' is impregnated by the 'male' sun, and this is perhaps a version of the sleeping beauty myth. If we may see the poem in such terms, but with the myth only as helpful and implicit symbolism, certain tragic meanings can be perceived. The opening injunction, 'Move him into the sun', applies a version of that test where one holds a mirror before a man's face for his breath to cloud. Is the soldier still alive?

> If anything might rouse him now
> The kind old sun will know.

This might be irony. Either the sun is *not* kind and, though able to quicken, mocks the soldier, knowing him to be already dead; or, although the sun *is* kind, its power is, ironically, unavailing. Perhaps the intention is not one of irony, although this would make 'kind' verge on sentimentality. Thus: we trust to the natural and benign power of the sun; if it cannot help us in this case, it can at any rate be trusted as a constant and integral part of a context benign to man.

   If, however, one follows the ironic possibilities of the first stanza, corroboration can be found in the second in that the bitter sun, which once woke the 'clays of a cold star', is, nevertheless, impotent to bring back to life a man whom another has killed. Thus, the benign power of the sun suffers ironic depreciation because it cannot restore to life the life it has helped to form (a life killed by that of another similarly quickened by the sun); the cosmic power lacks as much particularized capacity as God today is seen to. This contrast, between the killing of one man and the immense power of the sun to originate all life, is conveyed in the movement of the lines:

> Woke, once, the clays of a cold star.
> Are limbs, so dear-achieved, are sides,
> Full-nerved—still warm—too hard to stir?

The punctuation withholds any quickening of movement which the tetrameter would otherwise have. The bitterness is given final emphasis if we think of man, in any sense, as nature's highest achievement, or process, which man, in an instant, destroys. Man kills one of his slowly evolved species whom the sun, with all its power, cannot enliven. In such a case, the 'toil' of the sunbeams is turned into a mockery, as is everything else associated with the quickening of the cold clay. It is good to create, but better the sleep of earth had never been broken if the creatures that come of this wakening destroy the life they have been given, as well as the lives of other creatures not of their species.[1]

Owen sees nature in one of two ways: either as a benign sustaining entity (which may or may not be the handiwork of God—as it *was* for the Deists), or as a force hostile to man for as long as he makes war. Unlike Blunden, he does not make nature in war a principal sufferer; for him, man is war's central victim. And in this scheme of man and nature, man is responsible for his own suffering, and nature merely endorses his error with her own retribution. That at least is principally his scheme, and rarely is nature permitted to take matters into her own hands. If she does, the whole scheme alters in emphasis. Then hostile nature is one more punitive act by God for violating His moral laws, but with the sense of God directly intervening in man's affairs. Once that happens, man's direct control over his fate suffers reciprocal diminution as God's direct intervention increases. It takes from man not only a sense of his own actions being his own, but of their consequences being a direct result. If you introduce into man's actions an alien and for ever incalculable factor that is outside man's capacity to effect, you diminish his sense of his own ability to act effectively. And with this diminution you absolve him of responsibility for his actions and their consequences and make of him a child. This would not do for Owen who came I think, whatever his religious upbringing, to believe that man's actions were what affected man. Thus, nature's variousness or duality *may* be a reflection of God's attitude, but it is also an image of man's actions and his own judging of them. The point at which nature is seen to be most at variance with her usual benignity is the point at which man's self-destructiveness is most intense.

If rage is a primary response to the inflictions of war, then Owen's poems of anger are more truly 'war poems' than any others he wrote. Perhaps this is the meaning of Blunden's remark that Owen 'was, apart from Mr. Sassoon, the greatest of the English war poets. But the term "war poets" is rather convenient than accurate. Wilfred Owen was a poet without classifications of war and peace.' One might add that, even in his poems of anger, Owen is often more complex than Sassoon. Interestingly, with regard to Sassoon's

[1] Compare with *The Dynasts*, pp. 36–7 above.

influence on Owen, one of the first of the poems in this category (that can be dated) is amongst his harshest and most didactic; one, that is to say, most akin to Sassoon's war poetry.

Welland says that 'Dulce et Decorum Est' was written during August 1917, the month in which Owen and Sassoon first met. Owen had just been reading the war poems in *The Old Huntsman* (see above p. 207). Perhaps, as one of his earliest poems of anger, it represents the tapping of a fresh source of energy (fresh in the sense of a previously unworked area) with confidence for the undertaking newly acquired through his *contact* with Sassoon. The language, although not yet colloquial, is, as it is in some of Sassoon's poems, nearer to speech than the language of 'Exposure', for example. Perhaps this change underscores Owen's recognition in himself of a tendency, especially in his poems of sacred pity, to use a poeticized, over-aureate language and tone that has recognizable affinities with the language of sanctification and euphemism. There is nothing of this in 'Dulce et Decorum Est'. The title itself points to one of the poem's targets: the sacredness of the sacrifice, and the glamorized decency of the danger ('adventure') one's own side undergoes. By contrast, the poem opens rawly:

> Bent double, like old beggars under sacks,
> Knock-kneed, coughing like hags, we cursed through sludge,
> Till on the haunting flares we turned our backs
> And towards our distant rest began to trudge.
> Men marched asleep. Many had lost their boots
> But limped on, blood-shod.

This has the dignity of honestly reported fact and implicitly acts as a corrective to the reporting of most journalists, whom both Sassoon and Owen loathed. Then comes the gas attack and Owen heightens our sense of terror by using, and thus making complex, a word that has associations contrary to the context in which it is used: 'Gas! Gas! Quick, boys!—An ecstasy of fumbling'. Ecstasy can produce fumbling, but this is not the ecstasy that accompanies the knowledge of the possibility of escape, but the fevered sense of the terrified fumbling itself, which *appears* akin to that of joy, but is in fact so opposite to it. Owen uses this bifurcated yoking together in other poems, but this is a comparatively early instance of it. One soldier fails to fit on his gas-mask in time. His agony haunts

the narrator, as it horrifies the reader in front of whom it passes as
though it were the experience itself. The intensity of it is such that,
with the narrator, we have a sense not merely of being there but of
identity with the gassed man. The scene shifts finally to where it is
evident that the experience itself has melted into a narration of it
and a ruminating on it (as well as into the narrating of the false
subsequent narrative), and this shift, from experience to recall,
contains the didactic element:

> If you could hear, at every jolt, the blood
> Come gargling from the froth-corrupted lungs,
> Obscene as cancer, bitter as the cud
> Of vile, incurable sores on innocent tongues,—
> My friend, you would not tell with such high zest
> To children ardent for some desperate glory,
> The old Lie. . . .

The recall is folded into rebuke. And as the experience cancers the
innocent flesh of its victims, so the thoughtless retelling of the
story to children, and to adults, corrupts their imagination; and
this, quite apart from the distortion of the suffering. Had the
chauvinist been a participant, it is implied, he would not be perpetuating the old Lie that it is sweet and fitting to die for one's
country, whatever the death.

'The Dead-Beat' reports the fate of a man whose body has
apparently collapsed under the strain of war, although the medical
officer chooses to believe he is malingering. In fact, the collapse is
even more pervasive, although the mind in its desperation retains
some convictions so strongly—that the ruling powers on both
sides are callously responsible for the war's continuation—that it is
able to voice its aggression.

> —Didn't appear to know a war was on,
> Or see the blasted trench at which he stared.
> 'I'll do 'em in,' he whined. 'If this hand's spared,
> I'll murder them, I will.'
>   A low voice said,
> 'It's Blighty, p'raps, he sees; his pluck's all gone. . . .'

In the *Collected Poems*, C. Day Lewis provides both an earlier draft
of the poem and a note. The latter reads: 'In a letter to LG [Leslie
Gunston, the poet's cousin] dated 22 August 1917, enclosing this

draft, Owen said, *after leaving him, I wrote something in Sassoon's style.*' This is the second stanza of the earlier draft:

> He didn't seem to know a war was on,
>   Or see or smell the bloody trench at all . . .
>   Perhaps he saw the crowd at Caxton Hall,
> And that is why the fellow's pluck's all gone—

Owen's comment—'in Sassoon's style'—is shrewd self-criticism, and certainly the final version, paragraphed narrative, in comparison with the earlier draft in stanzas, shows a move away from Sassoon. Yet, interesting though the changes are, the matter perhaps owes something to Sassoon's concerns. Especially interesting is the reference to Caxton Hall, where some pacifist meetings were held. The point here is that, although the pacifists are blamed for causing the man's pluck to vanish, and are even, it is implied, in themselves lacking courage, the hint from the poet that comes through is that perhaps the soldier only too well recognizes and understands both what the pacifists have to say and the contingent political implications. Needless to say, the imputations put on the pacifists were not shared by Owen, if his own pacifist declarations provide any guide.

The poem continues with a telling scrutiny of mischiefs that perhaps frequently happened at home. Tactfully Owen does not permit the soldiers to be explicit on why they (and he, Owen) believe the soldier has collapsed; perhaps a self-protective tact ensured no explicit references to such subjects:

> Maybe his brave young wife, getting her fun
> In some new home, improved materially.

'Improved materially' implies what amounts to prostitution. It further initiates the idea that, if she is better off financially, she has spiritually degenerated, although I do *not* think that Owen is advancing the suggestion that moral degeneration is produced by financial betterment. The poem ends:

> Next day I heard the Doc.'s well-whiskied laugh:
> 'That scum you sent last night soon died. Hooray.'[1]

---

[1] Against the earlier form of these lines in the first draft Owen wrote: 'Those are the very words!'

The officer's drunkenness may be the result of an attempt to relieve the pressure of work, but I prefer the less charitable explanation—which I think Owen intended—that the doctor lacks sympathy and even minimal kindness, and that his being 'well-whiskied' is an emblem of this lack. Such interpretation accords with Owen's puritan cast. Finally, the belief that the non-combatant part of the army had less sympathy and compassion finds its expression I think in the line: 'Malingering? Stretcher-bearers winked, "Not half!"'

'Soldier's Dream', the earlier version of which was almost certainly written at Craiglockhart, works by opposing the 'kind Jesus' with an efficient vindictive God who has something of the character of Blake's 'Selfish Father of Men!' ('Earth's Answer'). Kind Jesus 'fouled the big-gun gears', but God empowers Michael to repair them, which he does. In the earlier version, the prototype of an efficient God had been an authoritative 'man from U.S.A.'. In a sense the poem remains on the level of fantasy, since no one in a battle would want the guns to be in disrepair unless the enemy's were also. As with 'The Dead-Beat' and 'Strange Meeting', the significant alterations are away from particularity and towards universalizing statements. With the first poem especially, one regrets, for both the matter and expression, some of the inevitable loss of particularity. Yet in this poem, the shift is at least towards its proper subject and towards real considerations. The poem is concerned not with man's ploys with respect to a passive ludditism, but with attitudes. Of these, one symbolizes the kind, merciful, pacific; the other an impersonal, efficient bureaucracy.

'Wild with all Regrets' and its later version, 'A Terre', together with 'Disabled', 'Mental Cases', and in a certain sense 'The Chances', expose and examine the effects of war on survivors, wounded, maimed, and often doomed to early death or the asylum. Sassoon had written what are in some ways similar poems, such as 'Does it Matter?' and 'Repression of War Experience'; and Owen, consciously I think, acknowledges his debt in his reference to the 'buffers'. In 'A Terre' Owen's 'I'd willingly be puffy, bald,/And patriotic' recalls Sassoon's scarlet majors in 'Base Details', who are 'fierce and bald', have 'puffy petulant' faces, and are of course patriotic. Owen's officer in 'A Terre', however, has little of the staff officer's illusions, pretensions, or even patriotism, but merely a tragic disablement. Wrenched from his secure pre-war context,

he faces up to the post-war years with honesty. The tag 'to earth'
suggests both a man 'as good as dead' and also the pre-war, fox-
hunting era. The foxy victim is now replaced by the officer himself.

   The changes in 'Wild with all Regrets'[1] which produce 'A Terre'
are considerable.[2] Compare the early

>   not to renew
>   My boyhood with my boys, and teach 'em hitting,
>   Shooting and hunting,—all the arts of hurting!
>   —Well, that's what I learnt. That, and making money. . . .

with the corresponding lines in 'A Terre':

>   I suppose
>   Little I'd ever teach a son, but hitting,
>   Shooting, war, hunting, all the arts of hurting.
>   Well, that's what I learnt,—that, and making money.

The characteristic half-rhyme appears in the earlier version, but in
a partially distracting context of colloquial speech, with staccato
phrasing (Sassoon's verisimilitude, with a dash of Masefield);
whereas the latter is smoother, more in the manner of discourse.
The tone of 'Little I'd ever teach' gives more thoughtfulness to the
passage and suggests a man talking to himself as much as someone
else.

   The differences are not only of manner. The earlier version
simulates truculence and even petulance, directed at a background
that failed to provide the officer with adequate means of coping
with the post-war world. He has of course to come to terms with
disablement, but what Owen manages to show (as Sassoon, in
'Repression', does not) is how ill the man's background equips him
to deal with his situation. The new social shuffle causes him
humiliation:

>   My servant's lamed, but listen how he shouts!
>   When I'm lugged out, he'll still be good for that.

This is roughly Clifford Chatterley's position in Lawrence's *Lady
Chatterley's Lover*, although the similar points of departure serve
very different destinations. In Owen's poem the officer resents the

---

   [1] The phrase 'wild with all regret' comes, of course, from Tennyson's *The Princess*
('Tears, idle tears'). The first stanza shows Owen's bitter contrast with it.
   [2] For obvious reasons, this theme was occupying Owen at Craiglockhart; see his
Collected Letters, p. 499.

fact that his superior social status cannot purchase him even as partial a handicap as his servant has. He would gladly exchange his status for his servant's bodily wholeness:

> I'd like to kneel and sweep his floors for ever,—
> ('Wild with all Regrets')

and

> How well I might have swept his floors for ever.
> I'd ask no nights off when the bustle's over,
> Enjoying so the dirt.
>
> ('A Terre')

So far does the officer's condition humiliate him that he compares himself to 'a dug-out rat'.[1] The prospect of death reminds him of those yet lower forms of life, which, through parturition, never die:

> Dead men may envy living mites in cheese,
> Or good germs even. Microbes have their joys,
> And subdivide, and never come to death.

This leads to agonized speculation about his condition after death:

> 'I shall be one with nature, herb, and stone',
> Shelley would tell me. Shelley would be stunned:
> The dullest Tommy hugs that fancy now.
> 'Pushing up daisies' is their creed, you know.

In *Adonais*, Shelley had written of Keats:

> He is made one with Nature: . . .
> He is a presence to be felt and known
> In darkness and in light, from herb and stone. . . .

The Romantic poet survives through nature, both literally and metaphorically. The difference, crucial for Owen, is that 'to be one with Nature' in death is nothing, and in this he does not, as Welland argues, constitute a bridge between this century and the last, but a break. That kind of organic merging with nature is now seen as no compensation for death, and certainly not for a life truncated by war. To survive through nature is nothing:

> To grain, then, go my fat, to buds my sap,
> For all the usefulness there is in soap.
> D'you think the Boche will ever stew man-soup?

---

[1] Compare this with Rosenberg's 'Break of Day', discussed on pp. 276–81.

This is a reference to the popular belief that the Germans manufactured soap from the fat of the dead. The officer sardonically,
but despairingly also, consigns his flesh to nature where it will
serve healthier and more beautiful ends than his body has in war.
Inasmuch as he is maimed, he will

> . . . be better off with plants that share
> More peaceably the meadow and the shower.

'Peaceably' marks his weariness, and shows a hankering for a
paradise he would like to believe in. But even this hope is diminished
in the line, 'Soldiers may grow a soul when turned to fronds'. He
cannot be certain of even a fern-like consciousness, though he
believes he will nourish the fern. This knowledge implies a partial
assent to the process, but the response is also sardonic. One may
nourish beauty but not be conscious of doing so. The word 'fronds'
also occurs in 'Miners', where it is the crushed fronds that turn to
coal. So the officer will enter nature's cyclic process.

'Disabled', a less rich and resonant poem, remembers, like
Sassoon's 'Does it Matter?', the former civilian health of those who
are now maimed. Comparison is made between the pre-war heroics
of the football field and those of the battlefield, the telling discrepancy between the two achieved in 'blood-smear':

> One time he liked a blood-smear down his leg,
> After the matches, carried shoulder-high.
> It was after football, when he'd drunk a peg,
> He thought he'd better join.—He wonders why.

This last line echoes the close of Sassoon's poem 'In the Pink',
'And still the war goes on—*he* don't know why'. Characteristically,
Owen makes more attempt to enlarge the man's motive—pride that
imagines it will do as well on the one field as the other; pride,
excited by drink, and the presence of his woman.

> Someone had said he'd look a god in kilts,
> That's why; and may be, too, to please his Meg. . . .

His disabling wounds expose the reality of male vanity:

> To-night he noticed how the women's eyes
> Passed from him to the strong men that were whole.

If the subsequent judgements on his motives for enlisting are harsh,
the feeling for the man himself in his disillusioned and disabled

condition is compassionate. This sets Owen apart from Sassoon
who will only imply compassion in his anger. The implied sexual
incapacity, which the women sense, is the test of how little they
really comprehended the sacrifice the men made in enlisting, and
that which they have since made. It was not the sacrifice but the
glamour of heroism which kindled them. They want their heroes,
but they want them whole. Their attitude is not the same as that
found in Newbolt's '*Vitai Lampada*', but it stems from a similar
lack of insight. For Newbolt the necessary heroisms of the two
fields were identical, but Owen's remorseless contrast is followed
through to the poem's end:

> Some cheered him home, but not as crowds cheer Goal.
> Only a solemn man who brought him fruits
> *Thanked* him; and then inquired about his soul.

Owen seems to imply that the pious visitor is as much—if not
more—concerned with his own do-gooding as with the patient's
spiritual welfare. The passive suffering, which Yeats rejected as a
theme for poetry, is emphasized by the rhyme 'Goal' (something
actively achieved) and 'soul' (whose condition is drastically qualified
by the bodily one). The tactless inquiry as to the soldier's spiritual
condition, when it is his physical one that is so overwhelmingly
evident, indicates the real neglect that he suffers.

The same 'blood-smear' appears in 'Mental Cases', another poem
about disability. Physical mutilations and distortions are seen as
the outward and visible evidence of inward dereliction:

> Drooping tongues from jaws that slob their relish,
> Baring teeth that leer like skulls' teeth wicked?
> Stroke on stroke of pain,—but what slow panic,
> Gouged these chasms round their fretted sockets?

As in 'The Chances',

> —These are men whose minds the Dead have ravished.
> Memory fingers in their hair of murders,
> Multitudinous murders they once witnessed.

We get some sense of their madness functioning as an index of
their guilt or even, perhaps, as retribution for their murderous acts;
but this compassionately gives way to a sense of their madness
resulting from what they have witnessed and endured. In such a

double situation of murderer and sufferer the soldiers' duality is never glossed over by Owen, but compassion is never finally withheld. As conscripts, they are essentially victims.

'Smile, Smile, Smile', probably Owen's last poem, makes a fairly detailed analysis of the clichés current in the justifications for continuing the war. A press that aimed at promoting its circulation and civilian morale habitually made the casualties seem less grievous by insisting on the gain in captured machinery (only of use in winning the war):

> Head to limp head, the sunk-eyed wounded scanned
> Yesterday's *Mail;* the casualties (typed small)
> And (large) Vast Booty from our Latest Haul.

The promise of 'Cheap Homes' for the deserving soldiers after the war—and therefore 'not yet planned'—gives way to a consideration of their present requirements. If they are to win the war, they will (as Kipling indicated; see Chapter Three) need to be better and better equipped:

> Meanwhile their foremost need is aerodromes,
> It being certain war has but begun.
> Peace would do wrong to our undying dead. . . .

More men must be sacrificed to obtain that victory for which the dead have died. The official voice speaks carefully of the 'undying', lest the sacrifice of millions seem a disproportionate price for victory. The euphemism 'undying', which means 'immortal through noble actions', also attempts to diminish the sense of loss which death brings the relatives. Thus, 'undying' has it both ways; the dead continue to fight for us (some literally believed this) while we continue to fight and die for them so that their deaths (why then 'undying'?) shall be vindicated. The contemptible manipulations of these illogicalities are familiar enough, but it is worth following the twist which Owen gives to them:

> The sons we offered might regret they died
> If we got nothing lasting in their stead.

'Lasting' is a loaded word, since it brings mortality to mind, but how can the dead be compensated for their 'unlastingness'? They die, and we are given material compensation. 'Lasting' also associates with the cliché, 'lasting peace', which I believe Owen thought society was unlikely to obtain. It should also be noted that the quasi-religious terminology, used self-justifyingly by the modern state, underlines the active dissociation from Christianity as Owen understood it.

The older generation encourage the young to persist in their efforts:

> We must be solidly indemnified.
> Though all be worthy Victory which all bought,
> We rulers sitting in this ancient spot
> Would wrong our very selves if we forgot
> The greatest glory will be theirs who fought. . . .

The thrust in this passage centres on 'solidly indemnified'. There is much urgent sincerity in 'We'; we will be indemnified, the soldiers can have the glory. Owen skilfully expresses the fraudulent mixture of blandishment and pious exhortation, and in examining these performs a political act.[1] I would not, as I have before remarked, agree with Welland that 'The political situation which Owen had "emotionally experienced . . . and assimilated" [Welland is quoting Day Lewis] is war, but it was not primarily as a political situation.' It depends, of course, on the amount of emphasis one puts on 'primarily' and what is left if that word is removed. Here, at least, Owen seems to have fully understood the political method of balancing patriotic sacrifice with material compensation. He finally points to such a balancing: 'How they smile! They're happy now, poor things.' By transparently imposing over the wry, knowing smiles of the soldiers the civilian image of their supposedly peaceful smiles (happy in noble death), he exposes the final vacuity of the belief.

---

[1] The political nature of 'Smile, Smile, Smile' is emphasized, I think, by a passage from a letter to Sassoon dated 22 September 1918, one day before the poem was written:

Did you see what the Minister of Labour (George Henry Roberts) said in the *Mail* the other day? 'The first instincts of the men *vfter the cessation of* hostilities will be to return home.' And again—'All classes *acknowledge* their indebtedness to the soldiers & sailors. . . .' About the same day Clemenceau is reported by the *Times* as saying: '*All* are worthy . . . yet we should be untrue to ourselves if we forgot that the *greatest* glory will be to the splendid poilus, who, etc.' [Owen's italics]

The poem shows direct transcriptions from the two politicians, and the fact that he picks on two suggests not so much an isolated response to an isolated piece of political fatuity, as a *political* mind conjuncting evidence.

'The Parable of the Old Man and the Young' depends for its meaning and effect on the discrepancy between the Biblical story and Owen's re-telling of it. In the Hebrew original, Abraham's reluctant sternness and the sacrifice are both averted on to the 'ram caught in a thicket by its horns'. The angel requires the father to 'offer the Ram of Pride instead',

> But the old man would not so, but slew his son,
> And half the seed of Europe, one by one.

Joseph Cohen disturbingly suggests that Owen's re-creation embodies an instance of Christian 'Greater Love' in the slain youth of Europe. The crux is hard to argue in that the Hebrew story indicates complete filial obedience, which in theory involves love, but which, even then, might not in fact have coincided with it. In any case, in the Hebrew story the greater test is put on Abraham, who binds Isaac, thereby making him a passive participant. My sense of Owen's re-creation is that he does *not* approve of the old man's sacrificial killing, so the poem can hardly at the same time be intended to demonstrate the youth's greater love. Moreover, the angel, representative of God's love, explicitly forbids the killing, which is then undertaken.

The innocence of youth is further explored in 'Arms and the Boy':

> Let the boy try along this bayonet-blade
> How cold steel is, and keen with hunger of blood;
> Blue with all malice, like a madman's flash;
> And thinly drawn with famishing for flesh.

This has its ancestry in Shelley's *Mask of Anarchy*:

> Let the fixèd bayonet
> Gleam with sharp desire to wet
> Its bright point in English blood
> Looking keen as one for food.

This is not the kind of luddite transference found in the sonnet 'On Seeing a Piece of our Artillery Brought into Action', because the bayonet is not the true focus of attention so much as the capacity of its user. The weapon may look evil, but it reflects the minds of its designer and user; indeed the object, through the mind of another, reveals the appetite of its user. Thus both Shelley and Owen are concerned with the corruption of the one who commits the violence.[1] Both are concerned with the essential community of human beings—'We are all brethren'—and the corruption of the young soldier in Owen's poem (as well as the corruption of those who force him into such a situation) is partly the result of their violation of this. Shelley wrote:

> Let them ride among you there,
> Slash, and stab, and maim, and hew. . . .

This may be hopelessly idealistic counsel, but Shelley has a valid point. The soldiers were of yeoman stock and would be of the same class as those they were striking down in the Peterloo massacre of 16 August 1819; certainly they were all English and, more important for Shelley, they were all 'brethren'. They had been no more than hired by the tyrant. In Owen's poem the innocent boy suffered similar corruption. The moral treachery is not against those of his nation (although it *might* be argued that to kill an enemy soldier ensures a continuation of the struggle); the treachery is against humanity—'I am the enemy you killed, my friend'—and, in the last instance, a violation of his own innocence. In the third stanza the reader is assured that

> There lurk no claws behind his fingers supple;
> And God will grow no talons at his heels,
> Nor antlers through the thickness of his curls.

It is questionable, however, how long such innocence can retain its nature in time of war. Moreover, the denied transformation is raised too powerfully for the mind to reject the imaged possibility altogether. This theme of war's corrupting influence—found also in Herbert Read's 'The Happy Warrior', for instance—is present in both 'At a Calvary near the Ancre' and 'Le Christianisme'. Both poems, in their different ways, are attacks upon the Church which, Owen felt, had become erastian. Blunden must surely have felt something similar when he prefaced his *Undertones of War* with the Article of the Church of England (No. xxxvii), 1553: 'It is lawful for Christian men, at the commandment of the Magistrate, to wear weapons, and serve in the wars.' Placed in this context, the

---

[1] See also Simone's Weil's 'The *Iliad*, or the Poem of Force'.

Article draws to the Church some of the dubious morality of the State.

Owen wrote of the role of the Church:

Already I have comprehended a light which will never filter into the dogma of any *national* church [my italics]: namely that one of Christ's essential commands was: Passivity at any price! Suffer dishonour and disgrace; but never resort to arms. Be bullied, be outraged, be killed; but do not kill. It may be a chimerical and an ignominious principle, but there it is. It can only be ignored: and I think pulpit professionals are ignoring it very skilfully and successfully indeed. . . . And am I not myself a conscientious objector with a very seared conscience?[1]

The 'pulpit professionals' ignored the question because, he implies, the Church as a body had become erastian and found it expedient to be so. Certainly, in 'At a Calvary', the contrast is between the 'gentle' Christ and the priests who 'were fleshmarked by the Beast'. It is the soldiers (by paradox but not only by paradox) who are now Christ's suffering disciples:

> But His disciples hide apart;
> And now the Soldiers bear with Him.

The third verse make all these ideas explicit:

> The scribes on all the people shove
> And brawl allegiance to the state,
> But they who love the greater love
> Lay down their life; they do not hate.

The last two lines, however, might seem to agree with the proposition that the 'greater love' and patriotism are synonyms, but in the letter quoted above Owen wrote also: 'Greater love hath no man than this, that a man lay down his life for a friend.' In the poem, the phrase 'Lay down their life' is admittedly ambiguous, in that it might mean by extension 'for their country', but it seems highly unlikely that the poet intended this.

'Le Christianisme' also rebukes the Church, but here, for its

---

[1] His conscience, of course, was seared by his own violation of the fifth commandment. See, for example, his letter of 4 or 5 October 1918 to his mother:

I can find no word to qualify my experiences except the word SHEER. (Curiously enough I find the papers talk about sheer fighting!) It passed the limits of my Abhorrence. I lost all my earthly faculties, and fought like an angel. . . . I only shot one man with my revolver (at about 30 yards!); The rest I took with a smile.

failure to extend its powers of sympathy and beneficent perception
to those enduring the war:

> So the church Christ was hit and buried
> Under its rubbish and its rubble.
> In cellars, packed-up saints lie serried,
> Well out of hearing of our trouble.

The implication is that the Church, with 'its rubbish and its rubble'
and its inanimate statues, is oblivious to human need and that, by
its present nature perhaps, it cannot be otherwise. The Church has
retained its 'immaculate' spirituality and unworldliness, but at the
price of inhumanity.

Owen's difficulties are partly located in his perplexed self-
questioning, 'And am I not myself a conscientious objector with a
very seared conscience?' If he indicts the Church for its failure to
accommodate this 'light', he also accuses himself. A combatant
conscientious objector shares in the suffering but also in the killing.
Owen did not and could not resolve the 'Victor-victim' paradox,
but he tried. By fusing anger with compassion, he indicated that
the only solution lay in people so rethinking their attitude to war
that they would never wage it again. The sense of physical horror,
anger, and pity must co-exist as mutually qualifying and interacting constituents. The presence of the anger and the physical
horror prevents the sacred pity, which seems to be Owen's especial
contribution, from neutralizing or shrouding war's enormities. But
where the pity tends either to exclude the horror, or to operate in
isolation, Owen risks our sense of the horror being dissolved in
euphoria or religiosity, through his own incapacity (as I see it) or
through others' (sometimes deliberate) misreading. By indulging
the 'haloesque', readers are released from the horror and the guilt, or,
at the least, their awareness of what has been done, and are thus
enabled to accept fresh wars whenever it is expedient for their
governments to start them.

It seems possible that Owen coped with the dual role of pacifist-
killer partly by encompassing the miseries of the German, French,
and English soldiers in a universal pity. The Allies' victims are given
pity, which in some sense acts as a neutralizer to the excruciating
pain he must have felt as their slayer. This antimony, this situation
where the killing seems unavoidable and the pity necessary, perhaps

accounts for the tendency of the poems of pity, and those of horror, to exclude each other's constituents. Pity, however, needs anger and physical horror; they are its material source. Conversely, if the anger is not to become a fiery hatred reducing the person to an entirely destructive particle, pity, if for the sacrificed alone, needs to be present. It too, in a qualified and active way, can order and direct the intelligence, and re-direct it towards the victims themselves.

Seen in this light, 'Greater Love' appears constructed from a set of comparisons, in the first instance between the terms and movements of love and of dying:

> Red lips are not so red
> As the stained stones kissed by the English dead.

Love and death are linked by the adjective 'red'. By associating the colour of lips with shed blood, Owen is able to make not merely a comparison, but an implicit criticism of the inherited Romantic view of death which subsumes ideas concerning love as if they were variants of each other. Sassoon had used this technique, and Swinburne made a similar conjunction of dissimilar elements in 'Faustine':

> Wine and rank poison, milk and blood,
> Being mixed . . .

and also in 'A Cameo':

> There was a graven image of Desire
> Painted with red blood on a ground of gold. . . .

But where Swinburne joins death with sex to intensify his experience of the latter (and perhaps to sexualize the former), Owen brings them more contrastingly together. His zeugmas are capable of undoing the entanglement Swinburne had made by pointing to his own set of contrasts. Owen, however, was too close to Swinburne (who died in 1909) and his eroticism entirely to escape contagion. Thus, in the second stanza of 'Greater Love',

> Your slender attitude
> Trembles not exquisite like limbs knife-skewed,

the 'slender' sexuality, which is meant *not* to 'tremble' as exquisitely in death as it will do in sex, sets up the unmeant suggestions so powerfully as to overcome the repeated assertions that this is not how the man dies. Such ambiguity is due partly to the syntactical position of 'like', but I am unsure that the ambiguity, whatever its immediate mechanical causes, can be entirely accounted for by this.

> Rolling and rolling there . . .
> Till the fierce love they bear
>   Cramps them in death's extreme decrepitude.

Their potentiality for loving, expressed in a desire to continue living, is made with such intensity that the cramp of death is intensified by the man's desire for life. Perhaps Owen intended an interfusion of opposites, but if so it works against the truthfulness of any description of war, and in particular, against the meaning of the poem's first two lines as I understand them.

The last stanza contains another zeugma in 'pale', which initially refers to pallor caused by love but which, at its second appearance as 'Paler', refers to the paleness of the 'greater love' (and perhaps from fear). Owen keeps the order of the terms he began with:

> Heart, you were never hot
> Nor large, nor full like hearts made great with shot. . . .

The reader expects the 'Heart' to be, as he reads the word, alive; then immediately after, to be dead.[1] The comparison centres on 'hot' and 'large', in that the adjectives induce expectations of love; but the heart is filled not with love but with 'shot', as a result of its 'greater love'. Thus, the real comparison is here not between love/life and death, but between the two kinds of love. The same comparison ends the poem:

> And though your hand be pale,
> Paler are all which trail
> Your cross through flame and hail:
>   Weep, you may weep, for you may touch them not.

The hand in the first line is the lover's hand, pale with *fin de siècle* sensuality; the others are pale with the pallor of the battlefield. These men seem deserted by God, who 'seems not to care', and beyond the reach of most human beings, especially those absorbed in passionate love. By offering his compassion to the living rather than the dead Owen makes the kind of preference he makes in the

---

[1] The implied comparison, throughout the poem, is between the civilian lover and the soldier sacrificed through his 'greater love'.

last lines of 'Asleep.' But the weakness of his compassion here is that it forces us to think of their willing sacrifice (greater love) as something we must all endorse; when, by endorsing it, we condemn more human beings to pain and death.

There are other problems. 'English dead' is a weighted phrase and draws Owen towards Brooke. But given the set of comparisons in 'Greater Love', there is a much more sensitive apprehension of distinctions than there is in Brooke's 'Peace', which surely adumbrates a whole nation somehow being regenerated by the demands of war, inasmuch as he, Brooke, rejects 'all the little emptiness of love'.

There is also the problem of the meaning of the phrase 'greater love'. Even if Welland's dating—1916—is correct, Owen's ideas probably underwent considerable change; but as he defined the phrase in a letter a year later (May 1917), it then seemed to mean 'that he lay down his life for a friend'. Clearly, it involves many associations of sacrifice, but the real question is whether one permits it to extend to one's country or limits it, literally, to one's 'friends'. I think he came to mean the latter, but that in the poem the phrase does have attachments with patriotism. Owen's emphasis, however, is on the love itself, virtuous, suffering, and innocent. The quality of the love is of more importance *for him* than what it serves.

Owen's best-known poem is 'Strange Meeting'. Its date of composition is uncertain, but Welland argues convincingly that it is not his last poem and that any attempt to regard it as his swan song is injurious to our interpretation of the poem (and perhaps to Owen's work as a whole). Its ancestry can be traced to *The Revolt of Islam*, but to say that Owen recognized the situation formulated in Shelley's poem to be his own ethical one, is perhaps to say no more than that he got from Shelley confirmation of something he had begun to formulate himself. Shelley wrote:

> 'Soldiers, our brethren and our friends are slain.
>   Ye murdered them, I think, as they did sleep!
> Alas, what have ye done? the slightest pain
>   Which ye might suffer, there were eyes to weep,
>   But ye have quenched them—there were smiles to steep
> Your hearts in balm, but they are lost in woe;
>   And those whom love did set his watch to keep
> Around your tents, truth's freedom to bestow,
> Ye stabbed as they did sleep—but they forgive ye now.

'Oh wherefore should ill ever flow from ill,
    And pain still keener pain for ever breed?
We are all brethren—even the slaves who kill
    For hire, are men; and to avenge misdeed
On the misdoer, doth but Misery feed. . . .

When I awoke, I lay mid friends and foes,
    And earnest countenances on me shed
The light of questioning looks, whilst one did close
My wound with balmiest herbs, and soothed me to repose;

  And one whose spear had pierced me, leaned beside,
    With quivering lips and humid eyes;—and all
Seemed like some brothers on a journey wide
    Gone forth, whom now strange meeting did befall
    In a strange land, round one whom they might call
Their friend, their chief, their father, for assay
    Of peril, which had saved them from the thrall
Of death, now suffering. Thus the vast array
Of those fraternal bands were reconciled that day.

(Canto V, x-xiii)

The situation is by both poets called 'strange', in that such re-conciliation between enemies is not customary; but it is strange (both imply) that it is not. 'We are all brethren.' This constant hostility is echoed, one guesses, by the half-rhyme, a dissonance that expresses frustration, or pessimism. Michael Roberts made the good observation that 'In Owen's War poetry, the half-rhymes almost invariably fall from a vowel of high pitch to one of low . . . producing an effect of frustration, disappointment, hopelessness.'[1] The half-rhyme in 'Strange Meeting' proceeds in this way, and one might add that its dissonances express some of war's inflictions and men's responses to them—'groined/groaned' for instance.[2]

Owen, who had been stationed with the Reserve Battalion at Scarborough since November 1917, sailed for France on 31 August 1918. A list—which included 'Strange Meeting'—of those poems he was shaping into a book for publication was, according to Welland, drawn up before September 1918. If this is so, and unless Owen was including in his list a poem he had not yet written, 'Strange Meeting' must have been written before his last experience of the trenches and made, as most of Rosenberg's 'war poems' were not, in a calm

[1] *The Faber Book of Modern Verse* (2nd ed., 1951), p. 28.
[2] For an interesting account of Owen's half-rhyme, and a discussion of his possible indebtedness to various sources, see Welland's *Wilfred Owen: A Critical Study* (1960).

period of home service. Careful work can of course be done under circumstances that seem hopelessly distracting, but as his brother indicates,[1] Owen was acutely conscious of how little time was left for his poetry, and would have appreciated any respite he could get.

The figures that confront each other in the poem have shed their class and are in the process of shedding nationality, although it is perhaps an intentional irony that they do not achieve this until one—or both—is dead. Classless and nationless individuals peaceably confront each other only perhaps in a visionary 'otherworld', in the nether world of death. To get the full effect of this, 'Strange Meeting' should be compared with the whole of the fifth canto of *The Revolt of Islam*, for although Shelley's poem is extremely ramified (and in a sense the entire poem, from the narration's commencement in Canto I, stanza vi, is contained in the parentheses of a vision), what occurs inside these parentheses is in many ways more actual and less parenthetical than the events in Owen's poem. The soldier who swoons from his wounds is brought back by Shelley, not into an underworld, or a vision, but into life, and within the situation he had known prior to his swooning. Everything about the situation embodies the 'hereness' of a problem that demands resolution, in living terms, and which cannot be postponed until after death or put into a visionary aside. It depends, of course, how one reads Owen's poem. Perhaps, after all, he felt that the war and its causes yielded no solution other than in death and the otherworldness of afterlife. Yet in view of Owen's earlier upbringing as a Christian it is unfortunate that his religion should appear so conveniently to provide that non-human sac into which many human problems demanding human resolution have been thrust. This may well not have been what Owen intended—a track infinitely extending an escape 'out of battle'—but the parallel suggests itself. Counter to this is the impression that despite the assertion that there 'no guns thumped, or down the flues made moan', nevertheless, the battle continues above, and that, alive or not, the two men are conscious of this. Owen ensures that his reader, too, retains the sense of the war's continuation, and that the two men exist in relation to it: 'probed', 'blood', 'thumped', 'flues', 'jabbed', 'parried', 'encumbered' (with kit as well as with death) are each un-aureate words in various but very physical ways related to combat. To complete the counter-suggestion, the two men might

[1] Harold Owen, *Journey from Obscurity*, vol. III, p. 163.

be seen to have 'escaped' into a 'Hell' that is the product of war. It is a place which previous 'titanic wars had groined'—and this war is larger even than titanic. There would seem to be a link with the opening of *Hyperion*, but where Keats is ostensibly concerned with fallen divinities, Owen's 'groined' is painfully human. The 'friend' is 'strange' not because he is unfamiliar (although at first apparently unrecognized),[1] but because, in the ferocity of the combat, any friendly meeting between 'enemy' individuals would be 'strange'. The word 'friend' is also ironic in that the other subsequently reveals to him that he is the man he killed. Of course, within the context of Owen's 'we are all brethren', the irony works in either direction, as it does with 'strange'.

In this second phase of the poem the meanings become more complex and difficult. The opening lines of *Endymion*,

> A thing of beauty is a joy for ever:
> Its loveliness increases; it will never
> Pass into nothingness;

(with the emphasis on 'thing' or attribute perhaps, rather than person) provide some gloss here. Compare these lines with Owen's:

> I went hunting wild
> After the wildest beauty in the world,
> Which lies not calm in eyes, or braided hair,
> But mocks the steady running of the hour. . . .

Both passages assert the eternal, lasting thing to exist within 'beauty'; but whereas both say that (eternal) beauty is resistant to 'process of time', Keats's resistance to it is as unruffled and natural as the process of time itself; 'it will never' being hardly even a deliberate but unquestioned expression of confidence. For Owen, eternal beauty (not found in women—'not calm in eyes, or braided hair') seems by comparison a defiant, slightly anxious, expression of time's otherwise inescapable erosion, of which war is the concentrating agent. In both cases it is beauty's context which qualifies its particular resistance, and the difference between the two articulates Owen's contribution to the Romantic idea of beauty and permanence, as well as his departure from it. 'Wild' certainly appears as residual romanticism, borrowed, if only because logically a frenetic beauty could hardly as it were compete with war's wildness which, by implication, is what it must do here. Nor does there seem any

[1] See Eliot's meeting with Dante in *Little Gidding*.

satisfactory reason why beauty should be wild—other than because
it was so with some Romantic poets—who infused it with a wildness
associated with sexuality. But resistant beauty has, or should have, a
monolithic calmness. Yet despite these objections, Owen, like
Keats, makes his point: beauty endows immortality of a kind. The
word 'richlier' is Keatsian, but the line taken as a whole—'And if
it grieves, grieves richlier than here'—is puzzling. It could mean
'beauty grieves, perhaps; but it grieves more richly on earth than
it does here in Hell'. But why should beauty grieve if it is eternal?
It could, of course, be grieving at the spectacle of time and of war
in particular, which is depriving it of its celebrants. One might,
alternatively, take the verb transitively: 'beauty grieves, that is,
afflicts *us* because war makes us feel so impermanent and so much
the reverse of all that endures; grieves the living who may lose it,
more than the dead who have so already. I favour the latter reading
because it strengthens the relation between this passage and the
rest of the poem, which the former reading weakens. These lines
come close to Keats's 'Beauty is truth, truth beauty', but where the
ultimate permanence of beauty exists in the truth, 'the true Poets
must be truthful'. Thus, it is probably truth which 'mocks the
steady running of the hour', where the truth is 'the pity of war'. If
war teaches us anything, Owen implies, it teaches compassion. In
everything else it destroys our small contact with beauty and
hinders our telling the truth to the 'future'.

Were the poem to end here, one might see it expressing, or
struggling for, some kind of angelic optimism or meliorism to
the effect that, however much war inflicts, it nevertheless teaches
us pity for one another, so that we may not unconfidently expect
some ultimate millennium. I cannot accept this interpretation, but
in any case the poem continues:

> For of my glee might many men have laughed,
> And of my weeping something had been left,
> Which must die now. I mean the truth untold,
> The pity of war, the pity war distilled.

Even this admits a slight hope in that, although man's understanding
of war—its pity—has been lost, there is his reader who will broad-
cast the idea. But

> Now men will go content with what we spoiled,
> Or, discontent, boil bloody, and be spilled.

This couplet asserts that what we have befouled future generations will placidly accept; or failing that, will again go to war, achieving their own destruction. In disagreement with Enright's elegant gloss that ' "trek from progress" is a rather [how much?] abject concession to the exigencies of rhyme', I believe that Owen deliberately sustains his irony with this phrase. 'Trek' would in his time still be regarded as something associated with Europeans courageously and laboriously settling portions of African wilderness, extending civilization, in fact. By joining the word and its aura of approval with 'from progress' Owen bitterly indicates how little the lessons of war have been assimilated into our civilization, or perhaps that the experience was too destructive for the pity to have survived it. In this case, the passage would carry the kind of warning we receive from 'Exposure' and 'Futility'. But in any case the man who could have told the truth is dead. In future none will defect from their admirably disciplined trek towards destruction. A point to notice about the half-rhyme 'tigress/progress' is that the former end-word connotes all that is predatory and destructive; the latter all that is constructive and beneficial. The two words should by definition contrast, but in this context 'tigress' and '*from* progress' —while pointing the contrast—are in agreement; the half-rhyme emphasizes this. A similar meaning emerges from 'swift', which suggests something of the quick, responsive vitality of life, but it is the vitality of the predator.

'Strange Meeting' ends with a recapitulation of what happened between the two men, and of how disturbingly ironic their meeting is. I believe the poem does not end optimistically, despite the reconciliation—'I am the enemy you killed, my friend'—since this is achieved only through and after death, perhaps the death of both. 'Let us sleep now' is often read as the angelic placating of men's enmities, where 'the wolf shall lie down with the lamb', but the millennium Isaiah is creating is a metaphor that wants the existing fact and which in experience would entail an unthinkable alteration in society's unpeaceable kingdom.

Owen implies, rather, that although there is reconciliation in death, that is the only place where it can be achieved (the war had not yet ended and most were anticipating its extension into the following year); we may, indeed must, understand this need for reconciliation, but we may only understand it after death, although our need is to have this knowledge before it. We die in the knowledge, and it dies with us. The poem is thus admonition of an extreme kind, and I would instance Owen's 'Preface' in support of this. The threat which he substantiates through the poem is all the more ominously powerful for the survivors, in that those who perished did so without hope for our future and despite posthumous reconciliation. What hope can there be for us, who remain un-reconciled and without the guidance of their knowledge of pity?

I should like at this point to consider the poem's opening, because it has particular bearing on the interpretation of its close. 'It seemed that out of battle I escaped' concentrates most of the problems in 'It seemed'. The phrase permits 'it seemed but was not the case', or its reverse. This problem may seem finicking, but it is relevant because the 'solution' defines the meaning of 'escaped'. Did the men escape from battle into Hell, or did they only seem to escape from battle? Was their escape from destruction into understanding? Was it a real remission or one that promised but did not fulfil its offer? If we could answer these questions, we might determine the nature of the context which permits, I think, at least three pos-sibilities:

(1) that the figures are part of an actual reality as opposed to an imaged, visionary, or symbolic one.

(2) that the narrator exists within an actual reality, but that what he narrates is a dream or vision.

(3) that the whole poem and the figures in it are a vision of the poet (who is not in the poem), and not the narrator; that the poet and the narrator are two distinct entities working on two different levels of reality. This may seem a casuistical version of (2), but I am trying to determine Owen's intention. Does he intend an ex-perience which we would assent to as part of our normal—but war-torn—life; or is it a visionary experience partly the product of, but separate from, our habitual and actual experience? 'It seemed' is crucial because it suggests that some temporary respite was obtained; although in view of the confrontation between the two men, 'escape', in the sense of setting aside the commitments of war, appears unlikely. Ultimately, the narrator is seen as not escaping (in this sense), and I suggest that if one takes this view together with the conclusion of the poem, the two will seem to confirm this idea of entrapment. I wish, that is, to subvert my categories and suggest that the situation combines (1) and (2), and that the apparent dream process is an imaginative recreation of a

supposed happening after death, or is even a process in the imagination of a living man picturing himself after death.

Welland interprets the poem in psychological rather than sociopolitical terms, his tendency being to remove Owen from political commitments. Thus, he sees the enemy as every person's 'alter ego'. The imaginative force of the poem consists in its uncovering the evil, aggressive portions of the soul: 'The point is well made by the enemy's identification of himself with his killer in lines that are in effect Owen's own elegy.' This is right, and clearly wars are sustained on the basis of authority being able to deploy such instincts, where the fear of the enemy is partly the image, and source, of one's aggressions. But wars are actually waged, and for many reasons sustained, on colder, less immediately instinctual levels, although we may call these evil too. Owen and thirteen million others were killed by an actual 'enemy', and if you rob the poem of its literal referents you deprive it and the situation that engendered it of their bitterest poignancy. To prove this, one should read the following lines, firstly as something 'that happened' and then on a psychological level.

> I am the enemy you killed, my friend.
> I knew you in this dark: for you so frowned
> Yesterday through me as you jabbed and killed.
> I parried; but my hands were loath and cold.

Owen's 'seared conscience'—even though, to re-apply a line from 'At a Calvary', 'he did not hate'—resulted from his killing. If he speaks to his other self, it is to a self that had participated.

One final point might be made. The earlier version of line 40 read, 'I was a German conscript, and your friend', and it can be argued that he abandoned concreteness to stress inward and psychological enactment. Of course, by changing the line to its received version there was a gain in conceptual immediacy, in the universalizing compassion; but there is a loss in particularity, where the sacred pity gains at the *expense* of the literal situation. This is not to say, however, that the situation and the figures in it do not still correspond more with actual than with psychological referents. Owen may admit a 'haloesque' quality into the poem, but with the earlier version of the line in mind, one cannot doubt that the emphasis was for him on actual battle, suffering, and deaths.

Whereas 'Strange Meeting' is in a sense a narrative poem,

'Insensibility' could be called an ode. Certainly what formal distinctions exist—an exalted subject, feeling, tone—fit the poem. From this, one might expect it to be more detached from its subject than 'Strange Meeting', but this is not the case. It works more synoptically, but progresses through a series of precise, particularized statements always fixed upon the subjects of the poem. The first stanza may be linked with assertions in Owen's 'Preface':

> Above all I am not concerned with Poetry.
> My subject is War, and the pity of War.
> The Poetry is in the pity.

Compare this with

> The front line withers,
> But they are troops who fade, not flowers
> For poets' tearful fooling. . . .

Nature is here introduced to confirm that *humanity* is Owen's central concern, and to indicate that a poetic trivializing of nature does justice neither to nature nor to human beings. This kind of literary concern is contrasted with the response of pity, with which Owen is concerned. The poetry is said to be subservient to it. This may seem narrow, and may even seem to be evading the whole question of expressive language, language as a total assent of the feelings and intelligence. On the other hand, it forces the emotions to discover the appropriate language, and at the same time provides a hidden aesthetic embedded in an openly moral basis (beauty is truth). It fuses the two elements—often in danger of separation; in time of crisis, as Wordsworth observed in the Preface to the *Lyrical Ballads*, 'The subject is indeed important!'

The first stanza of 'Insensibility' ended with a wearied 'but no one bothers', recalling the sense of apathy and frustrated expectation in the 'But nothing happens' of 'Exposure'. This leads directly into the second stanza:

> And some cease feeling
> Even themselves or for themselves.

The contrast here implied is between the civilian without sufficient imagination or feeling to recognize what the soldier endures, and between the soldier whose feelings and sensitivity have been eroded by the war; eroded in the area one might least expect—the concern with self. The unease, that is part of Owen's and our own recognition of this, centres on 'for', on which the principal emphasis of the line falls. The rhythmical emphases of the line then dissolve, so that 'themselves' gets lost, detached from the essential rhythmical expectations set up by the previous line; and this erosion of the rhythmical notation mimics the way in which the men's feelings are seen to dissolve. In the third stanza, this loss of sensitivity is amplified into loss of imagination on the part of soldiers, who 'have enough to carry with ammunition'. The imagination and the terrors it breeds are merely an additional burden. Exposed to the cruelties of war, such loss is a gain of sorts for as long as the war continues, although for such amputation to be considered a gain is an indictment of war. If it is not a loss Owen himself suffered, needless to say he does not condemn its occurrence in other soldiers. This blunting might be contrasted with Rosenberg's assertion in a letter of 1916 to Laurence Binyon:

> I am determined that this war, with all its powers for devastation, shall not master my poeting; that is, if I am lucky enough to come through all right. I will not leave a corner of my consciousness covered up, but saturate myself with the strange and extraordinary new conditions of this life, and it will all refine itself into poetry later on.

Owen tersely comments on the soldiers that 'Their hearts remain small-drawn.' Stanza four introduces a fresh idea, sustained through this and the next stanza, which is comparable with what Sassoon does for the boy in 'Suicide in the Trenches'. Owen wrote:

> Happy the lad whose mind was never trained:
> His days are worth forgetting more than not.

This might be coupled with

> I heard the sighs of men, that have no skill
> To speak of their distress, no, nor the will!
> A voice I know. And this time I must go.

The first passage, from 'Insensibility', and the second, from 'The Calls', both presuppose an unexpressed distress in those who have not been educated and are therefore not articulate enough to express their distress. But, whereas the benign paternalism of 'The Calls' merely pleads on their behalf, in 'Insensibility' it is said that, because the boy has no training—no formal education—he does nothing worth his (our ?) remembering. This leads to the further implication that because 'Alive, he is not vital overmuch', his feelings are therefore less intense than those with educated minds, and that he therefore *suffers* less. The difficulty here is that he is not singular but representative. If this is a correct reading of the passage, the patronizing element, however benignly intended, is strong and the logic surely at fault, since it by no means follows that those who are faultily educated (through no fault of their own) therefore *feel* less. Thought and education may interact with feeling but they are not thus synonymous with it. It is not established that to be articulate, or trained in mind, necessarily increases the depth of feeling or the capacity for suffering. Rather, perhaps, feelings that are denied expression tend to induce frustration. Sorley understood the problem better in his 'To Poets' (September 1914):

> We have the evil spirits too
> That shake our soul with battle-din.
> But we have an eviller spirit than you,
> We have a dumb spirit within:
> The exceeding bitter agony
> But not the exceeding bitter cry.

Written so early in the war, these lines are extraordinarily perceptive. Owen balances the idea of the under-educated 'lad' with that of the fully educated, whose imagination is, on the contrary, over-active. Activity of this kind and in such a context is certainly a burden, but in other circumstances it is also a privilege. Is it the prerogative of the educated, as it may be of the more experienced?

> We wise, who with a thought besmirch
> Blood over all our soul,
> How should we see our task
> But through his blunt and lashless eyes?

Whether 'we' are educated or 'wise' only through experience, the suggestion is that of an indulgent imagination corrected by passing its (our) feeling through the unconscious if catalytically healthful mind of the 'lad'—the 'blunt and lashless eyes'. 'We' imagine what the boy's state of mind is and then use it correctively for ourselves.

In the final stanza there is a switch of reference, in that so far Owen has been writing of different kinds of insensibility to suffering, but always, as I understand it, with reference to the soldiers' own feelings, which are eroded by experience. As opposed to the compassion he feels for the soldiers, here he expresses rage for the civilian who, as Sassoon also thought, lacked the imagination or inclination to feel what the soldier endured, and thus conspired in perpetuating his ordeal.

> But cursed are dullards whom no cannon stuns,
> That they should be as stones;
> Wretched are they, and mean
> With paucity that never was simplicity.
> By choice they made themselves immune
> To pity and whatever moans in man. . . .[1]

This is one of the most satisfactory approaches to change that Owen makes because, I suggest, where anger is present with compassion, then change may be seen to be determined upon. The anger does not lose sight of the suffering, and the compassion is forced into acting on behalf of the sufferer because of the presence of the anger. To put it differently, the soldiers are seen, in relation to the civilians for whom they suffer, and the indifference of the latter exacts from the reader the recognition that drastic change of thought, leading to action, is demanded.

The culminating pressure of the half-rhyme builds up a fierce 'on-behalf-of' quality, even though the poem ends in a kind of peaceableness. This quality lifts through a complexity of half-rhyme and internal assonance to the high pitches of vowel, at the top of which (mawkish though it may sound) is heard 'tears'. In 'Strange Meeting', the tendency of the half-rhyme, sounding the discords of despair and social disharmony, is to drop from a higher to lower pitch; and certainly the poem ends on just such an emphatic descent with 'killed/cold/now'. Perhaps this also backs up my sense of the compassion in 'Strange Meeting' as tending to be dialectically static and culminating in despair, albeit of an admonitory kind. Whereas in 'Insensibility' compassion is a factor contributory to desired change. The compassion that in 'Strange Meeting' is (for some) slightly haloesque, is here active. It is with these considerations in mind that some basis for comparing Owen and Rosenberg is formed.

Owen was killed on 4 November 1918 while trying with his men to improvise means for crossing the Sambre Canal. There were

[1] Day Lewis, in the *Collected Poems* (p. 38), reads 'mourns in man', but I prefer Blunden's reading.

9

many casualties and a fellow-officer, Lieutenant Foulkes, records
that 'The battalion eventually crossed lower down by means of a
bridge near the village of Ors'. On 12 October 1918 Owen had continued his letter of the previous day:

> I am glad you are finding courage to speak. In a previous letter you
> said you kept quiet. I was not proud of that. The 4th Army General has
> had to issue an Order:
> 'Peace Talk must cease in the Fourth Army'.

It was too late for Owen. A week later the war ended.

Not long before his death Owen had noticed Horatio Bottomley's
dissent from peace talk:

> I am not even depressed by Bottomley's 'NO! NO! NO!' . . .
> It has had the effect of turning the whole army against its John Bull at
> last. My heart has been warmed by the curses I have heard levelled at the
> *Daily Mail*.

Bottomley had written in *John Bull*, on 12 October 1918:

> I have no intention, as far as I have any power, of allowing the Gentle-
> men of Whitehall to come to an arrangement with the Kaiser. I don't
> want any more talk of not being out to destroy the German nation—that
> is just what I am out for. . . . I shall be there.[1]

That is what war had come to mean by 1918; the destruction of
nations. Perhaps the despair and admonition of 'Strange Meeting'
was not unjustified. What was handed to the Germans after the war,
without pity or any sense of the need for reconciliation or for change
of any kind however difficult that might have been to achieve, was
driven back into Europe twenty-one years later.

---

[1] Bottomley had started *John Bull* in 1906. In 1918 he returned to the House of Com-
mons, after having lost his seat in 1912 when he was declared bankrupt. Nothing
deterred him. In 1922 he was convicted for fraudulent conversion in connection with
the 'patriotic' Thrift Prize Bond Club with which he had been engaged during the
war, and was sent to prison for seven years.

CHAPTER TEN

ISAAC ROSENBERG

The Lambeth Guardians yesterday decided that, in order that the Poor Law School children might have an opportunity of appreciating the position of national affairs, the usual practice of allowing each child an egg for breakfast on Christmas morning be suspended this year. The Chairman of the Board remarked that it was better to let the children go without eggs than to give them shop eggs.

The Times, 12 November 1914

Rosenberg was born in Bristol on 25 November 1890. His parents were emigrants from Russia, and like many others who settled in England in this period, they fled from eastern Europe to avoid either the brutalities of the Czar or else the persecution of the peasants, whose prejudices expressed themselves through the residual biases of Christianity. When he was seven, his family were persuaded to move to the East End of London, where, they were told, they would earn more. They became poorer and Rosenberg's health, which had never been good, deteriorated to the point at which he developed a lung condition. These two factors—his Jewishness and his poverty—will form the basis of my examination of his work. It should be added that, although he knew no Hebrew, he did (according to his sister) speak Yiddish—the lingua franca of European Jewry, and it might be this which Kenneth Allott unconsciously refers to in his remark that Rosenberg's poems '. . . are spoilt for me by his appetite for the extravagant and his rebarbative poetic diction' (later modified to: 'unpleasing poetic diction'). The preference Allott shows for a more mellifluous diction contrasts with Rosenberg's language, with its bunches of harsh, obtruding consonants (Yiddish is German slightly Hebraicized and written in Hebrew characters).

Until he was fourteen Rosenberg attended the elementary schools at Stepney, and was then apprenticed as an engraver—work he hated, writing (before 1911):

It is horrible to think that all these hours, when my days are full of vigour and my hands craving for self-expression, I am bound, chained to this fiendish mangling machine, without hope and almost desire of deliverance. . . .[1]

In the evenings he went to the Art School at Birkbeck College, and in 1911 his wish to take up painting professionally was substantially implemented through the generosity of three Jewish women (Mrs. Delissa Joseph, Mrs. E. D. Lowy, and Mrs. Herbert Cohen), who paid for his studentship at the Slade School of Fine Art.[2]

His earliest dated poem is 'David's Harp' (1905), although he was not generally known to be writing poetry before 1909. In a letter prior to 1911 he says:

I really would like to take up painting seriously; I think I might do something at that; but poetry—I despair of ever writing excellent poetry. I can't look at things in the simple, large way that great poets do.

This is no place for a discussion of his work as a painter, but from the beginning he clearly longed to be a poet. Despite the encouragement of the painter J. H. Amschwitz in the Birkbeck period, and his association with Gertler, Bomberg, Kramer, Roberts, Nevinson, and Stanley Spencer at the Slade, he began to feel that his capacities were more those of a poet than a painter. 'I find writing interferes with drawing a good deal, and is far more exhausting', he wrote to Laurence Binyon in 1912, and to Mrs. Cohen:

I feel very grateful for your interest in me—going to the Slade has shown possibilities—has taught me to see more accurately.—but one especial thing it has shown me—Art is not a plaything, it is blood and tears, it must grow up with one; and I believe I have begun too late.

He told Edward Marsh, in about 1915, that 'I believe in myself more as a poet than a painter. I think I get more depth into my writing.' Rosenberg was by this time in the army, so that the possibilities of his being able to paint with any scope or regularity were non-existent. It was courageous of him to write this to Marsh, who was one of the few purchasers of his paintings, and had considerably less interest in him as a poet.

---

[1] Unless otherwise stated, all quotations from Rosenberg's poems and letters are taken from *Isaac Rosenberg: The Collected Works*, edited by Gordon Bottomley and D. W. Harding (1937).

[2] Rosenberg's work as a painter is discussed briefly by Maurice de Sausmarez in *Isaac Rosenberg 1890–1918/Catalogue with Letters*, the catalogue to an exhibition of his work held at the University of Leeds in June 1959.

Rosenberg thought that it was just possible for him to live from his painting, and he did some portrait work; but in 1914 he was told that his lungs were weak ('I have no tuberculosis as far as I know, but a weak chest', he told Marsh in May that year), and by June 1914 he was in Cape Town, staying with a married sister. South Africa provoked social comment found, obliquely, in his poetry, but it is explicit in a letter to Marsh, in which he energetically unfolds his plans to one who has been his patron and who will presumably be so again:

I am in an infernal city by the sea. This city has men in it—and these men have souls in them—or at least have the passages to souls. Though they are millions of years behind the time they have yet reached the stage of evolution that knows ears and eyes. But these passages are dreadfully clogged up, —gold dust, diamond dust, stocks and shares, and heaven knows what other flinty muck. Well Ive made up my mind to clear through all this rubbish.

Something unguarded (rather than naïve) emerges from the tone, in the way that Rosenberg takes the affluent Marsh into his confidence, realizing as much as Lawrence, say, the thriving if contradictory connection between culture and money. Rosenberg thought, as appears in a later passage of the same letter, that art would cauterize the rubbish, but the remedial powers he attributed to art did not create in him a naïve blindness to his own and others' poverty:

Im living like a toff here. Early in the morning coffee is brought to me in bed. My shoes (my only pair) are polished so brightly that the world is pleasantly deceived as to the tragedy that polish covers. I don't know whether there are snakes or wild animals in my room, but in the morning when I get up and look at the soles of my shoes, every morning I see another hole.

In 1915 he returned to England, and in November or early December that year he enlisted in the Bantam Regiment ('I was too short for any other'). Apparently he did not enlist out of patriotism, and although both he and Owen hesitated before joining up, they hesitated for different reasons. Thus, in June 1915 Owen writes to his mother:

So [Peyronnet] renews his proposition of an Eastern Voyage; to begin in Sept. if possible; but *not* until the Campaign of the Dardanelles be finished. I told him therefore that if the way were still blocked when I return home in Sept. I should try to join the Army. For I noticed in the Hotel in London an announcement that any gentleman (fit, etc.) *returning to England from abroad* will be given a Commission—in the 'Artists' Rifles'. Such officers will be sent to the front in 3 months. Thus we shall watch the Dardanelles with a little more interest than before. And, in very sooth, I rather hope things there will last out as long as the war, which will be through the winter. Still more Frenchmen have been mobilised since I left France; and the outlook is not one shade brighter. I don't want the bore of training, I don't want to wear khaki; nor yet to save my honour before inquisitive grand-children fifty years hence. But I *now do* most *intensely want to fight*. In redoubting the exercises during these months of July & August I have perfectly sufficient reason for *not* '*joining*' *yet*. But when I learnt that Peyronnet prefers me to wait until the East is more settled I felt full of peace—and of war. So the most patriotic thing I can do is to hope for non-success in the Dardanelles! In a month or so from now, forces will be as certainly lacking as munitions are now.

This is in some ways a naïve letter. One senses with some embarrassment the egocentric involvement of 'Thus we shall watch the Dardanelles . . .'; 'I rather hope things there will last out as long as the war'; and 'But when I learnt that Peyronnet prefers me to wait until the East is more settled'. This last suggests that Owen is being pushed into enlisting by the scent manufacturer Peyronnet's casual response to the war. One respects more 'I now do most intensely want to fight', if one is concerned more with the individually honest response. More admirable still is 'I don't want to wear khaki; nor yet to save my honour before inquisitive grand-children fifty years hence'—which one associates with a particular recruiting poster, and with his 'Dulce et Decorum Est'. Yet in this letter there is something of the perhaps compensating attitude of the 'I am a young gentleman on his travels and will attend my duties in due order'. That Owen was nothing of the kind is revealed in his letters by the frequent mention of his being short of money, and by his reiterated concern with railway tickets. The latter is puzzling until one recalls that his father was a railway official and that this enabled the son to travel at what were reduced rates. Owen never had the 'gentleman's release from money cares', and more importantly never had the attitude which accompanies such release. One senses in the tone of his letters, as much as in their substance, that with his petit-bourgeois background he was sometimes at a loss to know where he stood socially and in what direction he should be going.

With Rosenberg—as with Sorley—there is no confusion of this kind, which must surely be attributable to Rosenberg's unambiguous social background—'Im living like a toff here' being a comment that would pass more easily between himself and his family than it would between Marsh and himself. The publication of Owen's *Collected Letters* in 1967 reveals him to have only gradually acquired during the war the kind of seriousness that Rosenberg had before it; seriousness, not merely in art, but in respect of society and his responses to it. In Rosenberg's case there is a more evident debate with himself over enlistment (which is not to say that Owen may not have kept some of it to himself), perhaps because, unlike Owen's father, Rosenberg's family, who were 'Tolstoyans', were resolutely against war. But whatever the reasons, Rosenberg's argument with himself is clearly a painful one:

I am thinking of enlisting if they will have me, though it is against all my principles of justice—though I would be doing the most criminal thing a man can do—I am so sure my mother would not stand the shock that I dont know what to do.

I have changed my mind again about joining the army. I feel about it that more men means more war, —besides the immorality of joining with no patriotic convictions.[1]

I wanted to join the RAMC as the idea of killing upsets me a bit, but I was too small. The only regiment my build allows was the Bantams.[2]

I never joined the army for patriotic reasons. Nothing can justify war. I suppose we must all fight to get the trouble over. Anyhow before the war I helped at home when I could and I did other things which helped to keep things going. I thought if Id join there would be a separation allowance for my mother.

As to your suggestion about the army I think the world has been terribly damaged by certain poets (in fact any poet) being sacrificed in this stupid business. There is certainly a strong temptation to join when you are making no money.

This last, an apparently unfinished letter to Ezra Pound, 1915, brings into question what precisely Pound's suggestion to Rosenberg was. And in connection with the last but one letter (to Marsh) quoted, was it not open—even naïve—of Rosenberg to tell Marsh, who was

[1] How sharply this contrasts with Johnston's concerns with duty and the moral imperatives; he sees Rosenberg as equally, but oppositely, concerned with *his* duty.
[2] The first three quotations are from *Catalogue with Letters*, pp. 8, 10, 12.

then Churchill's private secretary, that he never 'joined the army for patriotic reasons'? The letters from this period suggest a searching self-analysis, a questioning of himself in relation to war and its issues, exceeding Owen's at this time. The obsessive quality of Rosenberg's misgivings emphasizes the starkness of his emerging responses.

Both the manner and substance of his letters contrast most strongly with Brooke's, whose response to the war was unambivalent (in 1914 Brooke was 27 and Rosenberg 24; Owen was 21). Thus, as we have seen, Brooke wrote in February 1915: 'I've never been quite so happy in my life, I think. Not quite so *pervasively* happy; like a stream flowing entirely to one end.' One may question the quality of happiness conveyed in such an image perhaps, and should recall Hassall's biographical enlargement on the nature of Brooke's disturbance in the period prior to the war. It must have been a great relief to have 'the call of duty' to answer. But to account for his motivation is not to justify his decision. The contrast sharpens when one compares the enlistment circumstances themselves. Brooke, the Fabian socialist, at first thought of joining as a private, but in August 1914 accepted a commission, obtained for him by Churchill, in the Royal Naval Division. Owen had similar ideas, but also changed his mind and took a commission. Aldington and Rosenberg, on the other hand, enlisted as privates. It is unfair perhaps even to seem to rebuke Brooke for what he did, since Owen did it also, and since in any case Rosenberg's class would have militated against his obtaining a commission (even had he wanted one), at that stage of the war. But one also recalls how Rosenberg refused promotion—to lance-corporalship. Other aspects of Brooke's responses to the war are disturbing. He refers to the chaos of retreating soldiers and Belgian refugees as 'an extraordinary and thrilling confusion'. By contrast, Rosenberg's army letters reveal constant misery. One crucial difference between the two men, apart from the evident one of matured personal convictions and responses, is that of class. Brooke was well-connected and middle-class, as the circumstances of his commission indicate. Describing his first contact with 'the men', he calls them 'dear things'. Rosenberg's experience was harsher: 'my being a Jew makes it bad amongst these wretches'; and 'I have a little impudent schoolboy pup for an officer and he has marked me—he has taken a dislike to me I dont know why.' He told Marsh: 'I find that the

actual duties though they are difficult at first and require all one's
sticking power are not in themselves unpleasant, it is the brutal
militaristic bullying meanness of the way they're served out to us.
You're always being threatened with "clink".' Early on in the war
he remarks: '. . . as for the others, there is talk of mutiny every day.
One reg close by did break out and some men got bayoneted'
(*Catalogue with Letters*, p. 14).

His isolation, as a man and as a poet, was complex. The comment
in his letter to Sydney Schiff about being a Jew (consult also his poem
'The Jew') indicates the isolation he could expect amongst both the
proletariat and others. As one of the first generation of English-
speaking Jews, he would find also a gap between his and his parents'
(mainly Yiddish-speaking) generation, although, as Welland indicates in his study of Owen, there existed a vigorous Jewish culture
in the East End of London which would have advantaged Rosenberg. Ethnic differences, however, cut across class solidarity as
much as 'intellectual' differences obtained via English culture did;
and inasmuch as his intellectual concerns placed him more with the
bourgeoisie, he would have found certain subtle factors militating
against him. On the other hand, it must be admitted that he was
not an easy man to have dealings with, as is shown by his relationship with one of his patrons (although patronage in itself has inherent strains). He wrote to Mrs. Cohen: 'I am not very inquisitive
naturally, but I think it concerns me to know what you mean by
poses and mannerisms—and whose advice do I not take who are in
a position to give—and what more healthy style of work do you
wish me to adopt?' It is hardly surprising that he writes—to Miss
Wright in 1912: 'I have thrown over my patrons they were so un-
bearable, and as I cant do commercial work, and I have no other
kind of work to show, it puts me in a fix.'

Rosenberg had a different kind of relationship with Marsh. For
one thing he was not beholden to Marsh as he seems to have been
to the three women who provided him with the Slade School fees.
Marsh, wisely perhaps, seems to have responded generously to what
Rosenberg as a painter produced, but seems not to have become
involved with him in any continuous way. The wisdom reveals
the limitation. Marsh became involved, it seems, on a work-by-work
basis, rather than with the man as a whole. This gave Rosenberg the independence that he so evidently lacked with his former
patrons, but, in the other sense of the word, some element of

patronage seems to have existed, if Rosenberg's humble letters to Marsh are any guide. For Marsh does not seem to have given Rosenberg the recognition he needed. Apart from printing the song from 'Moses', 'Ah Koelue', in his *Georgian Poetry* (1916–17), he published nothing of Rosenberg's, although he was sent plenty. He had no room for 'Dead Man's Dump', though it 'so impressed [him] that he copied it out before returning it, lest it should be lost'. Of 'Moses', Marsh wrote to Bottomley: 'I wrote him a piece of my mind about *Moses*, which seems to me really magnificent in parts, especially the speech beginning "Ah Koelue" . . . but as a whole it's surely quite ridiculously bad'; and again, to the same correspondent, 'I wrote to [Rosenberg] with the utmost brutality, telling him it was an outrage on humanity that the man who could write the Koelue speech should imbed it in such farrago.'

Given therefore Marsh's kind of cultural attachments, it is not surprising that the patronizing note should emerge even more strongly after Rosenberg was dead. In *A Number of People*, he wrote: 'poor little Isaac Rosenberg, who never came into his kingdom, surely one of the most futile sacrifices of the War, for except courage he had no quality of the soldier and if he had lived, he must have done great things.' There is something dismayingly second-hand about these assertions, and distant also, in the re-creation of 'the soldier' as an epitome of the human condition, which destroys any sense of a suffering, active human being such as Rosenberg's letters reveal him to have been. Moreover, there is more attachment to the poetry claimed than was ever enacted. The exaggeration of the phrase 'must have done great things' reveals the vacuity of the feeling. The professed conviction that Rosenberg 'must have done great things' (assuming he had not) seriously questions Rosenberg's capacity to do so. The emphasis of 'must' is rhetorical rather than an expression of conviction, and the elegant subjunctive amounts to no less than a tasteful turning off of the entire question. Finally, it is the word 'little' which persists: 'I spent the whole afternoon writing my speech for opening an exhibition of poor little Isaac Rosenberg's pictures in Whitechapel', Marsh wrote to Hassall. Then Hassall himself catches the trick: 'Eddie Marsh was still coping with the impoverished little Rosenberg's literary affairs.'

It may seem unjust so to criticize Marsh for his failure to take Rosenberg seriously, but his responses and failure to respond are reasonably representative of many of Rosenberg's admirers. With the exceptions of F. R. Leavis and Denys Harding, critics have since echoed Marsh's view that Rosenberg's poetry has promise but little that was 'perfect', little that was not marred by excess or obscurity. He had his interested readers, even during his lifetime, but none interested enough to secure substantial publication. Apart from 'Koelue's Song' in the *Georgian Anthology*, 'Break of Day in the Trenches' and 'Marching Song' both appeared in *Poetry* (IX, 3, Dec. 1916), probably through the offices of Ezra Pound; and Laurence Binyon introduced the selection edited by Gordon Bottomley, which was published by Heinemann in 1922.

Rosenberg then was effectively isolated from a public, from large sections of society, and from any critic at all perceptive to his work, which, considering the kind of literary fashions then prevailing, is not surprising. That he felt his isolation as a poet he makes clear in a letter to R. C. Trevelyan (c. 1916): 'it has made me very happy to know you like my work so much; very few people do, or, at least, say so; and I believe I am a poet. Here in the trenches where we are playing this extraordinary gamble, youre letter made me feel refreshed and fine.' Rosenberg had privately printed (though not with any vanity press) three pamphlet collections: *Night and Day* (1912), *Youth* (1915), and 'Moses', a play (1916). The second was printed at Marsh's expense, for which Rosenberg offered him three drawings. None of these pamphlets made any money and one might guess that they were of satisfaction to Rosenberg only in that a few people read his work; or else satisfied him by objectifying his work and giving it an authenticity which it had hitherto lacked. His remark to Marsh, 'I think I get more depth into my writing', is interesting in that his concern was so different from that of the new Georgian movement then rapidly consolidating itself, under Marsh's guidance. In *The New Poetic*, C. K. Stead discusses the impact of the first Georgian anthology (1912) on the received taste of the time. He notes the hostility with which the newer poets, like Brooke, were regarded by 'imperialist' poets such as Newbolt, although the anthology, with the adroit publicity it received, sold well. There is evidence in his letters that Rosenberg had some liking for a few of the Georgians—Bottomley for instance—which would not have precluded his admiration for Rossetti and Francis Thompson. There is one instance of his recasting a poem, 'The One Lost', in such a way as to draw Marsh's approval. The result is an unwitting parody of the Georgian manner. It seems unlikely that Marsh's acceptance could for long have diverted his powerful, original talent, but from our point of view (however painful it may at the time have been for Rosenberg) we can have little regret for Marsh's dislike of Rosenberg's poems. He could only have encouraged the weaknesses in his work. Rosenberg was not a Georgian.

Nor had he any connection with the Imagists who, unlike the Georgians, did not court the favour of the public. Rosenberg belonged to no movement and apparently followed none of the critical dicta offered either by groups of poets or by individual critics. He had read some F. S. Flint and wrote to Miss Seaton in 1912:

> I suppose [his] poems give me pleasure because of their newness to me. . . . they seem to me just experiments in versification except some, which are more natural . . . those are the ones I like best. I like of the first lot, 'The heart's hunger', for the energy intensity and simplicity with which it expresses that strange longing for an indefinite ideal; the haunting desire for that which is beyond the reach of hands. I like the one call[ed] 'Exultation', very much. The image in the last stanza; of the—
>
> > *'birds, unrooted flowers of space,*
> > Shaking to heaven a silver chime of bells',
>
> I think is fine

What he identifies in Flint accords with what he elsewhere claims to admire in poetry: 'the energy intensity and simplicity' and, from his reading of Donne, the comprehensive, metaphysical handling of, and insight into, naturally occurring phenomena. Rosenberg's 'more natural' may seem at first to be overly reserved, but it remains a useful corrective. It points to his centrally poised achievement in which he is not symbolically, metaphysically, or realistically weighted in any one direction. His imagination nearly always illuminates observed phenomena, and is not an egocentric reworking of these as a metaphor for his thinking. However necessary we may still find the Imagist demands, their concentration on linguistic means, their fragmentation of the problem is implicitly commented on by Rosenberg's achievement. Only the best imagistic poems, such as Read's 'The Happy Warrior', and 'Hugh Selwyn Mauberley', are as *whole*, as entirely congruous, as the best of Rosenberg. Eliot's 'The Hollow Men', for instance, remains disappointingly thin.

Perhaps what Rosenberg most responded to in the Flint passage quoted above was the imaginative use of the strongly visual root image. There are few traces of Imagism in his work, although there are instances of a corresponding economy of expression—perhaps the clearest being 'August 1914':

> Iron are our lives
> Molten right through our youth.
> A burnt space through ripe fields
> A fair mouth's broken tooth.

These last two lines strike the imagist tone, partly I think because of their apparent impersonal handling of observed phenomena; but examination shows that these lines are in apposition to the previous two, that is, they extend an avowedly personal assertion.

What Rosenberg was working for was the 'idea', and it is something he repeatedly visualizes in his letters. As he wrote to Miss Seaton in 1916,

> It is much my fault if I am not understood, I know; but I also feel a kind of injustice if my idea is not grasped and is *ignored* [my italics], and only petty cavilling at form, which I had known all along was so, is continually knocked into me.

To Bottomley, on 23 July of that year, he writes with extraordinary complexity and insight:

> Simple *poetry*,—that is where an interesting complexity of thought is kept in tone and right value to the dominating idea so that it is understandable and still ungraspable. . . . I am always afraid of being empty.

This concern with 'idea' and its negative fear of emptiness are neither the concern of the Georgians nor the Imagists.[1] For Rosenberg the idea was not only important, but was the controlling impulse driving the technical means. Denys Harding, one of his editors, believes that the operating idea began for Rosenberg at an early stage in the language-inducing process:

like many poets in some degree, one supposes—[he] brought language to bear on the incipient thought at an earlier stage of its development. Instead of the emerging idea being racked slightly so as to fit a more familiar approximation of itself, and words found for *that*, Rosenberg let it manipulate words almost from the beginning, often without insisting on the controls of logic and intelligibility.

[1] See p. 169 above.

I suppose that for those who look askance at Rosenberg, Harding's last comment will seem appropriate, but what Harding is speaking of is the poet's process of making. It might be added that, by implication, much of that over-finished quality in English poetry before and since Rosenberg is criticized by his poetry, and perhaps, even, by Harding's commentary.

It seems as if Rosenberg's capacity as a painter, as a thinker in images, impelled him into regarding the 'idea' as the crucial component in the 'made thing', and that, although language was for him an apter medium than paint, the idea even so must never be 'racked' by something already familiar and existing *in language or diction*; but must select for itself the right, singular language incepting the image and tone, as close to the original but composed force as possible. The fumbling in his early work seems not that of a searching for a theme, but the attempt to find that language for his ideas which had not before him existed. It is his struggle (which becomes a present but never obtrusive part of the made thing)—a refusal to simplify a complex set of powerful active ideas—which makes his work rich and responsive. This is perhaps one sense of the 'root', which appears so persistently in his work, and which approximates a cluster of concerns gradually discovered, worked, and expressed, the 'flower' of which is the explicit, 'naturalistic' part of the poem. The idea which is 'understandable and still ungraspable' is inherent in the poem and cannot be abstracted from it, because its full and proper expression is its sensuous ramification—the poetry itself. The experience of the idea is the poem. To extract the idea would be to destroy it, because that would mean destroying its profound sensuous connections with the society that nourishes it. An idea is a social thing (and an individual one) organic to the society it grows in, and to the natural forces that society itself draws on for nourishment. That society is made aware of itself and those forces by the emerging idea. The individual particularizes the idea.

Since the 'root' is one of Rosenberg's pervasive images, it has both complex and individualized associations with society, and it expresses in different contexts, however indirectly and allusively, the change, upheaval, and decay in the society of that time. A relatively simple, if inaccurate, use occurs in 'Midsummer Frost':

> Dead heart, . . .
> Hidden as a root from air or a star from day. . . .

but the intention at least is clear—to express an environment that destroys vitality.

'All poets who are personal—see things genuinely, have their place', he wrote to Marsh in 1914, and one supposes that Rosenberg is using his own response as a particular instance of a general *malaise*. But even if he is not, as he indicates, the genuine personal response is always valuable. Rosenberg, however, was not making a response that had only individual validity; he more and more came to clarify his personal response in such a way that it took on general applicability without losing its individuality.

In the playlet 'Moses' (printed 1916), the social implications of the 'root' are offered:

> See in my brain
> What madmen have rushed through,
> And like a tornado
> Torn up the tight roots
> Of some dead universe.
> The old clay is broken. . . .

'Moses'—'all written since I joined [the army]'—demonstrates how unlike Owen's development Rosenberg's was. Before the war he already had a complex of attitudes, and symbols for these; whereas, if Owen's early poems are a guide, he had none of any significance. The war had less impact on Rosenberg's work than upon Owen's; it confirmed Rosenberg in the direction he had already taken.

The idea in Moses' brain is the creative impulse which tears up the old 'dead' idea that the Jews must bear perpetual slavery. The old clay is broken. The new (in fact, ancient) Maccabean idea—to reapply a later historical event—is creative because it proposes to root out the enslaving, fatalistic one from the minds of the Jews, who must then destroy it in the Egyptian mind. Rosenberg regards this process as creative in that it initiates a form of action from which human life for the enslaved Jews will result. It may deprive the Egyptians of their slaves, but if tyrants can derive no benefit from a morally superior condition, they deserve nothing. The 'idea' is used here with full force, that is, as a form of mental activity that advances a group of people by leading them to beneficial action through the idea (the same kind of force implicit in Owen's 'Insensibility'). The Maccabean theme is itself Jewish, although not in its application confined to Jews, but it is interesting to see Rosenberg give it overt universal application. In this, too, he differs from Owen, who tends to sharpen his perceptions into didactic particularity; the perceptions funnel into didactic narrowness. This is not the disadvantage it is normally taken to be, but the method does in general contrast with Rosenberg's.

In 'Moses' he raises several related issues. Since the Jews were then labourers, a form of Egyptian proletariat, although without even the nominal privileges of an Egyptian, Rosenberg, by implication, invokes the class struggle. The inevitable suspicion, coming from both Jews and Egyptians (which compares with Rosenberg's own position; see above p. 255), centres on Moses who, some Jews think, is not only betraying his own ethnic group, but, by involving himself with a highly placed Egyptian woman, is dissociating himself from the condition of the Jews as labourers enslaved to the Egyptians. The Jewish grievance, although Judaically orientated, picks this out precisely:

> OLD HEBREW
> He is a prince, an animal
> Not of our kind, who perhaps had heard
> Vague rumours of our world, to his mind
> An unpleasant miasma.

This is immediately qualified by the Young Hebrew's reply:

> Is not Miriam his sister, Jochabed his mother?
> In the womb he looked round and saw
> From furthermost stretches our wrong.

The young man joins Moses to the Jews ethnically, and by distinguishing between the two issues—ethnic and class—he immediately again merges them. Rosenberg touches here on the two principal currents of nineteenth-century action and reaction, those of radicalism and nationalism. As I suggested in Chapter One, these are anything but identical impulses, but for Jews in this situation they inevitably combine, and for Moses they must remain inseparable too. Nationalism and the class struggle were, however, for Moses only apparently synonymous so long as the Jews were struggling with a common oppressor. Had the Egyptians not enslaved the Jews as labourers but treated them as a tribe, within their own hierarchic divisions, some of whom could penetrate the

ruling Egyptian echelons, Moses' position would have been distinct from the Jewish *labourer*. But because the Egyptians enslaved
the Jews as a whole, and because as a result the ethnic and the class
issues became inseparable, Moses' ethnic and radical impulses
merge. It is not possible in Rosenberg's 'Moses' to determine what
emphasis to put upon the ethnic impulse and what on the radical.
For Rosenberg, one suspects that the two issues were in common. To
be Jewish in England then was to be, in the main, working class. If
for some Jews the emphasis was ethnic, for Rosenberg the emphasis was radical, although we should not therefore be misled into
imagining that he would have countenanced an obliteration of the
cultural differences between the English and Jewish working class.
As he wrote to his mother: 'I hope our Russian cousins are happy
now. Trotsky, I imagine will look after the interests of his co-
religionists.' The expectation defines the position. To say this is
to show, not a confused mass of unshaped data, but a thinking
mind that had pieced together the issues which had grown from
comparable roots. The 'madmen' who have

> Torn up the tight roots
> Of some dead universe

have destroyed the coherence of the excluding and oppressive old
order and have cleared the way for new ideas and new coherences to
take root in their place; or rather, for the interests already rooted
there, to grow.

These are some of the issues which cluster round the image of the
root in 'Moses'. 'The Unicorn', which Rosenberg was working on
(but did not finish) up to his death on 1 April 1918, explores the
same image. But whereas in 'Moses' the root stands for the basis
and remaining structure of the old order (where to leave such root
in place is to accept that order), in 'The Unicorn' it is a referent for
primitive male sexuality and its engendering:

> Bestial man shapes ride dark impulses
> Through roots in the bleak blood, then hide
> In shuddering light from their self loathing.

In a different context, the image has something in common with the
idea of the root in 'Moses', but the difference is that, while in
'Moses' it emphasizes an idea (leading, it is true, to action) initially
operating internally, the 'Unicorn' root image is an apprehension
of things in external condition, which have their own objective

existence but which correlate with and reflect the changing condition of man's social relations:

> The roots of a torn universe are wrenched,
> See the bent trees like nests of derelicts in ocean
> That beats upon this ark.

Rosenberg's deepening experience of the war, and thus of external
reality, produced a response that delineated objects and creatures
more richly and powerfully; and in this enrichment, the relations
between inner response and outer reality are strengthened. The two
fetch and carry for each other, in mutual correspondence, more than
they did before.

One notices that the static root image often stands in relation to
violent change. And yet the image itself is immediately simple and
graspable. Before 1911, Rosenberg had written to Miss Seaton: 'I
despair of ever writing excellent poetry. I can't look at things in the
simple, large way that great poets do'; and to Bottomley, on 23
July 1916: 'Simple *poetry*, —that is where an interesting complexity
of thought is kept in tone and right value to the dominating idea
so that it is understandable and still ungraspable.' He seems to
mean not that the ideas should be simple, but that the vehicle
should present a simple 'graspable' surface. Rosenberg had already
established some of his postulates, many of which have since
been taken up in criticism as the constituents of a complete and
responsive poetry.

One final and opposite example of the root occurs in 'Chagrin',
which was printed with 'Moses' in the pamphlet of that name. It
was probably, however, written between November 1915 and June
1916 (but see his letter to Marsh with its reference to the 'inspired
"suntreaders" '). The image of Absalom hanging by the hair
articulates the rootlessness of the Diaspora (and English) Jew. As
the soul chokes in isolation, the subject of the poem asks Christ,
the spiritual emblem for the society in which the man is suspended,
to end his spiritual dying. Rosenberg finishes the poem with an
instance of the (seemingly unending) condition of rootlessness:

> We ride, we ride, before the morning
> The secret roots of the sun to tread,
> And suddenly
> We are lifted of all we know
> And hang from implacable boughs.

'The secret roots of the sun' are those nurturing, life-giving organs without which all human life would die. The Jews, and other groups similarly subsisting, enjoy this nurturing only in patches. At the moment when all their energies are unwarily exerted ('We ride, we ride'), their appetites and expectations fully roused, suddenly they are lifted of these. The image of the roots sensuously re-creates here something desirable, where in other instances (such as the 'Moses' passages above) the roots are of an older dead stock or, as in 'The Unicorn', need revitalizing. The image of the root serves a number of complex ideas, but whether the image represents a desirable force or not (and in the later poems the question of desirability and undesirability is more complexly handled), all the ideas are related, rooted in, a referent that is imagistically simple to grasp and connotes growth, or the dying of growth, whether desirable or not. Rosenberg used what he called the 'Herculean world of ideas' as a means of engaging something; the image is rarely decorative or photographic, but interpretative and experiential.

Rosenberg's idea of God can be described with greater precision than can his 'root' image, in that he presents it as idea and not as symbol. The Divine is an idea which, if he ceased to believe in as an anthropomorphic being, he nevertheless continued to draw on. But the Judaic nature of the Divine undergoes reinterpretation. Initially, as an idea (and not for what it represented), God was for him one who prescribed certain laws, codified through scholarly and rabbinic care; one whose nature was understood in complementary completeness to man's vulnerability and mortality. Any interpretation of, or relationship with, Him was therefore subject to the strength of that belief which saw man's nature and position as dominated, or rather, fixed, by manifold specific demands made by God upon man. Such beliefs were maintained by the Jews in the teeth of, as well as partly through, persecution; and the strength of the human response to the codified beliefs (through whatever motivation) may be attested by any who knew that generation of Jews adult by the end of the nineteenth century. Rosenberg's idea of God changed, but because this image in its various stages was composed of fairly precise elements (which is an oblique comment on their protective nature), one can see the idea changing progressively rather than, as in the symbolic handling of the root, being used for differing and agglomerative purposes.

In 'Spiritual Isolation', printed in *Night and Day* (1912), the relationship between God and the human speaker involves a diseased or malignant partner and, of course, in the earlier stages of conscious belief here, where the image of a deity is a benign one, it is the human that is defective. Arnold in *Culture and Anarchy* strikingly anticipates the plot of Rosenberg's poem with his comment on 'The discipline of the Old Testament [which] may be summed up as a discipline teaching us to abhor and *flee from sin*' (my italics). These are the tactics of Rosenberg's poem.

> My Maker shunneth me.
> Even as a wretch stricken with leprosy
> So hold I pestilent supremacy.
> Yea! He hath fled as far as the uttermost star. . . .
>
> Yea! all seeing my Maker hath such dread,
> Even mine own self-love wists not but to fly
> To Him, and sore besped
> Leaves me, its captain, in such mutiny.

In 'The One Lost', printed in *Youth* (1915) but probably written in 1914, Rosenberg introduces the idea that structures 'God Made Blind':

> And I, lying so safe
> Within you, hearing all,
> To have cheated God shall laugh,
> Freed by your thrall.

The paradoxical, but quite workable, idea here is of human imprisonment being voluntarily used in such a way as to cheat the divine agent of a spiritual imprisonment. Compare the above with this, from 'God Made Blind':

> And then, when Love's power hath increased so
> That we must burst or grow to give it room,
> And we can no more cheat our God with gloom,
> We'll cheat Him with our joy.
> For say! what can God do
> To us, to Love, whom we have grown into? . . .
> We are grown God—and shall His self-hate be?

The idea of bursting or growing with love is, however, found in the last line of Rosenberg's even earlier poem 'Tess': 'Ah, why has God made love so great that love must burst her heart?' Love, it seems, must pay a price for itself to God, or 'cheat' (meaning rebel against) God. Thus, not only is 'God Made Blind' a more amplified and involuted version of the idea in 'The One Lost', but it has also an idea from 'Tess' ramified into it. One sees Rosenberg bringing his ideas together, and composing them into more complex and fuller wholes. In both 'God Made Blind' and 'The One Lost' the only way he can see for two human beings to enact their love is for them to cheat their God; but one might rephrase this, saying that the idea of love as the rival imprisoner to God disappears, as does the emphasis on cheating, and that the human beings share their love as they deliberately league against a God jealous of their love for each other. 'For thou shalt love the Lord thy God with all thy heart and with all thy soul' is the Judao-Christian view of man's relationship to his God. The human relationship, it adds, may be of another and lower kind. By making his lovers in 'God Made Blind' rebel against God, Rosenberg forces that attitude into question:

> . . . what can God do
> To us, to Love, whom we have grown into?

We are love, we are therefore God? The rebellion explicitly depends on the ingenious manipulation of the paradox, but implicitly it depends on the courageous rejection of the priorities that religion has hitherto insisted on. The rendering unto Caesar of what is Caesar's (Love) is ingenious superficially, but on a deeper level profoundly antagonistic. That God is love is the merest of verbal declarations here. The emphasis in the poem is upon growth; love must grow subterraneously, like a root.

In 'Midsummer Frost', probably written before June 1914, Rosenberg uses a tension in which one polarity is made to contain its opposite—as in 'The One Lost' and 'God Made Blind', although there less for the purpose of exploring the tension itself. In 'God', this suspension of one opposite in another constitutes the entire poem's tension:

> In his malodorous brain what slugs and mire,
> Lanthorned in his oblique eyes, guttering burned!
> His body lodged a rat where men nursed souls.

The Divine body nurses the soul of a rat. This is complex theology, if only because Judaism does not in the main recognize the Neo-platonic division of the human being into a mortal body and im-mortal soul. Thus, what Rosenberg the Jew is rendering to both Christians and Jews (who alike believe in a *benign* God) is a Neo-platonically divided, anthropomorphic God, whose soul is malign: and not malign merely, but a rat-soul. This treble hierarchy and concentration of contrasting entities (God : man/man : rat/rat : God) helps to emphasize the idea of the divine, but not in-dividually immortal, soul of man as nurtured in a human and mortal frame. Whether this immortal soul is within a malign God's competence to give is at least questionable. One implication of Rosenberg's thought here is that the benign God system, so far from changing the human system is, rather, itself qualified by it. Rosenberg has changed round the relationship that existed between man and his God in 'Spiritual Isolation'. In 'God', it is man that stands firm, representing a comparatively ideal condition, in which he is, after all, striving for that unattainable goodness not however found in God. And to speak of goodness in this context is entirely too static; it is the process and flux of life in which decency is con-tinually evolved, rather than a static condition, to which Rosenberg aspires. But in the progression of these three poems concerning God, Rosenberg has taken an ultimate step; for, if in 'God Made Blind' the divinity was to be cheated, he was at least in his authori-tarianism thought of as supreme; here he is rejected. And if in the former poem he was jealous, he is here malignant and not to be treated with except as an enemy to be fought, a bully.

> On fragments of an old shrunk power,
> On shy and maimed, on women wrung awry,
> He lay, a bullying hulk, to crush them more.
> But when one, fearless, turned and clawed like bronze,
> Cringing was easy to blunt these stern paws,
> And he would weigh the heavier on those after.

The bully's only real response to fearless opposition is cringing, which blunts the magnanimous claws of the truly strong. All he has is his authoritarian weight with which he crushes his subjects. The heavier he weighs, the more you may know his power is waning. God is seen as a changing entity; his once real power

has now 'shrunk'. Rosenberg also images God's bullying as psychological as well as physical, in that he creates conditions impossible
for humanity to fulfil:

> And he has made the market for your beauty
> Too poor to buy, although you die to sell.

'You die to sell' suggests 'you die in the attempt' as well as the
colloquial sense of 'very much want to'; an extremity of wanting
that is also of God's creation, tormenting since he has also created
those very impediments to your attaining your goal. As in 'God
Made Blind' the controller is envious:

> Your wealth
> Is but his cunning to make death more hard.

And again, as in the earlier poem,

> Only that he has never heard of sleep;
> And when the cats come out the rats are sly.
> Here we are safe till he slinks in at dawn.

The power is not merely less dominating; it is also decayed and
sleazy. The confusing part in this passage is, I think, due to the
fact that the rats are the human beings (not God), and that God
is the cat. But perhaps this is an inevitable difficulty forced on
Rosenberg by his pushing on with the main idea, in which, at this
juncture, we, the humans are not always fearless. Sometimes it is
better we are sly than always in open confrontation with our enemy.
Survival dictates the best tactics. Thus, I do not think we should
carry over much (if anything) of the rat-like character of God on to
ourselves who are now in a rat-*like* predicament. If the rat-like
character is there, it is because we temporarily adopt some of
God's character, an adoption forced on us by aspects of his conduct.
The last stanza, in its relation to the previous two, is extremely complex, and this interpretation is tentatively offered. The rat-God has
'gnawed a fibre from strange roots', he has eaten at the roots of an
alien community, as perhaps the Jews have, or as any alien minority
must do subsisting in a larger alien host. As a result, the Jewish
God is no longer entirely Judaic; if it weakens, its Judaism has
weakened with it. The two results are inevitably even if not directly
interrelated. The larger community housing the smaller alien one
is of course an instance of the tension of one polarity containing its

opposite, as indeed is the idea of God having a rat-soul. This may seem very like an argument (a partial one since Rosenberg is not altogether deploring the situation) for racial purity, but it might be remembered that racial purity is more terrifying when imposed by the larger community on to its minorities. I am of course trying to explain the Jewish position as a minority group, not upholding its intolerances, but indicating that these are intensified by fear. The problem of relating these two ideas, that of the Judaic strain being diluted, and an authoritarian God suffering similar dilution, remains. That they are related is suggested, I think, by the fact that at the end of the poem, we, opposed to a weakened God, are ourselves weakened and listless, not perhaps as a result of energy expended in the struggle so much as because we are in relation to a weaker God:

> And in the morning some pale wonder ceases.
> Things are not strange and strange things are forgetful.
> Ah! if the day were arid, somehow lost
> Out of us, but it is as hair of us,
> And only in the hush no wind stirs it.

We are so motionless that not even the wind stirs us. The hair image recalls 'Chagrin' (Absalom) and suggests the same kind of depending vulnerability. The only way to avoid 'this miasma of a rotting God' and the infecting decay of authority is to change the character of the authority (if indeed it is to be kept at all) and one's relationship with it. This struggle to change the terms of one's existence is much more overtly the single, dramatic theme of 'Moses', and in a more oblique way that of 'The Unicorn' and all its versions. It is, of course, the crucial problem of the individual in a process where democratization has given so much power to the state.

This theme, of changing the terms of one's existence, is Maccabean. Rosenberg is a ramifier of ideas—ramifier in that he never sees the theme simply or the change as easy. Change involves struggle, whether with one's God or one's society, and for Rosenberg the struggle meant being perpetually open to the present and its pressures. He found the past valuable for what it yields us and not for its injunctive force, as a repository of ideal states and artifacts, and in this he differs from Yeats. Although the present might not be ideal, he felt he must experience it rather than berate it. As he

wrote to Schiff in 1915(?): 'One might succumb be destroyed—
but one might also (and the chances are even greater for it) be renewed, made larger, healthier' (*CWL*, p. 12). By this time he was
in the army (as we know from the address of this letter). He wrote
in a similar way to Laurence Binyon in 1916:

> I am determined that this war, with all its powers for devastation,
> shall not master my poeting; that is, if I am lucky enough to come
> through all right. I will not leave a corner of my consciousness covered
> up, but saturate myself with the strange and extraordinary new con-
> ditions of this life, and it will all refine itself into poetry later on.

Rosenberg was of course extremely vulnerable *and* open to experience. As a Jew, a working-class man, and a private soldier, he
knew about vulnerability and its relation to oppression, whether
by God (as he conceived it), a moral code, a class, the military
authority, or the hostile weight of the English. Finally, with millions
of others he learnt about vulnerability in war:

> Thank you for the cheque which is as much to me now as all the
> money in America would be to the Allies. . . . As to what you say about
> my being luckier than other victims I can only say that one's individual
> situation is more real and important to oneself than the devastation of
> fates and empires especially when they do not vitally affect oneself. I can
> only give my personal and if you like selfish point of view that I feeling
> myself in the prime and vigour of my powers (whatever they may be)
> have no more free will than a tree; seeing with helpless clear eyes the
> utter destruction of the railways and avenues of approaches to outer
> communication cut off. Being by the nature of my upbringing, all my
> energies having been directed to one channel of activity, crippled from
> other activities and made helpless even to live. It is true I have not been
> killed or crippled, been a loser in the stocks, or had to forswear my
> fatherland, but I have not quite gone free and have a right to say some-
> thing. (*CWL*, p. 19)

After the impulse of the complaint, the strength of the less heated
judgement on himself (by comparison with those less fortunate) is
striking, and attests that the kind of strength he possessed was not
so much forceful as robust, the energy of emotion balanced by a
deliberate, conscious fortitude. It is an intelligence that could not,
to judge from this letter, be shamed into silence by the accusation
of selfishness, and could after all speak up for the man.

   In the struggle to change the conditions of his own life, and others',

through his writing and in his daily living, one senses that Rosenberg struck down the orthodox image of a benign God *and* of a
benign authority which (paternalistically) cared for its subjects, but
did not hesitate to overrule them if its own interests were at all
threatened. Rosenberg wrote the fourth of the 'God' poems before
he sailed for France in May or June 1916, so it seems unlikely that
he revoked the image of a benign God through a disillusionment
induced by his first experience of the trenches. His was no swift
change but, rather, a gradual shift through long harsh exposure to
a variety of pressures; a shift that Brooke, for instance, could hardly
have experienced. The war merely confirmed Rosenberg's direction;
and, having taken this direction, his apparent abandonment of the
struggle with a divine image of God released him for a closer
examination of change and its contingent problems. This is not to
say that he was unresponsive to the war but that, like Clausewitz,
though from an utterly different position, he treated war as an
intensification of pre-war social struggle. He believed that 'War is a
continuation of State policy by other means'. And unlike C. E.
Montague, who did, it seems, suffer disillusion,[1] he appears not to
have believed that there should exist one morality for peace and one
for war.

Rosenberg's struggle with the image of God (a jealous Old
Testament and Christian Neoplatonic one) is to be associated,
emblematically, with his social struggle as projected in his Moses
wrestling with the Egyptians. Moses' flirtations with the luxuries
and benefits obtainable through co-operation with the Egyptians
may, to some extent, have parallelled Rosenberg's flirtation (it was
little more than this) with the richer English literati, of whom
Marsh was the principal example. And how distant, despite his
generosity, Marsh was from Rosenberg, I have already suggested.

Rosenberg eventually realized that he could not join with this
God; He had to be fought, as Moses had to fight with the Egyptians.
Rosenberg had to grapple with the various pressures of both Jewish
authoritarianism and the English authoritarian structures with
which he was also intimately involved. He was involved as a Jew
and as a human being with no ultimate allegiances other than those
which make basic human demands (these last are discussed in 'The
Unicorn'). I distinguish basic from primitive, for Rosenberg was
concerned with social relations and the growth of the individual

---

[1] See *Disenchantment* (1922), chapter 8, 'The Duty of Lying'.

as he comprises the social organism (see the end of 'Moses'). He brilliantly projected this human struggle by speaking in personal terms of his experience of the Anglo-Jewish predicament, and by relating it to an ultimately human wrestling with divine demands. In this he showed the inter-relation between the inner and outer complexities and the way in which they modified each other; what the individual gave up by force of circumstance, or choice. He did this without experiencing the lassitude Brooke complained of both in himself and in others of his class and generation; and without, too, Brooke's experience of alternating prostration and optimism.

Rosenberg's experience of the war seems not to have made a poet of him in the way that it forced on Owen a rapid development. Not that Owen was 'made' by the war, but his development was spectacular by comparison with Rosenberg's.

Of course, as Sassoon asserted, one should never speak of the war as having done anything for anybody, except the armaments industry; and those who see Owen's development as even the merest justification for war are vulgarly insulting not merely the other thirteen millions killed in it, but Owen's own moral indignation and pity. Thus even the celebration of a 'war poet' creates unease. What appeals to us is the expression of outrage at the irony and the waste. This is as it should be, and yet it is not, if we expend our watchfulness in the easing of our guilt, our outrage. Once these are spent society is vulnerable to further wars. There are other grounds for unease. What happens to the war poet is that the sacrifice becomes pictorialized. Owen's death is made to dramatize and illustrate the irony and tragedy of which he was unwillingly a part. He did not return to the front to get killed, but to share as best he could the others' suffering, as a pleader. Yet what the image pictorializes is not so much Owen's judgements as the brilliant revelation which his death uncovers.

Rosenberg's death, on the other hand, does not as easily satisfy any such categories. It is true he was young—twenty-eight—when he died, but the circumstances of his death were uncertain. It is thought that he went out with a wiring party, and it is certain that whatever he did go out to do, he did not return, although we lack witnesses even for this. It is uncertain how much Rosenberg's working-class origins and Jewishness contributed to his comparative oblivion between the two wars, but it is not a factor to be dismissed. What nationalistic country can be expected to honour one who was in many ways so alien to the culture? Disraeli of course was a Jew, yet not only was he converted to Christianity but with piratic expertise expanded the empire, and in this sense was a man of his own country as much as of any nineteenth-century European state. Rosenberg, like Owen, hated war, but he joined up without any convictions, and from poverty as one reason. This made him an unwilling mercenary, and perhaps he felt that there was nothing else he could have done; but he maintained his unwillingness. He lacked patriotic belief, though he had cosmopolitan and Tolstoyan ones.

Owen has seemed to be more a 'war poet' than Rosenberg. Apart from his poems concerning war little remains of value. This is not the case with Rosenberg, although I believe that he wrote some of the most interesting poems concerned with the war. Owen's achievement centres on his poems of hatred, irony, and pity; Rosenberg's on struggle and change, of which the war was a part but not a culmination. There is no sense of the war climaxing his ideas. Not belonging to either conveniently classifiable context, but making each context a part of his work, Rosenberg will fit no category. I believe that Owen would have continued to develop as a poet had he survived the war, but his work does, in an illusory way probably, convey a sense of completeness, which death contrived. But because Rosenberg developed before the war, and moulded war into his thinking, he ought not to be the less regarded. It is all the more ironic that his achievement is so often casually spoken of as fragmentary.

His 'war poems' are nearly all contained in his so-called 'Trench Poems' (1916–18), if, that is, we exclude the versions of 'The Unicorn'. These do not alter the direction of the work, but sometimes ramify the ideas, and more often concentrate certain aspects of them. Yet these poems necessarily introduce elements of experienced struggle which his work had lacked before.

'On Receiving News of the War', written in 1914 when he was still in Cape Town, expresses two attitudes. The first is the corrosive effect of war:

> Some spirit old
> Hath turned with malign kiss
> Our lives to mould.

Noticeable is the word 'kiss', which qualifies, with frightening complexity—or is it romanticism, merely?—the malignity of war. It does not seem to be used to emphasize the differences between love and war, although the implicit paradox depends on such a distinction being made. It conveys the sense of something insidiously and deliberately harmful being done (as if by Rosenberg's female deities); yet, also implicit is the sense of it being beneficial, ultimately through purgation, which of course is Rosenberg's intended meaning. The word has, too, the properties of euphemistic romanticism, but even if Rosenberg is using 'kiss' in this way it does not smother the poem. The war/kiss moulds our lives into temporary evil but finally purges us of our sickness:

> O! ancient crimson curse!
> Corrode, consume.
> Give back this universe
> Its pristine bloom.

There are striking similarities of meaning between this poem and parts of *Maud*.[1] Rosenberg hoped war would restore man's first innocence, but the stylization prevents us from taking the idea with absolute literalness. That he swiftly changed his belief all his 'Trench Poems' show. And however much he hoped war might cleanse, neither in the poems nor in his letters was he in any doubt that war was an affliction. No such recognition is deeply present in *Maud*, or, for that matter, in Brooke's '1914'. I deliberately cite Brooke again because his defenders sometimes suggest that, as with Owen, he would have adopted, had he lived, as scrupulous an anti-war position as Owen did. This seems to me to devalue Owen considerably, but it also seems fair to point out that, Rosenberg's (and Sorley's) initial reaction to the war notwithstanding, neither of them had seen any more of conflict than Brooke had. Contrast Brooke's perception of war in 'The Dead'—'they gave, their immortality'—with Rosenberg's 'Red fangs have torn His face'. Rosenberg's poem was written shortly after the declaration of war; Brooke's sequence was published in *New Numbers*, November–December 1914.

Rosenberg's strength as a 'war poet' arises partly from his ability to particularize powerful physical horror and take it, without losing its presence, to a further stage of consciousness. Owen's

[1] See above pp. 26–7.

particularities sometimes get *absorbed* into his universals, as I have suggested in Chapter Nine. Rosenberg admitted most of his experience in a conscious attempt to form his poetry from it:

> I will not leave a corner of my consciousness covered up. . . . I have thoughts of a play round our Jewish hero, Judas Maccabeus. I have much real material here, and also there is some parallel in the savagery of the invaders then to this war. I am not decided whether truth of period is a good quality or a negative one.

The thoughfulness of the final comment bears an interesting relation to Sassoon's realism, although there is no evidence that Rosenberg ever read his work.

A version of 'Break of Day in the Trenches' was probably completed by the end of July 1916, if this is the poem he refers to in his letter to Marsh of 6 August: 'I am enclosing a poem I wrote in the trenches, which is surely as simple as ordinary talk. You might object to the second line as vague, but that was the best way I could express the sense of dawn.' If this is 'Break of Day', it would seem that he wrote it after one month's experience of the trenches. This is an astonishingly swift development of insight into the horror *and* absurdity of war, although, given the depth of insight already revealed in 'Moses', we ought not to be surprised.

> Only a live thing leaps my hand—
> A queer sardonic rat—
> As I pull the parapet's poppy
> To stick behind my ear.
> Droll rat, they would shoot you if they knew
> Your cosmopolitan sympathies.

Since rats haunted the trenches, it is not surprising to find them represented in poetry which has any pretence to realism; both the rat and the poppy (another familiar war creature) occur in Herbert Asquith's 'After the Salvo',[1] for instance. Superficially, in fact, the poems are curiously similar, but whereas in Asquith's poem the rat's purpose is to emphasize, photographically, the general dereliction created by shellfire, Rosenberg's creature appears without

[1] See *Up the Line to Death*, ed. Brian Gardner (1964), p. 81.

such graphic intention.[1] The rat commutes freely between the two enemies' trenches. By bringing in the idea of cosmopolitanism— the expression of which (except between allies, and then in moderation) was a political offence—Rosenberg indicates the absurdity of the situation by permitting the rat, a supposedly lesser creature, to do what men dare not.

In 'God Made Blind' and 'God', man may be in rebellion against God but he occupies a rational position, in that if God is envious and cruel it is rational to resist His demands, by guile in the former case, force in the latter. Rosenberg emphasizes this rationality in man by giving God the supposedly irrational rat-soul ('God'). And as with his image of the root, he here creates relationships between his poems and ideas by using an image of the same referent but giving it a differing meaning through a different context. By the time he had come to write 'Break of Day', man and God had exchanged attributes, or, at least, man had acquired those which he had previously and only attributed to God. Man may rule the earth, but war is a man-made irrational activity which brings with it absurd, irrational restrictions—national boundaries demarcated with hatred and death. Man absurdly incarcerates himself in the battlefield for an unknown number of years, but the rat freely traverses these demarcations:

> Now you have touched this English hand
> You will do the same to a German—
> Soon, no doubt, if it be your pleasure
> To cross the sleeping green between.
> It seems you inwardly grin as you pass
> Strong eyes, fine limbs, haughty athletes
> Less chanced than you for life. . . .

[1] Creatures in malign relationship to man appear forcefully in several of Rosenberg's poems. The 'rotting God' image appears in 'God' and 'Moses' (*Works*, p. 51) and so does the wolf (ibid.); a toad 'shifting his belly' in 'Moses' (*Works*, p. 59); the worm in 'A Worm Fed on the Heart of Corinth' (*Works*, p. 74), one of the few Greek references in his work; lice appear in both 'The Immortals' and 'Louse Hunting' (*Works*, pp. 78 and 79). Like Owen, Rosenberg sees nature as sometimes in malign relationship to man, but it is not so much a transformation caused by war (man's making) as the emphasis of perception caused by the man's unpleasant or fearful context. Partial exceptions to this exist, as, for example, 'the swift iron burning bee' in 'Dead Man's Dump' (*Works*, p. 82).

As the rat commutes, he mocks the absurd plight of the supposedly superior creatures—'It seems you inwardly grin'—an attitude that rationally we are forced to endorse, however painful and offensive we may find it. The harshness of this judgement does not impair the tenderness with which the poem ends, as the harshness does not impair the tenderness in 'Dead Man's Dump'.

Because Rosenberg has elsewhere given God a rat-soul we may associate the complexity and draw some of the meaning there into this poem. Thus the normal[1] attitude in the context of war would be to envisage a benign God sorrowfully regarding the agony of His supreme creation—a perhaps presumptuous assumption for man to have. In 'Break of Day' God is noticeably absent. The implication may be drawn that, since man can do no better than murder his own kind, he deserves no better witness to his suffering, and no better comforter, than the rat (rat-God) who in this poem usurps the rational position man has abandoned. Whatever the original rights were, in the poem conflict has obliterated them. There remains the tragic and absurd destruction of living creatures. The rat's mocking is rational but heartless; but then so here is the position of man, and it is this that the animal mirrors, while at the same time profitably sharing those conditions unprofitable to man. This mockery is the judgement man receives for his conduct. It is not a destructive retribution such as nature provides for man in Owen's 'Exposure', it might be noted, although the judgement in Rosenberg's poem is more explicitly harsh and disheartening. No further punishment needs to be given. It is both judgement and evaluation.

The lesser creature sees its condition as fortunate by comparison with the 'strong athletes'. It 'grins' at a perceived absurdity, but also perhaps in revenge for man's oppression. It is as much an answer to the oppressor, as is the mice's rejoicing in 'Exposure'. The rat's grinning is an image at the core of Rosenberg's achievement, an image complex, vital, and informed by a tragic apprehension. For, in abandoning God and any religious mode, man no longer has a scapegoat on which he can disburden blame for his actions; he is forced into a position of responsibility. Only he can terminate the activities he has set in train. In holding up to us the rat-image, Rosenberg holds up a partial complement to man's self. To recognize

---

[1] A word with many users, and uses. Newbolt regarded Owen's disgust at the war as 'hardly normal'. (Quoted by C. K. Stead, *The New Poetic*, p. 57.)

the rat is to recognize our absurdity; but if we can recognize our absurdity, we may arrest those activities which otherwise threaten to destroy us. In recognizing that he has lost God, man gains himself; but if he recognizes and still refuses responsibility, he is entirely lost, without the more traditional assistance of religion, and without the power to act on his own behalf. He is his own burden but not his own action, and the tragic implications are that, so burdened, he may perish. The relationship between the rat and the men is a hierarchical one, but it is also a mirror that answers much more than reflecting merely what is presented to it. The grin is the answer, the point at which man has almost lost the capacity to save himself, and tragedy must issue from such loss of potentiality. This is what the rat's grin recognizes and conveys. The point of offence at which men feel judged by a rat has been passed, for more is now at stake than man's rather pitiful pride ('haughty athletes')—pitiful also in that man judges himself as superior to the rat but cannot act as freely. From this point in the poem, Rosenberg develops the tragic extent to which man is mutilating himself, and everything else in nature within the area of conflict.

This mutilation is implied in the phrase 'the torn fields of France'. Rosenberg manages to envisage a landscape but synchronizes the image of it with the image of something smaller. 'Torn' would normally be applied to paper, an object or substance in scale with human beings (made by, and thus in scale with, them). 'Torn' implies a relationship between the object and the person, and the scale adjusted between the two. Also, the verb *tear* has a deliberate, human sense to the action. Landscape, on the other hand, cannot be torn, at least not by human hands and in the way paper is. By making the landscape 'torn', by merging the two scales, the poet suggests that the ground is torn with as much ease as hands tear paper, a suggestion that indicates the power in the implements of war and the vulnerability of man and nature. At this point (line 15) the poem becomes more violent, but one feels that Rosenberg has earned the right at this stage of the poem's development to release his sense of war's violence:

> What do you see in our eyes
> At the shrieking iron and flame
> Hurled through still heavens?

The poem ends tenderly:

> Poppies whose roots are in man's veins
> Drop, and are ever dropping;
> But mine in my ear is safe,
> Just a little white with the dust.

The poppies, of course, represent the dead, their violently shed blood, and in using the image Rosenberg is employing a familiar emblem. The poppy in his fantasy (and everyone else's, one imagines) is nourished by blood that has soaked into the earth and turned the petals red. Rosenberg took this common fantasy a stage further. In return for nourishing the flower and the plant as a whole, the poppy gives man the ambiguous gift of mortality. Its 'roots are in man's veins'; or rather, though this is circular, the poppies feed off man but they feed off his *mortality*, and therefore emphasize it. They too 'Drop, and are ever dropping'. The extension of meaning that Rosenberg has given to the original fantasy is organic to it; the graft seems entirely natural, as primitive and folk-like as the original he has extended. Such achievement attests the strength and tact of his imagination; for it is one thing to invent, quite another to submit one's imagination to another's, or to the collective imagination, and extend it, adding something new and harmonious.

Yet even here Rosenberg has linked this poem with 'Daughters of War', for the same kind of logic operates in both poems. Death is nourished by mortal life; the Daughters lust for soldiers who must however be killed (for them) in their prime. There is also an echo in this of 'God Made Blind', for the female deities are envious of the male human activity—'envy of the days of flesh'—as much as God was of the human lovers.

The last two lines of 'Break of Day in the Trenches' quietly emphasize the perception of death that is not due to age. 'Just a little white' may evoke 'just a little while', a phrase of everyday speech 'as simple as ordinary talk', which in its turn suggests not only the comparatively brief span of a man's life, and a flower's, but the likelihood of the soldier's life being foreshortened. The device subtly underlines the transience of life in war.

'Break of Day in the Trenches' is a fine poem, and its metrical and rhythmical composition is integral to its meaning.[1] The line

---

[1] 'Regular rhythms I do not like much, but of course it depends on where the stress and accent are laid' (*Works*, p. 317).

length is controlled by stress and rhythm rather than by a specified counted number of syllables operating in a single metrical frame. In the main there are three or four stresses per line, but the number of syllables may vary, just as the kind of unit itself may; the line is neither basically iambic nor trochaic. Rosenberg moves his rhythm to originate his meaning:

> The dárknĕss crúmblĕs ăwáy—
> Ĭt ĭś the saḿe olď dŕuiď Tiḿe ăs évĕr. . . .
>
> Nów yŏŭ haV̆e toúched thĭs Eńglĭsh hánd
> Yŏŭ wĭll dó the sáme tŏ ă Gérmaň—

One notices how, in the second set of lines, the shift of stress and the alteration in pace (between the two lines) not only emphasizes the opposition between the English and the German hand, but also initiates a sense of the rat moving from one set of trenches to another; each line initiates a location on the battlefield.

Rosenberg's longest war poem, 'Dead Man's Dump', contains most of what he had to say about the war. In a letter to Marsh dated 8 May 1917, he wrote, 'I've written some lines suggested by going out wiring, or rather carrying wire up the line on limbers and running over dead bodies lying about.' The poem may at first seem picaresque, but what Rosenberg does is to present a number of complex responses to combat, and then unify them into a single realization of how war entails one damaging, continuous impact on the body and the mind. The poem opens with what may seem a biased complaint of the enemy's brutality:

> . . . the flood of *brutish* men
> Upon our brothers dear.[1]

This may seem like gratuitous half-honesty: honest only in that war is brutish, and therefore the enemy behaves brutishly, but only half honest because we behave by the same token as brutishly. It seems unlikely, however, that a man of Rosenberg's intelligence, in one of his central poems and with his professed attitudes to war, should see, or profess, only half the situation. He might of course have changed in his attitude towards the Germans, but nothing in his letters indicates this. External evidence is ambiguous, although his letters are usually corroborative of the attitudes and

[1] My italics.

ideas in the poems. So that in the absence of any expressed belief
that the Germans are more brutish than the English, and taking into
account the cosmopolitanism of 'Break of Day in the Trenches', it
might be reasonable to try another explanation. Rosenberg is saying
perhaps that when you are fighting, the enemy will always seem
brutish, and that you will not notice your own behaviour. If this
seems viable then the poet is re-creating, not immediate judgements,
but the *responses* which he felt he and others made to the enemy's
attack. And surely it is a correct one, as correct as what the Germans
would similarly feel when the British attacked. Again, if this is
correct, it shows, as Harding indicates, how Rosenberg managed to
remain, as he said he wished to, open to 'the strange and extraordinary new conditions. . . . I will not leave a corner of my consciousness covered up'. Now he is not pre-judging the issue with
ready-made ideas, but responding to the situation, and making his
judgement on it when he has responded as fully and finally as
possible.

The second stanza contains the 'limber' passage referred to
above:

> The wheels lurched over sprawled dead
> But pained them not, though their bones crunched,
> Their shut mouths made no moan.

'Lurched' is the painful, exact word. Limbers (carriages for ammunition and equipment) running over bodies will lurch. The word
also seems to use Rosenberg's device of transposition, for 'lurch'
may also refer to the feelings of the person as he empathetically
'feels' the limbers running over the bodies. Rosenberg presumably
felt this enough for him to have remarked on it to Marsh. What is
painful in this passage is the sense that the limbers' weight will
damage the body as much as if it were alive. The watcher *feels* that
if he can see the body he cannot feel that it is dead; the corpses are
still perhaps too nearly human. The 'crunched' bones emphasize
this, and emphasize too how close to the dead the living were drawn
by the shared experience of conflict in which chance decimates
some and not others. Finally the reader, like the watcher, identifies
himself with the crushed corpses. The seemingly unnecessary 'But
pained them not' confirms this sense of the dead not being so, by
telling you something you know, but cannot fully feel, partly because the identification is so strong. The conscious intelligence and

the emotional responses suffer dissociation. The passage moves into a recognition of how all suffer in war, and surely contradicts any possible partiality in the first stanza. 'Friend and foeman' lie together 'And shells go crying over them'. Here again Rosenberg makes 'crying' have two agents. The shells cry out, as do the humans mutilated by fragments of exploding shells. The same kind of device is used in 'Break of Day in the Trenches':

> What do you see in our eyes
> At the shrieking iron and flame. . .?

The third stanza brings in a theme expressed by most of the war poets (the non-combatant ones also, as F. S. Flint in 'Lament'):

> Earth has waited for them,
> All the time of their growth
> Fretting for their decay:
> Now she has them at last!
> In the strength of their strength
> Suspended—stopped and held.

This stanza, which as Dennis Silk observed is often omitted or truncated in anthologies,[1] is an important one, being in many ways a fuller version of a passage in 'Daughters of War':

> I heard the mighty daughters' giant sighs
> In sleepless passion for the sons of valour. . . .

Both passages assert that the earth/daughters desire 'the sons of valour' at the peak of their virility (as art, in Keats's 'Ode on a Grecian Urn', arrests and fixes youth at its most graceful and passionate). In 'Dead Man's Dump' such suspending of the youthful lives is shown to be more evil than in 'Daughters of War'; Rosenberg keeps the question open until the end of the latter poem, since to have done otherwise would be to have made redundant the accumulating of dramatic responses and ideas which structure the poem. In 'Dead Man's Dump' he is not working for one compact movement towards a final accumulation of response and meaning, but towards a series of different but cohering responses.

To return to the stanza itself, 'stopped and held' is powerful in that each participle corroborates and seems to contradict the other: 'held' suggests a tenacious holding on, as the soldier would hold on to

[1] 'Isaac Rosenberg 1890–1918', *Judaism*, XIV, No. 4 (Autumn 1965), p. 466.

his life; but 'held' is also consonant with 'stopped', because it is the earth that does the holding of their lives, which are obtained at their peak. But where, in Keats's poem, art fixes the youthful lives in such a way that both the lives and the image interact on each other and produce a sense of immortality, in Rosenberg's it is death which does this; and, as Harding indicates, shows up even more the value of what is being destroyed. As Owen perceived in 'Strange Meeting', it is 'the truth untold' (pity), and the value lost sight of, one might add, that are so often casualties in war.

Stanza four begins to question the immortality habitually attributed to the soldier dying in battle. Where do the dead go, and what becomes of them?

> Earth! Have they gone into you?
> Somewhere they must have gone,
> And flung on your hard back
> Is their soul's sack
> Emptied of God-ancestralled essences.

The question is exclamatory and in part deliberately tautological, since it is clear to Rosenberg that their journey is no further than into the earth. They have no other immortality, except of a metaphysical kind. Life is brutally foreshortened and its value, if we are lucky, fully realized at that moment of death. The real question is placed at the end of the stanza: 'Who hurled them out? Who hurled?' We may realize that man has done the expulsion, but the question that answer raises is, for what reason and to what end?

Stanza six expresses not only the *illusion* of safety, created by survival, but also the feeling of immortality which youth lends to the one illusioned, 'ichor', the food of the immortals, is only seemingly fed 'as' to the soldiers, and 'lucky limbs' stresses the fiction of such immortality:

> Or stood aside for the half used life to pass
> Out of those doomed nostrils and the doomed mouth,
> When the swift iron burning bee
> Drained the wild honey of their youth.

The terms are Keatsian, with 'wild' recalling a similar debt in 'Strange Meeting': 'I went hunting wild/After the wildest beauty'. In Rosenberg's poem the wildness of the shells is made to qualify the wildness of youth, but without reducing that wildness.

'Half used', in fact, shows Rosenberg not so much concerned with
the soldiers' being dead, as with the instant of their death, and
with that fraction of their lives so far lived. The moment of their
death is ever-present, and it is a way of enforcing the value of what
has been lost. Rosenberg's Keatsian moment differs in emphasis,
however, from Owen's in 'Strange Meeting', in that he makes his
moment of understanding synchronize with the actuality of the
battlefield. Thinking about the event is not separated from its
happening. In this sense, at least, Rosenberg's apprehensions are
more intimate because more immediately connected with the event
itself. There is less evident distancing than there is in Owen's
poem, but then the problem of distancing is a less necessary or
mechanical problem than *we* have perhaps, with Eliot's help, supposed it to be. It is not the distance that matters so much as the
quality of the relationship between the poet's ego and what he is
writing of; and to speak of distance and recollection, in Owen for
instance, as demonstrating a superior human response or a better
poetic one is, to say the least, not proved. It would be just, I think,
to say that Owen's responses are more retrospective, in his poems,
than Rosenberg's are. Compare almost any passage in 'Dead Man's
Dump' with, say:

> If anything might rouse him now
> The kind old sun will know.

In stanza seven of 'Dead Man's Dump' Rosenberg still concentrates on the specific response:

> In bleeding pangs
> Some borne on stretchers dreamed of home,
> Dear things, war-blotted from their hearts.

Event for event, some comparison with this might be made with
'Dulce et Decorum Est':

> If in some smothering dreams you too could pace
> Behind the wagon that we flung him in,
> And watch the white eyes writhing in his face. . . .

Owen's lines are vivid, precise, terrible; but the difference between
the two, apart from Owen's more dramatic rendering, is the energy
of 'war-blotted' and the way in which the mass of the noun 'war' is
converted into descriptively verbal force. The effect of Rosenberg's

energy here is to bring the scene upon the reader with extra insistence, although it might be said that 'Dulce et Decorum Est' presents the event in such a way as to make the reader re-enact it. Nevertheless, the comparison between the one poet's immediacy and the other's recollectedness will in general hold. The didactic nature finds it easier to manipulate the event if it is recollected rather than immediately experienced, and this accounts I think for the shift in Owen's poem from the re-enactment of the gas-attack to the subsequent recollection of some man thrilling the 'children' with tales of danger.

Stanza eight of Rosenberg's poem shows man as his own destroyer:

> What dead are born when you kiss each soundless soul
> With lightning and thunder from your mined heart,
> Which man's self dug, and his blind fingers loosed?

'Blind' of course suggests unheeding; incapable of heeding by how much man has lost the capacity to recognize what he is doing to himself. The admonition implicit in the line extends through the next stanza in an overt expression of tenderness:

> A man's brains splattered on
> A stretcher-bearer's face;
> His shook shoulders slipped their load,
> But when they bent to look again
> The drowning soul was sunk too deep
> For human tenderness.

The violence of the first three lines emphasizes the tenderness of the three following; but one gets no sense of manipulation because Rosenberg's direct and immediate expression does not permit one to think the variation a dramatic device operating separately from his feelings. The tenderness gets emphasis because it is of no practical value to the wounded—and then dead—man. The poet's registration does not heartlessly include him as one more item in his rehearsal of war's brutalities, and it disdains this precisely in that his tenderness is of no practical use to the man. Rosenberg, that is, was not a propagandist, in the bad meaning of that word. On the contrary, precisely because the man is included, we feel the value of the poet's tenderness and thus, ultimately, of his judgement of war's destruction. The 'uselessness' of his tenderness, a precursory echo of the poem's ending, turns out to be another fully experienced instance of futility in war; and the single death becomes represent-ative.

I speak of tenderness rather than pity, because I would make a distinction between Rosenberg's and Owen's response to war's brutalities. Owen's compassion may be unhesitating in its generosity, as I am certain it is, but it moves over war's victims as they are recollected. The pity is universal. His tendency (not with his anger and satire) is to move from specificity to an inclusive ethic that will cover all war's victims. He represents all men. The whole stands for each part assembled together. With Rosenberg it is otherwise, and the difference lies between Owen's compassion and Rosenberg's tenderness. Compassion is sacred, and distanced. Rosenberg's tenderness is that of a man intimately speaking of one death. It does not try to include the others. This specific tenderness for a particular man makes the man representative without losing his specificity.

Even in the next stanza, Rosenberg does not lose sight of the particular death:

> They left this dead with the older dead,
> Stretched at the cross roads.

In the second line an emblematic and more generalized implication emerges; the cross-roads may represent the dilemma of man's future. The dead accumulating at this 'juncture' are both admoni-tory and accusing. But even these, in stanza ten, are identified, although negatively, by their loss of human identity:

> Burnt black by strange decay
> Their sinister faces lie,
> The lid over each eye,
> The grass and coloured clay
> More motion have than they,
> Joined to the great sunk silences.

'Strange' in the sense of alien, not now belonging to the human tissue, the bodies will soon be a part of grass and clay, which have more life now. 'Sunk silences' suggests the silence of the earth, but also the silence and space of the air which they filled when alive. It suggests, moreover, the tomb-like spaces which they now fill with their death. Silence. A silence of speculation left for the living; a void where nothing is known except that the dead are inert to us.

The question of an afterlife is raised, but answered only with silence. It is raised earlier in the poem with the platonist image 'soul's sack', but in this second instance, more tentatively. Even in the first case, no sense of the platonist's belief in the soul returning to its spiritual and collective home after the death of the body is permitted:

> And flung on your hard back
> Is their soul's sack. . . .

—all that is rejected. If the body is treated thus, can there really be a soul, which is any better treated? The spiritual part of man dies with his body. The body is parted from life, not from a soul.

The last two stanzas move from this question, for, in the poem's terms, even if man has a soul, its existence seems incapable of affecting the way in which we treat each other—as the 'soul's sack' is treated. The poem returns after one line of scene-setting ('Here is one not long dead') to the expectations of a dying man, who is waiting for help that, in this instance, would seem to be of no use. He is expecting it from a party of men who know nothing of his need until it is too late. Rosenberg makes a distinction between actively wishing for death and passively accepting it:

> Swift for the end to break
> Or the wheels to break. . . .

When they reach him, he is dead, and at the end he had even wanted them to arrive:

> 'Will they come? Will they ever come?' . . .
> So we crashed round the bend,
> We heard his weak scream,
> We heard his very last sound,
> And our wheels grazed his dead face.

The man's death is particular and representative. The failure to reach him in time represents the war's process of inevitable erosion. The tenderness, on the other hand, without destroying the representative quality, holds our attention upon this man and his death. The tenderness and the barbarity in the situation modify each other, and will continue to do so, even perhaps as one man kills another. And perhaps the tenderness will itself become hardened.

This is also a cost of war; to elicit the tenderness which itself is consumed.

'Dead Man's Dump' is as admonitory as 'Strange Meeting', and as sombre in its conclusions. It creates a sense of these conclusions being obtained in the middle of conflict, but this is a part of the particularity of Rosenberg's art, a characteristic which De Sausmarez has remarked on in his work as a painter:

'Sacred Love', the most mature of his works, and the 'Self-portrait in a Steel Helmet' and other works of the 1914-15 period, have a quality that is intensely personal and suggest the probable direction of a later development. This quality is not easy to characterize, but it includes a simplification that moves towards compression of experience rather than towards the schematic. . . . The symbol always retains the sensuousness of the original experience and he mistrusts an art that uses 'symbols of symbols'. . . . By the time he produced these works he had clearly realized that 'an idea in painting is only one because it cannot be put into words', and that 'mere representation is unreal, is fragmentary. The bone taken from Adam remains a bone'. (*CWL*, p. 29)

Rosenberg wrote to John Rodker, probably between June and September 1917, that he thought 'Daughters of War' was, up to that time, his 'best poem'; and to Marsh in a letter dated 30 July of that year:

I believe my Amazon poem to be my best poem. . . . It has taken me about a year to write; for I have changed and rechanged it and thought hard over that poem and striven to get that sense of inexorableness the human (or unhuman) side of this war has. It even penetrates behind human life for the 'Amazon' who speaks in the second part of the poem is imagined to be without her lover yet, while all her sisters have theirs, the released spirits of the slain men; her lover yet remains to be released.

I have already anticipated this poem in several places, since its thinking is relevant to other poems. An explanation of the 'plot' is adequately accounted for in the quotation above:

'My sisters have their males
Clean of the dust of old days
That clings about those white hands
And yearns in those voices sad.
But these shall not see them,
Or think of them in any days or years;
They are my sisters' lovers in other days and years.'

The triumph of the sisters, which this one does not yet share, must of course be at the expense of the living, of both the soldiers and those related to them, 'But these shall not see them'. The 'dust of the old days' belongs to the life of the living, for their dust associates with their soldiers' *mortality*. But for the sisters, dust signifies the impure substance associated with that mortal *life;* which is why the sisters 'have their males/Clean of the dust'. Rosenberg does not seem to have regarded such 'immortality' as desirable, but given their death, he is concerned with a kind of immortality—of the ever-present moment—in which their value is seen. This is what Denys Harding identifies:

> The value of what was destroyed seemed to him to have been brought into sight only by the destruction, and he had to respond to both facts without allowing either to neutralize the other. It is this which is most impressive in Rosenberg—the complexity of experience which he was strong enough to permit himself and which his technique was fine enough to reveal.

Fine though this is, I would quibble with 'only'—'only by the destruction'—since I believe that it was not a case of the value being then brought into sight so much as of it then being emphasized, and in a particular way. To say that the value was only then brought into sight is, I think, to simplify and over-stress the evaluative ever-present moment in which the life was destroyed. Death may force the living to reassess the value of the person they had been in relation with, but such valuation then does imply that valuation of a more continuous and responsive kind must constantly have been made in the flux of the relationship itself. Crises of relationship, it is true, will bring on such valuation, but the kind I am thinking of is implicit in the active continuation of the relationship. But to imply that the value of that person was not brought into sight (perhaps 'sight' is the key word here) is to over-stress the act of evaluation at the expense of a response to what is continuously valuable, such response being implicit in the sustaining of such a relationship.

Of the more literal side of Rosenberg's apprehension, of the young men

> In the strength of their strength
> Suspended—

one remembers, of course, the physical fitness which the army perforce needed to bring out in each man. This, it would seem, was only achieved to be destroyed. A subsidiary question here (those who would justify war, or a part of war, will ask it) is whether this high point in the individual's development can or will be brought out in circumstances other than war.

Although Rosenberg is not opting for war, he is saying that he has observed such high levels to occur in it. Yet comradeship, which such officer poets as Owen, Read, and Sassoon mention as being one of the generous and valuable human responses produced in war, Rosenberg does not touch on either in his letters or poems; and one guesses that what isolated him before the war continued to produce the same effect during it. Moreover, one has heard of such genuine comradeship and friendship during the war which evanesces after it; and one supposes that the arbitrary conditions of war which cast people together can sometimes produce relationships dependent on the arbitrariness of the situation rather than on something less forcedly valuable. This is perhaps as true of relationships in peacetime, but of course the argument is that war produces something valuable which peace could not.

One further aspect of the poem should be considered, which is raised by a perception of Rosenberg's series of God poems, already discussed. It is a question raised in Dennis Silk's article on Rosenberg:

> Just as an earlier series of poems about God culminates in the explosion of 'Moses', in the same way a series of earlier poems preceding and leading directly to 'Dead Man's Dump' and 'Daughters of War' are tentative attempts to cope with the visionary experience of the two later poems.

There are connections between 'Daughters of War' and 'The Female God' (1914), and between 'The Female God' and 'Returning, We Hear the Larks'. Before exploring these one might add that the poems about the female deities also predicate a malign force. Silk moreover suggests that, although God may be fought, 'The pain inflicted ... by a Goddess ... becomes necessary suffering.' For Rosenberg there remained not a malignant universe brooded over by benign deities, approximately the orthodox Judao-Christian picture, but a universe potentially good but nevertheless ruled or, at any rate, over-looked by malign forces. I am not sure, however, that Silk is correct in concluding that for Rosenberg the female deities and their infliction of pain had to be endured. If God could be struggled with, why had the female deities such fatal power? Yet of course man's connection with woman, his necessary relation with her and her fecundity—these are the unavoidable forces, involving death, in that every act of creation initiates the death of the created thing. Of 'The Female God', Rosenberg says:

> You have dethroned the ancient God,
> You have usurped his Sabbath, his common days,
> Yea! every moment is delivered you,
> Our Temple, our Eternal, our one God.

Seen from this poem, the female god is clearly superior to the male who even, perhaps, attracts some of Rosenberg's attachment. This, although an undated poem, almost certainly precedes 'God' and perhaps even 'God Made Blind', but is probably later than the conforming 'Spiritual Isolation'. It is, however, one thing to say that God is usurpable; it is another to say that the female deity is not.

Rosenberg produced an earlier visualization of 'Returning, We Hear the Larks' (a poem probably written sometime during 1917), which he called 'Hark, hark, the Lark' (in monochrome wash and charcoal, 1912).[1] This shows six nude figures—two women, three men, and one whose sex is unidentifiable. Three—one man and two women—are ecstatic, greeting the fall of larksong. The two remaining male figures have a withdrawn quality (as has the ambiguous figure); one withdrawn as if in thought, another seemingly distraught. Certainly the impression is that the principal welcomers of the song are the women. The picture has the familiar duality we expect to find in his work, although the duality in the poem divides differently from that in the picture. The poem also takes the reader further and more complexly into the relations between beauty and death, between men and women:

> Dragging these anguished limbs, we only know
> This poison-blasted track opens on our camp—
> On a little safe sleep.
>
> But hark! joy—joy—strange joy.
> Lo! heights of night ringing with unseen larks.
> Music showering on our upturned list'ning faces.

---

[1] See *CWL* facing p. 33.

The last line accurately describes the ecstatic elements in the picture, but in the poem Rosenberg has developed the premonitory elements that in the picture remain mysterious and unrelated. In the poem he could of course draw on war as a unifying context for the duality, but in fact war is only one unifying factor in the poem, and then, very much the contextual one. 'On a little safe sleep' indicates how little of this the soldiers might expect, and foreshortens even this by associating itself with the euphemistic cliché for death. By bringing death close upon the birdsong the two are made to reflect—almost to seem versions of—each other, with death predominating. In this way the birdsong, which once gave joy, by being associated with death, now seems menacing; the more so in that it wears a pleasurable disguise, like the woman's beauty at the end of the poem.

> Death could drop from the dark
> As easily as song—
> But song only dropped. . . .

In the context of death everything takes on its appearance—as everything to a blind man is a metaphor of his pervasive disability. At the end of the poem Rosenberg uses just such a metaphor; and in such a way that the image of the blind man and the girl become as much versions of death's menace to the soldiers, as the soldiers' vulnerability is a version of the others'. For even if Rosenberg is writing a poem about war, he manages it in such a way that war is shown as a condition which has lethal counterparts in other contexts:

> But song only dropped,
> Like a blind man's dreams on the sand
> By dangerous tides,
> Like a girl's dark hair for she dreams no ruin lies there,
> Or her kisses where a serpent hides.

Thus the hidden danger is brought to the surface and shown as a possible characteristic of beauty; and brought to the surface to indicate that the danger is unperceived. The poem ends with a double comparison: the danger within beauty—unperceived by the woman herself—being compared to the blind man's inability to recognize the danger of the tides. His dreams are as dangerous to him, because of the tides, as the girl's unconscious potential for destruction is to any unwary lover. But by showing in the last two comparisons inability to recognize danger, Rosenberg shows that war, whether the soldiers recognize the danger at every moment or not, is capable of destruction in a way that the situations in the end of the poem are not. Nothing can guard against war. In the poem's final image Rosenberg is using the menacing material in 'Daughters of War' and 'The Female God' especially. Compare the ensnaring image of the girl's hair in 'Returning, We Hear the Larks' with this stanza from 'The Female God':

> Queen! Goddess! Animal!
> In sleep do your dreams battle with our souls?
> When your hair is spread like a lover on the pillow
> Do not our jealous pulses wake between?

The predatory quality of the beautiful deity is not necessarily a theme of war poetry, but it shows how Rosenberg was capable of taking ideas from a different context to metaphorize his apprehension of war. And by using similar material in different contexts he allows the emphases inherent in the metaphor to interpenetrate and enrich each other.

Two of Rosenberg's poems are concerned with the incidence of war on human sexuality: 'Soldier: Twentieth Century' and 'Girl to Soldier on Leave'. The first re-creates the phenomenon C. E. Montague recorded in *Disenchantment*, where women, who before the war were suffragettes, suddenly found the soldier desirable, regardless of his personal quality. What attracted them seems to have been the generalized image of his predatoriness and power, his heroic dimensions which the war, of course, and his actions in it, provided. It is from apprehensions of such a situation that the poem develops, but they show too how the soldier is used in such a situation. What the woman offers him is an emotional and sexual reward, touching his ego with an image of his own predatoriness that the woman claims is intrinsically his, and desirable/good:

> Cruel men are made immortal,
> Out of your pain born.
> They have stolen the sun's power
> With their feet on your shoulders worn.

The pain that the soldier heroically bears—note the pun on 'born'—permits a new race of cruel men to be generated, who are immortal.

The soldier himself is

> Out of unthinkable torture,
> Eyes kissed by death,
> Won back to the world again,
> Lost and won in a breath,

which partly reverses the situation of 'Daughters of War', since here it is the power-admiring *mortals* who have won their soldiers; but won them 'back' to what kind of world?

> Let them shrink from your girth,
> That has outgrown the pallid days,
> When you slept like Circe's swine,
> Or a word in the brain's ways.

One remembers Brooke's strictures:

> Glad from a world grown old and cold and weary,
>   Leave the sick hearts that honour could not move. . . .

It is not, of course, Rosenberg who is dispraising a situation that in some ways resembles what Brooke describes, but the woman, stimulated by the aura of power:

> I love you, great new Titan!
> Am I not you?
> Napoleon and Caesar
> Out of you grew.

Moreover, the proper alternative to stagnant peace is not 'invigorating' war. What one reads is not Rosenberg's praise of war but his observation of a woman's distorted view of the soldier. The poet, however, keeps sight of the soldier's suffering and it is this that qualifies the woman's distortions. Rosenberg's terse comment on Brooke confirms this reading: 'Rupert Brooke has written one fine poem with depth, "Town and country". I don't like his other work much, they remind me too much of flag days.'

In the second of these poems, 'Girl to Soldier on Leave', similar imagery and phrases occur. The pre-war period is compared to the present:

> Pallid days arid and wan
> Tied your soul fast.
> Babel-cities' smoky tops
> Pressed upon your growth. . . .

We again see the coherence of Rosenberg's imagery, which in this instance focuses on the sun (that in 'Chagrin' provided life-giving energy). Here its lack is located in the word 'Pallid'. In the previous poem the sun appeared in the guise of Titan, the sun-god; here a similar Titan image is used:

> I love you—Titan lover,
> My own storm-days' Titan.
> Greater than the sun of Zeus,
> I know whom I would choose.

The Titan image is more complexly used here where Rosenberg makes the two facets of his sun image interpenetrate. At its first appearance in the poem it again signalizes the woman's adoration of power (one of the sun's aspects), but that other facet of the sun as life-giving appears negatively in 'Pallid days arid and wan'. Rosenberg contrasts these two aspects of the sun-symbol and makes them evaluate each other, as well as the contexts in which they appear. For, while it is perhaps true that aspects of the pre-war period were 'arid and wan' and lacked the health-giving attribute of the sun, it is presumably preferable to the power of the sun which the woman now so eagerly grasps at, and which characterizes the war-time ethos:

> Titan—my splendid rebel—
> The old Prometheus
> Wanes like a ghost before your power—
> His pangs were joys to yours.

Rosenberg enlarges on the distorted image of the hero. Sassoon in 'Glory of Women' says much the same:

> You love us when we're heroes, home on leave,
> Or wounded in a mentionable place.
> You worship decorations. . . .

By showing the woman enacting her attitudes, Rosenberg plots more closely the sensuous conditions of the situation. And by bringing in the Promethean myth he is able to show how the heroic attitude is inevitably distorted by war's pressures, and how society loses sight of what Prometheus—and Rosenberg—felt to be the more valuable understanding of courage and suffering.

Prometheus, the beneficent sufferer, was a descendant of the Titans and, inasmuch as their father Uranus was a tyrant, their

rebellion would be seen by Rosenberg as a necessary and productive act. The Titans themselves, however, were overthrown by
Zeus, a son of Rhea, who was a daughter of Uranus and also one of
the Titans. Zeus' overthrow of the Titans seems to have been a
morally ambiguous act, and Zeus is invariably shown, by contrast
with Prometheus whom he tortured, as a tyrant. Hence Aeschylus'
Prometheus and Shelley's *Prometheus Unbound*. Prometheus, who
will commit no violence on his tormentors, wanes in the woman's
mind compared with the Titans. In devaluing Prometheus (the
name signifies 'forethought') she emphasizes a certain aspect of the
Titans, which images them not in their struggle against the tyrannic
Uranus but as a vague and unidentified emblem of power. Once
again it appears that the excitement and glamour of sexualized power
is the *only* preferable alternative to the 'Pallid days arid and wan'
of peace, or beneficent suffering. Rosenberg would find such unthinking choice intolerable. He even contrives to guard against an
indiscriminate admiration of suffering for its own sake with the
line 'His pangs were joys to yours'. It is as though the woman says:
I measure my admiration for you not only by your predatoriness,
but also by the amount of suffering in excess of Prometheus' you
can endure. And so she binds herself to her image of the Titan
soldier.

> One gyve holds you yet.
>
> It held you hiddenly on the Somme
> Tied from my heart at home. . . .

Admiration equally ties him to her because his ego is enlarged by it:

> O must it loosen now? I wish
> You were bound with the old old gyves.

The 'old gyves' (shackles) are presumably the bonds of their present
relationship; or else, ironically, the old pre-war ties. War breaks
or threatens to break them, but 'One gyve holds you yet'. This
could mean no more than that a part of their relationship still
exists. Dennis Silk suggests that 'the girl addresses her lover, who
is a kind of Titan enlarged by his sufferings and released from
servitude to an ignoble civilization'. I have tried to show that this
is only fractionally true, the civilization, however *partly* ignoble it
may be, in no sense being given a viable alternative in the release
(as he implies) of war. The soldier's 'enlargement' is dubious and,
in any case, one must weigh against it the cost to him and to others,

as well as to the woman ultimately, demanded by such distortions. Rosenberg, I am sure, takes these into account when he is speaking, if he does so speak, of any 'spiritual' gain produced by war. Silk adds that:

> The girl is losing in her competition with death, and behind death stand the Amazons. She figures in 'Daughters of War', she is one of the mortal women who lose their earth-men to this fierce supernatural will. Her Titan lover will soon be dead, when the last gyve of heroic life is loosened, and he is fetched home by his Amazonian lover.

Much as I am indebted to parts of this argument, I should like to point to the ambiguity of 'Tied from my heart'; one would expect 'tied to'. 'From' is preferred not merely for its vowel length, for instance, but to suggest, I think, that the new gyve of the Amazons (war, if one prefers it) is tied ('with' and 'out of') 'from' the same gyve of heroism and admiration with which the mortal woman is tied, and with which she is tying her mortal soldier. Thus 'from' not only means 'made from' (manufactured) but has prepositional meaning. So that we have an ironic situation expressed without irony, for the very bond of admiration which she used to tie her soldier to her is the one that is tying him to the war and ultimately to the Amazons. What ties him to his mortal woman also loosens him from her, since the Amazons will inevitably—and with a bond made of the same 'substance'—claim him. This is why I think Rosenberg uses the word 'from'. He had to express in compressed form two opposing but related ideas, without losing sight of either. He does this by using a preposition alien to the syntax it is placed in, but which will readily recall its grammatically correct opposite and which contains his other meaning.

His two louse-hunting poems probably date from January–February 1917. The second is more typical, its rhythms being an integral expression of the poem's meaning, the expression itself being less tradition-bound. The first exploits the convention via the assumptions built round the metronomic structure; the second uses the rhythms to originate the meaning. Rosenberg uses scale in both poems, the discrepancy in size between the man and the hunted louse releasing much of the energy and the meaning:

> See gargantuan hooked fingers
> Pluck in supreme flesh
> To smutch supreme littleness.

The poem moves from the perspective of the louse to that of the human. 'Smutch' is well chosen, because it suggests both the dirt which accompanies infestation and also the dark stain to which the creature is aggressively reduced between the fingers. Even in small poems, Rosenberg introduces into his picture of war another facet of its experience.

Two further poems may be considered as a pair: 'The Burning of the Temple' and 'The Destruction of Jerusalem by the Babylonian Hordes'. The first may be dated as no later than March 1918: 'I thought it was poor, or rather, difficult in expression, but G. Bottomley thinks it fine.' And, though the second has no external evidence for its dating, its similarity of theme and expression suggests that it was written about the same time. Both refer to the destruction of the temple, and of the Jews as a nation, by the Babylonians. Here again it is interesting to see Rosenberg drawing on Old Testament sources, where British writers would go to Celtic legends or to ancient Greece.

It would be easy to make parallels between the actions in these poems and the reverses and successes of the Allies, and wrong to do so. Some generalized sense of war's devastation made its way into Rosenberg's work, but not in such simplified politics as this. He uses the Jewish and Babylonian historic episodes as a metaphor for his sense of destruction; and, although one might say that the Babylonian hordes who destroy the Jewish civilization represent in their struggle the destruction of what was civilized in Europe (regardless of nationality), a more complex division is made, than between Jewish civilization and Babylonian barbarism, in 'The Destruction of Jerusalem by the Babylonian Hordes'. Much as he, a Tolstoyan, deplored demonstrations of martial strength, Rosenberg is honest enough to admit the impressiveness of the conqueror:

> They who bowed to the Bull God
> Whose wings roofed Babylon,
> In endless hosts darkened
> The bright-heavened Lebanon.

What gives the chilling image of the Bull God its energy is the way the noun 'roof' is given participial as well as verbal character, so that the whole image acquires the mass of a noun but also the additional force of a verb. What gives the image its size and strength is again the poet's use of scale. It is the flesh of a living if mythological creature which 'roofs' the entire city of the Babylonians, themselves conquerors. The discrepancy between a creature and a city is of course immense and it is this which Rosenberg uses to establish his creature's size and power.

The Babylonian destruction is successful in several ways. It destroys not only the physical structure of the civilization, but also any remembered, valued, and continuing sense of it in its captive survivors. One needs to set against the stanza quoted below the opening of Psalm 137:

By the rivers of Babylon, there we sat down, yea, we wept, when we re-
    membered Zion.
We hanged our harps upon the willows in the midst thereof.
For there they that carried us away captive required of us a song; and
    they that wasted us required of us mirth, saying, Sing us one of the
    songs of Zion.
How shall we sing the Lord's song in a strange land?
If I forget thee, O Jerusalem, let my right hand forget her cunning.

Rosenberg wrote:

> They washed their grime in pools
> Where laughing girls forgot
> The wiles they used for Solomon.
> Sweet laughter! remembered not.

'Laughing girls' may be a characterization of their behaviour to Solomon prior to the dispersal (I think it is not, in fact), but 'forgot' confirms my sense of their laughter easily disposing of the social tragedy of which Zion was the victim. 'Forgot' has a lightness about it; it is not the gradual softening of a harsh memory that is characterized here. Thus the same Jewish laughter which belonged to the civilized world of Solomon forgets the Jewish tragedy, and finds its laughter in Babylon. The sensual quality is no longer balanced by a corresponding civilized and moral one, as the sensual quality in the stanza above, in its emphasis, indicates. Such forgetting, which is war's especial triumph, is similarly understood in Owen's 'Strange Meeting': 'None will break ranks. . . .' Thus the laughter is 'sweet' and not sweet. It is sweet inasmuch as it is the laughter of beautiful women; it is sweet in that it emerges from a sensual context; but it is not sweet in that it is a careless, forgetful laughter. Nor is it sweet in the final stanza:

> Sweet laughter charred in the flame
> That clutched the cloud and earth
> While Solomon's towers crashed between,
> The gird of Babylon's mirth.

The sweet laughter of the Jews is contrasted with the barbaric, malicious mirth of the (vigorous) conquering Babylonians. The Jews' laughter and civilization are each charred in the fire that destroys them. The towers fall between both the flames and heaven-and-earth. Their pride is reduced; and as they fall between the flames, so they fall between the 'gird' (measurement) of Babylonian mirth. The flame is the measurement of Babylon's mirth, and the extent of their destruction enlarges its measure. Solomon's aspiring wisdom falls; man's ability to destroy is more powerful than his wisdom. This is much the same complex of ideas found in Owen's 'Strange Meeting'.

'The Destruction of Jerusalem by the Babylonian Hordes' and 'The Burning of the Temple' are additionally concerned with the conflict between national entities, and in this sense are war poems. But they have other aspects, one of which is Jewish in character. It is the destruction of Judea and the wise, Solomon-imaged nation —this has decayed, and is finally overcome by a more barbaric yet more forceful nation. One may not entirely support such a reading of history, but for Rosenberg this struggle between the civilized-decadent and the barbaric may have found echoes in the war. It must have occurred to him to evaluate the struggle and to consider what changes would occur and whether they would be for the better.

Sometime in 1916 (?) Rosenberg wrote to R. C. Trevelyan: 'I have an idea for a book of war poems. I have already written a few small things but have plans for a few longish dramatic poems.' 'Moses' had already been written and it seems possible, therefore, that he had in mind 'The Unicorn', which, interestingly, he relates to the war. Dennis Silk sees the 'earlier series of poems about God [culminating] in the explosion of "Moses"', and in the sense that Moses' conception of an old world being torn up by its roots (the Egyptian autonomy) corresponds to the idea of opposing a bullying

God, I would agree. Certainly there is imagery common to the
play and these 'God' poems.

'Moses' is concerned with two aspects of struggle—inner and
outer—the latter dependent on the outcome of the former. Moses
has several factors to struggle with. These have already been discussed on pages 261–3, and it remains to include the surrendering
of his Egyptian mistress Koelue amongst them. Rosenberg did not,
of course, see any of these sacrifices as easy, but what he does let
Moses perceive is that his sexuality is bound up with his sense of
power, which he can thus use in the service of his new ideas:

> While the new lips my spirit would kiss
> Were not red lips of flesh,
> But the huge kiss of power?
> Where yesterday soft hair through my fingers fell
> A shaggy mane would entwine,
> And no slim form work fire to my thighs.

The complexity of Moses' energies, rather than a static delineation
of his character, emerges in the succeeding four lines, which end
the first scene:

> But human Life's inarticulate mass
> Throb the pulse of a thing
> Whose mountain flanks awry
> Beg my mastery—mine!
> Ah! I will ride the dizzy beast of the world. . . .

The sexual implications of 'ride' show how Rosenberg lets Moses
not only use his sexuality as a metaphor for power, impregnating
the earth with it so that it conceives new ideas; Moses also trans-
poses his sexual strength into (potential) action of a quite different
kind. Sexuality is both the metaphor for and the representation of
power. The 'mountain flanks' are like a beast to be ridden, but they
are also awry, and this challenge to master and right it excites him
to action. In implicating Moses' sexuality with moral concerns,
Rosenberg provides him with a psychology. Moses is not a moral
cipher but a human creature whose energies, patterned in a particular way, infuse his purpose.

There is of course a Jewish (if anachronistic) character to his
actions, in that Rosenberg gives them a Maccabean emphasis,

which by implication they have already. Certainly, there is a Maccabean theme of resistance in Jewish tradition known to Rosenberg:
'I have thoughts of a play round our Jewish hero, Judas Maccabeus',
he wrote to Laurence Binyon in 1916. The Maccabees were a Jewish
family, sometimes known as the Hasmonaeans, founded by the
priest Mattathias, who died in 166 B.C. He and his sons led the
struggle for independence against the Syrians in the second century
B.C. Judas reconquered Jerusalem in 165 B.C., and Simon established Jewish independence in 142 B.C. The historical tradition is
interesting, not merely because it records successful resistance so
utterly at variance with the subsequent history of Diaspora Jewry
in Europe, but also, as Rosenberg implies, because he is handling
a tradition which still had vitality.

Koelue's father, Abinoah, has an obsessional hatred of the Jews,
and this Rosenberg adequately re-creates:

> ABINOAH
> You puddle with your lousy gibberish
> The holy air, Pharaoh's own tributary.
> Filthy manure for Pharaoh's flourishing.
> I'll circumcise and make holy your tongues,
> And stop one outlet to your profanation.
> [*To the* OLD HEBREW]
> I've never seen one beg so for a blow,
> Too soft am I to resist such entreaty.
> [*Beats him*]

Rosenberg uncannily fixes the deviousness of racial intolerance. The
intolerant group arrogates to itself a sacred superiority which it then
accuses the oppressed group of profaning. The accusation itself
provides a further pretext for oppression. The oppressors will seize
on one essential characteristic of the oppressed (in this instance,
circumcision) and use it against them.

The play works along two movements which are projected until
they at last meet. One is the holding down of the Jews as slaves, but
not for slave labour only. They are despised as much as they are
needed. The other movement, dependent on the intensity of the
former, is Moses' gradual making up of his mind until, as he
witnesses the beating, he is (like Hamlet, perhaps) forced into
precipitate action which he might not have taken, or taken then,
had he been in full emotional control. But it is of course his emotions

which force him to decide, and the decision in some senses precedes
the precipitate action. Perhaps the subsidiary action—the murder of
Abinoah—itself completes the decision: 'Egypt was in the way;
I'll strike it out.' When Moses reaches this point of decision, the
character of the verse changes; the rhythms become more urgent
and the images, expressing the complexity of the change Moses
undergoes, interfuse with one another:

> I have a trouble in my mind for largeness,
> Rough-hearted, shaggy, which your grave ardours lack.
> Here is the quarry quiet for me to hew,
> Here are the springs, primeval elements,
> The roots' hid secrecy, old source of race,
> Unreasoned reason of the savage instinct.
> I'd shape one impulse through the contraries
> Of vain ambitious men, selfish and callous,
> And frail life-drifters, reticent, delicate.
> Litheness thread bulk; a nation's harmony.
> These are not lame, nor bent awry, but placeless
> With the rust and stagnant. All that's low I'll charm;
> Barbaric love sweeten to tenderness.
> Cunning run into wisdom, craft turn to skill.
> Their meanness threaded right and sensibly
> Change to a prudence, envied and not sneered.
> Their hugeness be a driving wedge to a thing,
> Ineffable and useable. . . .

Again we have the 'root' image, and a hint of the direction in which
we should look for its value, 'old source of race'. The value of the
root contrasts here with Moses' earlier use of it in Scene I, where he
conceives of tearing up the Egyptian—and thus Jewish—order so
that a new ordering of things (freedom for Jewry) may happen. The
quality of the intelligence that intends such change is characterized
in the lines:

> When from a cave a leopard comes,
> On its heels the same red sand,
> Springing with acquainted air,
> Sprang an intelligence. . . .

It contrasts with the over-refined, static orthodoxy and hierarchy
of Egyptian society:

I am sick of priests and forms,
This rigid dry-boned refinement.
As ladies' perfumes are
Obnoxious to stern natures,
This miasma of a rotting god
Is to me.
Who has made of the forest a park?

The root image in the long passage above (beginning 'I have a trouble in my mind') has its nature expanded in this 'Unreasoned reason of the savage instinct', where 'reason' means 'cause/justification', 'origin', but also 'rationality', indicating that Rosenberg sees instinct as having its own rationality. He then goes on to show how reason, rightly guided by instinct, but instinct also corrected by reason (the 'contraries'), will produce the energized result that he envisages. For the 'vain ambitious men, selfish' have too much will; whereas the 'frail life-drifters', sensitive to the forces of life, are too little in contact with the directing will. Moses' energy will draw these together and, bringing their different impulses and attitudes, they will fuse into a fertile and energetic whole.[1] Moses' energy will be the 'litheness' that threads the Jewish 'bulk' and, by assisting in fusing these 'contraries' into a new social whole, will see produced 'a nation's harmony'. Rosenberg envisages not only a harmonious society, but one in which each individual is energized and made new by contact with his opposite kind, and all, by being a part of a freed, changing, and gradually energized social whole. But he, Moses, will also help to transform each individual; he will act catalytically to bring out what is creative in them:

Cunning run into wisdom, craft turn to skill.
Their meanness threaded right and sensibly
Change to a prudence, envied and not sneered.

And what for the Jews he might catalytically achieve, he could, by implication, achieve for other nations, such as the Egyptians; for 'bulk' could, I think, conceivably refer to both the Jews and Egyptians. In any case, if the Jews are not sneered at by the Egyptians, but perhaps envied, the next step for them is respect, and clearly, such an attitude is desirable for both groups. Near the close

---

[1] *Vide* Blake, whom Rosenberg had read: 'Without Contraries is no progression'.

of this passage Rosenberg speaks of the new 'hugeness' of the Jewish group as 'a driving wedge', and of its being 'ineffable and useable'. This phrase connects with what he wrote of the *idea* in a poem relating to its whole structure: 'the dominating idea [is to be] understandable and still ungraspable'. The phrase 'ineffable and useable' is congruent, I think, with the terms 'ungraspable' and 'understandable'; and Rosenberg may be seen placing the idea in the same kind of relationship to life as he does to a poem. The idea in each may be 'useable', because it is 'understandable', but the context (sensuously, for instance) remains in either 'ungraspable'. It may be experienced, but not reduced to the understanding of an idea; aspects of life and of a poem may be understood, but others may only be experienced. What *meaning* has the *desire* for freedom, for instance, or the love for a human being? We may point only to the experience. Similarly, a poem may not be reduced to an idea; it cannot be robbed of its sensuous and experiential nature. Rosenberg is guarding against utilitarian reduction such as he must himself have experienced; he does not wish to lose the 'all-eyed' quality of living.

Moses would 'fashion' his Jews

> Into some newer nature, a consciousness
> Like naked light seizing the all-eyed soul,
> Oppressing with its gorgeous tyranny
> Until they take it thus—or die.

He would not rule them, beyond making them fully conscious of their creative potential. Yet it is not the Jews' freedom, for Moses, that is essential but what it permits: an expanded and fertile sense of living. Of course Rosenberg is not so naïve as to imagine that the Jews could have obtained this under Egyptian tyranny, any more than they could within the European experience, while it remained oppressive and discriminatory. Yet he is not the kind of idealist who imagines that, once the material circumstances of life are wholesome, Utopia is instantly graspable. But whatever else, the material circumstances are essential. Without these, human beings cannot create. With his image of 'naked light. . . Oppressing with its gorgeous tyranny' we see Rosenberg offering the remedial opposite to persecution. The tyranny of oppression is turned into the demands freedom makes upon a community. He indicates, with the second use of 'tyranny', that freedom has its obligations. Consciousness may overtake the Jews; they will die if they do not take it. As a figure, Rosenberg's Moses is built in an active, practical, and visionary form.

Despite the trench conditions Rosenberg was working under, he became extremely excited over his idea for a play round Judas Maccabeus. In June (?) 1917 he wrote to Marsh:

'The Amulet' Ive asked my sister [the late Mrs. Wynick] to send you.... Its a kind of 'Rape of the Sabine Women', idea. Some strange race of wanderers have settled in some wild place and are perishing out for lack of women. The prince of these explores some country near where the women are most fair. But the natives will not hear of foreign marriages and he plots another rape of the Sabines, but he is trapped in the act [Orthodox Jews are forbidden intermarriage].

He told Bottomley, on 3 August 1917, that his play was 'called "The Unicorn". Now, it's about a decaying race who have never seen a woman; animals take the place of women, but they yearn for continuity.' To Miss Seaton he wrote 8 March 1918:

If I am lucky, and come off undamaged, I mean to put all my innermost experiences into the 'Unicorn'. I want it to symbolize the war and all the devastating forces let loose by an ambitious and unscrupulous will. Last summer I wrote pieces for it and had the whole of it planned out, but since then I've had no chance of working on it and it may have gone quite out of my mind.

His ideas kept changing, and he had no time to complete the work as a whole. As he wrote to John Rodker, even on 23 February 1916:

I suppose I could write a bit if I tried to work at a letter as an idea— but sitting down to it here after a days dull stupefying labour—I feel stupified. When will we go on with the things that endure? (*CWL*, p. 20)

We need not make allowances for the work itself, but merely understand why it was unfinished. I quote from several letters to show how Rosenberg explored and changed his ideas, gradually arriving at the difficult complexity he was struggling to express. The principal change is connected with the central character, the 'supernatural' Nubian of 'The Amulet', and Tel of 'The Unicorn', who also has powers that are either supernatural or else related to the supernatural beast, the Unicorn. Nubian is a less desperate, gentler being than Tel, and his power lies in his enormous frame, his wisdom, and in his amulet which contains a small scroll of written knowledge. (Jewish religious knowledge is represented in the synagogue by a pair of scrolls.) Tel is the chief of a decaying race perishing through lack of women. Unlike the Nubian he has no written wisdom; his magic, if it exists, derives from the Unicorn. He is more barbaric. Both men are physically immense— Rosenberg was small—and strong; both are sexually fascinated in different ways by the blond Lilith, and in some sense enmeshed by her, but Tel is still able to act in spite of this. He is also less scrupulous. In 'The Amulet' Saul's love for his wife seems to have died; this is not the case in the last version. In both versions Saul is weaker than either Nubian or Tel, overawed, and vulnerable to the strange power possessed—but not deliberately exercised—by them. In the former, Lilith is fascinated (though not sexually) by Nubian; in the latter, frightened by Tel. In the first version there is a child, in the second there is not. The domesticity of the first version is absent from the last, and this permits a more naked confrontation between Lilith and Saul, and Lilith and Tel.

In making both Nubian and Tel desire Lilith, Rosenberg is exploring the sexuality Moses abandoned, and it is through this that Tel's unscrupulousness is finally unloosed. With Moses the concern is social; with Nubian and Tel, Rosenberg's social concern is seen in how he observes the sensuous and powerful responses of the central figures to Lilith, and how this effects the two races. Finally, both Nubian and Tel are obsessed not merely with sexuality, but with beauty, and this is the theme that Rosenberg ramifies.

Nubian breaks into passion only when his amulet is broken, the amulet that held the power to restore Saul's and Lilith's decayed relationship, and which he is generously willing to use on their behalf. When his possibilities as healer are destroyed, destroyed with it is his restraint and a part of his wisdom. In many ways this is a covert parable concerning war, but here Rosenberg's principal efforts are towards shaping the passions of men and women as they affect society.

Tel's responses to Lilith in 'The Unicorn' are as overwhelming as Nubian's, but he is more domineering (less masterful of himself), more violent, and less benign. His first responses are qualified, it is true, by a puritan-like consciousness of his desires:

> Bestial man shapes ride dark impulses
> Through roots in the bleak blood, then hide
> In shuddering light from their self loathing.
> They fade in arid light—
> Beings unnatured by their craving. . . .

But such consciousness of self is tersely cut across. Saul's sudden appearance prompts and reveals his unscrupulousness:

> By now my men have raided the city,
> I heard a far shrieking.

The language is flat and practical. Any external barrier to his desires serves to remove conscience and remorse. This subtly draws attention to his unscrupulousness, which overmasters any compunction he has, and indicates also the inherent violence in his puritanism. The unscrupulous quality is carefully defined by the partly sentimental (partly sincere) nature of his compunction. But in his desires he is violent. For although Tel's final apostrophe of Lilith has lines in it belonging to Nubian's praise of her, the movement of his speech is jagged and less decorous. Psychologically, the two versions of response, from Nubian and Tel, emerge not so much as successive reachings after a final artifact as realized aspects of the different ways in which desire may be expressed. Tel exclaims:

> Marvellous creature.
> Night tender beast.
> Has the storm passed into me,
> What ecstasy, what lightning
> Has touched the lightning in my blood.
> Voluptuous
> Crude vast terrible hunger overpowers . . .
> A gap . . . a yawning . . .
> My blood knocks . . . inarticulate to make you understand,
> To shut you in itself
> Uncontrollable. [*He stretches his arms out*]
> Small dazzling face I shut you in my soul—

Rosenberg's concept of beauty is one of the complex puzzles that emerge in both 'The Amulet' and 'The Unicorn'. And, contingent on it, are his preoccupations with change and re-orderings. Beauty is a disturbing element in the first play's situation (another is Saul's lack of desire for his wife); beauty, in the second, is a principal factor, in that Tel and his race have only their potentially fulfilled desire together with a yearning for continuity. Faced with beauty, Tel must possess it. But, as I have already indicated, this breaking in on Saul's and Lilith's relationship, such as it is, is a problem for Nubian. On the other hand, for Lilith, in 'The Amulet', beauty is an almost depersonalized personal problem (as it is unconsciously so for the girl in 'Returning, We Hear the Larks'). For Lilith, it is not the beauty that is her problem, but those problems which it brings her as a human being. Her beauty is not only no use in stirring Saul; it is what against her will stirs other men into desiring her, and then into falsely accusing her of being wanton, when she refuses them. Lilith says to Nubian:

> I think beauty is a bad bargain made of life.
> Men's iron sinews hew them room in the world
> And use deceits to gain them trophies. . . .
> They without song have sung me
> Boldly and shamelessly.
> I am no wanton, no harlot; . . .
> I am a wife with a woman's natural ways.

Beauty has caused her sorrow and she sees a strong and persistent connection between them:

> LILITH
> I think there is more sorrow in the world
> Than man can bear.

> NUBIAN
> None can exceed their limit, lady:
> You either bear or break.

> LILITH
> Can one choose to break? To bear,
> To wearily bear, is misery.
> Beauty is this corroding malady.

Nubian's gentle rebuke is both just and strong. Of this passage Denys Harding wrote in *Scrutiny* (March 1935):

Here as in all the war poems his suffering and discomfort are unusually *direct;* there is no secondary distress arising from the sense that these things *ought not* to be. He was given up to realizing fully what *was*. He expressed his attitude in 'The Unicorn'.

Lilith has in fact been bemoaning how things 'ought to be' and Nubian does correct her; but to suggest that this is *entirely* what Rosenberg's attitudes consisted of is extreme. For, besides showing the correctness of Nubian's firmness here, he also shows the justice of Lilith's complaint. Stoicism may help you to bear suffering, but of itself, it does not change the situation, and it seems to me that change is what Rosenberg is partly concerned with; it is this concern that Harding's 'given up to realizing fully what *was*' omits. Rosenberg was certainly concerned with what was, but in relation to change, for behind both attitudes is his concern with re-orderings. Nubian's attitude may be a good enough expression of how to confront the facts, but on reflection Lilith's complaint shows his attitude to be inadequate for her (although it may, in its restraint, be adequate for him). 'The Amulet' fragment does not fully express this concern with change, but it surely forebodes it in Nubian's expressed desire for Lilith. What of his is broken (the amulet) takes him to *his* breaking point; after that he changes, and in doing so produces a potential change in the situation. It would then have been necessary for both Lilith and Nubian to determine as best they could the character of that change. It might be argued that Rosenberg was deploring a change of this kind, but I do not think that the situation will bear this out; Saul's listless disinterest in Lilith combined with Nubian's scrupulousness very carefully qualify, at least, such an argument.

Beauty then is at the centre of the problem. Nubian and Lilith are so to speak at right angles to each other; they converge on each other at this point, although their problems are neither identical nor opposed. For each it is, among other things, a moral problem; but where for Nubian the concern is with his inner responses (as it was initially for Moses), for Lilith, it is the response of others to her beauty, and how she will meet these in relation to it. Beauty demands acceptance, as Nubian implies, and in this sense it is a fact that stabilizes relations between people; or rather it clarifies the nature of the responses once it has been accepted. Beauty had originally 'ordered' the lives of Saul and Lilith into marriage.

In 'The Unicorn' Lilith says:

> Beauty is music's secret soul,
> Creeping about man's senses.
> He cannot hold it or know it ever. . . .

but this is precisely what Tel is trying to manage. She continues:

> He cannot hold it or know it ever,
> But yearns and yearns to hold it once.
> Ah! when he yearns not shall he not wither?
> For music then will have no place
> In the world's ear, but mix in windless darkness.

Tel's characteristic response to this is one of non-connection; he even responds with a quite different sensuousness:

> Am I gone blind?
> I swim in a white haze.

Beauty is at first a disturber; it moves man to desire and, as long as he thinks he can possess it, it continues to disturb him in this way too. Yet without it there is no desire, and without desire, he withers. And, she adds, in the last two lines of hers quoted, if he does not yearn music will be placeless and unattended. What then is music, and what is beauty's relation to it?

Beauty is what, in the engendering and spiritual sense, makes man survive. But it is also what unlooses Tel and his unscrupulous race, who had only their Unicorn. The Unicorn, I think, represents both their questing energies and, related to this, their unmated sexuality. Or, more precisely perhaps, this is what their relationship to the Unicorn represents. These are the creatures who 'wail their souls for continuity'. In the final seizing of the women, Enoch and Saul leap into a well—a particularly suggestive form of suicide. Clearly, beauty here is a component of disorder, but one has to remember that Tel's race has now found the beauty in which their continuity lies. Beauty is a re-orderer but it is one which involves violence, as Moses' re-ordering did.[1] Of course Moses had acceptable reasons for opposing the Egyptians, but one must recognize the needs of Tel's race. It is Rosenberg's achievement to have conveyed this recognition prior to the moral evaluation of their actions.

What then is music? If 'beauty is music's secret soul' and impels in man a quest for it, music is established by beauty's existence. Music is the orderedness of elements needing and complementing each other. For Saul, music was an orderer of a kind, but in the more conventional sense of something that soothes and placates: 'This is some fantasy: play music till I come.' It is Lilith's

---

[1] I am here indebted to an unpublished essay by Charles Tomlinson on the concept of beauty and music in Rosenberg's plays.

apprehension of beauty and music that is hers alone, and it is deeply of the imagination, and undecorative. Saul attempts to retain order by soothing the surface. This cannot work. Order cannot be imposed or retained when the whole structure is changing; order develops out of change. It is something impersonal, the result of forces working together. Nubian's philosophic version of reality (and one that he tries hard to retain) is robust; one bears or breaks. Tel's version, though immoral in his application of it, is one that involves change. In his case it is a question of change at whose expense, but he could not ask such questions in the way that Nubian asked them. He cannot resist his necessities. The difference between the two male figures finally involves not a routine morality, but insight. It is a question of how they each understand beauty, for beauty *in itself* is without moral demands. Morality comes into sight with the way it is quested. For Nubian, beauty involves morality because he can see that it is not a mere question of obtaining it. He says:

> Beauty is a great paradox—
> Music's secret soul creeping about the senses
> To wrestle with man's coarser nature.
> It is hard when beauty loses.

Beauty civilizes in that it must be quested; it wants to be sought in relationship, but not seized, so that, in this sense (to contradict myself) it does have moral power. But if beauty loses, there is either withering or the chaos of rape. Beauty disturbs then, but it brings with it the possibility of order, if it is rightly responded to. That is why it is 'music's secret soul'; it needs the correct response, which involves the creation of order. Tel shows that 'beauty is a great paradox' by being prostrated by it at first, but instead of recovering himself into order he returns, without restraint, and, by implication, eliminates the race who are in relation to the women he and his race require. Nubian could have healed Saul's and Lilith's relationship, and this would have constituted his response to Lilith's beauty. But his amulet and its contents were destroyed (Lilith suddenly decided she would wear it!), although it certainly seems that he did contemplate making this healing act; he says of Saul and of himself:

> I am justified at my heart's plea.
> He is justified also.

Tel, on the other hand, could medicine only to his own and his race's needs. Moses did the same for his race, if justifiably. One of the distinctions between Nubian and Tel (and Tel and Moses) provokes the question of justification—over which the war was ostensibly fought. In an earlier version of 'The Unicorn' Tel says:

> . . . yearning is
> Beauty and music, faith, and hope and dreams,
> Religion, love, endeavour, stability
> Of man's whole universe.

Here he is somewhat nearer to Nubian, but the question persists as to what happens when the yearning fulfils itself violently.

If moral actions mean anything they have meaning in relation to everybody. Rosenberg, as a Jew and a working-class man, would feel this especially strongly. To re-order is to include, and this, I think, is what he means by music. Music is the result of inclusive change in which equipoise is reached. Some means must be found to reconcile and include; otherwise we will have merely the rule of the stronger. Music means relationship, not rule. And if change and completion are implicit in desire whose stimulus is beauty and whose summation is music, this is health. Change must work towards completion and inclusion and not towards anarchy caused by exclusion. It is these two impulses, of change and desire for completion, which Rosenberg had to hold in relation (with the war showing him the difficulties); for change may often seem like anarchy. Tel's changes produce anarchy because they exclude. It may sound too plausible an account, but these are the results, and they stem from exclusion. Change and completion are not identical, and Rosenberg had to hold the two together, each as the other's necessary and qualifying counterpart. They had continually to remain so because there is no such thing as permanent completion.

I have tried to suggest that 'The Unicorn' is a play concerned with war and with the pre-war situation of imminent change. It is also concerned with what happens when change occurs. Rosenberg understood very well that war causes suffering which demands pity, but pity on its own is a luxury. It must induce a change that removes suffering. Rosenberg was familiar with Nubian's stoicism; he judged it as entirely necessary, but as insufficient on its own. He drew on his experience of war, poverty, and his Jewishness to nourish his last work. Incomplete though this is, perhaps an undesigned incompleteness also provides a way of understanding the war.

CHAPTER ELEVEN

DAVID JONES

In his Preface to *In Parenthesis* (1937), David Jones made certain distinctions in an attempt to define the kind of poem it is, or was intended to be:

> I did not intend this as a 'War Book'—it happens to be concerned with war. I should prefer it to be about a good kind of peace—but as Mandeville says, 'Of Paradys ne can I not speken propurly I was not there;[1] it is fer beyonde and that for thinketh me. And also I was not worthi.' We find ourselves privates in foot regiments. We search how we may see formal goodness in a life singularly inimical, hateful, to us.
>
> (pp. xii–xiii)

Perhaps the context as well as the substance of this is important because 'This writing has to do with some things I saw, felt, & was part of. The period covered begins early in December 1915 and ends early in July 1916.' The poem was not begun until after the war, in 1928, and published four years after Read's *The End of a War*, in 1937. In disclaiming *In Parenthesis* as a 'War Book', Jones had in mind perhaps the mass of publications which followed the war—not only poetry, but generals' memoirs, autobiographical and diaristic narratives, and novels. Much of these treated the war as an isolated and in some cases exciting phenomenon; and some saw it as different from previous wars, although the asserted differences had in some instances a servile bias. Again, some implied that the war had little to do with events prior to it.[2] As a result, their work, denied a necessary relationship with the past, had no perspective on itself and could offer none on an even immediate past. Moreover, their subject was war; as though war and peace were unconnected phenomena. It is perhaps with this latter,

---

[1] See the Boast on pp. 79–84 of *In Parenthesis*.

[2] Judge Smith, summing up for the jury in the trial of Roger Casement, recommended a similar position to them in helping them to come to their decision. The recommendation was that they ignore the political condition of Ulster which, it appears, was one of the crucial factors in shaping Casement's actions. Only his actions, stripped of their political context, in which the British acted with peculiar bias, were to be judged as relevant.

especially, that Jones is disclaiming association, although his remarks may be taken in a different sense. For as Clausewitz's dictum
that 'War is a continuation of State policy by other means' indicates that peace is a version of war, so Jones, from an opposite
position, may see war as an 'inimical' version of peace, or Paradys.
Of course, in many senses *In Parenthesis* is a 'War Book'. Its
'subject is war' and, in certain aspects of the work, 'the pity of
War'. The narrative, even when it associates with events outside
the war, most often draws on others wars and conflicts, which of
course give to the present a particular perspective as much as the
past is given perspective by the present. It might be objected that
Jones does not however vulgarize history ('the living past') by
reducing it to an explanatory metaphor for the present; that the
past is (almost) as alive as the present, and that in any case both
are temporally indistinguishable elements in the heap of timeless,
meaningful 'recordations', which he has contributed to and brought
into fresh juxtaposition; that for Jones each event is local and particular, and that whatever similarities they may have also show up
the dissimilarity and particularity of each fresh event. All this is
true but, in pointing to the orientation of a writer's preferences, one
has also to say that he cannot help but in some sense be contemporary as well; and that, having suffered in the war, his writing
about it is likely to have more experiential density (whatever the
significance of the Boast) than his writing about the past.

Jones was born in 1895, also the year in which Sorley, Graves,
and Leavis were born—the year of the Franco-Russian alliance; he
enlisted in January 1915, and served as a private in the Royal
Welch Fusiliers, the regiment in which Sassoon and Graves were
officers. As Peter Levi expressed it in *Agenda*, he was 'simply
human cannon-fodder torn away from his local origins [London],
the poet as a young soldier'. His relation with the war seems to have
remained what it was when he entered it, as a young and innocent
man, and in this he resembles Blunden. 'Innocent' seems as much
the right word for Jones as it does for Blunden, in that it implies
not so much a protective if permeable membrane worn over his
psyche, as an unworldliness which kept him in some senses separate
from the war; so that the war related to him as a terrifying metaphor
for his own condition and outlook rather than as something which
totally dominated and moulded his attitudes. Perhaps in this sense
his poem was not intended as a War Book. The war provided

specialized material, but although it re-emerged as the matter of war, it did so as Jones's creation, as that of a special 'kind of peace'. Saunders Lewis's comments, in his note on *Epoch and Artist*, express the sense in Jones's work of the continuing presence of the war:

> Yet in all sorts of context, discussion of sacrament, of Arthurian lore, of the work of Eric Gill or Christopher Smart, or in answer to criticism of the *Anathémata* the most frequent metaphors and prevailing imagery all come from the experience of infantry in the 1914–18 war. This book [*Epoch and Artist*], almost as much as *In Parenthesis*, is a soldier's book, a soldier of 1916. That soldiering gave David Jones a view of himself and of his comrades in trench and sap-head, and so of the normal human male in Western Europe through most of its history.
> It was the dominant practical experience of his life. It remains with him. He sees it still, evokes it. It is the source of his argot and of his rhetoric, moulds his philosophic explorations.[1]

One might add to this Levi's comment that 'David Jones's Romans [in the *Anathémata*] are old soldiers of the Boer War or 1914.' With his 'good kind of peace' in view, these positings of the war as Jones's dominant 'physical' experience might seem to him extreme, yet as Saunders Lewis implies, the soldiers (of the First World War) who represent the soldiers of all ages are not merely the conduit for Jones's matter; their experience is a part of the matter itself. One might say that he remains intensely preoccupied with the particularity of his then-contemporary experience, and not merely in terms that would make the present into usefully illuminating metaphors of a concern with the past. The problem is to interpret as precisely as possible the relationships between the past as Jones is concerned with it, and his present.

Before approaching this problem directly it is worth considering an instance in which the infantryman is used to explain a seemingly totally different situation. In his essay 'The Utile' the subject is not war but the dilemma for the artist, among others, who finds in this age between *Homo Faber*, man the artist and maker, and man the theoretician, a discrepancy. Evidently for Jones it is the nature of the discrepancy and its results which cause him difficulty; the practical and the utilitarian man emerge as different creatures:

> Ars is adamant about one thing: she compels you to do an infantryman's job. She insists on the tactile. The artist in man is the infantryman in man, so that unless the central contention of these pages is

[1] *Agenda*, V, Nos. 1–3 (Spring–Summer 1967), p. 112.

untrue, all men are aboriginally *of* this infantry, though not all serve *with* this infantry. To pursue the analogy, this continued employment 'away from the unit' has made habitual and widespread a 'staff mentality'. Today most of us are staff-wallahs of one sort or another.

(*Epoch and Artist*, p. 183)

It is as though Jones, in the middle of this passage, realizes that he is caught up in reconstituting the experience of the war, however subterraneously, and readjusts himself—at the point where he says 'To pursue the analogy'. The point at which choice and pervasive unconscious pressure can be distinguished is almost indeterminable. Yet given that unconscious pressure to some extent provides the pervasive metaphor, there is also the question of choice; Jones as *Homo Faber* is also a creature of choice, as well as one haunted by a particular context, and one must ask what the soldier and the whole complex of the military image mean to him; what kind of poem *In Parenthesis* is, and what its attitudes to war are. It may be about a 'kind of peace', but it is from and through the war that the poet's vision works.

J. H. Johnston has described the poem as an epic and, therefore, a more complete version of the experience of war than was offered by any other war poet. I do not see it as this, although it has some epic elements—its narrative and its proportion. On the other hand, it is hard to manoeuvre the term so that it will fit any sustained piece of writing since *Paradise Lost;* long narrative poems such as Scott's *The Lay of the Last Minstrel* have neither the texture nor the narrative structure of an epic; and if we were to admit Scott's poem, or Wordsworth's *Prelude*, it would be hard to include *Paradise Lost*. In a special sense, Scott's retrospection has superficially more in common with Jones than with Milton. The impact of the French Revolution on Wordsworth is an epic theme, but in the most obvious sense the poem focuses on the figure of the poet in such a way as to de-dramatize a sense of a society's fate hinging upon a group of individuals engaged in altering its course. Scott is concerned with the valedictory nuances of a dead tradition and not with the problems of a living society. For that reason his work is largely romance and not, in Leavis's term as he applies it to Lawrence, social history. Wordsworth makes his own life the subject of his poem, but the point is mainly conceived through the individual's change being wrought by society; in the last resort, intense as the concentration on social change is, it is the individual change and not the social that is his principal concern. I would not labour these points but for Johnston's persistent claim that *In Parenthesis* is an epic, and his devaluation of the work of the other war poets by comparison.

Only in an ironic sense can one speak of change in Jones's poem. The work relies on the intractable certainty of human annihilation, its narrative interwoven with previous similar human vicissitudes. And if we think of the meaning of *heroic*—large, individualistic feats nevertheless wrought on behalf of a particular group—these seem hardly to have been possible, or at least to much effect, in the context of modern war. Certainly, leaving aside for the moment the meaning of the Arthurian and Celtic matter in the poem, Jones is careful, in his Preface, to make us aware of the discrepancy as he understood it between the war he fought in and the earlier wars:

Some of us ask ourselves if Mr. X adjusting his box-respirator can be equated with what the poet envisaged, in
'I saw young Harry with his beaver on.'
We are in no doubt at all but what Bardolph's marching kiss for Pistol's 'quondam Quickly' is an experience substantially the same as you and I suffered on Victoria platform. For the old authors there appears to have been no such dilemma—for them the embrace of battle seemed one with the embrace of lovers.[1] For us it is different. ... I only wish to record that for me such a dilemma exists, and that I have been particularly conscious of it during the making of this writing.   (pp. xiv–xv)

Honour for those killed in such a condition of reluctance is more ambiguous and complex than honour for the earlier 'heroic' man; and Jones's art is nothing if not complex. Ultimately one must trust the poem more than the poet. Battle and death are described in detail often domestic:

And white faces lie,
(like china saucers tilted run soiling stains half dry, when the moon shines on a scullery-rack and Mr. and Mrs. Billington are asleep upstairs and so's Vi—and any creak frightens you) or any twig moving. (p. 175)

The way in which the contrasting comparison is taken through the domestic situation, and out again, carefully excludes the con-

[1] But see Simone Weil's 'The *Iliad*, or the Poem of Force', *passim*.

ventional feel of the heroic, although not the sense of suffering and
fear (I use the word heroic here to refer to the sense of fearlessness
as it is coupled with the desire for martial glory; courage, despite
fear, is something different). Jones's intention, I think, is to compare the condition of the dead—or, more likely, the troops' anxious
waiting faces—with the snug peacefulness of the civilian, and to
open the reader's mind to some sense of terror which it has experienced, by interleaving it with the domestic landscape.

Jones's pervasiveness, achieved through the accumulation of
small, predatory detail, is moreover something that works away
from the more generalized heroic mode (which has, significantly,
been broken up into intimate detail such as much twentieth-
century writing apparently demands). Whatever the intention of
such domestic similes, they have the effect of balancing the foreshortened life of the soldier against the seemingly durable and
static domestic situation. The facts of civilian life—one of which
may be ignorance of the soldiers' plight—are set up in qualifying
relationship not only with the terrors of modern war but with the
co-existing but tacit mode of the heroic. It might be argued that the
domestic order is there to be shown up, by an implied heroic mode,
for what it is, a life of shameless ease; but what is achieved here is
not an upgrading of the worth of the heroic so much as a revaluing
of the soldiers' suffering.

Structurally the narrative of the poem is extremely simple. It
consists of a sequence of events leading into and including the
annihilation of nearly all a 'new-army' battalion of a Welsh Regiment. Much of the narrative centres on John Ball, one of the few
(wounded) survivors. The name, as René Hague indicates, is 'that
of the priest executed for his share in the peasant rising of 1381
[and] stresses the continuity of Welsh and British tradition'. It also
stresses what Hague calls the 'troglodytic culture of the trenches'.[1]

The poem is in seven parts, and each assembles in it a homo-
geneous activity. Part 1 contains the parade and embarkation; Part
2, the training in France, a period of respite, followed by the march
towards the trenches. Part 3 involves further marching which ends
in the relieving of another regiment holding the trenches. It is a
fairly quiet sector. Part 4, the longest, gives a detailed account of
trench life, the physical hardship and the periods of boredom. In

[1] *Agenda*, V, Nos. 1–3, p. 58.

Part 5, a further spell in the trenches is followed by a period of rest behind the line and a march towards an area of the front that was to become part of the Somme battlefield. Part 6 speaks of the period of rest preceding battle, in which recollections of one's life are lovingly exchanged with one's friends. The regiment moves into position. Part 7, the final and second longest, re-creates that part of the battle experienced by Private Ball and his battalion, in which nearly all his comrades are destroyed.

This summary, though obviously inadequate, indicates how little 'story' there is. Events occur, people co-exist, but there is no plot, no action of one person or group of people dependent upon another. There are no oppositions in the story except in the battle itself. The narrative consists of a progression towards the single opposition they encounter, which annihilates them, and which then stops, after the elegiac concluding passage. It is much more a 'recordation' than an unfolding of interwoven events and impulses. The one significant change is from life to death. There are many conclusions one could draw from such a sequence, but the narrative itself is not easily abstracted or generalized from. The writing has a haecceity which insists on its referents and context:

You loose the thing into the underbush.
    Dark-faceted iron oval lobs heavily to fungus-cushioned dank, wobbles under low leaf to lie, near where the heel drew out just now; and tough root-fibres boomerang to top-most green filigree and earth clods flung disturb fresh fragile shoots that brush the sky.
    You huddle closer to your mossy bed. . . .   (p. 169)

Even when he synthesizes the details from two processes he does not lose sight of the individuality of each:

But it isn't like that for the common run and you have no mensuration gear to plot meandering fortune-graph nor know whether she were the Dark or the Fair left to the grinding.   (p. 159)

The complexity here consists in the soldier's helplessness to guess the cycle (mensuration) of fortune; his cycle is Fortune's. The interleaving of mensuration, Fortune's cycle, and his own unguessable track is complex and precise. A similar precision is part of this

man-flower complex, where both creatures have been vulnerable
to the fire of weapons:

> they could quite easily train dark muzzles
> to fiery circuit
> and run with flame stabs to and fro among
> stammer a level traversing
> and get a woeful cross-section on
> stamen-twined and bruised pitilline
> steel-shorn of style and ovary
> leaf and blossoming
> with flora-spangled khaki pelvises . . .
> where adolescence walks the shrieking wood.
>
> (pp. 170–1)

The transferred 'shrieking' does this intermingling terrifyingly well;
a few lines later, each part of the man-plant comparison (having
life and vulnerability in common) coalesces in three puns, as the
blood of the human and the 'dye' of the flower mingle even more
intensely:

> shin and fibula
> and twice-dye with crimson moistening
> for draggled bloodwort and the madder sorrel.   (p. 171)

Bloodwort is the name of a plant with red roots or leaves, supposed
both to staunch and draw blood. Ironically, it does not here
medicine the wounded, its 'dye' (dying) as much spread over the
shattered bodies as their blood is over the bloodwort leaves. The
plant cannot staunch this much blood and its properties, like those
of the men, are squandered. There is the additional sense (as with
Rosenberg's poppies in 'Break of Day in the Trenches') of the
blood nourishing the bloodwort, quite contrary to its use in medicine.
Thus the first pun 'dye' prepares for the second, which plays on the
plant's name. This kind of punning is found again in the last lines of
the poem, where the German and English soldiers, regardless of
rank, are interleaved in death:

> Lie still under the oak
> next to the Jerry
> and Sergeant Jerry Coke.   (p. 187)

The potentially pacific part of us links the two, as death does, and
this is made explicit through a pun—Jerry—the slang name for the

German soldier.[1] Owen achieves a more explicit linkage in the line 'I am the enemy you killed, my friend.'

This setting side by side and mingling of images and ideas is done throughout *In Parenthesis* on other levels, as for instance, with Celtic mythology and history. The mixture of Londoners and Welshmen in Jones's regiment reflects the mixture of contemporary British and historical Celtic matter. Johnston writes that the poem 'offers an historical perspective by bringing in the struggles of other national cultures of older times, which should, and to some extent does produce a "significant historical continuity"'. One wonders, however, if 'historical continuity' is as precise as it first seems if, as Jones indicates in the Preface, there is this discrepancy between his war and earlier struggles. Such a discrepancy between the heroic-and-never-count-the-cost matter and that of the First World War forces us to question that 'continuity' and the inferences drawn from it. History, of course, can be viewed as a sequence, rather than a continuity, where wars follow each other and the accumulating knowledge of human response to combat is added to the heap of human 'understanding'; but such knowledge is surely as dead as the men killed in combat.

Harold Fisch, in his essay 'Blake's Miltonic Moments', suggests that one difference between the two poets, and one that distinguishes many of the Romantics, is their abandoning of historical

---

[1] Ian Parsons in the Introduction to his anthology *Men Who March Away* (1965) notes an interesting passage in Shakespeare's *3 Henry VI* (II, v, lines 73–5 and 121–2):

> [*Enter a son that hath killed his father, bringing in the dead body*]. . . .
> HENRY: O piteous spectacle! O bloody times!
> Whiles lions war, and battle for their dens,
> Poor harmless lambs abide their enmity. . . .
>
> [*Enter a father, bearing his son*]. . . .
> FATHER: I'll bear thee hence, and let them fight that will,
> For I have murdered where I should not kill.

Shakespeare distinguishes between murder and the taking of life legalized by the state at war. 'Kill' is, on first inspection, a morally neutral word used to point the more judgemental meaning of 'murder'; but in the particular context (as opposed to the received meanings) both words take on a judgemental quality, since not only should each of them not have murdered but should not have killed. The moral judgement is given by making the distinction between the two words, evaluating both in the particular context, and then merging the distinctions. The father unwittingly doubles the killing into murder, in that he kills his son (and by implication any person—'We are all brethren'—'For I have murdered where I should not kill'). Fortune retributively punishes him by making him kill his son.

consciousness (continuity as cause and effect) for a consciousness that eclipses all the past within the eternal moment. With Jones, the contemporary material is scrupulously sequential, but in the relations between the historical and contemporary material there is a sense in which the historical is so vividly present, so contemporaneous, as on occasion to blur the differences between them, and thus to make some evaluation of the present (and the past) struggles difficult. It is true, for instance, that those killed in this sector of the Somme get mourned, and thus, by implication, all those slain in war; but it is also true that the Boast 'I was there' implies pride in service and a very different response to war than the elegaic conclusion. This kind of ambiguity makes it possible for Johnston to speak of Jones in relation to his concept of 'duty' and its 'moral imperatives' and so to enlist him, by implication at least, into the fold of the epic poets and (such is the nature of his divisions) as in opposition to those poets who protested against the war. Jones, to summarize the argument, may be seen as fulfilling a historical continuity[1] if the Boast of pride in service is more dominant than the pity he evokes.

Some of his historical matter has a lustre to it which Simone Weil and much contemporary opinion could not support. Even so, not only is the historical material not always in continuous and *supporting* recession to the contemporary; it also in some senses contrasts with it; although whether this is Jones's intention, and what is his evaluation of the differences between the two, is hard to determine. Historical continuity, congruity, and tradition are all different, and would not be the same even were there complete historical continuity and congruity in *In Parenthesis*.

I do not know if Johnston would claim that historical continuity and tradition are synonymous, but I sense such a loose assumption underlying his arguments. The assumption about tradition is that, being a body of accumulated historical events and one nation's responses to them, it can at any time be dragooned into serving the immediate interests of that nation, regardless of the nation's present attitudes, moral impulses, and economic position. How would Garibaldi or Mazzini have felt about the Italian tradition being 'used' in support of the invasion of Ethiopia with poison gas in 1935?

---

[1] I mean here by 'continuity' the repeated instances of soldierly pride in service.

There are other—by now almost traditional—discrepancies between groups within the one nation, who have different interests:

and into it they slide . . . of the admirable salads of Mrs. Curtis-Smythe: they fall for her in Poona, and it's worth one's while—but the comrade close next you screamed so after the last salvo that it was impossible to catch any more the burthen of this white-man talk. (pp. 154–5)

Jones catches admirably the whole situation of the supposed superiority that is both racist and class-ridden. Peter Levi remarks that although Jones 'is a morally formidable human being . . . there is no moral crisis in *In Parenthesis* as there was for the officer poets of that war'. That *may* be so; but what Jones is implying in the passage quoted above is that the ordinary ranker stands in much the same relation to his ruling class and its interests as the colonized human being; both have the same kind of demands put upon them by the group with the power (the affectation of the name connotes the class). Perhaps 'it's worth one's while'; but this is immediately qualified by 'the comrade close next you screamed so'—all for a culture represented by 'the admirable salads of Mrs. Curtis-Smythe'. I do not think that Jones is advocating the heroic ideal as the worthy opposite to such a culture, but contrasting the suffering with both. For what, one asks, have the cockneys and the Welsh in common with her; in what sense can she represent for them the ideal worth their sacrifice that they should die for her? Indeed, what ideal can dictate that one individual *must* die for another? It seems that here Jones, whether in full knowledge or not, is questioning the value of a tradition that insists on a continuity in which all relationships, such as they are, are kept intact and without question. Soldiers in earlier wars might have thought it worth while, but were they right to think so, and must we continue to think similarly? The problem here raised runs throughout the poem. Occasionally it is raised in a different form:

Two armies face and hold their crumbling *limites* intact. They're worthy of an intelligent song for all the stupidity of their contest. A boast for the dyke keepers, for the march wardens. (pp. 88–9)

What then *is* the value of the historical material in the sense that Johnston can claim that it 'to some extent does produce a "significant historical continuity"'? For the problem of aligning the contemporary struggle with earlier battles seen in heroic terms is that it suggests the continuing necessity of the moral imperatives of

duty, for all those who took part in the First War. The notion of
duty is not repellent to everyone, although the word itself deadens
the activity it is applied to. But considering the way in which many
enlisted, with some enthusiasm and certainly with good conscience, surely some better word could be found for their actions?
On the other hand, it might be remembered that some saw pacifism
as their duty and that, in any case, pacifism aside, not all wars
demand equally the allegiance of a nation's citizens.

Seen in relation to this kind of debate, the Boast in Part 4
acquires a certain ambiguity. It is made by a soldier and may be
taken in contrasting comparison with the two sentences of Mande-
ville's quoted by Jones: 'Of Paradys ne can I not speken propurly
I was not there', whereas of the matter of boast ('The long boast in
these pages I associate with the boast of Taliessen at the court of
Maelgwn', Jones writes in his Notes) the soldier can and does say:
'I was with. . . . I was the. . . . I saw. . . . I marched. . . . I
heard. . . .' The nature of the Boast has at least two implications,
one of them, evidently, being experiential. The other is less certain,
and is linked with the discussion above on the nature of duty, the
moral imperative, and allegiance. For it may be that the soldier's
Boast has not only to do with how he bore suffering but also with
loyal service. In a general way the point concerning loyalty would
hold despite the instances of individuals, armies, and even of
nations changing sides,[1] whether through the murder or defeat of
their ruler. But the Boast may have further implications, apart from
establishing an international claim to experience, endurance,
courage, and allegiance (despite the fact that soldiers on either side
may make a similar claim of allegiance and go on to kill each other);
for it feeds into the contemporary material the kind of lustre and
heroism which the contemporary would otherwise seem to lack.
Possibly the Boast picks out its corresponding aspect in modern
warfare which might otherwise be obscured. Possibly it shows a
contrast between the past and the present, even to the latter's
disadvantage. And possibly, the heroic mode is itself qualified by
the presence of the contemporary drabness and terror. So that, if
we have tended to see battle in the past as a heroic activity, we shall
have to modify our image of it so as to make it correspond more with
the evidence the present offers us, evidence not to be despised because it is contemporary with us. What causes me uneasiness in the

[1] See Cavafy's 'In a Township of Asia Minor'.

relation between Jones's historical and contemporary matter, however, is the remark in his Preface that 'Roland could find, and, for a
reasonable while, enjoy, his Oliver. In the earlier months there was
a certain attractive amateurishness, and elbow-room for idio-
syncrasy that connected one with a less exacting past. . . . [This]
seemed to terminate with the Somme battle.' At the risk of seeming
priggish, I should say that this is not frank enough; for it seems to
suggest that some people enjoyed the individualistic pursuit and
killing of an enemy soldier. I suspect that this was true of Grenfell
(see page 72 above) and that it might have been true of others,
although it would have been more open of Jones to have said as
much without implying, with the use of Roland and Oliver as types
and personifications, that such actions have justifications perhaps
through precedent. It might have been put baldly, and have been
more interesting if it had been. But can the remark be accepted as
having general implication? What interests me more is the attitude
which Jones himself brings to bear on the situation: 'there was a
certain attractive amateurishness'. What, one might ask, is the
attitude of the writer partly masked perhaps by 'attractive'?
Perhaps the individualistic exploit seemed more attractive in comparison with the embittered and increasingly mechanized develop-
ments in war, but these are surely severely limited comparisons,
both being tied to one's awareness that in either case we are speaking of the taking of life. And moreover, although Jones may 'not
have been there', he might have remembered the humiliating
casualties and defeats of the French armies in the early months of
the war as qualifying his sense of the 'attractive amateurishness' of
the war prior to 1916. If he may bring in historical matter, there
was plenty near him which might be thought to have been
relevant.

At all events, in relation to this passage in the Preface, one has to
ask what the nature of the Boast is and what its relation to our
present apprehension of the war and war in general. The Boast has
written into it a respect for the experiential; it is as if each soldier
is drawn from the dead to swear and testify to his value through his
presence. Whitman, in 'Song of Myself', says 'I was the man, I
suffer'd, I was there'. The first soldier begins: 'My fathers were with
the Black Prince of Wales', and then is made to identify with a
mythical witness: 'I was with Abel when his brother found him',
having the ability to transmigrate through each generation of soldiers,

or witness of killing, while at the same time possessing the individual quality of the man who was there, long since dead:

> I built a shit-house for Artaxerxes.
> I was the spear in Balin's hand. . . .   (p. 79)

The range of reference is wide, but each of the figures is brought together by the common context of death:

> the Dandy Xth are my regiment;
> who diced
> Crown and Mud-hook
> Under the Tree. . . .
> I heard Him cry:
> > *Apples ben ripe in my gardayne*
> I saw Him die.   (p. 83)

In this particular passage, in each of the Boasts, the references are to Christ. 'The Xth Fretensis is, in Italian legend, said to have furnished the escort party at the execution of our Lord', Jones writes in his Notes. Here one might ask if he intends the presence of the sacrificed Christ to qualify one's attitudes not only to the soldiers who 'furnished the escort party', but to all soldiers.

Perhaps 'intention' is here irrelevant in that one should really be considering what the effect of the Christ–soldier juxtaposition is. But again, I feel some ambiguity both in Jones's possible intentions and in his results. Christianity itself is ambiguous here, for some sinners, according to the Gospels, will on no account enter heaven, whereas those who participated in deicide seem to have acquired (with the exception of the Jews) a quasi-sacredness from their very association with Christ. Certainly Christ reserves much of His condemnation for the hypocrites, those Pharisees, for instance, who know what does and what does not constitute a sin, and yet continue with their acts, observing only the forms of morality; whereas forgiveness seems reserved especially for those sinners who 'know not what they do'. If one brings the person of Christ into a modern context, the historical reference is as liable to some qualification by contemporary ethics as the modern is by the historical; the equation is not entirely one-way. Is one saying, for instance, that all soldiers are innocent because 'they know not what they do', and especially because of their association, by tradition, with those soldiers who escorted Christ? By comparison with their Pharasaic rulers, perhaps they are; but contemporary attitudes condemn those who press the button as well as those who order it to be done. Contemporary ethics have a kind of homogeneity, although this is only one side of Caesar's coin, for the soldier also suffers.

By introducing Christ into the military Boast, Jones implies, I think, a comparison with the suffering Christ, a comparison that other war poets have also made: Read, in 'My Company'; Sassoon, in 'The Redeemer'; and Owen, especially in his letter to Osbert Sitwell from Scarborough in July 1918:

> For 14 hours yesterday I was at work—teaching Christ to lift his cross by numbers, and how to adjust his crown; and not to imagine he thirst till after the last halt; I attended his Supper to see that there were no complaints; and inspected his feet to see that they should be worthy of the nails.

Few would think this comparison over-generous, but I am concerned with the nature of the soldiers' martyrdom. Although it acquires emphasis from association with Christ's, it is the kind of honour which this martyrdom solicits from us that we should be especially cautious of offering. And we should be so, not only with the honour, but with the implicated attitudes of the soliciting. This kind of debate runs throughout this book, but it is here especially difficult to evaluate. If we honour the soldiers' martyrdom are we also to honour the tradition of soldiering, which involves killing as well? Sometimes, it seems, we are not to: 'They're worthy of an intelligent song for all the stupidity of their contest.' Would Jones dissociate Johnston's moral imperatives from the soldiers' suffering? Or do the traditions and the accumulations of the Boast ask us to associate, deliberately and inevitably, the soldiers' martyrdom with the cause? Can the cause be condoned because of the suffering? Or can we honour the one and reject the other, whether or not the soldier would want this? Does a tradition of soldiers' experience involve Jones, and us, in honouring patriotism, or can one honour the courage but reject the patriotism, even though the courage operates in a general way on its behalf? These are for me the principal questions raised by the Boast, and I have to say that I cannot answer them with any precision. If the clear answer were that Jones does demand of us that we honour the suffering and must therefore honour the cause, Johnston's assertions would be in order. But Jones does not fully accept or reject such a possibility; he simply raises the questions.

The Boast concludes with 'Old soldiers never die'. This may well have an ironic meaning in an (anti-) war poem, but there can be no doubt that it subscribes to the myth of the 'heroic' soldier. With the doubts now raised, it may not be over-meticulous to ask, service for whom, and fortitude to what end? The Boast also praises the 'secret princes' (see 'Dedication') who are explicitly referred to in the opening of the elegiac passage, Part 7:

> The secret princes between the leaning trees have diadems given them.
>   Life the leveller hugs her impudent equality—she may
> proceed at once to less discriminating zones.   (p. 185)

This is a medieval-like democratization—in that death is the leveller—but here the idea has been inverted. If democracy insists (which it does not) on a levelling *sameness*, which death certainly does, then nature plaits different torques and diadems for each of the dead. And these dead are the men not named in history, but whose effort in a cause, whether it was worth their sacrifice or not, make them, it is implied, equal in virtue with princes. They are princes in that their endurance and sacrifice establish their worth, and from this we see that it is these qualities that make men princes, and not their birth. They are hidden because no man names or individualizes them, except the poet. And by making nature honour the men, Jones is placing his tribute upon them too. But whether he intended it or not, there is a certain irony in the fact that nature and not society honours them; for society cannot honour so many dead, except collectively. John Ball himself honours them indirectly, but he is concerned with survival and can do no more than witness:

> The 'Queen of the Woods' has cut bright boughs of various flowering. . . .
>   Some she gives white berries
>   some she gives brown
>   Emil has a curious crown it's
>   made of golden saxifrage.
>   Fatty wears sweet-briar,
> he will reign with her for a thousand years.
>   For Balder she reaches high to fetch his.
>   Ulrich smiles for his myrtle wand.
>   That swine Lillywhite has daisies to his chain—you'd
> hardly credit it.
>   She plaits torques of equal splendour for Mr. Jenkins and
> Billy Crower.   (p. 185)

Nature does not distinguish in rank. 'That swine Lillywhite', by being killed, has as much right to be honoured as the others; whereas, had it been left to human agency, he might have been excluded. Unlike society, which honours its dead soldiers collectively, nature honours each individually.

Three essays in *Epoch and Artist* are relevant to the Celtic and Arthurian material in *In Parenthesis*: 'The Heritage of Early Britain' (1952), 'The Arthurian Legend' (1948), and 'The Myth of Arthur' (1942)—'a much corrected and largely re-written' version of an essay 1940–41. The poem was published in 1937, five years before 'The Myth of Arthur', but the date should provide no reason for assuming an unrelatedness between the poem and the essay. Moreover, there are hints in the essay which support the nature of the writing in the poem. In the essay Jones refers to 'the concrete (without which all art falters)', and later he writes:

[Malory's] data (his visual, felt, data I mean), were accurate, experiential and contactual. And something of that sort is a necessity to the making of a work, there can be no getting round that necessity in the long run. The imagination must work through what is known and known by a kind of touch. Like the Yggdrasil of northern myth, the roots must be in hard material though the leaves be conceptual and in the clouds; otherwise we can have fancy but hardly imagination. (p. 244)

As relevant to *In Parenthesis* is this, four pages on:

The notion that [Malory's] *Morte Darthur* lacks construction has always seemed to me somewhat superficial, for it gathers depth and drive as it proceeds toward the final disaster. (p. 248)

These comments are as true of the parts of the poem as of the work as a whole. In Part 4, for instance, the details of trench life in a quiet sector are shown; physical hardship is mixed with boredom, and the minutiae of experience offer a perspective on every war. And in the last part, as the action quickens, the speed and density of the writing also increase. The rapidity with which the action is taken through the changing images creates the sense of rapidity with which events are said to happen in battle, as well as creating that sense of speed the mind has when the senses are excited. The 'depth and drive' permeate the accumulated and necessarily haphazard events of combat and, as the battle moves towards its climax, so one has a sense of the whole narrative rising to its own.

This Joycean accumulation gives the poem a shape and unity, and one sees how Jones allows the events on just one sector of the Somme to help give his material a shape and unity. He offers a solution to those polar difficulties of unrecognized 'recordation', on the one hand, and on the other, of too great an intellectual organization which can remove a poem from the events it is struggling to contain. When Jones, writing of the end of *Morte Darthur*, says that 'The tension snaps or rather there is a ruinous explosion', there seems at least a parallel between the end of *In Parenthesis* and Malory's work. Of course, both do end in disaster—as did the Somme offensive—but the telling factor here is that the Arthurian and other disasters permeate the end of Jones's poem as well as the work as a whole.

Other resemblances between the past and the present, of a more local kind, are observed:

Any conflict at an egress, or collision of wills in a narrow space at stair-head or at door ... have, as in the case of confined struggle at trench-block or crater-lip, a particular quality of tension.   (p. 249)

Again, when Jones writes that

over the Celtic West ... [a] sudden activity came into being. ... Whatever the hair-splitting, the severities, the taboos, the background is the flora and fauna of Thule, where the contours are lost and found, where intuition refracts the shape of definition, where men speak true only when they speak as poets.   (pp. 254-5)

There is for me in such a 'background' a parallel found in the nature-elegy which concludes the poem. The pervasion of nature reminds us that, prior to the Industrial Revolution, the sobered stillness of a battlefield would consist of an interleaving of nature with the dead, as we have it in the poem's elegy. Here it seems that such a past is placed within our own time-system (although we know it is the past) so as to modify our imagination and create in our minds some sense of criticism as we should apply it to our own society; the 'consciousness of the beauty of the created world not always found in aesthetics'—found here, in both nature and Jones's aesthetics.

I offer another, more tentative, reading of the nature-elegy. Jones, in *Epoch and Artist*, refers to Spengler's cyclical idea of history as involving 'periods of decline', but the idea almost axiomatically includes periods of refurbishing such as, Jones tells us, occurred in earlier Welsh society. This refurbishing is perhaps hinted at in the crowning of the dead by nature in *In Parenthesis*. It is a measured, beneficent act, which has none of man's desperation in it; but the soldiers' deaths are too near for us to think of any immediate regeneration. The cost has first to be counted. But such mourning shows a valuation of life and, where that is present, some regeneration is possible, on man's side at least. And the interleaving of the dead with nature surely hints at such a possibility of renewal, both by nature and with man. That at least may be the implication of John Ball's assertion at the end of the poem, for an understanding of war's devastation is the prerequisite of society's growth: 'The geste says this and the man who was on the field . . . and who wrote the book . . . the man who does not know this has not understood anything.' If man can learn anything from nature, it consists in his understanding of its beneficence; nature is rarely hostile, as sometimes with Owen. Nor is the destruction that nature suffered much emphasized by Jones, as it was by Hardy and Blunden. Nature remains a moral—because benign—scale against which man's destructiveness and suffering can be measured, but the point is not pressed.

Some further indication of the way in which mythic and historical material is used in *In Parenthesis* may be gathered from two of Jones's statements:

To conserve, to develop, to bring together, to make significant for the present what the past holds, without dilution or any deleting, but rather by understanding and transubstantiating the material, this is the function of genuine myth, neither pedantic nor popularizing, not indifferent to scholarship, nor antiquarian, but saying always: 'of these thou hast given me have I lost none.'　　　(E. & A., p. 243)

and

it is certain that in our anabasis across [our 'wasteland'] we shall have reason to keep in mind the tradition of our origins in both matter and spirit.　　　(E. & A., p. 242)

To return to the resemblance between our age and the Celtic past— but this time in relation to the decline of the latter (and perhaps of our own age): 'it is possible that we are once again obliquely and by analogy, confronted with a *reflection* [my italics] of actual events'. Jones is in fact speaking of Malory, but he suggests I think that the final defeats reflect earlier 'successive' ones; as perhaps the prior battles and defeats as they occur in *In Parenthesis* reflect, and are reflected in, the contemporary ones. To tell the truth about the past and the present would therefore impose on Jones a necessity beyond that of the recorder of the past and present. The truth of these might indicate the possible (but perhaps avoidable) disintegration of our society in the future.

One further unifying effect of the Arthurian matter in *In Parenthesis* is, as I have already suggested, that of seeming to provide for the Welsh and the English in Jones's regiment a common myth:

> the tradition of Arthur (even when reintroduced in Angevin disguises) was, for the Welsh, an authentic part of their historical mythus, whereas for the English it was a literary convention mixed with locality-traditions.
> (*E. & A.*, p. 227)

This seems to deny the unifying possibilities but, as he goes on to say, the disintegration 'of the old synthesis',

> the self-destruction of the Wars of the Roses, in which [Malory] was himself involved, was the outward sign of the break-down of the old synthesis—the conflict from within, of the Marxists, that makes inevitable the new order.
> (*E. & A.*, p. 244)

Thus, although there are two Arthurs in Malory, one for the English and one for the Welsh—or, to put it differently, although there are mirrored in the *Morte Darthur* through the accumulating nature of the myth two cultural disintegrations, the Welsh and the English —these are both united in the one work, which is a description of a further and third disintegration, of which the Wars of the Roses was the syndrome. This bringing together also reflects the interleaving, however unwillingly, of the two cultures. One cultural myth is hidden in another, of which the former is the germ of the latter. By juxtaposing the Arthurian matter with that of the First War, one is seeing mirrored at least three disintegrations—Welsh, English, and European, each stage including in itself a particle of the previous one, with the Welsh element shrewdly being the germ of the total accumulation.

From Jones's viewpoint then there would seem to be every reason for insisting on the 'necessity of preserving the many elements'.

The past mirrors and defines the present in its processes. The past is always worthy of preservation, but with our own disintegration in view we seek more understanding, and more ways of controlling war. This may be partly achieved, some believe, through our understanding of the past. 'All must be safely garnered in', Jones quotes Stanley Spencer as saying to him. (Spencer first of all served as a Red Cross orderly in the war.)

Jones remarks on the difference between combat with firearms and that prior to the discovery of gunpowder. This was in use before the end of the fourteenth century although, interestingly, firearms are seldom mentioned in Shakespeare's plays. Perhaps the difference between the modes of combat and their instruments implied a moral evaluation which Shakespeare wanted to endorse. It is generally assumed that the more recent the combat (certainly since the invention of gunpowder) and the more highly developed the weapons, the less heroic are the participants.

John Hale writes in an article entitled 'War and Opinion in the Fifteenth and Sixteenth Centuries':[1]

Yet alongside this glamorization, it was clear that war was in hard fact becoming more impersonal, brutal and squalid. There was less hand-to-hand combat; in spite of considerable advances in their treatment, gunwounds remained more dangerous than those made by steel.

I accept Mr. Hale's point about the impersonality of firearms, to some extent; but one must question his inference that the new weapons made combat more 'brutal and squalid'. From the writing of the Great War, it would seem that the bayonet aroused more fear and horror than the rifle. Hand-to-hand fighting, of course, involves great physical effort and therefore perhaps offers a greater sense of 'achievement', but this is surely not 'heroic'. Mr. Hale continues: 'it was conventional for works on gunnery and fortification to apologize in this way for the brutality of their subject matter: a last twitch of embarrassment in the long debate about the legitimacy of gunpowder'. Apparently, 'The main arguments against its use were religious, humanitarian and social', the first two being subsumed under objections to blasphemy ('to imitate God's thunder') and cruelty. But 'The social argument was that gunpowder was a coward's weapon which destroyed the dignity of

[1] *Past and Present*, No. 22 (July 1962).

knighthood by allowing a common soldier to kill a gentleman from afar'. He then supports this with a quotation from Ariosto:

> Through thee is martial glory lost, through thee
> The trade of arms become a worthless art:
> And at such ebb are worth and chivalry
> That the base often plays the better part.

Unless it is assumed that the 'common soldier' must in contrast to the gentleman be a coward because he was of 'base' birth, there are really two arguments here. One is that it was a coward's weapon, but the other is made on behalf of the gentleman, presumably by those of his own class and interests. The first argument asserts, merely, and the second offers prejudice. Yet in spite of it, it would seem that gentlemen of the same social standing were not lastingly concerned with preserving themselves from the weapons fit only for the common man (perhaps because the weapons were all the time proving more lethal). Why otherwise would they have come into such use as to outmode the earlier more chivalric weapons? Presumably such chivalry decayed as it was confronted by superior force. This would hardly constitute a moral argument against chivalry, but it may help to question the strength of the chivalric tradition, in that one mode of fighting gave way to another. Hale asserts that

> The knightly argument that gunpowder was a coward's weapon has been taken too seriously. . . . Gunpowder was a grievance for the horseman who had invested his fortune on his equipment, and for the individual fighting for personal glory (rather than for a state or a cause), but it was accepted by the overwhelming majority of knightly soldiers. It was even accepted by the church, which provided gunners with a patron saint of their own, St. Barbara.

Jones is careful to record how the spirit of the war changed after 1916, but perhaps the changes were not fundamentally very important. Malory after all, although speaking of heroism and the chivalric code, also speaks of a society in disintegration, provoked into war by treachery, and its disintegration finalized by war. Perhaps such disintegration was the result of the decay of chivalry; but perhaps the chivalry was itself a factor we have over-esteemed. Perhaps the condition of chivalry was always subject to certain pressures less palatable than the heroism we have shiningly abstracted from the brutalities of war.

David Jones thought three dates in his calendar worth mentioning, and the third concerns the inception of *In Parenthesis*. The first is the commencement of the war, and the second receives this gloss in *Epoch and Artist:* 'in 1917 somewhere in the neighbour-hood of Ypres . . . I first found myself wondering about the Catholic tradition. Four years later, in 1921, I found myself unable to do otherwise than subscribe to that tradition.' The need for religion, for belief of some kind in crises, is often demonstrated in time of war; not that I wish to suggest that the war was a direct cause of Jones's subscription. His mind is too complex for that, although the sense of impermanence and mortality that war would emphasize would naturally find in religion, and art, an attempt to see, or create, images of permanence and value. 'All must be safely garnered in.'

Some such attempts may perhaps be associated with Jones's reference to Catholicism as 'that tradition'; and in his profession of faith in 'Art and Sacrament' (1955) he associates *Ars* and *Prudentia*. He sees these as aspects of each other, and this way of seeing one may associate with his understanding of religion. To put it simply, what he sees as the sacramental (sign-making) act—the human act of making, or re-presenting—he sees as a parallel to the rites in Catholicism (which he differentiates from ritualism): 'Because the church is committed to "Sacraments" with a capital S, she cannot escape a committal to sacrament with a small s.' The signs and rites of the Church are not only representative but also become, at a certain stage, the things represented (the bread and the wine representing first of all the bread and the wine of the Last Supper and then becoming, as Christ declared, his own flesh and blood). Thus, different kinds of metaphors are not only metaphors but, because of their 'hereness' and particularity, have a substance of their own. The past operates in relation to the present very much in this way; it is itself, and what it represents in relation to the present event, or experience, it is perhaps reflecting.

An example of the way in which the past operates as itself and through the present occurs in the first lines of the poem:

'49 Wyatt, 01549 Wyatt.
Coming sergeant.
Pick 'em up, pick 'em up—I'll stalk within yer chamber. (p. 1)

The reference, of course, is to Wyatt's lines

> They flee from me, that sometime did me seek
> With naked foot, stalking in my chamber.

What the past does for this particular present is both to compare and contrast with it. The predatory elements of love and war are compared; but what of human sexuality war utterly lacks is shown in the conjunction of the past and the present situations. Other contrasts appear. The decorous quality of the love encounter, and the terse management of human beings bonded in modern war.

The representational application of the sign occurs in many passages of *In Parenthesis*, where sexuality is made to represent or, in some sense, parallel a very different kind of relationship. In Part 7, when, after Private Ball has been wounded, he finds his rifle a burden, a painful debate takes place in his head as to whether he should abandon it. At this point, his army teaching bears in on him:

> men must really cultivate the habit of treating this weapon with the very greatest care and there should be a healthy rivalry among you—it should be a matter of very proper pride and
> Marry it man! Marry it!
> Cherish her, she's your very own.
> Coax it man coax it—it's delicately and ingeniously made. . . .
> Fondle it like a granny—talk to it—consider it as you would a friend. . . .
> You would choose her from among many.   (pp. 183–4)

The last line is overtly about the rifle, but the delicate linkages in and out of friendly, marital, and sexual references make the relationship between the man and his rifle more vivid because they establish parallels in which the exaggeration of the case for the man and his rifle is the more persuasive because of what it is paralleled by.

A more obvious metaphor, a personification, again occurs in Part 7, where death is represented as a woman:

> But sweet sister death has gone debauched today and stalks on this high ground with strumpet confidence, makes no coy veiling of her appetite but leers from you to me with all her parts discovered.   (p. 162)

The personification of death is not original, and not intended to be, but the nakedness of the danger gains emphasis from the metaphor; the repellent demeanour of death is especially emphasized by the parallel horror of the incestuous sexuality, set up in so deliberate a way. Sex and death (a version of love and war) are linked to show a few predatory similarities, but are also contrasted.

Another example of the past living in and through the present occurs in the lines

> Where his fiery sickle garners you:
> fanged-flash and darkt-fire thrring and thrrung athwart thdrill
> a Wimshurst pandemonium drill with dynamo druv staccato bark
> at you like Berthe Krupp's terrier bitch and rattlesnakes for bare
> legs . . .
> > the gentleman must be mowed.   (p. 182)

The reference is to John Barleycorn. The mowing image appears either side of the onomatopoeic drill of machine guns, which indeed mow, and which have attributed to them something of the wanton malice of the terrier bitch, the sharp vindictive power of its teeth and yap. The mowing operation can be compared to that of the machine guns, although it is less deadly. The past levers through the present and helps to form a total but differentiating complexity.

As Sassoon does, Jones shows the relationship between blasphemy and supplication, but with more subtlety and less strain. In Part 4, as the rations are being distributed in the trench, he writes:

> Dispense salvation,
> strictly apportion it,
> let us taste and see,
> let us be renewed,
> for christ's sake let us be warm.   (p. 73)

The supplicating quality of the anaphora (repetition), 'let us . . . let us', invites formal association with prayer. And since, as Jones might have put it, men have bodies, unlike angels, and have (self) consciousness, unlike animals, the conscious 'prayer' for the body's nutriment is as sacramental as prayer for the soul's. This is emphasized by what is almost a pun on the phrase 'for christ's sake', which is not only a strong expression of human desires—consider the conversational tone of the line in contrast with the preceding ones—but is also a supplication to Christ: have mercy on us, in Christ's name.

Jones uses the representative quality of signs from the past, but as if the past were still visibly and actually present; as if the signs and their substance persisted. The meanings of these past accumulations are refracted into and through the present, as though at the bend of their refractions the interrelated meanings of past and present accumulate; as though he were gathering deposits of understanding with which to withstand, and help others to withstand, the stresses of war and turn it into a better kind of peace.

He places us and himself 'in the order of signs'. We are incorporated into the world he has made and the act presses on us an understanding of the past by our presence in it. The past is renewed by our presence, and therefore our understanding through it of our present.

CHAPTER TWELVE

CONCLUSION

A constant problem in the preceding chapters has been to balance my concerns and approaches, allowing them the right amount of interplay at the right points. A social and historical approach might have produced a plausible work; a political analysis would have tended to exclude the poems except in so far as they provided material for reconstruction—metaphors, or illustrations for a diagnosis, already paralleled in an examination of the social events. I have preferred to consider the poems for their response to the values they evolved in relation to the experiences they re-created. The danger of this approach is that of reading the poem as an autonomous object (just as the danger of the other approaches is of reading the poems as dependent ones); although no critic of the-text-itself would suggest that 'background' knowledge is harmful so long as the poem itself and the individual responses it embodied are kept central to one's reading. The problem here was that some knowledge of the Great War was inescapable. And further, that although the political era is no longer ours exactly, enough of its concerns remain ours, or are still relevant, for us to be directly responsive to them. The question then was whether one could grasp the social and political concerns, without this dispersing a direct relationship with the poem, or causing one to pre-judge it because of a general sympathy (or lack of it) with the poet's generally understood responses. Yet one had also to keep in mind the relation of the poem, in its responsiveness, to the values generated by the experience itself.

The problem is circular, so that, additionally, I have tried to keep in mind that an integration of these concerns resulted in a kind of duality. The poems were of worth for their independent responsiveness; but they were concerned with values which many would still consider crucial, and in considering these values one had not to lose sight of how the poems themselves kept contact with the experiences they in varying degrees *evaluatively* re-created. I had also to remember that the poet needed to guard against his work succumbing to his experience—in such a way as to reduce the poems to naturalistic horror, for instance, or homiletic fury. The degree to which the poems did not succumb would be a factor in my evaluation. It was useful to know a little about the poet as a man and where he stood in relation to society.

The distinction is relevant in that, although the poet is first of all an individual, his work will to some extent reproduce his responses to society and society's to him.

Most of the poets of the Great War were middle-class or petit bourgeois, the terms being used neutrally. Sassoon before the war had no need to earn his living; others worked in a context which, because of the social image of the work as well as by the nature of the work itself, protected them from the exposed situation of the manual labourer. This was only partly true of Rosenberg who, prior to his Slade School period, worked as an apprentice engraver and detested it. As members of the middle class, they were not overmuch oppressed by lack of money, by the conditions of their work, or by the direct and brutal contact that the manual workers had with their employers. As poets, few if any of them could have made a living from their poetry as some now do in England and the United States. Since the eighteenth century their status in society had ceased to be one of direct reliance on a patron, and their market was in the main composed of the middle classes who had become literate, large, and prosperous enough to change the conditions of publishing. Subsequently, the poet had some of the self-employed status of the writer (not for every writer one of actual self-employment) and had too some of the aura that had gathered, since Romanticism, about the 'figure' of the poet.

There is not always a simple and direct correlation between the immediate social position of a poet and his work; some of his influences will come not only environmentally but in relation to other writers, and then, not only in relation to poets contemporary with him, but also in relation to such a literary tradition as he interprets it and as it is evaluated by others. Not every poet will accept these evaluations, but it seems unlikely that any will escape them. The relationship between the war poets and their literary environment has already in many places been described: how Owen took much from Keats and Shelley and from Sassoon; how Sassoon himself learnt something from Byron's satire, and borrowed from Shelley and Keats. Rosenberg read Jonson, Blake, Donne, and Rossetti, and he may have learnt something from Bottomley's plays.

Read borrowed from the Imagists and perhaps from Wordsworth and William Morris. The debt in general was to the nineteenth century, in that the prevailing ethos was largely an adulteration of the Romantics, Tennyson, and the Pre-Raphaelites. The war poets' use of contemporary speech and vocabulary was not in the main the result of any alteration in literary attitudes, but, rather, the result of new and terrifying circumstances. Because it was the environment that changed their work (even Rosenberg's, to some extent), the change was deeper than linguistic and structural. The new circumstances necessitated a new vocabulary and, to a lesser extent, altered forms and syntax. The traditional forms were tested, not merely by the new substance they had to express, but by the intensity of response to it. It is at this point, the point at which the forms of the poets so differ, that one begins to feel the common pressure of experience and, at the same time and because of it, the differences of the poets as they use a common language. These differences are not confined to poetry, where the opportunity for variety of structure may more evidently be seen. One notices that Blunden in *Undertones of War* rarely describes physical injury, and that Graves, in *Goodbye to All That*, does:

[The wounded man] was making a snoring noise mixed with animal groans. At my feet lay the cap he had worn, splashed with his brains. I had never seen human brains before; I somehow regarded them as a poetical figment.

Alun R. Jones has remarked that Graves's wit 'is often self-directed, and his neat, tidy craftsmanship often hides some large, romantic gesture cut short'. Blunden would tend not to cut short the gesture, and would be even less likely to hide his sensitivity under wit, especially when faced with a situation such as Graves describes. Blunden's method would be to confront the situation with more emotional directness, or to leave it out.

It might be objected that, in the case of Read and Jones, who wrote much or all of their work several years after the war, there was time for the poet to write more slowly, and with less reliance on the pressure of the experience itself as a shaping force. Jones, however, wrote of *In Parenthesis* that 'Each person and every event are free reflections of people and things remembered, or projected from intimately known possibilities'. In *Epoch and Artist* he related how 'In 1927 or '28 . . . I began to write down some sentences which turned out to be the initial passages of *In Parenthesis* published some ten years later. . . . I had no idea what I was letting myself in for.' The implication is that he was not carefully shaping his work independently of the pressure of his war experiences, but re-creating those experiences out of some dire but not immediately productive pressure. Read wrote of 'The End of a War' in *The Contrary Experience* : 'the necessary element is the time-lapse implicit in Wordsworth's phrase, "recollected in tranquillity", an element of "aesthetic distance".' This would suggest that he was deliberately distancing the events, and, in so distancing the experience, altered perhaps the expressive responses of the poem. Yet a comparison with *Naked Warriors* (1919) shows an intensification of responses rather than structural changes remote from the modes of the 1919 group of poems. (The second section of 'The End of a War' with its use of stichomythia would be an exception to this.)

From the social and political view there is no evidence that the poets influenced the actions of the politicians as peacemakers, and evidence of influence upon the climate of opinion is not easily isolated. With regard to the former, E. H. Carr in *International Relations since the Peace Treaties* (1937) has written:

These unnecessary humiliations, which can only be explained by the intense bitterness of feeling still left over from the war, had far-reaching psychological consequences, both in Germany and elsewhere. They fixed in the consciousness of the German people the conception of a 'dictated peace'; and they helped to create the belief, which is now universal in Germany and is tacitly accepted by a large body of opinion in other countries, that the signature extorted from Germany in these conditions is not morally binding on her.

As Carr might have implied, the pacific anti-war impulses of the poets were not here reflected; that is, the war was continued by way of penalties imposed by the Allied upon the Central powers, who were even regarded by some as collectively 'war criminals'.

The climate of opinion (presumably one of the pressures that some of the peacemakers responded to) is hard to gauge as something impinged on by the poets. Such gauging, moreover, depends on the assumption that their poetry, its values and expressiveness, constituted a response separate from the society and its attitudes in which they were immersed. To some extent this is true, and is prematurely reflected in Owen's letter to his cousin of 25 October 1918:

I have found in all these villages *no evidence of German atrocities.* The girls here were treated with perfect respect. All the material ruin has been wrought by our guns. Do you still shake your befoozled head over the *Daily Mail* & the *Times?*

Additionally, the poetry may be differentiated from the climate of opinion in that the poets' expressiveness was an articulate organized fact. To the extent, therefore, in which the poet and his work may be distinguished from social opinion, one can speak of his influence on this opinion as a possibility. And inasmuch as the poet rejected patriotism and expressed his rejection in experiential terms, then his opinions might be separable from other social opinion, whether similar to it or not; and one can speak of his possible influence. Behind such a rejection one could speak of the more positive desire to realign society's forces so as to make it an inclusive and sharing organism. Nothing so deliberate as a formulation in experiential terms of the proletariat feeling its power and re-fashioning the state is expressed by the poets. Yet the implications of Sassoon's 'Fight to a Finish' (an isolated instance) carry the argument in this direction, and Rosenberg's realignments do not rule out such a conception as Lenin formulated it:

In the *Communist Manifesto* are summed up the general lessons of history, which force us to see in the state the organ of class domination, and lead us to the inevitable conclusion that the proletariat cannot overthrow the bourgeoisie without first conquering political power, without obtaining political rule, without transforming the state into the 'proletariat organized as the ruling class'; and that this proletarian state will begin to wither away immediately after its victory, because in a society without class antagonisms, the state is unnecessary and impossible. . . .

under capitalism we have a state in the proper sense of the word, that is, special machinery for the suppression of one class by another, and of the majority by the minority at that. Naturally, for the successful discharge of such a task as the systematic suppression by the exploiting minority of the exploited majority, the greatest ferocity and savagery of suppression are required, seas of blood are required, through which mankind is marching in slavery, serfdom, and wage-labour.

It is the inclusive fruitfulness which indicates that, whether or not Rosenberg was thinking specifically along the lines that Lenin proposes, his responsiveness, although variegated and emphasized differently, was orientated in this direction. What Rosenberg would have made of Stalin's dictatorship and his development of the state's power and its oligarchic instrumentalism may, however, be imagined.

There is another sensing of change in the poets and their work, as they recognized the horizontal allegiances between the soldiers of the different countries, which makes effect on social opinion a possibility. For although the changes in the various societies since the end of the First War that have altered the conditions of people's lives may partly be attributed to Marxism, it is also true that nationalism has continued as a strong, mainly negative force. It is questionable whether groups of people must pass through a national-istic stage before reaching a socialist or communist one; and possible that, entering this stage, they may never emerge from it. This may suggest that the poets did not succeed in making effective their anti-nationalist responses. But one might argue that, not only have their warnings remained intact, but that, had they not made them, Europe might have suffered even greater nationalistic aggression.

These questions shade off into debate on the value of poetry as a social force, and this is clearly no point at which to begin such speculation. Yet the question is insistent enough to need some res-ponse, if only to suggest that poetry is different from all the forms of search and examination it is used to implement, such as history, sociology, politics, religion, and psychology.

We see Owen using Keats in a variety of ways to help him define his own responses. It might also be said that Owen, in so using Keats, has his own mode, and what he has to say is shaped and eventually constricted by the other's. As I have already suggested, there was not in his poetry before the war, as there *was* in some of his letters, an active social response, and the limitations of the mode as he used it in his poetry are emphasized by a comparison of his pre-war verse with that written during the war, and by com-paring his earlier verse with his earlier letters. The mode limits the substance of the verse and, in a less responsive writer, his thinking too. The mode is at once the mode and its substance.

In general, we can relate the war poets to their own literary en-vironment, and ask if their work has had any impact on poetry subsequent to it. Their relation to the 'school of violence' is non-existent, their relation to Imagism (excepting Read, Aldington, and Ford) also negative. Georgianism, indistinguishable as it may now seem from the dilutions of the Romantics, Victorians, and Pre-Raphaelites, had some initial (and subsequent) effect on Sassoon. The tone of voice which seems to control not only the imagery but the whole rounded-off movement of the syntax makes its quiet, sybaritic selection from nature, and this it covers in protective mystery. The images are often clear and the objects familiar and 'well-loved'. Some of this may have had some attraction for Owen, but little for Rosenberg.[1] Edward Thomas's relation to it exists, but some of this may be seen by way of his relationships with several poets—W. H. Davies, for instance—whom he helped, for a period, out of his meagre resources. There is also a respect in his work for the quiet voice, albeit an insistent quietness. But differences exist; with Thomas there is a basic connection between his inner life and his responses to nature, which is consciously realized, and with which the Georgians were not at all concerned. It is noticeable that Thomas most resembles the Georgians when his poetry is content to visualize nature, lacking as a result intensity and precise selective detail.

What connects the war poets with our time is, among other things, the inescapable war—not only as they were committed to realizing the terror of their conditions, but as those conditions are relevant to poets now. Inasmuch as the war sharpens their alertness to their society as a whole, and of course to problems that cannot be contained by social groupings, it offers to establish between them and poets writing now a connection still crucial. Francis Hope, in a review of Johnston's book and Brian Gardner's anthology *Up the Line to Death*, remarks:

the poets involved in the First World War were not the best, perhaps, of their time, though it is always possible that, had they survived, Owen and even Sorley might have been. But as it is, the map read differently. What Pound and Eliot and Yeats had begun before the war they continued after it: a revolution in English poetry that leaves both unreformed and reformed Georgians in the loop of a by-pass. Owen and Jones and Graves are of sufficient stature to endure, but it could hardly be claimed that they influenced many successors. . . . In general they have had admirers rather than imitators. . . . In a not altogether rhetorical sense,

[1] I except Bottomley's plays from all this; but a further aspect of some of the Georgians was their indulgence in violence; see Lawrence's letter to Marsh of 24 May 1914 and his comments there on Abercrombie (*D. H. Lawrence: Selected Literary Criticism*, ed. Anthony Beal (1962), pp. 81–2).

all poetry written since 1918 is war poetry; and Yeats and Eliot and Auden have contributed more to it than Rosenberg or Blunden, or even than Owen and David Jones.[1]

It is true that Eliot and Pound (and in a different way, Yeats) leave the war poets 'in the loop of a by-pass', if the Eliot-Pound direction is regarded as the only desirable way forward for English poetry; but only someone totally committed to such a direction would see the poets as trapped in a disused by-pass. Francis Hope would seem to believe that not only did the war poets have few 'followers' but that, apart from the three he mentions, they are not of 'sufficient stature' (the cliché suggests the dead weight of the evaluating attitude) 'to endure'. Yet easy and obvious connections can be made between Rosenberg and Keith Douglas, between Edward Thomas and Alun Lewis, for instance.

Owen's rhetoric may not now be especially meaningful to us; but his steady fury—the last stanza of 'Insensibility', for instance—is. The mounting of one person's consciousness on another's, as in 'Dulce et Decorum Est' and 'The Sentry', is also viable, and so is the narrative capacity in which, in 'Strange Meeting', the right detail both sets the context and advances the action, the argument, and at the same time the unfolding movement of the emotion. More perhaps might be said for Rosenberg. His handling of creatures and objects—how they remain centrally poised between their creatureliness and their potency as symbols—is relevant to us as poets and readers. He has what Lawrence indicated as a desirable polarization in any writer: force and complexity.

'It is the hidden emotional pattern that makes poetry, not the obvious form', Lawrence wrote (partly in rebuke) to Marsh in November 1913. The intensity of the emotional pattern, 'the natural pause, the natural *lingering* of the voice according to the feeling'—these are modes in opposition to some of Eliot and Pound; 'lingering' implies a lingering within a *flow*. Yet to imply that such modes are no longer relevant or useful to us would be as inaccurate as to suggest that they were not a part of Rosenberg and Owen. It is through such fluctuations in the emotional flow that we make contact with the feelings, and perceive the connections between ourselves and the poem.

[1] Francis Hope, 'Tommy's Tunes', *The Review*, No. 15 (April 1965), pp. 52–7.

And lastly, one cannot say that no connection may exist between a poet in the past and some future writer. Rosenberg's reading of Donne, Jonson, and Blake—none of them valued then as they are now—shows how a poet will find his own alignments, not always in agreement with current critical evaluations. Wordsworth's Preface to the *Lyrical Ballads* (1800) relates to several points in Owen's Preface, even if Owen may not have read Wordsworth's. Emphases change and the relevance of a certain poet, or aspects of several, assume a new cogency, and define for us a helpful, or vital, similarity to some structure we may be working at. Donald Davie's earlier concern with Augustan syntax and diction reveals concerns of order, directness, and completed movement in his own poetry.

None of this, of course, defines the intrinsic value of the war poets, but Francis Hope's mild fanaticism would (according to his diagram of twentieth-century poetry) disregard their work at a time when we are in need of as much vitality—countering our disintegrative experiences—as we can find.

SELECT BIBLIOGRAPHY

The place of publication is London unless otherwise indicated. Dates are those of editions cited in the text.

POETRY

Richard Aldington, *Complete Poems* (1949)
Edmund Blunden, *Poems 1914–1930* (1930)
Gordon Bottomley, *Poems and Plays* (1952)
Bertolt Brecht, *Selected Poems*, translated by H. R. Hays (New York, 1959)
Rupert Brooke, *Poetical Works*, edited by Geoffrey Keynes (1946)
Keith Douglas, *Collected Poems*, edited by John Waller and G. S. Fraser (1951)
F. S. Flint, *In the Net of Stars* (1909)
—— *Otherworld/Cadences* (1920)
Ford Madox Ford, *On Heaven/and other Poems* (*Poems written on active service*) (1918)
—— *Buckshee*, with Introductions by Robert Lowell and Kenneth Rexroth (Cambridge, Mass., 1966)
—— *Selected Poems*, edited and with a Preface by Basil Bunting (Cambridge, Mass., 1971)
Roy Fuller, *Collected Poems* (1962)
David Gascoyne, *Collected Poems* (1965)
Robert Graves, *Fairies and Fusiliers* (1917)
—— *Collected Poems* (1959)
Ivor Gurney, *Severn and Somme* (1917)
—— *War's Embers* (1919)
—— *Poems*, edited with a Memoir by Edmund Blunden (1954)
Thomas Hardy, *Collected Poems* (1952)
—— *The Dynasts* (1930)
A. E. Housman, *Collected Poems* (1939)
David Jones, *In Parenthesis* (1963)
—— *The Anathémata* (1952)
—— *The Tribune's Visitation* (1969)
Sidney Keyes, *Collected Poems* (1945)
Rudyard Kipling, *Poems* (Definitive Edition, 1940)
D. H. Lawrence, *Collected Poems* (1928)

Alun Lewis, *Raider's Dawn* (1942)

—— *Ha! Ha! Among the Trumpets*, with a Foreword by Robert Graves (1945)

—— *Selected Poetry and Prose*, edited with a Biographical Introduction by Ian Hamilton (1966)

Emanuel Litvinoff, *The Untried Soldier* (1942)

—— *A Crown for Cain* (1948)

John Masefield, *Collected Poems* (1923)

Vladimir Mayakovsky, *The Bedbug and Selected Poetry*, translated by Max Hayward and George Reavey (1961)

Harold Monro, *Collected Poems*, edited by Alida Monro (1933)

Robert Nichols, *Ardours and Endurances* (1918)

Wilfred Owen, *Collected Poems*, edited with an Introduction by C. Day Lewis and with a Memoir by Edmund Blunden (1963)

Ezra Pound, *Personae/The Collected Shorter Poems* (1952)

Herbert Read, *Collected Poems* (1966)

Isaac Rosenberg, *Poems*, selected and edited by Gordon Bottomley with an Introductory Memoir by Laurence Binyon (1922)

—— *Collected Works*, edited by Gordon Bottomley and D. W. Harding (1937)

Siegfried Sassoon, *Collected Poems* (1947)

Charles Hamilton Sorley, *Marlborough and other Poems* (Cambridge, 1932)

Algernon Charles Swinburne, *Poems and Ballads* (1st Series) (1892)

—— *Songs before Sunrise* (1917)

Edward Thomas, *Collected Poems*, with a Foreword by Walter de la Mare (1936)

Georg Trakl, *Twenty Poems*, chosen and translated by James Wright and Robert Bly (Minneapolis, Minn., 1963)

—— *Decline/Twelve Poems*, translated by Michael Hamburger (St. Ives, 1952)

Giuseppe Ungaretti, two poems translated by Jonathan Griffin, *Stand*, XI, No. 4 (1970); four poems translated by Charles Tomlinson, *Stand*, XII, No. 2 (1971)

—— *Selected Poems*, translated by Patrick Creagh (1971)

ANTHOLOGIES

Ronald Blythe, ed., *Components of the Scene* (1966)

Patrick Bridgwater, 'German Poets of the 1914–18 War', in *The Journals of Pierre Menard*, 3 July 1969

Des Imagistes (1914) (No editor named.)

Brian Gardner, ed., *Up the Line to Death* (1964)

—— *The Terrible Rain* (1966)

Michael Hamburger and Christopher Middleton, eds., *Modern German Poetry 1910–1960* (1963)
Ian Hamilton, ed., *The Poetry of War/1939–45* (1965)
Norman Kreitman, ed., *The Dove in Flames/1939–45* (n.d.)
Galloway Kyle, ed., *Soldier Poets/Songs of the Fighting Men* (1916)
Bertram Lloyd, ed., *Poems Written during the Great War 1914–1918* (1918)
Edward Marsh, ed., *Georgian Poetry* (5 vols.) (1911–22)
Christopher Middleton, Wolfgang G. Deppe, and Herbert Schönherr, eds., *Ohne Hass und Fahne (No Hatred and no Flag)* (Hamburg, 1959)
I. M. Parsons, ed., *Men Who March Away* (1965)
James Reeves, ed., *Georgian Poetry* (1962)
Michael Roberts, ed., *The Faber Book of Modern Verse* (1936)
Julian Symons, ed., *An Anthology of War Poetry* (1942)
W. B. Yeats, ed., *The Oxford Book of Modern Verse* (1936)

AUTOBIOGRAPHY, BIOGRAPHY, LETTERS, FICTION

C. C. Abbott and Anthony Bertram, eds., *Poet and Painter/Correspondence between Gordon Bottomley and Paul Nash* (1955)
Richard Aldington, *Death of a Hero* (1929)
Isaac Babel, *Collected Stories* (1957)
Henri Barbusse, *Under Fire*, translated by Brian Rhys (1917)
Arnold Bennett, *The Pretty Lady* (1918)
Edmund Blunden, *Undertones of War* (1928)
Lady Violet Bonham-Carter, 'The Missing Generation', *The Sunday Times*, 11 November 1962
Wolfgang Borchert, *The Man Outside*, translated by David Porter (1952)
Stephen Crane, *The Red Badge of Courage* (New York, 1962)
e. e. cummings, *The Enormous Room* (New York, 1934)
Keith Douglas, *Alamein to Zem Zem*, edited by John Waller, G. S. Fraser, and J. C. Hall (1966)
—— 'The Little Red Mouth', *Stand*, XI, No. 2 (1970)
Eleanor Farjeon, *Edward Thomas/The Last Four Years* (1958)
Ford Madox Ford, *Parade's End* (1963)
E. M. Forster, *Howards End* (1960)
Robert Graves, *Goodbye to All That* (1960)
Jaroslav Hasek, *The Good Soldier Schweik*, translated by Paul Selver (1939)
Christopher Hassall, *Rupert Brooke/A Biography* (1964)
A. R. Jones, *The Life and Opinions of Thomas Ernest Hulme* (1960)
Keynes, Geoffrey, ed., *The Letters of Rupert Brooke* (1968)
Karl L. Liebknecht, *The Future Belongs to the People*, edited and translated by S. Zimand (New York, 1918)
Frederick Manning, *Her Privates We* (1967)

354 *Out of Battle*

Edward Marsh, *A Number of People* (1939)
Giuseppe Mazzini, *The Duties of Man*, translated by Ella Noyes, L. Martineau, and Thomas Okey (1907)
C. E. Montague, *Disenchantment* (1928)
Harold Owen, *Journey from Obscurity/Wilfred Owen 1893–1918* (3 vols.) (1963, 1964, 1965)
—— and John Bell, eds., *Wilfred Owen/Collected Letters* (1967)
Herbert Read, *The Contrary Experience* (1963)
Erich Maria Remarque, *All Quiet on the Western Front*, translated by A. W. Wheen (1929)
Frank Richards, *Old Soldiers Never Die*, with an Introduction by Robert Graves (1964)
W. K. Rose, ed., *Letters of Wyndham Lewis* (1963)
Siegfried Sassoon, *Complete Memoirs of George Sherston* (1937)
Maurice de Sausmarez and Jon Silkin, eds., *Isaac Rosenberg 1890–1918/ Catalogue with Letters* (Leeds, 1959)
Charles Hamilton Sorley, *Letters* (Cambridge, 1919)
Edward Thomas, *The Icknield Way* (1913)
Helen Thomas, *As It Was . . . World Without End* (1935)
General Sir Archibald Wavell, *Generals and Generalship* (1941)
Walt Whitman, *Specimen Days in America* (1931)

CRITICISM

M. H. Abrams, ed., *English Romantic Poets* (New York, 1960)
Matthew Arnold, *Culture and Anarchy*, edited by J. Dover Wilson (1961)
James O. Bailey, *Thomas Hardy and the Cosmic Mind* (Chapel Hill, N. Car., 1956)
Bernard Bergonzi, *Heroes' Twilight* (1965)
Francis Berry, *Herbert Read* (1961)
Marius Bewley, *Masks & Mirrors* (1970)
Edmund Blunden, *War Poets 1914–1918* (1958)
Joseph Cohen, 'Wilfred Owen's *Greater Love*', *Tulane Studies of English*, VI (1956)
—— 'The Three Roles of Siegfried Sassoon', *Tulane Studies of English*, VII (1957)
William Cooke, *Edward Thomas/A Critical Biography 1878–1917* (1970)
H. Coombes, *Edward Thomas* (1956)
Peter Dale, 'Collected Poems of Wilfred Owen', *Agenda*, III, No. 3 (December–January 1963/4)
D. J. Enright, 'Literature of the First World War', in *The Modern Age* (Pelican Guide to English Literature, vol. VII), edited by Boris Ford (1969)
Ifor Evans, *English Poetry in the Later Nineteenth Century* (1966)

F. S. Flint, 'Contemporary French Poetry', *Poetry Review*, I, No. 7 (August 1912)

Robert Graves, *The Common Asphodel* (1949)

Frederick Grubb, *A Vision of Reality* (1965)

John Hale, 'War and Public Opinion in the Fifteenth and Sixteenth Centuries', *Past and Present*, No. 22 (July 1962)

Michael Hamburger, *Reason and Energy* (1957)

—— 'No Hatred and No Flag', *Encounter*, No. 85 (October 1960)

—— *The Truth of Poetry* (1969)

Alec M. Hardie, *Edmund Blunden* (1958)

D. W. Harding, *Experience into Words* (1963)

—— 'Isaac Rosenberg', *Scrutiny*, III, No. 4 (March 1935)

T. R. Henn, 'Critics of Kipling', *Review of English Literature*, VI, No. 3 (July 1965)

—— *W. B. Yeats and the Poetry of War* (1965)

Geoffrey Hill, 'Selected Poems of Keith Douglas', *Stand*, VI, No. 4 (1965)

Philip Hobsbaum, 'The Road not Taken' [Edward Thomas], *The Listener*, 23 November 1961

Francis Hope, 'Tommy's Tunes', *The Review,* No. 15 (April 1965)

T. E. Hulme, *Speculations*, edited with an Introduction by Herbert Read, (1960)

R. A. Scott-James and C. Day Lewis, *Thomas Hardy* (1965)

John H. Johnston, *English Poetry of the First World War* (1964)

David Jones, *Epoch and Artist*, edited by Harman Grisewood (1959)

Victor Lange, *Modern German Literature 1870–1940* (New York, 1945)

Philip Larkin, 'The War Poet', *The Listener*, 10 October 1963

D. H. Lawrence, *Selected Literary Criticism*, edited by Anthony Beal (1969)

F. R. Leavis, *The Common Pursuit* (1952)

—— *Revaluation* (1956)

—— *New Bearings in English Poetry* (1963)

—— 'Ezra Pound: The Promise and the Disaster', in *Partisan Review Anthology* (1962)

Saunders Lewis, 'Epoch and Artist', *Agenda*, V, Nos. 1–3 (1967)

Geoffrey Matthews, 'Brooke and Owen', *Stand*, IV, No. 3 (1960)

Christopher Middleton, ed., 'Documents on Imagism from the Papers of F. S. Flint', *The Review*, No. 15 (April 1965)

Eric Newton, 'Art and the First World War', *The Guardian*, 27 February 1964

Mario Praz, *The Romantic Agony* (1960)

John Press, 'Charles Sorley', *Review of English Literature*, VII, No. 2 (April 1966)

Herbert Read, 'The Collected Works of Isaac Rosenberg', *The Criterion*, XVII, No. 66 (October 1937)

Pierre Renouvin, '1914/A French View', *The Listener*, 23 July 1964

Hans Richter, *Dada/Art and Anti-Art* (1965)

Andrew Rutherford, ed., *Kipling's Mind and Art* (Edinburgh, 1964)

Vernon Scannell, *Edward Thomas* (1965)

Roger Shattuck, *The Banquet Years/The Arts in France 1885–1918* (1959)

Jon Stallworthy, *Wilfred Owen* (Chatterton Lecture, British Academy) (1971)

C. K. Stead, *The New Poetic* (1964)

Michael Thorpe, *Siegfried Sassoon/A Critical Study* (1966)

Leon Trotsky, *Literature and Revolution*, translated by Rose Strunsky (Ann Arbor, Mich., 1960)

Raymond Tschumi, *Thought in Twentieth-Century English Poetry* (1951)

Paul West, *Byron and the Spoiler's Art* (1960)

Simone Weil, 'The *Iliad*, or the Poem of Force', *The Wind and the Rain* (1962)

D. S. R. Welland, *Wilfred Owen/A Critical Study* (1960)

Raymond Williams, *Culture and Society* (1962)

Austin Wright, ed., *Victorian Literature* (New York, 1961)

Edith Wynner, 'Out of the Trenches by Christmas', *The Progressive*, December 1965

INDEX

war poetry (*contd.*)
  language, 343; influence on politicians
  as peacemakers, 344; possible influence
  on social opinion, 345–6; rejection of
  patriotism, 345; and nationalism 346
Weil, Simone, 8, 50, 51, 58, 324; 'The
  Iliad, or the Poem of Force', 50, 231 n.,
  319 n.
Welland, D. S. R., *Wilfred Owen*, 207,
  209, 220, 225, 229, 236, 237, 243, 255
West, Paul, *Byron and the Spoiler's Art*, 23
Whitman, Walt, 120, 327
Wimsatt, W. K., 17
Winchilsea, Anne Finch Countess of, 'The
  Soldier's Death', 43, 135
Wordsworth, Dorothy, 9, 14, 16
Wordsworth, William, poetic concern
  with contemporary events, 2, 318–19;
  rejects early allegiances, 2–3; suspected
  of treason, 9; changing view of France,
  10, 11–12; revised attitude to reform,
  10, 14, 15–16; revolutionary sympathies,
  11; humanitarian commitment, 11;
  indictment of war, 12; rationalizes his
  early ideals, 13; image of the poet, 14;
  effect of political withdrawal, 14; and
  the poor, 15–16, 60; withdrawal to
  Grasmere, 16; criticized by Byron, 24,
  209; Hardy and, 52; Byron compared
  with, 209, Owen, 244, 349, Read

('Happy Warrior'), 172, Sassoon,
  148–9, Thomas, 93
    'Character of the Happy Warrior',
  172; 'The Female Vagrant', 14, 15;
  Lyrical Ballads (Preface), 14, 244, 349;
  The Prelude, 10, 11, 12, 13, 14, 15, 24,
  148–9, 318–19; 'Resolution and Independence', 15, 93; 'Tintern Abbey', 14,
  16, 17
World War, First (1914–18), 2; compared
  with Napoleonic struggle, 34; heroic/
  optimistic start, 50, 51, 59; working-
  class support, 58; casualties, 71; Somme
  offensive, 71; use of countryside in
  patriotic appeals, 138–9; post-war
  publications, 315; horror aroused by
  bayonet, 335; continuing relevance,
  341; penalties imposed on 'war
  criminals', 344. *See also* war *and* war
  poetry
World War, Second (1939–45), 44, 178,
  190
Wyatt, Sir Thomas, 337–8

Yeats, William Butler, 33, 82, 347;
  association with Pound, 32; affinity
  with Hardy, 44; dislike of Owen, 80;
  Read and, 173; exclusions from *Oxford
  Book of Modern Verse*, 177; rejection of
  passive suffering, 227; and the past, 270